The information age is here. Advances in technology have dramatically improved our ability to communicate electronically. Intra-company e-mail is now commonplace and the explosion of the internet has made worldwide communication possible. The downside of this new capability is an information overload. Today I receive ten times more correspondence than I did five years ago, and it continues to increase. In this environment it is more important than ever that you have the ability to communicate clearly and concisely. Make sure your great ideas don't end up in the electronic wastebasket.

—PHIL SEMMER
Vice President, Information Systems
General Mills

When you train scuba instructors from varied cultures, nationalities, and backgrounds, you quickly realize that you must communicate clearly. Proper grammar, sentence structure, and writing skill not only help you organize thoughts, but allow you to communicate them succinctly. In much of today's business world, standardized training practices form the door to success, and consistent, clear communication opens this door. I can't promise you that reading and applying the principles in *Business English for the 21st Century* will be as much fun as underwater exploration. This book, however, simplifies learning to use effective English and is an excellent investment in your future.

—JULIE TAYLOR SHREEVES
Vice President, Training and Education
PADI (Professional Association of Diving Instructors)

Communication skills, particularly skills in writing, are critically important in any business. You must learn to write and speak effectively in order to succeed in the modern business environment. If you can't express an idea, you don't have one.

—RICHARD J. MAHONEY
Chairman and CEO
Monsanto Company

Technical skill, a conscientious attitude, and a winning personality may help a person to gain employment in today's business community. Positions in management, however, are generally reserved for those candidates who can use the English language most effectively.

—**Maxine Ransom Von Phul**
President
Winmax Construction Corporation

The ability to communicate effectively is an important skill in the business world and one which I always look for in selecting people for key positions of responsibility.

—**James J. O'Connor**
Chairman of the Board
Commonwealth Edison Company

There will always be a place in the business world for the worker who has great technical skill. In order to reach the upper levels of management, however, an employee must be able to express ideas clearly and convincingly.

—**Romana A. Banúelos**
President
Pan American Bank

SECOND EDITION

Business English for the 21st Century

PAT TAYLOR ELLISON

ROBERT E. BARRY

with
JAMES SCANNELL McCORMICK

Prentice Hall
Upper Saddle River, New Jersey 07458

Library of Congress Cataloging-in-Publication Data
Ellison, Patricia Taylor
   Business English for the 21st century / Patricia Taylor Ellison,
  Robert E. Barry with James Scannell McCormick. —2nd ed., annotated
  instructor's ed.
      p.   cm.
  Includes index.
  ISBN 0-13-082667-7
   1. Commercial correspondence. 2. Business writing. 3. English
  language—Business English. I. Barry, Robert E.
  II. McCormick, James Scannell. III. Title. IV. Title: Business
  English for the twenty-first century.
  HF5726.B27 2000
  808′.066651—dc21   99-22514
                                             CIP

Acquisitions Editor: Elizabeth Sugg
Editorial/Production Supervision: WordCrafters Editorial
    Services, Inc.
Director of Manufacturing & Production: Bruce Johnson
Managing Editor: Mary Carnis
Production Liaison: Eileen O'Sullivan
Cover Design: Amy Rosen
Interior Design: Amy Rosen
Creative Director: Marianne Frasco
Development Editor: Judy Casillo
Cover Artwork: David Bishop
Manufacturing Manager: Ed O'Dougherty
Marketing Manager: Shannon Simonsen
Formatting/Page Makeup: Clarinda Co.
Printer/Binder: Banta Company

This book was set in Times Roman by Clarinda Co., and was printed and bound by Banta Company. The cover was printed by Banta Company.

This book was previously published under the title *Business English for the '90s*, © 1992, 1989 by Prentice Hall, Inc.

Printed in the United States of America

10 9 8 7 6 5 4 3 2 1

ISBN 0-13-082667-7

Prentice-Hall International (UK) Limited, *London*
Prentice-Hall of Australia Pty. Limited, *Sydney*
Prentice-Hall Canada Inc., *Toronto*
Prentice-Hall Hispanoamericana, S.A., *Mexico*
Prentice-Hall of India Private Limited, *New Delhi*
Prentice-Hall of Japan, Inc., *Tokyo*
Pearson Education Asia Pte. Ltd., *Singapore*
Editora Prentice-Hall do Brasil, Ltda., *Rio de Janeiro*

To Robert Barry,
who built this book almost 30 years ago
and has kept it cogent, useful,
and most important for so many years:
we extend our heartfelt thanks.

—Pat Taylor Ellison

When Robert Barry prepared
the original version of this book,
it was the first and only one of its kind.
Alone, with few signposts to guide him,
Professor Barry established a field of study.
Today, it proudly stands among similar texts
as the quintessential work in the area.

—The Editors

Contents

Preface

The first edition of this text, entitled *Business English for the '70s,* was published almost three decades ago. Since that time the world of business has changed dramatically. We live in an *information* society in which communication skills are ever more critical to our success as individuals and as a global community. This edition of *Business English for the Twenty-First Century* is not drastically different from its predecessor. Every chapter of the earlier edition has been scrutinized in order to update its examples and increase its value to you without eliminating those features that have made the book a valuable teaching tool.

NEW TO THIS EDITION

The greatest improvement to this new edition is a complete support package for Distance Learning. The Pearson Distributed Learning Group offers the latest in multimedia technology. This new programming makes it possible to combine new elements with a traditional textbook. The *Companion Website* and *Interactive Computerized Study Guide* provide support for both the classroom environment and for primary course directives in non-traditional teaching environments.

We have added two new features to the textbook: *Watching the Web* and an improved overhead transparency system. *Watching the Web* is a collection of 19 usage and spelling errors found on web pages and internet advertisements over the past year. The company names are fictitious, but the errors are real. We hope the students will find the examples both amusing and instructive and will engage in finding the errors and making the corrections. *Watching the Web* examples are scattered throughout the book, and the errors are identified in the key found on page 435. The new overhead transparency system offers instructors two transparency masters for each chapter, one that conveys key concepts and around which lecture and practice can take place, and one exercise or quiz that tests those concepts and can be used collaboratively if you wish.

All of these new features are part of the most complete teaching packages for Business English currently available:

1. Distance Learning Package
2. Companion Website
3. Interactive Computerized Study Guide on CD-ROM
4. *Watching the Web* boxed feature
5. An improved overhead transparency system

CONTINUING WITH SUCCESSFUL FEATURES

This edition also retains several helpful study and teaching features from previous editions:

1. Collaborative Learning Exercises, noted with the square icon in each chapter, which allow students to use a team approach to solving exercises (see the article on Collaboration on p. xiii)

2. *Word Tips from the Real World*, a collection of vignettes from real people responsible for making decisions about communication skills on the job
3. Material concerning dictionary use and spelling in the first chapters because of their importance
4. A section entitled Key Items (pp. 435–448) with answers and sometimes explanations for selected questions from each of the chapter worksheets
5. News items, puzzles, anecdotes, and classroom discussion questions
6. Chapters 8, 16, 24, 32, and 40 devoted to review so that students will never encounter more than seven consecutive chapters of new material

Of course there are many differences between the language of business and the language of familiar conversation. This text is concerned with English usage that would prove acceptable in every way to the most critical reader or listener. We will not pretend that all successful persons have mastered the intricacies of grammar or that they are all perfectly comfortable with our challenging language. It is certainly true, however, that the ability to communicate effectively can be very important to anyone attempting to climb the corporate ladder. If you have questions concerning the acceptability of particular words or constructions, perhaps this book will answer those questions for you.

This edition, like earlier ones, is concerned specifically with grammar, word usage, conciseness, clarity, punctuation, spelling, and dictionary study. The rules and recommendations it covers should help today's businessperson. If our language did not change with the passing of time, books such as this one would never become outdated. The truth is that language does change, and sometimes the modifications are not easily detected. Over a period of years many new words are added, a number of old words are assigned new meanings, a few informal words are accorded greater acceptability, and a few traditional rules of grammar are ignored because they no longer serve our changing needs.

Even our new title reflects the tensions between old and new, formal and informal. While Prentice-Hall's art department designed our cover graphics around the numeral ordinal *21st*, most careful writers still spell out the word twenty-first. We have tried, therefore, to consistently spell out this number whenever it occurs within the text itself, but our cover's version of the title was designed compactly with numerals. The dynamic nature of our language makes it responsive and forever fascinating.

The suggestions made in this text reflect the current practices of this country's finest writers, particularly those who serve in the business community. Our heartfelt thanks are extended to those busy executives who took time to express their opinions concerning particular grammatical constructions or to prepare statements on the importance of communication skills. Thanks also go to those many college instructors throughout the country who took time to share their ideas about material used in previous editions. Their willingness to offer suggestions based upon their classroom experiences has always enhanced the value of this text.

To the Student

Most of us have heard at least one person say, "I hate English." In questionnaires completed by the graduates of several California high schools, the majority of the respondents named English as the course they had enjoyed *least*. Yet English is a course that may lead to spectacular financial rewards in the years ahead. Here are a few random thoughts on the subject:

1. Top executives in our major corporations, almost without exception, possess the ability to communicate effectively.
2. Most people employed in corporate America are completely sold on the importance of language skills. Many enroll in evening classes (as adults) to learn the rules and principles that seemed unimportant to them before they joined the workforce.
3. Every year thousands of employees are denied promotions to better-paying positions simply because they lack the ability to write and to speak acceptably.
4. The rules of grammar are *not* difficult to understand. They *seem* difficult to anyone who fails to recognize their value and, as a result, does not make a serious attempt to master them.
5. Regardless of what you eventually do with your life, the language refinements covered in this text can help you to communicate with confidence (and without embarrassment) as you encounter people from all walks of life.

Collaborative Learning

The more we study adult learning, the more we must acknowledge that adults approach learning tasks in widely varying ways. This diversity is due to many factors, among them differences in learning styles, differences in earlier teaching methods, and the complex combinations of habits that individuals bring to any task. This diversity can seem to be a stumbling block to both students and teachers.

Add to the variations in individuals' approaches to learning the consistently confirmed opinion that English is a challenging course for many students, and we are left with a clear need: we must develop teaching strategies that are more helpful, more enjoyable, and more effective than ever if we are to offer students a worthwhile learning experience.

Collaborative learning can become such a strategy. Why? Collaborative learning allows each student to work with one or more partners to investigate, solve problems, reconstruct, and compose. True collaboration matches persons who might well approach learning from different style perspectives and, hence, see (or miss!) different elements of every lesson. Fashioning a classroom experience that includes partners or teams gives students a better chance of catching everything, or at least increases the likelihood that fewer concepts and processes will elude them. It also provides for a level of synergistic learning that individuals never reach alone.

But, more than simply a case of two heads being better than one, collaboration provides another opportunity. Although there is much we do not know about adult learning, we do know two things, proven over and over again in the laboratory of real life: people own what they help to create, and people internalize facts and concepts most effectively in the act of teaching them to others. Learning in collaborative partnerships puts students in the position of having to teach one another their reasons for making certain choices and for applying rules the way they do. They actually create their experience, which leads to more engagement in the classroom and better retention afterward.

We believe so strongly in collaborative learning's positive effects that we've designated some work in each chapter as particularly suitable for the partner or team approach. Of course, almost all of the worksheet exercises could be accomplished in teams, but we've selected those that develop a key chapter concept, require a judgment call on the part of the student, are suitable for completion by a group, or require discussion in support of a position. These designated pieces give students the optimum chance for success as they learn to learn collaboratively.

Students may be assigned to collaborative partnerships or teams by the instructor according to learning styles (a variety of styles within each group is most effective), or they may select their own partners or teams. During the term, the groups might be shuffled so that every person is exposed to many other students as they teach one another. By the end of the term, each student should have had the chance to learn from as many persons as possible. This increased number of learning partners often has a dramatic effect on how well students learn, how much they remember, and to what extent they enjoy the learning experience-another factor that determines how likely they will be to apply what they have learned. Whenever feasible, students should *own* the teaching of the lesson; it is only then that they will master its content.

About the Authors

Pat Taylor Ellison earned her B.A. in English and Speech-Communication at the University of Minnesota, her M.A. in Teaching at the University of St. Thomas, and her Ph.D. in Education at the University of Minnesota. She has taught English and speech classes for 25 years, mostly for business and broadcasting students, and has won several awards, among them the Award for Faculty Excellence from the Minnesota Association of Private Post-secondary Schools. Currently she coordinates three research teams and works as Developmental Editor for Church Innovations Institute. She advises doctoral students on matters of research and thesis construction. She also serves Minnesota School of Business and Globe College of Business as their faculty's professional development trainer.

Dr. Ellison has co-authored two books, *Learning Together* and *Being Together,* about interactive small group processes. She also wrote the extensive lecture notes and teacher materials for Prentice Hall's Instructor's Manual to *Applied English.* Her research into how adults learn and apply new collaborative skills has made her a sought-after speaker on teaching methods, particularly those that foster the creation of community in the classroom. Her own facility with English, among the three languages she speaks, helps her to write for and train other educators in the art of teaching. She believes in excellent listening and speaking as the primary tools we will need to build community into the future.

Robert E. Barry is a graduate of Salem State College in Salem, Massachusetts. He earned his Master of Arts degree at California State University in Los Angeles.

He had been teaching classes in Business English for approximately 15 years when he was induced to write his first textbook, *Business English for the '70s.* That book, published in 1970, was followed by a second edition in 1975 and, at five-year intervals, by two editions of *Business English for the '80s.* Two shortened versions of the text were published under the title *Basic Business English.*

Mr. Barry spent several years in banking and in selling before he entered the field of education. During his 30 years at Mount San Antonio College in Walnut, California, he taught 12 different courses in the business area. He is best known, however, for his expertise and research in the field of communications. Throughout his life he has taken a keen interest in the use and misuse of the English language.

James McCormick earned his B.A. and M.A. in English from the University of Wisconsin at Madison and his Ph.D. in English at Western Michigan University in 1995. He has taught English and business writing for 13 years at such places as Fullerton College in California, University of Wisconsin at Waukesha, Brown Institute in Minneapolis, Globe College of Business in St. Paul, and Marquette University of Milwaukee. He lives and writes in Milwaukee.

Assignment Sheet

Date Due		Assignment
_____	**1.**	Read Chapter 1; complete Worksheet 1.
_____	**2.**	Read Chapter 2; complete Worksheet 2.
_____	**3.**	Read Chapter 3; complete Worksheet 3.
_____	**4.**	Read Chapter 4; complete Worksheet 4.
_____	**5.**	Read Chapter 5; complete Worksheet 5.
_____	**6.**	Read Chapter 6; complete Worksheet 6.
_____	**7.**	Read Chapter 7; complete Worksheet 7.
_____	**8.**	Prepare to take the quiz (see text) on Chapters 5–7.
_____	**9.**	Read Chapter 8; complete Worksheet 8.
_____	**10.**	Prepare for an examination on Chapters 1–8.
_____	**11.**	Read Chapter 9; complete Worksheet 9.
_____	**12.**	Read Chapter 10; complete Worksheet 10.
_____	**13.**	Read Chapter 11; complete Worksheet 11.
_____	**14.**	Read Chapter 12; complete Worksheet 12.
_____	**15.**	Read Chapter 13; complete Worksheet 13.
_____	**16.**	Read Chapter 14; complete Worksheet 14.
_____	**17.**	Read Chapter 15; complete Worksheet 15. Prepare for a quiz on column 1 of the spelling list (see Chapter 2).
_____	**18.**	Prepare to take the quiz (see text) on Chapters 12–15.
_____	**19.**	Read Chapter 16; complete Worksheet 16.
_____	**20.**	Prepare for an examination on Chapters 9–16.
_____	**21.**	Read Chapter 17; complete Worksheet 17.
_____	**22.**	Read Chapter 18; complete Worksheet 18.
_____	**23.**	Read Chapter 19; complete Worksheet 19. Prepare for a quiz on column 2 of the spelling list (see Chapter 2).
_____	**24.**	Read Chapter 20; complete Worksheet 20.
_____	**25.**	Read Chapter 21; complete Worksheet 21.
_____	**26.**	Read Chapter 22; complete Worksheet 22.
_____	**27.**	Read Chapter 23; complete Worksheet 23.

Date Due	Assignment
_____	**28.** Prepare to take the quiz (see text) on Chapters 20–23.
_____	**29.** Read Chapter 24; complete Worksheet 24.
_____	**30.** Prepare for an examination on Chapters 17–24.
_____	**31.** Read Chapter 25; complete Worksheet 25.
_____	**32.** Read Chapter 26; complete Worksheet 26.
_____	**33.** Read Chapter 27; complete Worksheet 27.
_____	**34.** Read Chapter 28; complete Worksheet 28. Prepare for a quiz on column 3 of the spelling list (see Chapter 2).
_____	**35.** Read Chapter 29; complete Worksheet 29.
_____	**36.** Read Chapter 30; complete Worksheet 30.
_____	**37.** Prepare to take the quiz (see text) on Chapters 28–30.
_____	**38.** Read Chapter 31; complete Worksheet 31.
_____	**39.** Read Chapter 32; complete Worksheet 32.
_____	**40.** Prepare for an examination on Chapters 25–32.
_____	**41.** Read Chapter 33; complete Worksheet 33.
_____	**42.** Read Chapter 34; complete Worksheet 34.
_____	**43.** Read Chapter 35; complete Worksheet 35. Prepare for a quiz on column 4 of the spelling list (see Chapter 2).
_____	**44.** Read Chapter 36; complete Worksheet 36.
_____	**45.** Read Chapter 37; complete Worksheet 37.
_____	**46.** Read Chapter 38; complete Worksheet 38.
_____	**47.** Read Chapter 39; complete Worksheet 39.
_____	**48.** Read Chapter 40; complete Worksheet 40.
_____	**49.** Prepare for a final examination.

Pretest (Optional)

DIRECTIONS: Consider carefully each of the 25 sentences that follow. Underscore any word, word combination, punctuation mark, or abbreviation that would be unacceptable in business; then write the preferred form in the space provided. If a sentence is perfectly acceptable as printed, place a C in the space.

Example: The plan will succeed if <u>her</u> and Weibold cooperate.

_____she_____

1. In his speech Jon inferred that his goals are different from mine.

1. _____

2. I reached your office at 3 P.M., but you already left.

2. _____

3. Neither of the losers seem to feel bad about the outcome.

3. _____

4. If Fenster was here, he would help you and me with this problem.

4. _____

5. One of the lookers-on told me that the air smelled pleasantly.

5. _____

6. By the time we reach New Hampshire, Cassie already will graduate.

6. _____

7. The Flahertys expect us to pay six month's interest as a penalty.

7. _____

8. Lee's and Beth's new computer is identical with mine.

8. _____

9. The Jones's own a shop that offers ladies' dresses at reasonable prices.

9. _____

10. The winners are Molinski and I, just like you predicted.

10. _____

11. Lasser whom we all trusted, divided the profits among the four of us.

11. _____

12. We will try and reach our sales quota by September 20.

12. _____

13. The air conditioner runs smoothly now, but we seldom ever use it.

13. _____

14. If the climate here were more healthful, our employees would have less problems.

14. _____

15. He would have lain down if his telephone had not rung continuously.

16. His only employees are my two sisters-in-law and me.

17. Lynn Connery is one of the executives who are opposed to the new policies.

18. Let me know by Friday if either Medwig or I am eligible to go.

19. Wenzel & Bowditch, Inc., has closed their New Jersey plant.

20. He mentioned Anne's withdrawing from her two Science classes.

21. Both attorneys seem to favor three or four-day weekends.

22. Travis's involvement in the affair was a well kept secret.

23. He asked me if this building was older than his building on Tenth Street.

24. On my desk are a map and a compass that you may use.

25. The principal speaker gave us some real helpful ideas.

15. _____

16. _____

17. _____

18. _____

19. _____

20. _____

21. _____

22. _____

23. _____

24. _____

25. _____

Business Language and Dictionaries

■ POINT TO PONDER

The typical college-level dictionary is a
virtual treasure chest of useful information.

Recently a friend asked me why a book that deals with English must be revised every few years. He wanted to know if language really changes as time goes by. I had to admit that there have been no *major* changes in recent years. The rules of grammar are about the same now as they were in the 1890s.

As time passes, though, our language *does* change in a number of minor ways. Also, *the way that businesspeople use words* tends to change. Observe the following paragraph, which was written about 100 years ago.

> We wish to acknowledge your letter of recent date. Pursuant to your inquiry therein, permit us to say that we should like the order in question filled promptly. We would ask that you be so kind as to include an additional 20 reams of Chicopee bond paper (Stock #261B).

Not many people in today's business world would employ such a humble tone. In addition, the paragraph is much too wordy to meet today's standards. The formal tone of the paragraph is no longer acceptable in business. When writing, a person should attempt to sound *natural,* not formal. There is a difference, of course, between *business English* and the very informal language of relaxed conversation.

This first chapter offers a few recommendations for *business* writers. You will also find a number of comments on dictionary usage. Chapter 2 provides some valuable spelling rules, while Chapters 3 and 4 present several terms that are basic to an understanding of grammar. As you read, be aware that, ideally, business language is *clear, concise,* and *grammatical.*

RECOMMENDATIONS
FOR BUSINESS WRITERS

This text offers many recommendations for anyone who uses our language. Among the most important for business writers are these five:

1. Avoid the use of informal expressions that are unbusinesslike.

A person writing a business letter or report should try not to be too informal. It is generally wise to avoid those words that are marked *Slang* or *Informal* or *Colloquial* in your dictionary. Most of us, of course, use such words now and then in our business writing. The occasional use of words that are not considered standard English may help to make our writing more interesting. Most business writers, however, avoid words like those that are italicized in these sentences:

The other *guys* have a better product.

We are *dying* to hear the news.

Our dispatcher is a *dud.*

He didn't have an *alibi* for being late.

She is *crazy* about your idea.

The sales presentation was a complete *flop.*

Her attire was really *far out.*

All six of us felt that the boss was a bit *nutty.*

Your own judgment should tell you that expressions like those in italics would not be acceptable in business. If, however, you are not sure of yourself, a good dictionary can be extremely helpful. Labels such as *informal, colloquial,* or *slang* tell you that the word, as defined, is not standard English. Note that the noun *slew* has been labeled *Colloq.* in *Webster's New World Dictionary* (see page 4). Most business writers would not use the expression *a slew of people.* At least one popular dictionary, by the way, does not attempt to classify words as *informal* or *colloquial.*

2. Omit unnecessary words.

Perhaps nothing is more annoying to busy executives than wordiness. They don't want to spend time reading long, rambling reports that are wasteful of words. The person who writes *Please try our product for one month* will be better appreciated than the one who writes *Will you be so kind as to try our product for the duration of one month.* Here are other examples:

DON'T USE: visible to the eye   USE: visible

DON'T USE: for the reason that   USE: because

DON'T USE: along the lines of   USE: like

(You will find other examples in Chapter 26.)

3. Avoid needless repetition.

Our language provides us with many ways to express a single idea. The number of ways that come to mind may be limited by the size of one's vocabulary. Business writing, though, should not challenge the reader. Ideally, it conveys ideas in language that can be easily understood. A writer, of course, should not use a particular word over and over again. Each of us needs to know enough words so that we can avoid annoying repetition. No one should feel compelled to use the word *factory* five times in a single paragraph. After all, a word such as *firm, plant, concern,* or *subsidiary* might convey the basic idea. When *the right word* doesn't come to mind, check a dictionary or a thesaurus.

4. Use constructions that are grammatically correct.

Grammatical errors do not belong in business writing. Although most people don't enjoy the study of grammar, its mastery can be extremely helpful in business. Men and women who express themselves well are likely to be chosen for management training programs. Anyone who is planning a career in the business world should be deadly serious about the study of grammar.

5. Use your dictionary skillfully.

A careful business writer is likely to make frequent use of a reliable dictionary. To be really dependable, a reference book should have a fairly recent copyright date. The dictionary that was printed more than ten years ago contains too many entries that are out of date. Our language is undergoing constant change. New words are added frequently, and old words are being used in new ways. A serious student would do well to acquire a recent edition of a dependable dictionary.

DICTIONARY NOTES

A college-level dictionary contains a lengthy explanation of how the book should be used. It is likely to be found just before the main listing of words. You will also find that a number of chapters in this text contain suggestions concerning the use of a dictionary. Here are just a few general ideas:

1. **CHOICE** The best dictionaries for classroom use are *abridged;* that is, they do *not* contain every word in the English language. Because they are small, pocket dictionaries have proved to be popular. Every student, however, should have at least one college-level dictionary with 150,000 or more entries.
2. **GUIDE WORDS** Two words appear in large boldface at the top of each dictionary page. The one to the left is the first entry word on the page; the one to the right is the last entry word. All words in the dictionary, of course, are arranged alphabetically. By noting the guide words, a person can quickly determine whether a particular word is listed on that page.
3. **SYLLABICATION** Entry words, which appear in boldface, are likely to be divided into syllables by the use of dots or lines. On page 4 the entry *sleep • walk • ing* tells us that the word should be written without a space or a hyphen *(sleepwalking).*
4. **PRONUNCIATION** Just after an entry word you are likely to find its *phonetic spelling* in parentheses. There will also be marks to tell you exactly how the word should be pronounced. In most dictionaries an accent mark appears *after* any syllable to be accented. In many dictionaries a pronunciation key will be found at the bottom of every odd-numbered page. (Note such a key on page 4.)
5. **ETYMOLOGY** The etymology of a word (its history or derivation) may appear in brackets near the beginning of an entry, as in *Webster's New World Dictionary* (see first entry on page 4). Other dictionaries put the etymology near the end of an entry, as in *The American Heritage Dictionary.* Abbreviations used in etymologies (*OF, IE,* etc.) are explained in the front matter of a dictionary. Many of our words have been handed down from one language to another—and eventually to English. As you read the material that appears between brackets, bear in mind that the symbol < means *derived from.* The language mentioned *last,* therefore, is likely to be the language in which the word originated, possibly in a form we no longer recognize.
6. **ORDER OF ENTRIES** If a word has more than one meaning, the definitions are likely to be presented in historical order. The oldest, which now may be almost forgotten, will be given first. Definitions in a few dictionaries, however, are presented in

slay (slā) ***vt.* slew** or for 2 **slayed, slain, slay′ing** ⟦ME *slean* < OE < **slahan*, akin to Ger *schlagen*, Du *slagen* < IE base **slak-*, to hit > MIr *slacc*, sword⟧ **1** to kill or destroy in a violent way **2** [Slang] to impress, delight, amuse, etc. with overwhelming force **3** [Obs.] to strike or hit —***SYN.*** KILL[1] —**slay′er** ***n.***

SLBM submarine-launched ballistic missile

sld **1** sailed **2** sealed

sleave (slēv) ***n.*** ⟦< OE *-slæfan*, to separate; akin to *slifan*: see SLIVER⟧ **1** [Obs.] *a)* a fine silk thread separated from a large thread *b)* untwisted silk that tends to mat or tangle; floss **2** [Rare] any tangle, as of ravelings —***vt.* sleaved, sleav′ing** [Obs.] to separate or pull apart (twisted or tangled threads)

sleaze (slēz) ***n.*** ⟦back-form. < fol.⟧ [Slang] **1** the quality or condition of being sleazy; sleaziness **2** anything cheap, vulgar, shoddy, etc. **3** a shady, coarse, or immoral person: also **sleaze′bag′** (-bag′) or **sleaze′ball′** (-bôl′)

slea|zy (slē′zē) ***adj.* -zi|er, -zi·est** ⟦< *slesia*, var. of SILESIA⟧ **1** flimsy or thin in texture or substance; lacking firmness *[a sleazy rayon fabric]* **2** shoddy, shabby, cheap, morally low, etc. Also [Slang] **slea′zo** (-zō) —**slea′zi|ly** ***adv.*** —**slea′zi·ness** ***n.***

sled (sled) ***n.*** ⟦ME *sledde* < MLowG or MDu, akin to Ger *schlitten*: for IE base see SLIDE⟧ any of several types of vehicle mounted on runners for use on snow, ice, etc.: small sleds are used in the sport of coasting, large ones (also called *sledges*), for carrying loads —☆***vt.* sled′ded, sled′ding** to carry on a sled —☆***vi.*** to ride or coast on a sled —**sled′der** ***n.***

☆**sled·ding** (-iŋ) ***n.*** **1** a riding or carrying on a sled **2** the condition of the ground with reference to the use of sleds: often used figuratively *[the work was hard sledding]*

sledge[1] (slej) ***n.*, *vt.*, *vi.* sledged, sledg′ing** ⟦ME *slegge* < OE *slecge* < base of *slean*, to strike, SLAY⟧ SLEDGEHAMMER

sledge[2] (slej) ***n.*** ⟦MDu *sleedse*, akin to *sledde*, SLED⟧ a sled or sleigh for carrying loads over ice, snow, etc. —***vi.*, *vt.* sledged, sledg′ing** to go or take by sledge

sledge·ham|mer (-ham′ər) ***n.*** ⟦see SLEDGE[1]⟧ a long, heavy hammer, usually held with both hands —***vt.*, *vi.*** to strike with or as with a sledgehammer —***adj.*** crushingly powerful

sleek (slēk) ***adj.*** ⟦var. of SLICK, with Early ModE vowel lengthening⟧ **1** smooth and shiny; glossy, as a highly polished surface, well-kept hair or fur, etc. **2** of well-fed or well-groomed appearance *[fat, sleek pigeons]* **3** polished in speech and behavior, esp. in a specious way; unctuous **4** highly fashionable, or stylish; elegant —***vt.*** to make sleek; smooth: also **sleek′en** —**sleek′ly** ***adv.*** —**sleek′ness** ***n.***

sleek|it (slēk′it) ***adj.*** ⟦Scot var. of pp. of SLEEK⟧ [Scot.] **1** sleek, or smooth and shiny **2** sly, crafty, or sneaky

sleep (slēp) ***n.*** ⟦ME *slep* < OE *slæp*, akin to Ger *schlaf*, sleep, *schlaff*, loose, lax < IE **slab* < base **(s)leb-*, **(s)lab-*, loose, slack > LIP, LIMP[1], L *labor*, to slip, sink⟧ **1** *a)* a natural, regularly recurring condition of rest for the body and mind, during which the eyes are usually closed and there is little or no conscious thought or voluntary movement, but there is intermittent dreaming *b)* a spell of sleeping **2** any state of inactivity thought of as like sleep, as death, unconsciousness, hibernation, etc. **3** *Bot.* NYCTITROPISM —***vi.* slept, sleep′ing** **1** to be in the state of sleep; slumber **2** to be in a state of inactivity like sleep, as that of death, quiescence, hibernation, inattention, etc. **3** [Colloq.] to have sexual intercourse (*with*) **4** [Colloq.] to postpone a decision (*on*) to allow time for deliberation *[let me sleep on it]* **5** *Bot.* to assume a nyctitropic position at night, as petals or leaves —***vt.*** **1** to slumber in (a specified kind of sleep) *[to sleep the sleep of the just]* **2** to provide sleeping accommodations for *[a boat that sleeps four]* —**last sleep** death —**sleep around** [Slang] to have promiscuous sexual relations —**sleep away** **1** to spend in sleeping; sleep during **2** to get rid of by sleeping —**sleep in** **1** to sleep at the place where one is employed as a household servant **2** to sleep later in the morning than one usually does —**sleep off** to rid oneself of by sleeping —**sleep out** **1** to spend in sleeping; sleep throughout **2** to sleep outdoors —**sleep over** [Colloq.] to spend the night at another's home

sleep|er (slē′pər) ***n.*** ⟦ME *slepere* < OE *slæpere*⟧ **1** a person or animal that sleeps, esp. as specified *[a sound sleeper]* **2** a timber or beam laid horizontally, as on the ground, to support something above it **3** [Chiefly Brit., etc.] a tie supporting a railroad track ☆**4** SLEEPING CAR ☆**5** a previously disregarded person or thing that unexpectedly achieves success, assumes importance, etc. ☆**6** *a)* [*usually pl.*] a kind of pajamas for infants and young children, that enclose the feet *b)* BUNTING[1] (sense 3) ☆**7** *Bowling* a pin concealed by one in front of it, in bowling for a spare

sleep|i·ly (-pə lē) ***adv.*** in a sleepy or drowsy manner

sleep|i·ness (-pē nis) ***n.*** a sleepy quality or state

☆**sleeping bag** a large, warmly lined, zippered bag, often waterproof, in which a person can sleep, esp. outdoors

☆**sleeping car** a railroad car equipped with berths, compartments, etc. for passengers to sleep in

sleeping partner *Brit., etc. term for* SILENT PARTNER

☆**sleeping pill** a pill or capsule containing a drug, esp. a barbiturate, that induces sleep

sleeping sickness **1** an infectious disease, esp. common in tropical Africa, caused by either of two trypanosomes (*Trypanosoma gambiense* or *T. rhodesiense*) that are transmitted by the bite of a tsetse fly: it is characterized by fever, weakness, tremors, and lethargy, usually ending in prolonged coma and death **2** inflammation of the brain, caused by a virus and characterized by apathy, drowsiness, and lethargy

sleep·less (slēp′lis) ***adj.*** **1** unable to sleep; wakeful; restless **2** marked by absence of sleep *[a sleepless night]* **3** constantly moving, active, or alert —**sleep′less|ly** ***adv.*** —**sleep′less·ness** ***n.***

sleep·walk·ing (-wôk′iŋ) ***n.*** the act or practice of walking while asleep; somnambulism —**sleep′walk′** ***vi.*** —**sleep′walk|er** ***n.***

sleep·wear (-wer′) ***n.*** NIGHTCLOTHES

sleep|y (slē′pē) ***adj.* sleep′i·er, sleep′i·est** **1** ready or inclined to sleep; needing sleep; drowsy **2** characterized by an absence of activity; dull; idle; lethargic *[a sleepy little town]* **3** causing drowsiness; inducing sleep **4** of or exhibiting drowsiness

***SYN.*—sleepy** applies to a person who is nearly overcome by a desire to sleep and, figuratively, suggests either the power to induce sleepiness or a resemblance to this state *[a sleepy town, song, etc.]*; **drowsy** stresses the sluggishness or lethargic heaviness accompanying sleepiness *[the drowsy sentry fought off sleep through the watch]*; **somnolent** is a formal equivalent of either of the preceding *[the somnolent voice of the speaker]*; **slumberous**, a poetic equivalent, in addition sometimes suggests latent powers in repose *[a slumberous city]*

sleep|y·head (-hed′) ***n.*** a sleepy person

sleet (slēt) ***n.*** ⟦ME *slete* < OE **sliete*, akin to Ger *schlosse*, hail < IE base **(s)leu-*, loose, lax > SLUR, SLUG[1]⟧ **1** partly frozen rain, or rain that freezes as it falls **2** transparent or translucent precipitation in the form of pellets of ice that are smaller than 5 mm (.2 in.) **3** the icy coating formed when rain freezes on trees, streets, etc. —***vi.*** to shower in the form of sleet —**sleet′y** ***adj.***

sleeve (slēv) ***n.*** ⟦ME *sleve* < OE *sliefe*, akin to Du *sloof*, apron: for IE base see SLIP[3]⟧ **1** that part of a garment that covers an arm or part of an arm **2** a tube or tubelike part fitting over or around another part **3** a thin paper or plastic cover for protecting a phonograph record, usually within a JACKET (*n.* 2*b*) **4** a drogue towed by an airplane for target practice —***vt.* sleeved, sleev′ing** to provide or fit with a sleeve or sleeves —**up one's sleeve** hidden or secret but ready at hand

sleeved (slēvd) ***adj.*** fitted with sleeves: often in hyphenated compounds *[short-sleeved]*

sleeve·less (slēv′lis) ***adj.*** having no sleeve or sleeves *[a sleeveless sweater]*

sleeve·let (-lit) ***n.*** a covering fitted over the lower part of a garment sleeve, as to protect it from soiling

☆**sleigh** (slā) ***n.*** ⟦Du *slee*, contr. of *slede*, a SLED⟧ a light vehicle on runners, usually horse-drawn, for carrying persons over snow and ice —***vi.*** to ride in or drive a sleigh

☆**sleigh bells** a number of small, spherical bells fixed to the harness straps of an animal drawing a sleigh

sleight (slīt) ***n.*** ⟦ME < ON *slœgth* < *slœgr*, crafty, clever: see SLY⟧ **1** cunning or craft used in deceiving **2** skill or dexterity

sleight of hand **1** skill with the hands, esp. in confusing or deceiving onlookers, as in doing magic tricks; legerdemain **2** a trick or tricks thus performed

slen·der (slen′dər) ***adj.*** ⟦ME *slendre, sclendre* < ?⟧ **1** small in width as compared with the length or height; long and thin **2** having a slim, trim figure *[a slender girl]* **3** small or limited in amount, size, extent, etc.; meager *[slender earnings]* **4** of little force or validity; having slight foundation; feeble *[slender hope]* —**slen′der|ly** ***adv.*** —**slen′der·ness** ***n.***

slen·der·ize (-īz′) ***vt.* -ized′, -iz′ing** to make or cause to seem slender —***vi.*** to become slender

slept (slept) ***vi.*, *vt.*** *pt. & pp. of* SLEEP

Sles·vig (sles′vikh) *Dan. name of* SCHLESWIG

sleuth (slo͞oth) ***n.*** ⟦ME, a trail, spoor < ON *slóth*, akin to *slothra*, to drag (oneself) ahead: for IE base see SLUG[1]⟧ **1** [Rare] a dog, as a bloodhound, that can follow a trail by scent: also **sleuth′hound′** (-hound′) ☆**2** [Colloq.] a detective —☆***vi.*** to act as a detective

☆**slew**[1] (slo͞o) ***n.*** *alt. sp. of* SLOUGH[2] (sense 4)

slew[2] (slo͞o) ***n.*, *vt.*, *vi.*** *alt. sp. of* SLUE[1]

☆**slew**[3] (slo͞o) ***n.*** ⟦Ir *sluagh*, a host⟧ [Colloq.] a large number, group, or amount; a lot

slew[4] (slo͞o) ***vt.*** *pt. of* SLAY

slice (slīs) ***n.*** ⟦ME < OFr *esclice* < *esclicier*, to slice < Frank *slizzan*, akin to SLIT⟧ **1** a relatively thin, broad piece cut from an object having some bulk or volume *[a slice of apple]* **2** a part, portion, or share *[a slice of one's earnings]* **3** any of various implements with a flat, broad blade, as a spatula **4** *a)* the path of a hit ball that curves away to the right from a right-handed player or to the left from a left-handed player *b)* a ball that follows such a path —***vt.* sliced, slic′ing** **1** cut into slices **2** *a)* to cut off as in a slice or slices (often with *off, from, away,* etc.) *b)* to cut across or through like a knife **3** to separate into parts or shares *[sliced up the profits]* **4** to use a SLICE (*n.* 3) or slice bar to work at, spread, remove, etc. **5** to hit (a ball) in a SLICE (*n.* 4*a*) —***vi.*** **1** to cut (*through*) like a knife *[a plow slicing through the earth]* **2** to hit a ball in a SLICE (*n.* 4*a*) —**slic′er** ***n.***

slice bar an iron bar with a broad, thin end, used in a coal furnace to loosen coals, clear out ashes, etc.

slick (slik) ***vt.*** ⟦ME *slikien* < OE *slician*, to make smooth, akin to ON *slikr*, smooth < IE **(s)leig-*, slimy, to smooth, glide < base **(s)lei-*: see SLIDE⟧ **1** to make sleek, glossy, or smooth **2** [Colloq.] to make smart, neat, or tidy: usually with *up* —***adj.*** ⟦ME *slike* < the v.⟧ **1** sleek; glossy; smooth **2** slippery; oily, as a surface **3** accomplished; adept; clever; ingenious **4** [Colloq.] clever in deception or trickery; deceptively plausible; smooth *[a slick alibi]* **5** [Colloq.] having or showing skill in composition or technique but little depth or literary significance *[a slick style of writing]* **6** [Old Slang] excellent, fine, enjoyable, attractive, etc. —***n.*** ☆**1** *a)* a smooth area on the surface of

at, āte, cär; ten, ēve; is, īce; gō, hôrn, lo͝ok, to͞ol; oil, out; up, fur; ə *for unstressed vowels, as* a *in* ago, u *in* focus; ′ *as in* Latin (lat′'n); chin; she; zh *as in* azure (azh′ər); thin, *the*; ŋ *as in* ring (riŋ)
In etymologies: * = unattested; < = derived from; > = from which
☆ = Americanism **See inside front and back covers**

order of frequency of use. That is, the most common meaning of a word is shown first; the least common meaning is shown last.

7. **PARTS OF SPEECH** Before a dictionary presents definitions for a particular word, it indicates the part of speech. Your dictionary uses abbreviations such as *n., vt., vi., pron., adj., conj.,* or *interj.* Many words in our language may be used as more than one part of speech.

8. **USAGE LABELS** A dictionary entry may include a label that restricts the use of a word in some way. The label *Obs.,* which means *obsolete,* tells us that the definition given is out of date. The label *Informal* (or *Colloq.*) means that the word as defined may not be suitable in situations that call for the use of *standard* English. Make sure that you understand the meanings of labels such as these: *Rare, Brit., Illit., Dial., Non-standard, Slang, Bot.*

9. **TWO-WORD EXPRESSIONS** A dictionary provides entries for many common expressions that have two or more words. You are likely to find entries for *post card, half dollar,* and *social security,* among others. If your dictionary does not list a particular expression, do not write it as a single word. The lack of an entry for *peach tree* tells me that this expression should be written as two words.

10. **PREFIXES AND SUFFIXES** College-level dictionaries include prefixes (*ante, bi, circum,* etc.) and suffixes (*-able, -ous,* etc.) in the main listing. If your dictionary does not list a word such as *acrophobia,* you may have to look up the two *parts* of the word. *Acro* (the prefix, or beginning) means "top, summit, height." Your dictionary will tell you that *phobia,* the root word, means "an abnormal or illogical fear." *Phobia* is shown in most dictionaries as a word and as a suffix (a word ending).

11. **SYNONYMS** Synonyms are words that have similar meanings. If the meanings are not identical, your dictionary may provide a paragraph that points out any slight differences. The paragraph is always placed after the entry for one of the synonyms discussed. Note on page 4 the abbreviation *SYN.* following the entry for the word *sleepy.* In addition to *sleepy,* the words *drowsy, somnolent,* and *slumberous* are discussed. After the entry for each of these words you would expect to find this notation: —*SYN.* see *sleepy.*

12. **INFLECTED FORMS** A word that has several different forms is said to be inflected (*do, did, done,* etc.). Most dictionaries include only those inflected forms that are *irregular* (or unusual). You are not likely to find common *(regular)* inflected forms such as *buildings.* An irregular plural form like *women,* though, would definitely appear in your dictionary. You will become aware of many inflected forms as you study the eight parts of speech.

13. **SIGNS AND SYMBOLS** Most dictionaries contain a special appendix listing signs and symbols used in astronomy, chemistry, mathematics, and other such disciplines. In *The American Heritage Dictionary* you will find signs and symbols in the main listing.

FINAL THOUGHTS

Business English is really *standard English.* A dictionary definition that has no usage label (*Obs., Colloq.,* etc.) is considered to be standard.

The three words that best describe business English are *clear, concise,* and *grammatical.* The three are equally important.

Corporation presidents cannot tolerate employees who consistently waste words. They do not enjoy reading lengthy reports that make only a few minor points. In business, time is money. Conciseness is extremely important.

The unpopularity of grammar can work to your advantage. If you learn the rules well, you may one day find yourself among the comparative few who can qualify for a top-paying position in industry.

THE IMPACT OF LANGUAGE

A DICTIONARY PLUS

The American Heritage Dictionary is a fine reference work that any college student would find useful. Most dictionaries, you may have discovered, have little to say about controversial points of grammar. Some have even abandoned the use of labels such as *colloquial* or *informal* rather than impose judgments upon users.

Like most lexicographers, the makers of *The American Heritage Dictionary* accept standard usage as the authority of correctness, but they have firmly rejected the idea that a dictionary should contain no value judgments. To help determine correctness, they commissioned a panel of professional writers and speakers—about a hundred novelists, essayists, poets, journalists, science writers, sports writers, public officials, and professors. Although these authorities were asked several hundred questions, they agreed unanimously in only one instance: They all objected to the use of *simultaneous* as an adverb. Following are five of the sentences that these professional writers and speakers were asked to evaluate. Decide whether you would approve or disapprove of each construction; then note (at the bottom of this page) how the panelists voted.

1. There is no doubt *but what* he will try.
2. He invited Mary and *myself* to dinner.
3. Nobody thinks that the criticism applied to *their* own work.
4. This cigarette tastes good *like* a cigarette should.
5. It's *me.* (Spoken response to the question *Who is it?*)

—————————— HOW THE PANELISTS VOTED ——————————

(1) Disapproved 95–5 in favor of *that;* (2) Disapproved 95–5 in favor of *me;* (3) Disapproved 95–5 in favor of *her or his;* (4) Disapproved 84–16 in favor of *as;* (5) Approved 60–40 as opposed to *I.*

---

wWWw ———————— **Watching the Web** ————————

| **Back** | **Forward** | **Home** | **Reload** | **Images** | **Open** |

```
Make Money from your Home
Don't wait another day. Start to use your at-home time to
make you rich. Many people have already discovered success.
Please use this opportunity to take the chance to get to know
us, and we are sure that you will see we're on the level.
```

| order now | | no thanks |

_____WORKSHEET 1_____

BUSINESS LANGUAGE AND DICTIONARIES

An asterisk (*) in a space tells you that the answer is given in the section headed "Key Items." Attempt to determine the answer yourself before you turn to that section, which begins on page 433.

PART A.   Read the following paragraph from a business letter. Look for colloquialisms. Underscore each error, and then rewrite the paragraph together, using the best judgment of the group.

I am writing to complain about the order your company sent us this week. We are usually crazy about the quality of your stuff, but you can bet we had a fit over this order. Materials were ripped up and completely unusable. When I brought the package to my boss, she was really mad. Thanks to your poor packing, we lost one of our biggest orders in ages. It's up to you to make things right.

_____

* _____

_____

_____

_____

_____

_____

_____

PART B.   Each sentence contains an expression (in italics) that is too informal for business. In the space provided, suggest one that would be more acceptable. If you are working as a collaborative team, decide together on a better alternative.

Example: In January of last year his firm went
               belly up.   bankrupt
                                                    _____

   1. Our leading product this season seems to be
          a *flop.*   1. * _____

   2. He *made a mess of* the negotiations with our
          competitors.   2. _____

   3. She *got stuck with* the leftover office.   3. * _____

4. Hempley always looks *a little spacey* on
on Monday mornings.

4. _____

5. You don't have to *get mad* just because the
vote was negative.

5. _____

PART C.   Each sentence has an expression (in italics) tht is wasteful of words. You are to
suggest one that is shorter and more acceptable.

Example: Ms. Maggio agrees that the office
walls should be *green in color.*

_____green_____

1. The Senator's remarks were *in reference
to* our firm.

1. * _____

2. Every office *with the exception of* yours is
reasonably large.

2. * _____

3. Our manager has found a better copier for
the price of $1,000.

3. * _____

4. We will continue to meet each Tuesday *until
such time as* the merger is final.

4. _____

5. We have four profitable overseas offices *at
the present time.*

5. _____

6. Sam Duncan, the finance manager, says that
each and every department must conserve.

6. _____

7. We will need more office space *in the event
that* we add several new word processors.

7. _____

8. *Enclosed herewith* are two brochures
that describe our optical scanner.

8. _____

9. Our systems analyst will be in London for
the duration of one week.

9. _____

10. I will edit the accounting forms *due to the
fact that* the current forms are too confusing.

10. _____

PART D.   Use your dictionary to find the correct response. Write A or B.

1. The *word err* has (A) two, (B) three acceptable pronunciations, one of
which rhymes with *sir.*

1. * _____

2. The ornamental screw on top of a lampshade is a (A) *lintel,* (B) *finial.*

2. * _____

3. The word *ethic* comes at its earliest point from (A) Latin, (B) Greek.

3. * _____

4. A *concierge* is a (A) person, (B) building.

4. * _____

5. To change or modify defines (A) *alter,* (B) *altar.*

5. * _____

6. The word *nuclear* can be correctly pronounced noo-kyoo-ler.
(A) true, (B) false

6. _____

7. Someone who is *malevolent* has (A) bad dreams, (B) ill will towards
others.

7. _____

8. If something is *precarious,* it is (A) uncertain, (B) valuable.

8. _____

9. The word *mercurial* should be accented on the (A) first, (B) second
syllable.

9. _____

10. The first or preferred spelling of this word is (A) *judgment,*
(B) *judgement.*   **10.** _____

11. A word meaning *sincere* or *heartfelt* is (A) *ernest,* (B) *earnest.*   **11.** _____

12. The word *renaissance* originated in (A) Greek, (B) French.   **12.** _____

13. A *cartographer* makes (A) carriages, (B) maps.   **13.** _____

14. *Couture* is a field populated by (A) designers, (B) musicians.   **14.** _____

15. The noun *slide* has (A) three, (B) at least four meanings.   **15.** _____

PART E.   Write the syllable that should bear the principal accent when the word is pronounced. Use your dictionary whenever necessary.

Example: resuscitate _____sus_____

1. conducive   *_____   **6.** recalcitrant   _____

2. declaration   *_____   **7.** elasticity   _____

3. mischievous   *_____   **8.** degenerate   _____

4. amenable   _____   **9.** manifestation   _____

5. omnipotent   _____   **10.** ameliorate   _____

PART F.   Use your dictionary. Write the letter that identifies the correct response. If you do this exercise collaboratively, try using several different dictionaries and check for similarities and differences.

1. The prefix *ex* usually has this meaning.
   (A) after   (C) under
   (B) out   (D) before   **1.** _____

2. Which word has not been correctly divided into syllables?
   (A) symp-tom   (C) pro-mo-tion
   (B) ec-stas-y   (D) prob-lem   **2.** *_____

3. Which one of the following forms is correct?
   (A) grand-parent   (C) granparent
   (B) grand parent   (D) grandparent   **3.** *_____

4. If an idea is approved *tacitly,*
   (A) people agree in silence   (C) people don't approve it
   (B) people applaud it quietly   **4.** _____

5. The verb *recognize* has
   (A) at most four meanings   (C) a law-related meaning
   (B) at least five meanings   (D) B and C   **5.** _____

6. The word *ram* can be used as a
   (A) noun only   (C) noun and verb
   (B) noun and preposition   (D) verb only   **6.** _____

7. The word *maverick* comes from
   (A) Latin   (C) German
   (B) Greek   (D) Mr. S. Maverick   **7.** _____

8. *Immeasurable* and *immensurable* are words that
(A) contradict (B) are equal to one another

8. _____

9. *Fehling's solution* refers to a(n)
(A) astronomy problem (C) mixture of chemicals
(B) mathematics equation

9. _____

10. The word *range* has about 15 possible meanings when used as a(n)
(A) noun (C) verb
(B) adjective (D) adverb

10. _____

11. The word *even* can be used as a(n)
(A) noun or pronoun (C) pronoun or preposition
(B) adjective or adverb (D) noun or preposition

11. _____

12. Fort George is a
(A) fortress (C) river
(B) town (D) resort

12. _____

13. Pavlova was a
(A) dancer (C) singer
(B) scientist (D) director

13. _____

14. Orson Welles' real first name was
(A) John (C) William
(B) James (D) George

14. _____

15. The word *expletive* refers to words that fill out a sentence or a line but
(A) add no meaning (C) take away original meaning
(B) add a double meaning

15. _____

See Optional Exercises on following pages.

THE DICTIONARY SAYS . . .

Two colleagues of mine were conversing in my office when one of them used the word *harass*. Because he had accented the second syllable, his listener challenged his pronunciation. For several minutes they engaged in a lively discussion concerning the word *harass*. One was certain that it should be accented on the first syllable; the other was just as certain that the second syllable should be accented.

A few days earlier I had checked the word *harass* in four different dictionaries and discovered that *both* pronunciations are shown in all four of them. Interestingly, two of my reference books first show the word with the accent on the second syllable, while the other two dictionaries show that version *last*. The word in question, according to all four sources, *does* have two acceptable pronunciations.

It is important to note that the variant listed first is not necessarily preferred. The "Guide to the Dictionary" in *Webster's New World* has this to say: "When two or more pronunciations for a single word are given, the order in which they are entered does not necessarily mean that the first is preferred to or more correct than the one that follows." If usage is about evenly divided, the editor's preference generally prevails. When I had shared these insights with my colleagues, they stopped harassing each other.

Name _____ **Date** _____

OPTIONAL EXERCISES

OPTION 1   Use the dictionary excerpt on page 4 of this text to answer the following questions.

1. How many meanings does the noun *sleep* have?

2. Where is sleeping sickness common?

3. In what language did the word *sleuth* originate?

4. What word is listed as the past tense of the verb *slay?*

5. *Sledge hammer* can be used as any of what three parts of speech?

6. Which homonym means a fine wisp of thread separated from a larger thread? *Sleeve* or *sleave?*

7. How many meanings are listed for the noun *sleeper?*

8. What is the phonetic spelling of both *sleave* and *sleeve?*

9. Of six meanings of the word *slick,* how many are not labeled *colloquial?*

10. In which language did the word *slender* originate?

11. *Sld* can be an abbreviation for either of what two words?

12. A small star precedes *sleigh* and several other entry words. According to the notes at the bottom of page 4, what does the star mean?

13. Does the word *slice* have more meanings as a verb or as a noun?

14. The one-word synonym for *sleep walking* is what?

15. What is the phonetic spelling of the word *slick?*

1. _____

2. _____

3. * _____

4. _____

    *

5. _____

6. _____

7. _____

8. * _____

9. _____

10. _____

11. _____

12. _____

13. _____

14. _____

15. _____

OPTION 2   Use your dictionary. Write the letter that identifies the correct response.

1. Franklin Delano Roosevelt was born in the year
   (A) 1898   (C) 1882
   (B) 1890   (D) 1906   **1.** * _____

2. A *meerschaum* is
   (A) smoked   (C) eaten
   (B) folded   (D) printed   **2.** * _____

3. Joseph Pulitzer was a
   (A) scientist   (C) mathematician
   (B) novelist   (D) newspaper publisher   3. _____

4. What does the word *dissemble* mean?
   (A) to disrupt   (C) to congregate
   (B) to reveal   (D) to conceal or disguise   4. _____

5. A person may use *semaphore* to
   (A) signal someone   (C) take dictation
   (B) start an engine   (D) avoid infection   5. _____

6. Which word best describes people who wear very inexpensive clothing and deny themselves any form of luxury?
   (A) frugal   (C) thrifty
   (B) economical   (D) stingy   6. *_____

7. If you are an *anthropophile,* you
   (A) love human flesh   (C) love the outdoors
   (B) fear human beings (D) eat human beings   7. _____

8. You would probably make use of *rials* if you lived in
   (A) New Zealand   (C) Iran
   (B) Kenya   (D) Tibet   8. _____

9. An excited, enthusiastic person could be described as
   (A) esoteric   (C) eclectic
   (B) abstemious   (D) ebullient   9. _____

10. A *peripatetic* person spends considerable time in
   (A) thinking   (C) working
   (B) walking   (D) helping others   10. _____

OPTION 3 Some dictionaries (but not all) tell us that the word *jerk* is *informal* or *slang* in the sentence *Your agent is a jerk.* Should dictionary editors provide such labels? Are they qualified to do so? Express your views in a brief paragraph.

_____

_____

_____

_____

_____

_____

_____

_____

_____

_____

_____

_____

_____

_____

_____

_____

CHAPTER 2

A Few Spelling Rules

This chapter, which concerns the spelling of English words, is the second of four introductory chapters. It is presented early in the text because accurate spelling is important to virtually all writers of business communications. The mastery of spelling skills, however, is complicated by the fact that many English words are formed in strange, unexpected ways.

THE CHALLENGE OF SPELLING CORRECTLY

Several high-ranking business executives, as well as two U.S. presidents, have expressed a complete lack of confidence in spelling English words correctly. Throughout our society we find countless people who are thoroughly confused by letter combinations that seem inconsistent or illogical (*feign, vein, should, rough, bought, through, dew, lieu, sign, caught,* among others). Spelling mastery is, without a doubt, a formidable challenge to many writers. It is, however, of significant importance to anyone preparing for a career in today's business arena and should not be taken lightly.

Spelling tends to be difficult because English is made up of words borrowed from just about every other language known to humanity. Among those languages are Latin, Greek, French, German, Welsh, and Frisian, as well as others that have made less significant contributions. As a result, of course, the words in our language lack uniformity and can pose problems for even the most conscientious writers.

Unfortunately, many people in today's business world tend to question the basic intelligence of anyone who makes frequent spelling errors. Spelling mastery, they would point out,

13

is primarily a matter of memorization—and you probably agree. A person's most valuable aids in this area are a keen power of observation and a retentive memory. Every executive should be able to recognize spelling errors that appear in communications prepared by a secretary or an administrative assistant. No executive should feel that *correct spelling* is someone else's responsibility.

EIGHT HELPFUL RULES

The English language would be far less complex if every word were spelled phonetically (according to sound) or if each word were governed by a strict rule. Such is not the case. Several writers prefer to use the word *guidelines,* rather than *rules,* because there are so many exceptions. The eight presented in this chapter are well worth your attention, especially if you have ever found spelling to be difficult. The following rule can help you to spell hundreds of words correctly because it has frequent applications and very few exceptions. Study it carefully.

> **RULE 1** If a one-syllable word ends in consonant-vowel-consonant, double the final consonant before adding a suffix that begins with a vowel.

Note these examples:

	Suffix	*New Word*
wrap	er	wrapper
ton	age	tonnage
hum	ing	humming
star	ed	starred
drug	ist	druggist
big	est	biggest
tag	ed	tagged
bet	or	bettor
brag	ing	bragging

This rule does not apply if the final consonant is *x (boxes, mixed)* or if it is not pronounced. Note that in *row* the final consonant is silent. It is not doubled, therefore, in the word *rowing.*

In words such as *quit,* the *u* has the sound of *w,* a consonant. The rule, then, may be applied. Note these spellings; *quitter, quizzes.*

Because the next rule cannot be expressed briefly, it may seem complicated. Actually, in spite of its length, you should not find it difficult to master. That mastery may save you many trips to the dictionary because lexicographers, in compiling dictionary entries, seldom violate this rule. Learn it well.

> **RULE 2** If a two-syllable word ends in consonant-vowel-consonant and is accented on the second syllable, double the final consonant before adding a suffix that begins with a vowel.

Here are some examples:

	Suffix	New Word
occur	ence	occurrence
refer	ed	referred
expel	ing	expelling
transmit	er	transmitter
defer	ed	deferred
begin	er	beginner
acquit	al	acquittal
repel	ing	repelling
admit	ance	admittance
allot	ed	allotted

In some words, such as *reference* (REF er ence), the accent changes to the first syllable when the suffix is added. In most such cases the final consonant of the root word is not doubled. The rule does not apply to words such as *bestow,* in which the final consonant is not pronounced. Note these spellings: *bestowed, bestowing.* The word *programmer,* which became popular with the advent of computers, is usually spelled with two *m*'s even though it is accented on the first syllable.

RULE 3 If a word ends in *e* preceded by a consonant, drop the *e* before adding a suffix that begins with a vowel.

Note the following examples:

	Suffix	New Word
hope	ing	hoping
excuse	able	excusable
please	ant	pleasant
scarce	ity	scarcity
desire	ous	desirous
choose	ing	choosing
like	able	likable
obese	ity	obesity
freeze	ing	freezing
excite	able	excitable

The rule implies, of course, that the final *e* should be retained if a suffix beginning with a consonant is added.

move	ment	movement
tire	less	tireless
remote	ness	remoteness
strange	ly	strangely
appease	ment	appeasement

Unfortunately our language has few, if any, spelling rules that are completely dependable. Rule 3 has several noteworthy exceptions, such as these: *argument, judgment, ninth, truly, wholly, acknowledgment.*

Other exceptions include words that end with the *soft* sound of *ge* or *ce.* The *e* is generally retained when *able* or *ous* is added, as in these words: *changeable, manageable, noticeable, advantageous, courageous.*

Even though few spelling rules are completely reliable, they can be extremely helpful when a dictionary is not available. The next rule is one that you may have learned in grade school simply as "*i* before *e* except after *c*."

RULE 4   After a soft *c*, write the *e* before the *i* when these two letters appear in sequence.

deceive   receive   conceive   perceive   receipt   deceit

Also write the *e* before the *i* when these letters are to be pronounced with the sound of *long a.*

sleigh   skein   heinous   inveigh   neighbor   vein   reign

In most other words the *i* is written first.

believe   grieve   tier   mischievous   spiel   relief   shriek

Several common words are exceptions to the general rule. The correct spellings of these words will demand individual attention:

forfeit   height   counterfeit   sleight   seize   weird

RULE 5   Learn to recognize the two parts of any word that is made up of a prefix and a root.

Several of the most commonly misspelled words in our language are made up of a prefix, such as *un,* and a familiar root, such as *natural.* (Note that the word *unnatural* must be spelled with two *n*'s). An awareness of a few common prefixes can help a writer to avoid misspelling such words. Following are several words that may prove troublesome to those who fail to recognize prefixes.

dis	+ appear	= disappear	mis	+ spell	= misspell
il	+ legible	= illegible	over	+ ripe	= overripe
il	+ logical	= illogical	re	+ commend	= recommend
inter	+ racial	= interracial	under	+ rate	= underrate
mis	+ shape	= misshape	un	+ noticed	= unnoticed

RULE 6   If a word ends with *y* preceded by a consonant, generally change the *y* to an *i* before adding a suffix other than *ing.*

A variation of this rule will be discussed in Chapter 6, which is concerned with the plural forms of nouns. An understanding of the foregoing rule may help you to spell a significant number of nouns, verbs, and adjectives correctly. Note these correct spellings:

worry	+ er	= worrier	tasty	+ er	= tastier
worry	+ some	= worrisome	carry	+ s	= carries
hurry	+ s	= hurries	company	+ s	= companies
lazy	+ est	= laziest	jury	+ s	= juries
happy	+ ness	= happiness	BUT:		
merry	+ est	= merriest	carry	+ ing	= carrying
vary	+ s	= varies	worry	+ ing	= worrying

We come now to a rule for those who spell correctly most of the time but have difficulty with just a few challenging words.

RULE 7	Build a memory device, or mnemonic, for each word that is difficult to master.

The average troublesome word is likely to have only one challenging letter or combination of letters. Consider the word *asphalt.* The most common misspelling of this word is, without a doubt, *asfalt.* Students who habitually write *f* instead of *ph* might do well to build a mnemonic that will make the correct spelling *difficult to forget.* They may decide to associate the word *asphalt* with the word *pavement.* If they concentrate for a moment on the expression *asphalt pavement* and note the use of the letter *p* in each of those words, they will never again spell asphalt with an *f.* Elementary? Of course. The simplicity of such memory devices accounts for their effectiveness. In fact, the mnemonic that impresses you as being completely nonsensical may prove to be the most useful of all. Here are a few that have proved helpful to college students:

pursue (not *persue*)	Remember this sentence: *Pursue* the *purse* snatcher. Note the *pur* in each word.
parallel (not *paralell*)	*All* the lines are par*all*el. The word *all* appears in the word *parallel.*
personnel (not *personal*)	*Personnel* is basically a noun; *personal* is an adjective. Note the two *n*'s in both *noun* and *personnel.*
privilege (not *priviledge*)	You will not spell this word with a *d* if you remember this nonsensical sentence: It will be your privi*lege* to stand on one *leg.* The word *leg,* of course, appears in *privilege.*

RULE 8	Keep a good dictionary handy and use it whenever the need arises.

Many words in our language have more than one spelling. Dictionaries indicate preferred forms in a variety of ways. In *Webster's New Collegiate,* spellings that are equally acceptable are joined by *or* and printed in boldface type. If the first spelling given is more acceptable, the word *also* precedes the secondary spelling in both the *Collegiate* and *The American Heritage Dictionary.*

In *Webster's New World Dictionary,* definitions are given with the form known or judged to be the one most frequently used. Other spellings are likely to be cross-referred to that entry. A variant spelling that is used less frequently than the main-entry spelling may appear at the end of the entry block. If you read the guide to usage in the introductory pages of your dictionary, you will have no difficulty in determining the preferred spelling of a word.

A Spelling List

A number of years ago a researcher in the field of English made the claim that 95 percent of the spelling errors made by educated people occur in just 100 words. He apparently felt, rightfully or wrongfully, that many people could become excellent spellers simply by mastering those 100 words. Our language has undergone many changes in the past two decades, but many of the same words *do* continue to plague us. The list on the following page contains the 100 words in question as well as 100 others that historically have given trouble. Your instructor may choose to quiz you on any or all of the four columns.

200 TROUBLESOME WORDS

1	*2*	*3*	*4*
absence	conscience	indelible	physician
absorption	consensus	independent	plagiarism
accede	convenient	indispensable	plebeian
accessible	convertible	inimitable	possesses
accommodate	coolly	inoculate	potato
accumulate	corroborate	insistent	precede
achieve	criticism	intermediary	predictable
acoustics	definitely	irresistible	preferred
acquittal	description	irritable	privilege
advantageous	desirable	jewelry	procedure
affiliated	despair	judgment/judgement	proceed
aggressive	development	judicial	professor
alignment	dilemma	khaki	pronunciation
all right	dilettante	kindergarten	psychology
aluminum	disappear	labeling	pursue
analyze	disappoint	legitimate	questionnaire
anoint	disbursement	leisure	receive
apostrophe	discrepancy	license	recommend
apparent	discriminate	likable	repetition
appropriate	dissatisfied	litigation	rescind
argument	dissipate	loneliness	rhythmical
asphalt	drunkenness	loose	ridiculous
assistant	ecstasy	maintenance	sacrilegious
asterisk	eligible	mathematics	salable
athletics	embarrassing	mediocre	secretary
auditor	endorsement	minimum	seize
bachelor	envelop (verb)	misspelling	separate
balloon	exaggerate	necessary	sergeant
bankruptcy	exceed	necessity	sheriff
believable	exhaust	negligence	stationary (fixed)
benefited	exhilaration	negotiable	stationery (paper)
bicycle	existence	newsstand	succeed
brilliant	extraordinary	nickel	suddenness
bulletin	fallacy	noticeable	superintendent
calendar	familiar	occurrence	supersede
campaign	flexible	omission	surgeon
canceled/cancelled	fluctuation	opponent	surprise
canvass (verb)	forty	oscillate	tangible
category	gesture	pageant	tariff
ceiling	grammar	panicky	technique
cemetery	gratuity	parallel	tenant
changeable	grievous	paralyze	tranquilizer
clientele	haphazard	pastime	truly
collateral	hemorrhage	peaceable	tyrannize
committee	holiday	penicillin	unanimous
comparative	hosiery	permanent	until
competitor	hypocrisy	perseverance	vacillate
concede	illegible	persistent	vacuum
connoisseur	immigrant	personnel	vicious
connotation	incidentally	persuade	weird

——WORKSHEET 2——

A FEW SPELLING RULES

PART A. Keep Rules 1 and 2 in mind as you do this exercise. In each instance you are to build two new words by adding the suffixes indicated.

	Root	Suffixes		New Words
1.	clip	+ ed, ing	1.	_____
2.	outwit	+ ed, ing	2. *	_____
3.	refer	+ ing, ence	3.	_____
4.	drug	+ ed, ist	4.	_____
5.	deter	+ ed, ent	5.	_____
6.	wrap	+ ed, ing	6.	_____
7.	occur	+ ed, ence	7. *	_____
8.	rid	+ ing, ance	8.	_____
9.	acquit	+ ed, al	9.	_____
10.	prefer	+ ed, ence	10.	_____
11.	better	+ ed, ment	11.	_____
12.	permit	+ ed, ing	12. *	_____
13.	allow	+ ing, ance	13.	_____
14.	dim	+ ed, er	14.	_____
15.	cheap	+ er, est	15.	_____
16.	litter	+ ed, ing	16.	_____
17.	paper	+ ed, ing	17.	_____
18.	mix	+ ed, er	18.	_____
19.	new	+ ly, ness	19.	_____
20.	travel	+ ed, ing	20.	_____

COMPLETE THIS SENTENCE: The *t* is doubled in the word *submitted* because a suffix beginning with a vowel has been added to a two-syllable word that _____

_____

_____

PART B. Keep Rule 3 in mind as you complete this exercise. Review the exceptions to the rule before you begin.

	Root	Suffix		New Word
1.	judge	+ ment	1. *	
2.	manage	+ able	2.	
3.	compose	+ ing	3.	
4.	encourage	+ ment	4. *	
5.	compare	+ able	5.	
6.	revise	+ ion	6.	
7.	service	+ able	7.	
8.	delete	+ ing	8.	
9.	surmise	+ ing	9.	
10.	erase	+ able	10.	
11.	peace	+ able	11. *	
12.	remote	+ ly	12.	
13.	describe	+ ing	13.	
14.	relate	+ ing	14.	
15.	trace	+ able	15.	
16.	replace	+ ment	16.	
17.	grieve	+ ous	17.	
18.	devote	+ ing	18.	
19.	forgive	+ ness	19.	
20.	crude	+ ity	20.	

PART C. Keep Rule 4 in mind as you insert either *ie* or *ei* in each blank.

1. unbel _____ vable
2. fr _____ ght
3. dec _____ ving*
4. n _____ ghbor*
5. gr _____ f

6. rec _____ pt
7. rel _____ ve
8. r _____ gn
9. shr _____ k
10. br _____ f

11. misch _____ vous
12. caval _____ r
13. n _____ ce
14. perc _____ ve
15. h _____ nous

PART D. This exercise is designed to sharpen your awareness of a few common prefixes. You are to write in the answer space the single word that has the same meaning as the two words in italics. Use your dictionary whenever necessary. If you are collaborating, try several alternatives and decide together on the best one.

Examples: Your plan is *not practical.* → impractical

His apology was *not necessary.* → unnecessary

1. The fax tone was *not audible.*   1. * _____
2. Our version remains *not edited.*   2. _____
3. The signature was *not legible.*   3. * _____

4. The client was *not patient.*   4. _____

5. The group is *not governable.*   5. _____

6. His conclusion was *not escapable.*   6. _____

7. She was *not vulnerable* to his interrogation.   7. _____

8. Our hiring policiy is *not discriminatory.* 8. _____

9. When I heard his story, it sounded *not plausible.*   9. _____

10. The proposal was *not logical.*   10. _____

11. Their words seemed *not sincere.*   11. _____

12. Those results were *not foreseen.*   12. _____

PART E. Read through this letter of application and find the ten spelling errors that will cost this applicant the job.

222 East Lansing Street
Mineapolis*, MN 55414

Novemeber 19, 1995

Mr. Jack Collins
CIS Incorporated
3145 West Highway 12
St. Cloud, MN 55310

Dear Mr. Collins:

After speaking with you by phone the other day, I have decided to send you my resume and apply for the personel position you mentioned. The work sounded important and intresting, and I know I have the skills you are looking for in an employee.

My background and experience will speak for themselves; just read through my resume and you will see that I have done similiar work at Rancott Industries. No one at Rancott doubts my abilities. I just wish I had been able to stay with them passed there period of layoffs last spring. We had an excellent relationship. I also have extensive experience with computerized accounting and recordkeeping. Please feel free to contact any of my prevous employers; their glad to give me their heartiest reccommendations.

Hoping to hear from you soon,

Daniel J. Taylor

PART F. One of the three words in each group has been misspelled. Write the correct spelling of that word in the answer space.

1. ethical agressive nomenclature   1. *_____

2. dentistry corporate recievables   2. _____

3. indecisive imediately aggravated   3. _____

4. ocasionally steadiness financial
5. performance tariff preferance
6. referal denial edifying
7. insecurity severance correspondance
8. embarass mischievous delightful
9. accomodate niece recipient
10. omitted conservator respectible
11. elevate definate appreciate
12. reticule surprise rediculous
13. dicision insidious height
14. prevention waiver preceeding
15. predictible collate knowledge

4. *_____
5. _____
6. _____
7. _____
8. _____
9. _____
10. _____
11. _____
12. _____
13. _____
14. _____
15. _____

DOUBLE TROUBLE

Many words in our language would be easier to spell if they didn't contain one or more doubled letters. There is obviously something wrong with every one of the strange-looking words on the following list. In each of them one or two letters should be doubled. Are you confident that you can write the correct version of every word listed?

acumulate	embaras	oposite	recomend
afiliated	haras	opresive	regresive
agresive	mispel	penicilin	sherif
apetite	ocasion	posesion	tarif
asesment	ocured	rabit	unecesary

CORRECT SPELLINGS: accumulate, affiliated, aggressive, appetite, assessment, embarrass, harass, misspell, occasion, occurred, opposite, oppressive, penicillin, possession, rabbit, recommend, regressive, sheriff, tariff, unnecessary

---

A WORD TIP FROM THE REAL WORLD

Bonnie, who works in middle management at a company employing 200 persons, has the task of reading the resumes of job applicants. "We receive resumes from people all over the country who really want to work for our firm. We want to hire them, too. But we want to hire them to pay attention to our clients with great care and detail. Many of them send us letters of application and resumes that show little attention to the most basic items such as spelling. If they don't make an effort to present themselves well to us, how will they be able to represent our company?"

Bonnie is not alone in this concern. Several times in this book you will read similar stories from people who work in personnel-related positions. They will urge you to be careful in whatever you say or write because that careful attention is a job-getting and a job-keeping skill. What you say and write *does* make a difference!

OPTIONAL EXERCISES

OPTION 1   Determine the missing word; then write it in the answer space.

1. The letter combination *ei* is likely to follow the letter
   _____.

   1. _____

2. The word *controlled* has two *l*'s because the accent is on
   the _____ syllable.

   2. _____

3. We should double the *m* in *slam* if we add a suffix that
   begins with a(n) _____.

   3. _____

4. Before adding *est* to *foggy,* we should change the *y* to
   a(n) _____.

   4. _____

5. A memory device may be referred to as a _____.

   5. _____

OPTION 2   You will find 20 spelling errors in the following paragraphs. When you find a misspelled word, write its correct spelling in the blank at the end of the line. Use your dictionary whenever necessary. If you are collaborating, each person might scan a separate paragraph for errors first and then report.

There are several ways for office staff members   1. *_____

to improve their knowlege of computer software and   2. *_____

data communications options. The most convienient is   3. *_____

to invite an emminent consultant in to train the staff   4. *_____

during an in-service workshop. In such a situation,   5. *_____

personel can remain in their own work stations, using the   6. _____

equiptment that they will use every day. What is learned   7. _____

has imediate application to their daily work. The   8. _____

disadvantage of this method is that it usurpps the office   9. _____

for a day and little normal work can take place.   10. _____

Another method of upgradeing involves sending   11. _____

one or two staff members to a training simposium at an   12. _____

institute or technology classroom. The staff members   13. _____

aquire the new information and then return to teach the   14. _____

others in their office the new proceedures. This method   15. _____

keeps operations intac and running, but it also demands   16. _____

at least two days of time from the designaited staff   17. _____

members, and the rest of the office staff must be able to
learn from their peirs.

In the short run, the preferrable method seems to
be to bring in a real outsider with expertees in the
particuler desired upgrade. After all, operations only
suffer one day's interuption. But in the long run, staff
members who can investigate and learn on behalf of (as
well as educate and inspire) their team members
supply that team with a far more valuable resource than
an upgrade of technology: they build team self-relience
and comradery. And those attributes lead to quality.

18. _____
19. _____
20. _____
21. _____
22. _____
23. _____
24. _____
25. _____
26. _____
27. _____
28. _____

OPTION 3   Write a short paragraph on this subject: "The Importance of Spelling Correctly."

_____
_____
_____
_____
_____
_____
_____
_____
_____
_____
_____
_____
_____
_____
_____
_____
_____
_____
_____

OPTION 4 (CLASS DISCUSSION)   Assume that you are a capable speller but occasionally
have difficulty in remembering how to spell these words:
*accommodate, calendar, criticism, pageant, pronuncia-
tion,* and *superintendent.*

Suggest a mnemonic that you might use in mastering each one.

A Preview of the Parts of Speech

■ POINT TO PONDER

No one has ever mastered English grammar without learning the parts of speech.

There is nothing mysterious about the parts of speech. Every word that you and I use can be labeled as one of the eight: noun, pronoun, verb, adjective, adverb, preposition, conjunction, or interjection. If you learn to control the parts of speech, you will surely go on to control grammar. If you learn to control grammar, you will make yourself eligible for a top-paying job in industry.

Whatever you do, *don't* convince yourself that this chapter is difficult. After all, we are concerned with only eight terms, and each one should be at least somewhat familiar. Try to memorize their definitions as you read this chapter.

The eight parts of speech are simply labels. The label that we give to a particular word depends on how that word has been used (its *function*). A dictionary entry may show that a word may be used as more than one part of speech. Consider the word *bank*. We often use it to name an institution. When used in that way, it is a noun. We sometimes use it as an action word. When used in *that* way, it is a verb. We may also use it to describe something, that is, as an *adjective*. Note the different uses of *bank* in these sentences:

> The *bank* was closed on Monday. (*Bank* is a noun.)
> *Bank* the money as soon as possible. (*Bank* is a verb.)
> He may not qualify for a *bank* loan. (*Bank* is an adjective.)

A knowledge of the parts of speech is basic to any course involving the use of English. This chapter, though, is only a *preview.* It will briefly introduce these eight important terms. Each one will be covered in depth in later chapters. If you have already learned these terms, the chapter and the worksheet should be fun for you. If you find the work difficult, you have no reason to be discouraged. Simply do the best that you can.

Nouns

A **noun** is a name of anything. Look around you. What do you see? A *wall?* A *ceiling?* A *door?* A *pen?* A *person?* A *desk?* A *window?* The words in italics are all nouns because they name the things we see. Nouns, though, may also name things that cannot be seen—things like *patience, courage, luck, intelligence,* and *skill.* In the following paragraph, all nouns are in italics.

Many of our largest *corporations* are looking for new *employees* in the *area* of *marketing.* They want *men* and *women* who can sell *ideas* as well as *goods* and *services.* Many of these *firms* use the college *degree* as a screening *device. Applicants* who don't have a college *education* may be overlooked even though they have *intelligence* and *initiative.*

For now, simply remember that any word used to *name* (*Morgan, partner, Gloria, wealth, company, sympathy,* etc.) must be a noun.

Pronouns

A **pronoun** is a word that takes the place of a noun. Note how pronouns could be substituted for nouns in these sentences:

> *Barlow* (or *He*) recommends the use of voice mail. (*He* is a pronoun.)
> When did you last telephone *Mazak* (or *him*)? (*Him* is a pronoun.)
> *Pauley* (or *She*) deserves the promotion. (*She* is a pronoun.)
> Custer congratulated *Huff* and *Landry* (or *them*). (*Them* is a pronoun.)

Pronouns help to make our language smooth and manageable. Most of us would find it awkward to say *Abner prepared Abner's own tax return.* Most people would undoubtedly prefer to say *Abner prepared his own tax return.* In that sentence the word *his* is a pronoun, and *Abner* is referred to as its *antecedent.* The *antecedent* is simply the word that the pronoun replaces. In each of the following sentences, two words appear in italics. The first one is an antecedent; the second one is a pronoun.

> Mr. Justin is the *man who* saw the accident.
> *Larry* owes a large sum of money, but *he* is not concerned.
> *Grace* has opened *her* own law office.
> The *book that* Ms. Sachs requested is now in stock.

Keep in mind that a word used as a noun substitute is a pronoun. The word *everyone* replaces many nouns in a sentence such as *Everyone took part in the discussion.* Pronouns will be discussed in detail in Chapters 9 through 11. In the meantime, here is a short random list of words that generally are used as that part of speech:

I	who	all	they	you
me	which	some	their	we
he	that	everyone	any	everybody
him	one	it	nobody	none

Verbs

A **verb** is a word (or word group) that expresses action or state of being. *Every sentence must have a verb.* Most verbs tend to be *action* words, such as these: *do, write, speak, dictate, help, find, hesitate, go, read, educate,* or *build.* Action words in sentences should not be difficult to identify. Consider this sentence: *The president of the firm answered my question.* The action word (*answered*) tells us what the president did. It is, of course, a verb. Sometimes the verb is a group of words which show the action and which place it in time. In the following sentences, each of the verbs (in italics) expresses action. Some are single words and some are groups of words.

> She *uses* a Canon copier.
> Our managers *appreciate* its time-saving features.
> *Did* you *ask* the shipping clerk for help?
> The sales manager *should have been informed.*
> Ms. Winslow *frowned* as she *read* the letter.
> *Relax, work* slowly, and *concentrate* on what you *are doing.*

Verbs that do not express *action* are said to express *state of being.* They can also be called *linking verbs.* Here are several: *am, are, is, was, were, will be, have been, become, feel, seem, appear.* The italicized verbs in the following sentences express state of being:

> Ms. Sadecki *has been* with the firm for more than ten years.
> The dispatcher *is* not happy with his new job.
> The new accountant *appears* ready to assume more responsibility.
> At the start of the program everybody *seemed* friendly.

You have probably already discovered that a single sentence may have two or more verbs. Here is an example (verbs in italics): He *wrote* the letter on Monday and *mailed* it on Tuesday, but Hopkins *has* not *responded.*

Adjectives

An **adjective** is a word that modifies a noun or a pronoun. Don't be confused by the word *modifies;* it means simply "to describe or limit or restrict." Consider the word *employee.* It suggests, in a somewhat vague way, a person who works for someone else. Note how much clearer your picture of that employee becomes when adjectives are added. Here are several possibilities:

a dedicated employee	*a young, energetic* employee
an efficient employee	*an indispensable* employee
a talkative employee	*a dishonest* employee
a confused employee	*a well-dressed* employee

You will find that most adjectives are placed *before* the nouns that they describe, as in the examples just given. Some adjectives, however, are placed after the nouns or pronouns they describe. Consider these possibilities: The employee, *dedicated* and *ambitious,* worked overtime. OR The employee is *dedicated* and *ambitious.* In both sentences the adjectives in italics modify the word *employee.* Here is a random list of words that are used frequently as adjectives.

hard	soft	easy	difficult
large	happy	slow	fast
high	low	quick	rapid
recent	efficient	bright	helpful
tall	little	simple	complex
busy	distant	real	angry

You could probably fill a page or two with words of this type that you use every day. Remember that these words are *adjectives.* Use them to modify nouns and pronouns. Here is one more sentence with adjectives in italics: *An excellent* salary and *fringe* benefits are *available* to *a* person who is *capable* and *trustworthy.*

Adverbs

An **adverb** is a word that modifies a verb, an adjective, or another adverb (or adverb substitute). It is likely to answer the question *How?* or *When?* or *Where?* or *To what degree?* In the following sentences, each word in italics is an adverb; the word it modifies is in uppercase letters.

Adverbs Used to Modify Verbs:

Coggins WORKED *slowly* and *carefully.*
Ms. Baxter *hurriedly* SIGNED the contract.
The proofreader DID his job *well.*

Adverbs Used to Modify Adjectives:

Our systems analyst is *too* SLOW.
Mr. Lake is an *extremely* LARGE man.
This *very* OLD cabinet should be replaced.

Adverbs Used to Modify Other Adverbs:

The applicant accepted the position *somewhat* HESITANTLY.
You will meet him *surprisingly* SOON.
This new computer performs *exceedingly* WELL.

Keep in mind that adjectives and adverbs are modifiers. They are both used to *limit* or *describe.* Remember that adjectives modify nouns and pronouns, while adverbs modify verbs, adjectives, and other adverbs. Note also that a word ending in *ly* is likely to be an adverb.

Prepositions

A **preposition** is a word that shows the relation of its object to some other word in the sentence. A *prepositional phrase* is made up of a preposition, its object, and (sometimes) modifiers. Each phrase of this kind does the work of an adjective or an adverb. In other words, prepositional phrases are used as modifiers. Consider this sentence: *I will finish the project later.* The adverb *(later)* modifies the verb *(will finish).* We could easily substitute a prepositional phrase for the adverb in that sentence. Here is a possibility: *We will finish the project on Friday.* Now the prepositional phrase *(on Friday)* modifies the verb *(will finish).* In each of the following prepositional phrases, the preposition appears in italics.

in the meantime	*concerning* the merger	*on* Tuesday
from Chicago	*without* delay	*of* the errors
under his breath	*by* a prominent writer	*at* the end
after the meeting	*since* January	*with* the brown cover
before Wednesday	*about* the strike	*for* several minutes

Chapter 21 of this text covers prepositions in greater detail. Before you reach that chapter, however, be aware that prepositional phrases are simply modifiers. As such, they must be properly placed in sentences. Note the following italicized phrases: The batteries *in this carton* (this phrase modifies *batteries*) will be shipped *to Atlanta* (this phrase modifies *will be shipped*).

Although prepositions are small words, it is important that you learn to recognize them. Each one takes an object. If that object happens to be a pronoun, a difficult choice may be involved. Chapters 9 and 10 will discuss the possibilities.

Conjunctions

A **conjunction** is simply a connective. It may be used to join words or groups of words (phrases, clauses). Chapters 22 and 23 will discuss the proper use of conjunctions, which are sometimes called connectives. Following is a random list of words that often function as this part of speech.

and	because	if	where or wherever
but	unless	while	before
or	as	after	although
nor	since	provided	when or whenever

Even though it is a *connective,* a conjunction may be used at the beginning of a sentence, as in the last one of the following examples. All conjunctions have been printed in italics.

Mr. Durham *and* Ms. Sandusky did not report for work.

The new appraiser is slow *but* accurate.

Pay now *or* pay later.

Business has been slow *since* Mr. Crane left the firm.

You will get the promotion *if* your fine work continues.

We purchased the machine *because* it is economical.

Because the price was right, we made the purchase.

Interjections

An **interjection** is a word used to denote strong feeling or sudden emotion. It is generally followed by an exclamation mark or a comma. A pure interjection does not contribute to the basic meaning of a sentence. It simply suggests surprise, fright, confusion, wonderment, or any other such emotion. Note these examples:

Ouch! Something bit me.

Oh, do you really believe her story?

Hurray! The scanner is finally working!

FINAL THOUGHTS

This chapter has simply *introduced* the parts of speech. For each one of them we have given a definition along with a few examples. If you can now recall those eight definitions, you have made a fine beginning. Remember at least this much:

Nouns are names (room, Henry, Topeka, ability, box, character, noise).

Pronouns are noun substitutes (you, me, her, who, anybody, we, I, one).

Verbs express action or state of being (go, work, help, write, is, was).

Adjectives modify nouns and pronouns (short, kind, clear, faster, big).

Adverbs modify verbs, adjectives, and adverbs (not, clearly, surely).

Prepositions show relation of objects to other words (in, on, with, to).

Conjunctions are connectives (and, but, or, nor, if, since, because).

Interjections simply express feeling (gee, oh, gosh, wow).

Let's take a look at a sentence that contains all the parts of speech. The following statement has two nouns and two verbs. Every other part of speech has been used once.

Determine the proper label for each word; then check your answers with those at the bottom of the page.

1   2   3   4   5   6   7   8   9   10

Well, in June he unexpectedly sold both stores and retired.

SLOW UP OR SLOW DOWN?

For many years English has been considered the language of commerce. In spite of its worldwide popularity, however, there are some aspects of English that may cause any of us to question its logic. Here are a few questions that come to mind:

1. If a man is driving too fast, does it make any difference whether he slows *up* or slows *down?*
2. If natives of America are called *Indians,* what should natives of India be called?
3. If a poor worker may be referred to as *inept,* why shouldn't a capable worker be referred to as ept?
4. Why are all boxing rings *square?*
5. Why aren't there any *eggs* in *eggplants?*
6. Why do we refer to a fruit that contains neither *pine* nor *apple* as a *pineapple?*

—————————————————— FOR CLASS DISCUSSION ——————————————————

Can you think of other expressions that are not entirely logical?

Name *Alisha Hicks*   **Date** 1-9-02

_____WORKSHEET 3_____

A PREVIEW OF THE PARTS OF SPEECH

PART A. List the eight parts of speech in the order suggested by the clues.

1. This one appears in every sentence.
2. This one is a joiner.
3. This one always takes an object.
4. This one may describe how you write or speak.
5. This one simply expresses strong feeling.
6. This one is merely a substitute.
7. This one may describe my computer or my home.
8. This one may be your signature.

1. * *Verb*
2. * *conjunctions*
3. *preposition*
4. *adverb*
5. *interjection*
6. *pronouns*
7. *adjectives*
8. *noun*

PART B. Eight of the words in italics are nouns, and six are pronouns. Indicate the correct part of speech by placing an N (noun) or a P (pronoun) in the answer space. You may need your dictionary.

1. *Martha Heygate* will conduct a workshop on business travel.   1. * *N*
2. *It* will be offered on Tuesday and Wednesday at the downtown Hilton.   2. * *P*
3. It is designed for anyone who has been frustrated on trips in the *past*.   3. * *N*
4. Heygate will have several *topics* prepared.   4. *N*
5. As *you* know, she has written two books about low-cost accommodations.   5. *P*
6. She is also an *expert* on international travel.   6. *N*
7. Her specialty is European business travel, especially frequent monetary *exchanges*.   7. *N*
8. *She* has already prepared for the introduction of the Euro as the dominant currency.   8. *P*
9. Since she is well equipped to handle this *change,* she is much in demand.   9. *N*
10. Her opinion is that the Euro conversion will make life much easier for *us* all.   10. *P*
11. Heygate also reserves at least 90 *minutes* of her workshop for audience concerns.   11. *N*
12. Participants with particular *challenges* take center stage at that point.   12. *N*
13. Heygate's versatility allows *her* to handle any question quite readily.   13. *P*
14. It is recommended that *someone* from each division attend this useful workshop.   14. * *P*

PART C. Note each item in italics. Indicate its part of speech by writing the appropriate letter.

A. noun   B. pronoun   C. verb

(1) *Bronson* (2) *said* that (3) *someone*
(4) *was* in this (5) *office* when the
(6) *fire* (7) *started.* (8) *He* and (9) *I*
(10) *have spoken* with (11) *everyone*
(12) *who* (13) *works* here. (14) *We*
(15) *agree* that (16) *arson* (17) *is* a
(18) *possibility.*

1. * A
2. * C
3. * B
4. * C
5. * A
6. A
7. C
8. B
9. B
10. C
11. B
12. B
13. A
14. B
15. C
16. A
17. C
18. A

PART D. Write the correct choice; then add A or B in parentheses to indicate its part of speech. If you are working collaboratively, try to convince your group that your choice is correct using chapter ideas.

(A) adjective *describes*   (B) adverb *answers ?*

Example: Try to speak more (slow, slowly).
slowly (B)

1. Jen learned her duties (quick, quickly).
2. Coggins does not organize his work very (well, good).
3. Rankin is (enthusiastic, enthusiastically) about your idea.
4. The loan officer agreed (immediate, immediately).
5. Your new assistant is an (unhappy, unhappily) man.
6. The new data entry clerk certainly works (fast, fastly).
7. Von Hayes is a truly (remarkably, remarkable) person.
8. Swearington's plan worked (perfect, perfectly).
9. Templeton was (careful, carefully) as she scanned the document.
10. The plans we discussed on Friday were not (definite, definitely).

1. * quickly – B
2. * well – A
3. * enthusiastic – A
4. immediately – B
5. unhappy – A
6. fast – A
7. remarkable – A
8. perfectly – B
9. careful – A
10. definite – A

PART E. Write a word that may be used to fill the blank. Add A or B in parentheses to indicate its part of speech. If you are collaborating, each person should supply a word and argue in favor of it.

(A) preposition   (B) conjunction

Example: The agent _____ I disagreed.
and (B)

1. She put the contract into either this drawer _____ that one.
2. Ms. Katz told Briley to take his place _____ the platform.

1. * or – B
2. * on, A

3. I talked to Clagget, _____ Munson was not there.

    3. *Since - A

4. Only one of these welders has ever lived _____ Chicago.

    4. in - A

5. We will purchase 300 feet _____ sturdy cable.

    5. of - A

6. Baskin will not prepare the balance sheet _____ you help him.

    6. before - A

7. You can reach the airport in time _____ you leave immediately.

    7. if - B

8. I will go to Raleigh if you go _____ me.

    8. with - A

9. Several of these exotic products were sent to me _____ India.

    9. _____

10. Any check for more than $1,000 must be signed by both Berkowitz _____ me.

    10. _____

PART F. Write the only conjunction that you find in each sentence. You may have to use your dictionary.

1. When the office is reorganized, various machines will be in new locations.

    1. * _____

2. For example, the fax-scanner-printer unit and the speaker phone will stay here.

    2. * _____

3. The high-speed copier will be placed in the hall after Jensen's desk is moved in.

    3. _____

4. Postage meters will be in the reception area since it is closer to the mail room.

    4. _____

5. If Schultz wants his color printer, it will be installed in the supply room.

    5. _____

6. All of us will have access to any machine whenever we need it.

    6. _____

7. Each machine will have a storage cabinet for its supply of paper or toner.

    7. * _____

8. We will have to get used to the new locations, but that should not prove difficult.

    8. _____

9. Some of the designers have complained, yet they have offered no alternative plans.

    9. _____

10. We will try this new arrangement for six months and evaluate it at that time.

    10. _____

PART G. Underscore the only prepositional phrase in each sentence. You may have to use your dictionary.

Example: Two or three <u>of my colleagues</u> have purchased condominiums.

1. Our firm investigates its investments in foreign businesses.*

2. It seems that many multi-national corporations have ties to questionable factories.*

3. In some cases these factories operate unconscionably.*

4. They often employ children to do vigorous work under horrible conditions.

5. When our firm discovers such factories, we begin work on two tasks.

6. Our first priority is to stop any mistreatment without factory closure.

7. Our second move is to use our previous investment dollars to help the factory provide better conditions for its laborers.

8. Whenever we intervene, we study the entire community and learn from them what will work better.*.

PART H. When creating a resume, a good writer uses consistent patterns of expression. Notice the patterns of underscored words in this resume sample. Indicate which parts of speech form each pattern by writing the appropriate *letters* in the answer space.

A. noun   B. verb   C. adjective

Experience

1. • recorded transactions, transcribed phone orders, handled defaulted accounts

    1. * _____

2. • managed executive, expense, and delinquent accounts

    2. _____

3. • coordinated sales and marketing departments

    3. _____

4. • worked in administration, management, and outsourcing

    4. _____

Education

5. • majored in bookkeeping and accounting

    5. * _____

6. • wrote, edited, and published *Money Management,* a student finance journal

    6. _____

7. • will pursue further work in financial, investment, and tax counseling

    7. _____

8. • played on the intramural football, basketball, and golf teams

    8. _____

A WORD TIP FROM THE REAL WORLD

Tom, a career placement coordinator for a large midwestern college, is always on the lookout for good and bad word choices. "Faulty wording hurts people's chances of landing that great job," he claims. "Every spelling or word choice error on a resume can mean a rejection. Every poor description in an art portfolio means an employer has to think twice about hiring an applicant. We don't want that. We want employers to like everything they see."

Tom helps students check carefully through job placement documents, combing for errors to correct and searching for great descriptions. "I know how choosy companies can afford to be. The students I help to place deserve the best jobs we can find. The way they use words on paper makes all the difference in the world, both in their being hired in the first place and later in their ability to keep the job." He says that while most of his students believe they will be evaluated only on the skills of their special field, they must learn that all people are judged on the basis of the words they use.

Name *Alisha Hicks*   Date *January 22, 02*

OPTIONAL EXERCISES

OPTION 1   Write the verb in each sentence.

Example: Our plant engineer designed the
new work stations.

_____designed_____

1. The board has decided to expand the sale of
   private shares.

   1. * *has decided*

2. Complete the enclosed reservation before
   February 10. *you, understood*

   2. * *complete*

3. Sixteen employees of this plant lost their jobs
   last week.

   3. *lost*

4. This publisher has consistently produced
   quality books for 80 years.

   4. ~~consistently~~ *HAS PRODUCED*

5. No one could name the current president
   or C.E.O.

   5. *could name*

6. She was not present to accept her employee
   of the month award.

   6. *was present*

7. This year the company picnic will be held at
   Radisson Park.

   7. *will be held*

8. Will you vote for a strike? *(you, understood)*

   8. * *will vote*

9. The shipping department has high standards
   for packing materials.

   9. *has*

10. Our office products supplier is the best in
    the region.

    10. *is*

OPTION 2   Each sentence has one interjection. Write it in the answer space.

1. Westbrook said, "Gosh, how can we possibly compete
   with Allied Chemical?"

   1. _____

2. Well, someone has to serve our customers in the
   northern part of Minnesota.

   2. _____

3. The temperature was 115 degrees Fahrenheit and, oh,
   did we perspire!

   3. _____

4. Gee, we certainly didn't mean to offend one of our best
   customers.

   4. _____

A PREVIEW OF THE PARTS OF SPEECH   **35**

OPTION 3 Each word in italics is an adjective or an adverb. Indicate the correct part of speech by placing the appropriate *letter* in the answer space. Use a dictionary if necessary. If you are collaborating, convince each other of the correct answer.

A. adjective   B. adverb

Example: All *major* decisions are tested *rigorously* against a mission statement.

	A		B
Peck's (1) *enormous* salary was given a boost (2) *recently.*	1. * A	2. * B
Her speech urging everyone to give (3) *generously* was indeed (4) *compelling.*	3. * B	4. * A
Computer literacy is an issue for (5) *almost* every (6) *entry-level* job.	5. A	6. B
(7) *College* graduates are (8) *not* difficult to find but are often underprepared.	7. B	8. A
To our (9) *great* delight, Conigli was (10) *early* for the appointment.	9. A	10. B

OPTION 4 In a short paragraph, make an argument for using good grammar in a business setting.

_____
_____
_____
_____
_____
_____
_____
_____
_____
_____
_____
_____
_____
_____
_____
_____
_____
_____
_____
_____
_____
_____
_____
_____

Sentence Analysis

■■■ POINT TO PONDER

An idea can be expressed in a multitude of ways, some of which are far more acceptable than others.

This chapter will introduce you to several basic terms concerned with sentence building. Only those that are important to your understanding of language structure will be presented. You will not be expected to learn any terms that have no practical value or tend to make simple ideas obscure. A statement will be called a *statement,* not a *declarative sentence.* A command will be referred to as a *command,* not an *imperative sentence.* If three grammatical terms express a single idea, the most meaningful of the three will be presented; the other two will not appear in our discussion.

SENTENCES, SUBJECTS, PREDICATES

A **sentence,** as you have probably learned, is an independent group of words that contains at least one subject and one predicate (in a command or a request the subject is usually implied). The ability to distinguish sentences from sentence fragments is extremely important to the business writer. Note that each of the following word groups is a complete sentence. A vertical line has been used to separate each complete subject from its complete predicate.

> Some vital statistics | are stored on this magnetic tape.
>
> Our gross national product | has increased greatly in recent years.
>
> The New York Stock Exchange | is known as the Big Board.
>
> This bank draft | was received on Monday.
>
> | Help me.

The **subject** tells who or what is being discussed; the **predicate** tells something about that subject. In the last sentence of the foregoing examples, *you,* the subject, is understood. Sentences of this type express commands or requests. The subject of a sentence generally, but not always, is placed before the predicate. In attempting to determine the subject, you would do well to find the verb first. The parts of the following sentence appear in their usual order.

The quality control inspector objected to these cost-cutting changes.

If you recognize *objected* as the verb, you can determine the subject by asking this question: "What (or Who) objected?" The answer, of course, is *inspector.* The word *inspector,* therefore, is the **simple subject.** Note these labels:

SIMPLE SUBJECT:	inspector
SIMPLE PREDICATE:	objected
COMPLETE SUBJECT:	The quality control inspector
COMPLETE PREDICATE:	objected to these cost-cutting changes

The **complete subject,** you will observe, consists of the simple subject and its modifiers. The **simple predicate** is the main verb of the sentence. The **complete predicate** comprises the verb and all words governed by the verb or modifying it.

If a sentence begins with *There* or *Here,* the subject will usually come after the verb. In each of the following sentences the subject appears in italics.

Here are several important *issues* to be resolved.

There is no *money* left in the treasury.

Direct Objects

Let's consider this very conventional sentence pattern:

subject	*verb*	*object*

Our director of human resources purchased an answering machine.

If you recognize *purchased* as the verb in this sentence, you should be able to determine the following:

SIMPLE SUBJECT:	director
COMPLETE SUBJECT:	Our director of human resources
SIMPLE PREDICATE:	purchased
COMPLETE PREDICATE:	purchased an answering machine

To find the **direct object** of a verb, you should express the verb and then ask *What?* or *Whom?* For example, in the sentence under discussion you would find the direct object by asking the question *Purchased what?* The direct object, in a very real sense, completes the meaning of the verb and receives its action. The business writer who cannot recognize a direct object is likely to make several types of grammatical errors, each of which will be discussed in later chapters.

Indirect Objects

Occasionally an **indirect object** will appear between the verb and the direct object. Here is another common sentence pattern:

subject *verb* *ind. object* *direct object*

The manufacturer gave our purchasing agent considerable information.

subj. *verb* *ind. obj.* *direct object*

He would not tell the assistant manager the nature of his business.

The indirect objects in these sentences are *agent* and *manager.* Like all indirect objects, they could be expanded into prepositional phrases; for example, *He would not tell the nature of his business to the assistant manager.*

Complements

In expressing our thoughts, we make frequent use of **linking verbs,** the most common of which is *to be* (*am, are, is, was, were, have been,* etc.). Verbs of this type do *not* show action. The noun, pronoun, or adjective that follows a linking verb either renames or modifies the *subject* of the verb. It seems logical that we refer to such words as **subject complements.** Note how they are used in these sentences:

subject *verb* *subject complement*

Rachel Billingsley will be our next office manager. (the complement is a noun)

subj. *subj. v.* *complement*

It was she on the videotape. (the complement is a pronoun)

subj. v. *subj. complement*

Her talk was highly inspirational. (Subject is *modified* by its complement, an adjective.)

Linking verbs and subject complements will be discussed in detail in a later chapter.

Compound Elements

As you analyze sentences, you will need to recognize **compound elements.** As the name suggests, such elements are made up of more than one part. Observe these sentences carefully:

COMPOUND SUBJECT:	Many colleges and a few high schools offer such courses. (The simple subject is *colleges, schools.*)
COMPOUND PREDICATE:	The price of the stock rose slightly and then declined. (The simple predicate is *rose, declined.*)
COMPOUND OBJECT:	She studied law and economics for one semester. (*Law and economics* are direct objects of the verb *studied.*)

Clauses

A **clause** is a group of related words that contains both a verb and its subject. It functions as a part of a sentence. In a later chapter of this text, clauses will be classified and discussed in greater detail. You should understand now, however, the difference between independent and dependent clauses. An **independent clause** (or **main clause**) is one that can stand alone. It could be used as a separate sentence. A **dependent clause** is one that cannot stand alone, since it depends upon another clause for its meaning. Dependent clauses function as nouns, adjectives, or adverbs. The following groups of related words are clauses because each contains a verb and its subject. Each of the italicized clauses below is dependent and would function as the part of speech indicated in parentheses.

We will return to work *when the strike ends.* (adverb)

I will sign the proposal *if management agrees.* (adverb)

She knows *that the conference has been canceled.* (noun)

He guessed *that problems would arise.* (noun)

Take every course *which we have recommended.* (adjective)

I ordered the software *that was requested by Mr. Snow.* (adjective)

Consider the first italicized clause on the foregoing list. It could easily be substituted for the adverb in this sentence: We will return to work *soon. Soon* answers the question *When?* and modifies the verb *will return.* Our adverb clause has the same function in this sentence: We will return to work *when the strike ends.*

In the third sentence, *that the conference has been canceled* could function as a noun by replacing a more conventional direct object: She knows *that information.*

Did you hear the good *news*? (A noun is the direct object.)

Did you hear *that the conference has been canceled?* (A noun clause is the direct object.)

Phrases

A **phrase** is a group of related words that does *not* contain both subject and verb. It functions as a noun, a verb, an adjective, or an adverb. In each of the following sentences the italicized phrase functions as the part of speech shown in parentheses.

Our social security laws *have been amended* frequently. (This **verb phrase** is used as the simple predicate.)

Retired workers usually hope *to collect maximum benefits.* (This **noun phrase** is used as a direct object.)

Widows receive no benefits *during the blackout period.* (This **adverb phrase** modifies the verb *receive.*)

Some members *of the teaching profession* have separate retirement programs. (This **adjective phrase** modifies the noun *members.*)

You will note that the phrases do not contain subject-verb combinations. Perhaps you recognized the prepositional phrases in the last two sentences listed. Don't forget that prepositional phrases function as adjectives and adverbs. Other types of phrases will be discussed in the chapters that follow. Their names are not yet important to us.

An understanding of the *functions* of phrases and clauses is extremely important to the business writer. If a phrase or a clause is used to modify a word, it should be placed so that the meaning is perfectly clear. In general, the modifier should not be placed too far from the word modified. Try to spot the weakness in this sentence:

Our salesperson met a farmer just this morning who needs a new tractor.

Because the dependent clause modifies the word *farmer,* the sentence should read: *Just this morning our salesperson met a farmer who needs a new tractor.* In this wording, *farmer* is modified by the clause immediately following.

Appositives

An **appositive** is a noun or noun substitute that immediately follows another noun or noun substitute and tends to rename or identify it, as in these sentences:

Mr. Caruso, *our present treasurer,* does not favor this proposal.
The program was transmitted from Columbus, *the capital of Ohio.*

Sentence Patterns

The English language offers us a variety of ways in which to express ideas. Perhaps the most common basic sentence patterns in modern business writing are these:

1. **SUBJECT–VERB**

   subj.   *verb*
   The contest ended on Friday.

   subj.   *verb*
   The employees cooperated with me.

2. **SUBJECT–VERB–DIRECT OBJECT**

   subj.   *verb*   *obj.*
   Mr. Stone offered a fine suggestion.

   subj.   *verb*   *obj.*
   Ms. Francis prepared the agenda.

3. **SUBJECT–VERB–INDIRECT OBJECT–DIRECT OBJECT**

   subj.   *verb*   *indirect obj.*   *direct obj.*
   We offered Mr. Montgomery a new automobile.

   subj.   *verb*   *ind. obj.*   *direct obj.*
   Ms. Palefsky handed the gentleman an application.

4. **SUBJECT–LINKING VERB–SUBJECT COMPLEMENT**

   subj.   *verb*   *complement*
   Mr. Winters will be the sole beneficiary.

   subj.   *v.*   *complement*
   Those two firms are our principal competitors.

5. **THERE/HERE–VERB–SUBJECT**

   verb   *subj.*
   There may be a slight delay.

   verb   *subj.*
   There were several people in the office.

The flexibility of the English language allows us other sentence patterns that, although grammatical, are less common than those already mentioned. Here are three possibilities:

$$\overset{obj.}{\text{The most important question}} \quad \overset{subj.}{\text{our chairman}} \quad \overset{verb}{\text{ignored}} \text{ completely.}$$

obj.   subj.   verb

The most important question our chairman ignored completely.

prep. phrase   verb   subj.

To the victor will go the spoils.

comp.   subj.   verb

What a strange person our controller is!

More often than not a question should be expressed in the form of a statement before it is analyzed; for example, the question *Were you in the room?* can be analyzed more easily in this form: *You were in the room.* Some questions, such as *Who called this number?* (SUBJECT-VERB-DIRECT OBJECT), cannot be put into statement form. You will want to recognize the sentence pattern of a question introduced with a direct object or a helping verb, as in these examples:

subj.   verb   obj.

What color did the customer choose? (The customer did choose what color?)

subj.   verb

Does the supervisor agree with you? (The supervisor does agree with you.)

NOTES ON PUNCTUATION

1. A sentence that simply states a fact should be followed by a period. Here are two examples:

   The average business letter costs several dollars to produce.
   I cannot find my pen.

2. A sentence that issues a *command* or makes a *request* should also be followed by a period. Here are three:

   Open a checking account today.
   Handle your finances with care.
   Please help me with my budget.

3. A sentence that asks a question should generally be followed by a question mark. Note these examples:

   Have you prepared a will?
   Do you know precisely what will happen to your worldly goods if you die intestate?

In deciding whether to use a period or a question mark at the end of a sentence, consider the nature of the response expected. If the other person is expected to answer you in words, use a question mark. If that person is expected to act in some way, use a period. Note the punctuation following these sentences:

Will you please start working. (request in question form)

Where is the probate court? (question requiring a verbal response)

He asked whether you had talked to the judge. (indirect question)

4. An *exclamation,* which may or may not appear as a complete sentence, should be followed by an exclamation mark. Any strong emotion may be indicated. Here are a few examples:

You're in contempt of court!

Isn't the sunset magnificent!

Stop the performance!

Splendid!

Ouch!

Most business writers agree that the exclamation mark loses its effectiveness when used too frequently.

TO THE STUDENT

Please think of this chapter and the preceding one as the basis or foundation for what will follow. It is important that you be aware of the eight parts of speech and of the structure of English sentences before you attempt to master specific rules and concepts. If you profited from these two chapters, you have made an excellent beginning. If, on the other hand, you found them confusing, you have no reason to feel discouraged. In the chapters that follow, you will find detailed explanations of the terms and ideas to which you have now been introduced. Worksheet 4 is designed to *teach* more than to *test.* Simply do the best that you can.

FIND THE SYNONYMS

The prefix *in* is often used to convey the meaning of *no, not,* or *without.* The word *ineffective,* for example, may be used to describe something that is *not effective.* In seven of the following eight pairs of words, *in* has the meaning of *not;* that is, each of the seven pairs consists of two adjectives that are opposite in meaning.

appropriate, inappropriate	flexible, inflexible
capable, incapable	sensitive, insensitive
convenient, inconvenient	significant, insignificant
flammable, inflammable	sincere, insincere

—————————— FOR CLASS DISCUSSION ——————————

One of the foregoing pairs consists of two words that are similar (not *opposite*) in meaning. Identify the pair and then suggest a word that *does* mean the opposite.

THE IMPACT OF LANGUAGE

SIMPLIFIED SPELLING

In January 1983 Andy Rooney, a syndicated newspaper columnist, wrote about a Michigan organization called Better Education Thru Simplified Spelling, a group of people dedicated to the idea that we should simplify the way we spell many English words.

Several of this nation's presidents have expressed dismay at the complexity of English spelling. Certainly any language that requires us to pronounce a single letter combination *(ough)* in at least six different ways *(rough, bough, cough, dough, through, bought)* leaves something to be desired. It is not surprising that the Simplified Spelling Board was formed in the early part of this century to suggest improvements.

The learned individuals who made up that body spent many hours of deliberation before making their recommendations to the English-speaking world. They finally announced the preparation of a simplified spelling list of 300 words. It included spellings such as *tho* instead of *though, thru* instead of *through, laf* instead of *laugh,* and *bot* instead of *bought.* Well pleased with the list, President Theodore Roosevelt decided that all government employees should make use of the simplified versions of spelling. Because numerous heated articles appeared in the country's newspapers, the proposed changes were discussed at length in the halls of Congress—and bitterly opposed by almost all who expressed themselves. The President, as a result, was forced to rescind his order.

The recommendations of the Simplified Spelling Board have never been adopted, although many learned people, George Bernard Shaw among them, have written convincingly in favor of simplifying the English language.

—————————— FOR CLASS DISCUSSION ——————————

Should a serious attempt be made (possibly by a government agency) to simplify the spelling of English words? If so, would the majority of the American people be willing to accept the necessary changes?

THE IMPACT OF LANGUAGE

AMUSING AMBIGUITIES

An old edition of the *Reader's Digest* contains a feature concerning newspaper headlines that suggest meanings other than those intended by the writers. The following five ambiguous headlines, which actually appeared in various newspapers throughout the country, were mentioned in the magazine. All five undoubtedly confused (and amused) a few readers.

**SQUAD HELPS DOG
BITE VICTIM**

CHESTER MORRIS, 92, WAS FED SECRETARY

**DRUNK GETS NINE MONTHS
IN VIOLIN CASE**

CHINESE APEMAN DATED

**SHUT-INS CAN GROW
INDOORS WITH LIGHTS**

—————————— FOR CLASS DISCUSSION ——————————

Attempt to determine the intended meaning of each headline. The first one, of course, is confusing because the hyphen in *dog-bite* has been omitted.

_____WORKSHEET 4_____

SENTENCE ANALYSIS

PART A. In the space provided, write A or B to indicate the complete sentence.

1. (A) Even if we could afford to acquire the very best materials
   (B) Our sales goals are high

   1. * _B._

2. (A) Jergens will inherit the office
   (B) At least 20 people caught in the inevitable downsizing activities

   2. _A._

3. (A) As the stock market soared on Wednesday
   (B) We failed

   3. _B._

4. (A) My choice for department manager was Harry Yubanov
   (B) Anderson Lakes Parkway, a center for development and commerce

   4. _A._

5. (A) We unwisely left an incompetent person in charge
   (B) Because we thought he was aware of the problem and could fix it

   5. _A._

PART B. In the following excerpt from a letter of application, underscore the five incomplete sentences.

I think you will discover that I have the qualifications your company is looking for. Good problem solving skills. They are my strong suit. Followed by punctuality. All of my previous employers have complimented me on that score. Then of course I have a knack for getting along with fellow workers. Even when they have not gone out of their way to be friendly to me. Not many applicants can claim that skill. Finally, I must point out my ability to prioritize tasks. A talent which led to my most recent promotion. Also, a talent which no number of time management workshops can really improve. I hope that, because of these qualifications, you will consider my application favorably.

PART C Classify each element by writing the appropriate letter in the space provided. If you are working collaboratively, take time to teach one another why you think your classification is correct.

A. phrase   B. dependent clause   C. independent clause (sentence)

1. (For immediate use) *prep. phrase*   1. * ~~A~~
2. While we spoke, ~~DC IC~~   2. * ~~B~~
3. Max laughed   3. * ~~C~~
4. (Without the needed software) *prep. phrase* A 4. * ~~B~~
5. Failing to get a response   5. * ~~A~~
6. The new machines are compact   6. ~~C~~
7. Although the printout is missing   B 7. ~~A~~
8. Until next month's meeting   8. ~~A~~
9. Because he cooperated with us   9. ~~B~~
10. If the file name is not recorded   10. ~~B~~
11. The copier is broken   11. ~~C~~
12. She listened intently   12. ~~C~~
13. From the purchasing department   13. ~~A~~
14. If the sheet feeder malfunctions   B 14. ~~A~~
15. Our competitors understand the problem   15. ~~C~~
16. When clearing the paper jam   16. ~~A~~
17. In about one hour   A 17. ~~B~~
18. The effort was worthwhile   18. ~~C~~
19. After considering options   A 19. ~~B~~
20. Whenever we complain about wages   B 20. ~~A~~
21. Working very slowly   A 21. ~~B~~
22. Everyone cooperated   22. ~~C~~
23. To assist this company   23. ~~A~~
24. On the firm's anniversary date   24. ~~A~~
25. We witnessed something historic   25. ~~C~~

PART D In the answer space write the simple subject of the verb in italics. If the sentence is worded as a command, write *you (understood)* as the subject. If you are collaborating, complete five items at a time by yourself first, then check with the group. All prepositional phrases have been underscored.

Example: Our income tax laws *have undergone* some major changes. (To find the subject, ask, *What have undergone?*)

laws

1. Many people *take* control of home finances by using a software package.   1. * *people*

2. Many packages *are* currently available.   2. * *packages*

46   SENTENCE ANALYSIS

3. Some *offer* a system for checkbook managment.

4. Others *offer* effective instructions for income tax computation.

5. The type of software that you select *will depend* on your needs.

6. *Think* about your most frustrating financial operation.

7. For most people, the work of balancing a checkbook *is* tedious.

8. For that reason, they seldom *do* it and so increase their chance of error.

9. A stack of four months' statements and canceled checks *awaits* them.

10. Within that stack *lurk* errors in recording, addition, and subtraction.

11. Most checking customers, even careful ones, *make* mistakes.

12. By tracking accounts every month, with a computer's help, we *reduce* risk.

13. For one thing, the software *tells* the user what to carefully record.

14. Some applications actually *have* a voice to calmly coach the user.

15. A formerly tedious process *can* actually *become* somewhat enjoyable.

16. An enjoyable activity *is* more likely to be done regularly.

17. As a result, users *tend* their accounts more often and more accurately.

18. Banks *are* delighted at the rise in these home help software packages.

19. Their customers *are* more accurate, reducing complaints at the bank.

20. *Investigate* finance software for yourself to be sure of the best fit.

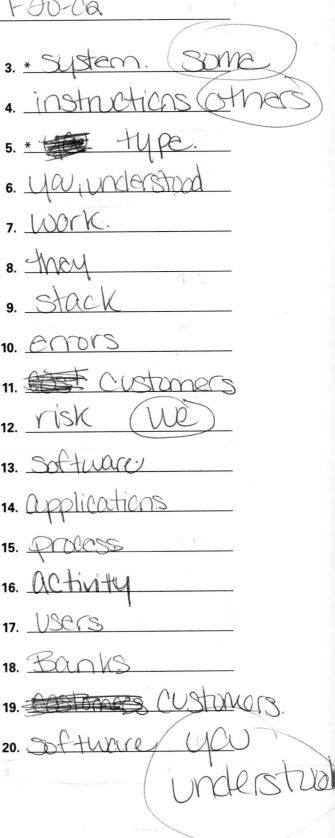

3. * system. (Some)

4. instructions (others)

5. * ~~will~~ type.

6. you, understood

7. work.

8. they

9. stack

10. errors

11. ~~cast~~ customers

12. risk (we)

13. software

14. applications

15. process

16. activity

17. users

18. Banks

19. ~~customers~~ customers.

20. software you understood

PART E. Each sentence contains one direct object of a verb. Write that direct object in the answer space. *All* verbs are in italics.

Example: He *studied* the pamphlet on automobile insurance. (To find the object, ask, *Studied what?*)

_____ pamphlet

1. Georgetown *will host* the international conference next year.

1. * *Conference*

2. We *didn't learn* the conference location until last week.

2. * *location*

3. Now every department *is making* plans (to travel) and (to ship) merchandise.

3. * *plans*

4. Clients often *experience* conventions as endless booths and seminars.

4. *conventions*

5. Georgetown's facilities, however, *build* greater hopes for the gathering.

5. *Hopes*

6. The convention center *offers* spacious and interesting display areas.

6. *areas*

7. The center *borders* the largest hotel complex (in the nation).

7. *complex*

8. Clients *can visit* restaurants catering to every taste on earth.

8. *restaurants*

9. Few conference locations *can claim* so many attractive features.

9. *features*

10. Georgetown's facilities *may have* nearly everything.

10. *everything*

ON WORD LENGTH

A friend of mine questioned me recently about a magazine article he had just read. It began with these words: "When you speak and write, no law says you have to use big words." The writer referred to the strength, grace, and charm of *small* words. He mentioned also that the 50 most common words in English are each one syllable.

When my friend scanned this text, he wondered about Chapters 37 and 38, which encourage students to study words such as *prevaricate, recalcitrant,* and *garnishee.* The article he had read seemed to suggest that a person can communicate effectively without using long words.

_____ FOR CLASS DISCUSSION _____

Suggest at least three reasons that a person might have for learning challenging words of more than one syllable.

OPTIONAL EXERCISES

OPTION 1 By writing the appropriate letter, identify the word(s) in italics. If you are working collaboratively, your group must decide together on an acceptable identification.

    A. simple subject   C. object of verb

    B. simple predicate   D. none of these

Example: A policy of this kind *provides* fine protection.   ___B___

1. Planning an effective meeting *takes* time and energy.   1. *_____

2. However, good *planning* pays good dividends.   2. *_____

3. Certain strategies are *very* important.   3. _____

4. The planning team should evaluate the *purpose* of the meeting.   4. *_____

5. They *must invite* all of the key players and no one else.   5. _____

6. *They* must set an agenda and distribute it to the attendees.   6. _____

7. They must be ready to consider changes in the agenda if the attendees request such *changes.*   7. _____

8. The planners *must encourage* the attendees to contribute in significant ways.   8. _____

9. Someone on the planning *team* should do some "pre-work" with key participants.   9. _____

10. This pre-work *gets* people ready and *makes* meetings more productive.   10. _____

11. It also uncovers *difficulties* and *barriers* that might affect the meeting.   11. _____

12. The meeting itself *should be managed* by a skilled negotiator.   12. _____

13. This *leader* tries to keep the group on task as much as possible.   13. _____

14. When digressions appear, the leader notes *them* and checks their *appropriateness* with the group.   14. *_____

15. *Meetings* can be very effective when they're 50 minutes long at the most.   15. _____

16. Another effectiveness *enhancer* is to hold meetings in unusual rooms.   16. _____

17. People often feel more *creative* in new surroundings.   17. _____

18. Most of all, meetings *should be* a source of synergistic work.   18. _____

19. Instead, they are often *poorly managed, boring,* and *unproductive.*   19. _____

20. With careful planning and good management, meetings *can help* organizations grow.   20. _____

OPTION 2   Write sentences as indicated.

1. A sentence with the word *attorney* as its subject: _____

_____

_____

2. A sentence with *attorney* as a direct object: _____

_____

_____

3. A sentence with *attorney* as a subject complement: * _____

_____

_____

OPTION 3   Each of the following groups of words could be a complete sentence. However, you are to add an appositive to each one. (You *are* permitted to use your imagination.)

1. The book he chose was written by Charles Dickens, * _____

_____

2. Our chairman is a descendent of John D. Rockefeller, _____

_____

3. The meeting of world leaders was held in the White House, _____

_____

4. He owns three copies of *The American Heritage Dictionary,* _____

_____

A WORD TIP FROM THE REAL WORLD

Marcie graduated from a major university with a journalism degree and a desire to enter the field of broadcast news. She landed a job almost immediately at a small television station, replacing a feature reporter. She was astonished to learn in her first week on the job that reporters and anchors write all of their own stories, that there are no news writers at most stations. Although she had a degree in journalism, she didn't know how to write well enough to express the information in breaking stories clearly and concisely. Within a week, she had lost her job.

When Marcie graduated, she believed the world of broadcast journalism would not require her to be a clear writer. Now she knows that it does. She has made specific efforts to improve her writing and now works at a different station as a reporter. She gives new hires good advice. "Listen, write, and write again. Then report."

CHAPTER 5

Capitalization

■■ POINT TO PONDER

If all nouns were easily classified as common or proper, this chapter would be extremely brief.

A word that begins with a capital letter attracts more attention than the other words in a sentence. Writers in special situations, therefore, sometimes use capital letters simply to command interest and attention. This practice is especially common in advertising and in legal writing. Some organizations compile their own stylebooks and vary the capitalization rules according to the nature of the business or the group of readers for whom the writing is being prepared. Employees of such organizations should, of course, follow the recommendations set forth in those stylebooks. In general, however, a writer who can distinguish between common and proper nouns should know when to begin a word with a capital letter.

COMMON AND PROPER NOUNS

A **common noun** indicates a general class of persons, places, objects, conditions, or qualities. A **proper noun,** which begins with a capital letter, indicates a *specific* person, place, or thing.

Common Nouns	*Proper Nouns*
(General Designations)	*(Specific Names)*
city	Milwaukee
book	*Wuthering Heights*
month	January
theater	Granada Theater

51

Common Nouns *(General Designations)*	Proper Nouns *(Specific Names)*
girl	Naomi
building	Richfield Building
river	Amazon River
highway	U.S. Highway 101
state	North Dakota
inventor	Thomas Edison
university	Fordham University
school	Springfield High School
holiday	Thanksgiving
war	Civil War
language	French
automobile	Chevrolet
company	General Motors
church	First Baptist Church
department	English Department
street	Madison Street

SPECIAL RULES FOR CAPITALIZATION

Although authorities differ on some details concerning capitalization, there are certain basic rules that careful writers observe. Most of these rules are easy to remember and to apply, but some will require special study because their use involves judgment.

When you cannot decide whether an expression should be capitalized or not, consult a good reference book. In dictionary entries, words that regularly function as proper nouns begin with capital letters. Because many proper nouns do not appear in your dictionary, however, it will pay you to study the following rules carefully.

(1) Proper Nouns and Derivatives

Capitalize the name of a *particular* person, place, or thing, as well as an adjective that refers to a specific name.

Canada	Canadian
Georgia	Georgian
Keynes	Keynesian

Capitalize descriptive names that are substituted frequently for the real names.

The Big Apple (New York) Here *The* is capitalized as part of the nickname.

the Big Board (New York Stock Exchange)

Honest Abe (Abraham Lincoln)

(2) Brand Names

Capitalize brand names and trademarked names. (A *manufacturer* or an *advertiser* is likely to capitalize the common noun following the actual brand name.)

Kleenex	Milky Way candy	Palmolive soap	Ford truck
Coca-Cola	Vaseline	Starbuck's coffee	Bic pen

If words derived from proper nouns have lost their specialized meanings, they should not ordinarily be capitalized. Because common usage has obscured their original identity, do not capitalize words such as these:

china (dishes)	pasteurize	arabic numbers
italics	watt	plaster of paris

(3) Compound Proper Nouns

Generally speaking, all words except articles (a, an, the), conjunctions, and short prepositions should be capitalized in names or titles that consist of more than one word. The *first* word and the *last* word must always be capitalized. Do not capitalize *the* if it precedes the name of an organization but is not actually a part of that organization's name. Capitalize any word with four or more letters in a compound proper noun.

The Rise and Fall of the Roman Empire (book title)

the Eastman Kodak Company (business organization)

Supreme Court (judicial body)

City Council (governing body)

the Ways and Means Committee (standing committee)

The First Ship-to-Shore Broadcast (Capitalize the parts of a hyphenated word in a title as you would capitalize them in the absence of hyphens.)

(4) The Government

Capitalize the names of governmental agencies and departments. If the word *union* or *commonwealth* refers to a specific government, it should be capitalized. The word *government, federal, nation,* or *state* should not be capitalized unless it appears as part of an official name or is being used in official government communication.

Department of the Interior	House of Representatives
Interstate Commerce Commission	New Jersey Legislature
Springfield City Council	Orange County Board of Supervisors

We should get authorization from the *Department of Housing and Urban Development.*

He has served the *Commonwealth* for 30 years. (*Commonwealth* refers to the state of Massachusetts).

A brilliant young attorney will represent the *government.*

He is no longer a member of the House. (Short forms such as the *House,* the *Bureau,* and the *Department* are capitalized when they designate national or international bodies.)

(5) Noun-Number Designations

Generally capitalize a noun that is followed by a number or letter used to identify a unit or division. Most writers do not capitalize the noun, however, if the unit or division is a very minor one. Note these examples:

Lot 14, Tract 7243	Volume III, Chapter 8, page 133
Catalog No. 212F	Exhibit A
Policy No. 347501	Building 5, Room 12
Section 16	paragraph 3

(6) Areas of Subject matter

Capitalize the names of areas of study only if they are derived from proper nouns.

English	speech	mathematics
German	accounting	history

(7) Course Titles

The names of specific courses should be capitalized.

She is enrolled in *Introduction to Data Processing 21A.*
Mr. Edward Stokes teaches *Business Mathematics 101.*

(8) Official Titles of Rank and Public Office

Here are four rules for capitalizing titles of rank, position, or public office:

a. Unless a comma intervenes, capitalize titles that precede names; generally, however, do not capitalize those that follow names.

I have never met *Congressman* Nelson. (BUT: I have never met our congressman, Herbert Nelson.)
Much of the research was done by *Professor* Flanagan.
Alice Matson, *treasurer* of our organization, will report on our financial condition.

b. Capitalize the title of a high-ranking national, state, or international official, however, even when it follows a name or serves as a substitute for that name.

The *President* will return to Washington on Monday of next week.
The dinner is in honor of Elizabeth, *Queen* of England.
We were present when the *Governor* signed the bill.
BUT: Ask the *lieutenant* if he knows Matthew Pitts, the *councilman.*

c. Do not capitalize titles of company officials when they follow or replace personal names.

Both the *president* and the *chairman of the board* are out of town. (Writers of internal communications, however, are likely to capitalize such titles when they prepare minutes of meetings, bylaws, etc.)

d. Capitalize a title that appears either in the address or after the signature in a letter.

Mr. William Covert, *District Manager*
Shannon Machine Tool Company
Centerville, MO 63633

(9) Words Denoting Family Relationships

A name that indicates a family relationship is usually capitalized unless it is preceded by a noun or a pronoun in the possessive case.

Uncle Ralph	my *aunt* Ada	Dad
Mother	Morton's *brother* Paul	my dad
Brother David	her *cousin* Rachel	Cousin Mark

(10) Points of the Compass

The names for the points of the compass (*north, south, east, west,* and their derivatives) are capitalized only when they are used to name regions. They should not be capitalized when they are used to indicate directions.

These silicon chips were produced in the *East.*

Buffalo is *west* of Albany.

We plan to visit *Western* Europe.

His territory is in the *northern* part of the state.

Her property is located on the *south* shore of the lake.

Our engineer was born in the *Midwest.*

(11) Days and Months

Capitalize the names of holidays, days of the week, and months of the year.

Independence Day   Monday   August

(12) Seasons

Capitalize the name of a season or the word *nature* only if it is strongly personified, that is, spoken of as if it were human.

Old Man Winter left a foot of snow on our parking lot.

In the *spring* we will purchase a word processor.

Business is slow during the *summer* months.

(13) Geographical Terms

Capitalize the names of countries, sections of a country, states, counties, cities, streets, avenues, oceans, harbors, and other geographical terms.

These microcomputers are manufactured in *New York State.*

Our ship will leave from *San Diego Harbor.*

Several textile mills in *New England* have been closed.

Property taxes are somewhat high in *Franklin County.*

BUT: His home is near the *Canadian* border. (There is no reason to capitalize *border.*)

a. Do not capitalize a geographical term that precedes a name unless it is a part of that name.

Our accountant has never been in the *state* of Florida.

He worked as an engineer for the *city* of Cleveland.

b. Do not capitalize a plural common noun that completes the meaning of two or more proper nouns.

We have offices in the Woolworth and Chrysler *buildings.* (If the plural noun appears first, as in *Lakes Erie and Ontario,* it should be capitalized.)

(14) Historical Events or Eras

Capitalize the names of important historical events or eras in history, as well as the names of well-known political policies.

the Civil War	the Louisiana Purchase	the Great Society
the Dark Ages	the Monroe Doctrine	Welfare to Work

(15) Religious References

Capitalize any reference to a supreme being, even a personal pronoun that refers to a supreme being but has no antecedent in the same sentence. Capitalize also the name of a religion, its members, and its buildings.

Jehovah	the Holy Spirit	St. Mary's Episcopal Church
the Almighty	Allah	Temple Judea
God	Catholics	Islam

They expressed their thanks unto *Him.*

There is a *Nazarene* church on Seventh Avenue.

(16) Additional Uses of Capitalization

Capitalize the *first word* in each of the following:

a. A complete sentence

The computer was programmed by Maria Sanchez.

b. A direct quotation that could function as a complete sentence

She said, "*Please* take care of the matter at once."

BUT: He said that Mae's weakness is "*her* inability to write well." (Quoted portion could not function as a sentence.)

c. A word or a phrase that substitutes for a complete sentence

Yes, of course. When?

d. The salutation of a letter

Dear Ms. Rosberg:

e. The complimentary close of a letter

Sincerely yours,

Yours respectfully.

f. An independent clause that follows a colon if it expresses a formal rule or provides a thought that deserves special emphasis

He forgot this rule: Use a dash before a word that sums up a preceding series. (Capitalize the first word of a formal rule or principle.)

He concluded with these words: "The odds are now in our favor." (Capitalize the first word of a quoted sentence.)

We apparently have the same goal: to increase profits. (An independent clause does not follow the colon.)

This is my opinion: We must accept the loan on their terms or face possible bankruptcy. (Because the important thought in this sentence follows the colon, a skillful writer would emphasize it by capitalizing the word *We*.)

Gena spent her time on two projects: she sorted the mail and proofread your manuscript. (The second clause, which simply explains the first one, does not require special emphasis.)

Note: If a colon is preceded by a single word, capitalize the first word of a sentence that follows the colon (this very sentence is a good example).

---

wWWw ═══════ Watching the Web ═══════

| Back | Forward | Home | Reload | Images | Open |

Limited time offer!
Exquisitely reconditioned cars available now!
No matter whether you come from North, East, West, or
South, when you see this offer your not going to believe
your eyes.

[see more]   [no thanks]

THE IMPACT OF LANGUAGE

ALL ABOUT EXPLETIVES

The word *expletive* has two meanings that may prove of interest to a business writer. First, it may be used to designate an oath or exclamation. Newspaper reporters who transcribe conversations or speeches sometimes substitute the word *expletive* in parentheses for any profanity that could prove offensive to their readers.

Second, the term *expletive* may refer to a word that facilitates the construction of a sentence but makes no contribution to its meaning. Note the italicized expletives in these sentences:

It is not likely that he will appear in court. (The expletive *it*, which does nothing more than introduce the thought, serves as a singular subject.)

There is no time to discuss the question. (Note that the singular subject, *time*, follows the verb.)

The words *it* and *there*, of course, do not always serve as expletives. In the sentence *I gave it to my secretary*, the word *it* is simply a pronoun, the object of *gave*. In the sentence *He put the book there on your desk*, the word *there* is simply an adverb that modifies the verb *put*.

———————————————— FOR CLASS DISCUSSION ————————————————

Inasmuch as the expletive is a mere function word and does not logically qualify as any of the eight parts of speech, should we consider it to be a ninth part of speech? Give reasons for your answer.

_____ WORKSHEET 5 _____

CAPITALIZATION

PART A. Indicate whether each statement is true or false by inserting T or F in the space provided.

1. Personal titles in addresses or letter signatures should always be capitalized.

    1. _____

2. The names of the seasons should never be capitalized.

    2. _____

3. The words *north, south, east,* and *west* should never be capitalized unless they are being used to name regions.

    3. _____

4. Historical events or eras do not require capitalization.

    4. _____

5. Every word in the complimentary close of a letter should be capitalized.

    5. _____

6. A complete sentence direct quotation always begins with a capital letter.

    6. _____

7. A word that follows a colon in a sentence should never be capitalized.

    7. _____

8. This capitalization is correct: the Ohio and Columbia rivers.

    8. _____

9. Both words should be capitalized in the expression *North Africa.*

    9. _____

10. Neither word should be capitalized in the expression *computer courses.*

    10. _____

PART B. Underscore every word or abbreviation that has not been capitalized properly. In the space provided, indicate the number of such items. If you are collaborating, discuss each correction as a group.

Example: The <u>President</u> of General <u>motors</u> wrote this article.

    2
    _____

1. My Mother sits on a citizens' panel for the House.

    1. * _____

2. The governor has often commended Patrillo's work.

    2. _____

3. Our staff uses IBM-compatible Computers.

    3. _____

4. Working in the Government takes drive and patience.

    4. _____

5. Michels is a Purchasing Agent for the State Department.

    5. * _____

6. The canadian embassy was a very difficult building to find.

6. _____

7. She ordered canadian bacon on her pizza.

7. _____

8. The cartoonist who draws Dilbert will be working on the project.

8. _____

9. He had no idea that the Bureau was tracking his movements.

9. _____

10. Seventy graduates hold majors in Systems Analysis.

10. _____

11. Our comptroller is considering the new Macintosh accounting program.

11. _____

12. Did you study English and Mathematics to prepare for this job?

12. _____

13. Tomorrow the Lafayette Bridge will be open to Eastbound traffic only.

13. _____

14. Jefferson County will build its new Government center in 2008.

14. _____

15. The President of our company is talking about merging with Ectron, Inc.

15. _____

16. Nan Ouren, our Executive Assistant, begins her term as Councilwoman today.

16. * _____

17. The Youngstown River flows North toward Collingsworth.

17. _____

18. Haven Waterworks is a typical small business for carroll county.

18. _____

19. A&M Records, Inc. has its Headquarters in Hollywood, California.

19. _____

20. U S WEST is offering a promotion for free second line installation.

20. _____

21. The Lindgren School offers free Parent Membership in the P.T.S.O.

21. _____

22. Wooddale lutheran church has acquired the adjacent lot for parking.

22. _____

23. The business meeting was handled by vice president Fogarty.

23. _____

24. I was expecting to have been promoted to vice president by this time.

24. _____

25. A quarter century of business has taken place in the Donaldson building.

25. _____

26. The Church down the street leaves its door open for those needing a telephone.

26. _____

27. Jenny's flowers will be open late on Valentine's day.

27. _____

28. This Antique Shop is known for unique china pieces and african carvings.

28. _____

29. The nineteenth century novelist wrote about a tour of the south after 1865.

29. _____

30. The Temple of the Scottish Rite stands on Morgan street and 15th avenue.

30. _____

PART C.   In this sample resume section, underscore the 20 letters that should be capitalized.

john henrich

33 madison way

oak city, michigan

EDUCATION

bachelor's in english from the university of michigan: june 1988

- took courses in general literature, shakespeare, and standard american grammar

- received scholarship from the johnson foundation

- studied with henry hunter, department chair

PART D.   Write sentences containing the words given in parentheses. Please note that five of the words are capitalized and should, therefore, be used as *proper nouns.*

1. (french) *_____

_____

_____

2. (French) *_____

_____

_____

3. (avenue) _____

_____

_____

4. (Avenue) _____

_____

_____

5. (lieutenant) _____

_____

_____

6. (Lieutenant) _____

_____

_____

7. (camera) _____

_____

_____

8. (Camera) _____

_____

_____

9. (publishing) _____

_____

_____

10. (Publishing) _____

_____

_____

THE PLIGHT OF FRESHMEN

The chancellor of a large Western university announces periodically that almost 50 percent of all incoming freshmen fail to pass the English pretest and are required to enroll in "bonehead" (remedial) English. Colleges and universities throughout the nation, in fact, have discovered that most high school graduates are woefully deficient in their understanding of English grammar; yet it is taught in all our public schools.

_____ FOR CLASS DISCUSSION _____

Why does the average student fail to master the principles of grammar?

Name _____ Date _____

OPTIONAL EXERCISES

OPTION 1 Underscore (with a ruler) every word or abbreviation that should begin with a capital letter but does not. The first three have already been underscored. If you are working collaboratively, each group member might find the errors in a separate paragraph and teach the others about what was discovered.

1 People in <u>north</u> <u>america</u> who run small businesses feel as though they are always in

2 a race with their bank. Dick <u>fortunato</u>, vice president of fillmore bank & trust knows this.

3 After all, dick started his career in a small business in toledo, ohio. "Each time expenses

4 exceed income, each time holiday or overtime pay are calculated, small business owners

5 shiver," dick says. "The question is this: can anything be done about how the bank and its

6 clients interact that will raise business owners' confidence and help them take good risks?

7 If we can figure that one out, small businesses will thrive, whether they're in ohio or

8 wisconsin, ontario or texas." Fillmore bank & trust believes that they *have* figured it out,

9 although their solution might surprise the average bank customer. "It's all about

10 relationships," says eileen waters, small business accounts manager. "We make it a point

11 to visit clients every three months." Last week waters made a personal visit to cleary

12 manufacturing, a frequent supplier of parts to wisconsin counties building commission

13 projects such as ironbridge historical village near the town of canfield. When waters

14 meets with cleary's owner, charles friedman, he shows her the progress on site and talks

15 about other projects cleary is bidding for in the canfield area. "When eileen waters shows

16 up, I know I'm accountable for my work, and I also know that fillmore bank & trust

17 supports what we're doing together. It feels like a partnership."

18 Working as partners is what waters wanted when she began as a banker. She and

19 fortunato decided together to begin the practice of site visits to both check and support

20 their clients. In november of last year, that local practice became a provisional policy for

21 the entire fillmore network. Site visits are only a part of the whole relationship system at

22 fillmore, which includes a website, monthly on-line chats between bankers and clients as

23 well as among clients themselves, and a one-page monthly newsletter fillmore makes

24 available by fax or e-mail. Cleary's friedman appreciates the chats and newsletter as much

25 as site visits. "We communicate better with the bank and with other small businesses in

26 canfield than we've ever done before. I never expected that kind of help from my bank.

27 On the first wednesday of every month, I'm ready to learn and connect."

OPTION 2   Some authorities believe that the following expressions in italics should be capitalized. Other authorities disagree.

1. She lives by the *golden rule.*
2. The property is in *western* Montana or *northern* Idaho.
3. The printer asked for three bottles of *india* ink.
4. Among his belongings was a small *turkish* towel.

Would you capitalize the expressions that are in italics? In a brief paragraph, tell how you would handle any or all of them. Give reasons.

Plural Forms of Nouns

■■ **POINT TO PONDER**

There are more than a dozen different
ways to build the plural forms of nouns.

For the student of English, the distinction between singular nouns and plural nouns is an extremely important one. Note that a noun is considered *singular* if it refers to only one of anything (person, place, thing, quality, idea, etc.). A noun that refers to more than one of anything is said to be *plural*. Words like *college* and *building,* therefore, are singular, while words like *colleges* and *buildings* are plural.

If you use *The American Heritage Dictionary,* you will find that it provides plural forms for virtually all nouns listed. Most college-level dictionaries, however, omit plural forms that require simply the addition of *s* or *es*. As mentioned in Chapter 1, plural forms that are unusual, or *irregular,* are almost always included. In your study of nouns and their various forms, you would be wise to keep the following principles in mind.

1. Most nouns are made plural by the addition of *s*.

automobile, automobiles	Martin, Martins
cabinet, cabinets	Orlando, Orlandos
computer, computers	Perry, Perrys
employee, employees	Zola, Zolas

2. Nouns that end in *s, x, z, ch,* or *sh* are made plural by the addition of *es*.

bush, bushes	watch, watches
business, businesses	Bendix, Bendixes
quiz, quizzes	Schwartz, Schwartzes
tax, taxes	Williams, Williamses

3. Common nouns that end in *y* fall into two classifications:

   a. If a noun ends in *y* preceded by a vowel, the plural is formed by the addition of *s*.

alley, alleys	fairway, fairways
alloy, alloys	journey, journeys
attorney, attorneys	key, keys

   b. If it ends in *y* preceded by a consonant, the plural is formed by changing the *y* to *i* and adding *es*. Plurals of nouns ending in *quy* are formed in this same manner.

beneficiary, beneficiaries	company, companies
boundary, boundaries	quantity, quantities
colloquy, colloquies	secretary, secretaries

4. The plurals of personal names accompanied by titles may be correctly expressed in more than one way. The modern tendency in business writing is to avoid the use of plural titles, such as *Messrs.,* because they are very formal in nature. Observe these correct forms:

PREFERRED:	We have sent letters to Mr. Wong and Mr. Lobe.
FORMAL:	We have sent letters to Messrs. Wong and Lobe. (*Messrs.* is an abbreviation of the French word *Messieurs.*)
PREFERRED:	Ms. Hanson and Ms. Stevens donated the prizes.
FORMAL:	Mmes. Hanson and Stevens donated the prizes. (*Mmes.* is an abbreviation of the French word *Mesdames.*)

   Note: In most of today's business offices, correspondents have discontinued the use of both *Mrs.* and *Miss.* These courteous titles have been replaced with *Ms.,* which does not reveal a woman's marital status. Many writers, of course, prefer to use no courteous title.

5. Most nouns that end in *f, fe,* or *ff* are made plural by the addition of *s*. In some nouns, however, the *f* or *fe* is changed to *v* and *es* is added.

bailiff, bailiffs	calf, calves
handkerchief, handkerchiefs	half, halves
pontiff, pontiffs	knife, knives
safe, safes	life, lives
staff, staffs	wife, wives

6. The principle that governs nouns ending in *o* is divided into four parts:

   a. If a noun ends with *o* preceded by a vowel, the plural is formed by the addition of *s*.

curio, curios	radio, radios
portfolio, portfolios	studio, studios

   b. If a musical term ends in *o,* the plural is formed by the addition of *s*.

alto, altos	piano, pianos
banjo, banjos	solo, solos
crescendo, crescendos	soprano, sopranos

c. If a noun ends in *o* preceded by a consonant, the addition of *es* may be required. The modern tendency, however, is to form the plurals of such nouns by adding just an *s*. Check a good dictionary when you are in doubt.

embargo, embargoes	canto, cantos
hero, heroes	dynamo, dynamos
potato, potatoes	palomino, palominos
tomato, tomatoes	silo, silos
veto, vetoes	tuxedo, tuxedos

d. Some nouns ending in *o* have two plural forms.

cargoes, cargos	mottoes, mottos
hoboes, hobos	provisoes, provisos
mementoes, mementos	volcanoes, volcanos
mosquitoes, mosquitos	zeroes, zeros

7. Some nouns are made plural by a vowel change.

foot, feet	mouse, mice
goose, geese	tooth, teeth
man, men	woman, women

8. A few nouns take *en* as a plural ending.

   child, children   ox, oxen

   Note: *Brother* has two plural forms, *brothers* and *brethren.* The word *brothers* is used to denote a family relationship, whereas *brethren* is used to indicate fellow members of fraternal or religious organizations.

9. Some nouns have plural forms that are identical to their singular forms.

corps	moose	series
deer	rendezvous	sheep

   Note: When *corps* is used in the singular, the *s* is silent.

10. A few nouns that end in *s* are singular in meaning and require singular verbs when used as subjects in sentences.

civics	mathematics	phonetics	politics
economics	news	semantics	

11. Plural nouns such as *scissors, pliers, thanks, goods,* and *riches* may be either singular or plural in meaning, but they are used only with plural verbs. They have no corresponding singular forms.

12. Compound nouns consist of a combination of two or more words that are written in one of these ways: in solid form as one word, as a hyphenated word, or as separate words.

   a. If the compound word consists of one or more nouns and an adjective or a preposition, the principal *noun* is made plural.

aide-de-camp, aides-de-camp	brother-in-law, brothers-in-law
bill of sale, bills of sale	looker-on, lookers-on

b. If no part of the hyphenated compound word is a noun, the final element is made plural.

follow-up, follow-ups   trade-in, trade-ins

strike-over, strike-overs   write-up, write-ups

c. If a compound noun is written as one word without a hyphen, the final element is made plural.

businessman, businessmen   letterhead, letterheads

cupful, cupfuls   stepchild, stepchildren

13. The plural of a lowercase letter or of a capitalized vowel is usually formed by the addition of an apostrophe and *s*.

four *e*'s   several *A*'s

five *l*'s   the two *U*'s

14. The plural of a number, a capitalized consonant, or a word referred to simply as a word is generally formed by the addition of *s* or *es*.

a few 7s   too many *ands*   many *yeses*

the 1990s   his *ifs* and *buts*   three *noes*

Note: Modern writers are likely to use an apostrophe only if the expression would otherwise be easily misread (*so*'s, *me*'s, etc.).

15. The plural of an abbreviation is generally formed by the addition of *s* to the singular form.

bbls.	pks.	YMCAs
hrs.	wks.	CPAs
mos.	yrs.	RNs
Nos.	Bros.	Ph.Ds

Note: A writer may choose to insert an apostrophe to prevent a possible misreading (*rpm's*).

16. Some abbreviations have the same form for both the singular and the plural.

ft.	foot *or* feet	deg.	degree *or* degrees
bu.	bushel *or* bushels	min.	minute *or* minutes
mi.	mile *or* miles	oz.	ounce *or* ounces

17. The plural of a contraction is formed by the addition of *s*.

don't   don'ts   can't   can'ts

Note: A contraction that already ends in *s* should not be used in the plural form.

18. Many nouns that are foreign in origin are commonly used in formal, scientific, and technical matter. Some of these nouns have only their foreign plurals; others have been given an additional (English) plural. You will note that the nouns listed have been taken from Latin, Greek, and French.

The plurals of foreign nouns are formed by changing the endings as indicated.

	Singular	Foreign Plural	English Plural
sis to *ses*	analysis	analyses	
	basis	bases	
	diagnosis	diagnoses	
	oasis	oases	
um to *a*	addendum	addenda	
	curriculum	curricula	curriculums
	datum	data	
	memorandum	memoranda	memorandums
us to *i*	alumnus (mas.)	alumni	
	gladiolus	gladioli	gladioluses
	nucleus	nuclei	nucleuses
	stimulus	stimuli	
ex or *ix* to *ices*	appendix	appendices	appendixes
	index	indices	indexes
a to *ae*	alumna (fem.)	alumnae	
	formula	formulae	formulas
	larva	larvae	
	vertebra	vertebrae	vertebras
on to *a*	criterion	criteria	criterions
	phenomenon	phenomena	phenomenons
eau to *eaux*	bureau	bureaux	bureaus
	tableau	tableaux	tableaus
	trousseau	trousseaux	trousseaus

OR WOULD YOU PREFER TWO HAMBURGERS?

To determine the correct plural of *Egg McMuffin*, employees of McDonald's Corporation wrote to 63 English professors at universities across the land. The results of the survey were not really conclusive. Of the 30 professors who responded, 17 favor *Egg McMuffins* as a plural form, but the other 13 prefer *Eggs McMuffin*.

_____ FOR CLASS DISCUSSION _____

If you decide one day to order more than one Egg McMuffin, which plural form will you use? Why?

THE *DATA* DILEMMA

The word *data,* which functions as the plural form of *datum,* is often used with a singular verb; in fact, 50 percent of the language authorities questioned in a recent survey are willing to accept as correct either of these sentences: *These data are inconclusive. This data is inconclusive.*

_____ FOR CLASS DISCUSSION _____

If you were preparing an annual report for a corporation, would you be more likely to use *data are* or *data is?* State your reasons.

HOW FAST ARE YOU?

If you are a serious student of English, you will be able to complete the following cross-word puzzle in a few minutes. Your only task is to put the eight parts of speech in their appropriate places.

![globe icon] **A WORD TIP FROM THE REAL WORLD**

In these days of company downsizing with emphasis on efficiency, it's quite common for one person to have to do the work that used to be done by two persons. Patrick, the president of a consulting group, manages all of his correspondence with no traditional secretarial support. "Each consultant, speaker, or trainer is responsible for his or her own written and oral correspondence," he says. "In this time of electronic mail and instant desktop publishing, people worth having as consultants should be able to undertake their own written communication. They do it themselves, or it simply doesn't get done."

Patrick's company is not the exception. It is the new rule of business. Students who pay attention at the college level to basic grammar and mechanical skills will be more than repaid when they find work that demands clear writing and speaking. They will, in fact, be ahead of the crowd.

Name _Alisha_   Date _2-13-02_

———WORKSHEET 6———

PLURAL FORMS OF NOUNS

Part A. Underscore any word that is unacceptable as a plural form; then write the correct form in the space provided. If you find no error in a sentence, put a C in the space.

Example: Several <u>alumnas</u> serve on the board.

alumnae

1. Alexander <u>Portz's</u> trial began last Tuesday morning.

   1. ~~Portz's~~ correct

2. Portz is one of the <u>CPA's</u> in our accounting department.

   2. * CPAs

3. He has worked for us since the late <u>1970's</u>.

   3. 1970s

4. He is being tried for misrepresentation of company assets when preparing reports for our corporate taxes.

   4. Correct

5. He reported that large <u>quantitys</u> of paper stock had been damaged.

   5. quantities

6. It was later discovered that he had used that stock to publish <u>portfolioes</u> for local struggling artists.

   6. * portfolios

7. He reported that several trucks lost their cargoes in highway mishaps.

   7. Correct

8. We later traced the contents of those trucks to five local <u>churchs</u> and their programs to help clothe the needy.

   8. Churches

9. At least 400 <u>familys</u> were helped by these diversions of supplies.

   9. families

10. Now a court will have to decide whether the Portzs (his wife was also involved in the schemes) should have to pay for crimes which resulted in good being done.

    10. Portzes

11. Two <u>companys</u>, ours and another local firm, have an interest in the trial.

    11. companies

12. Each company employed Portz as a tax accountant for a series of years.

    12. Correct

13. Each company took losses which later created community <u>beneficiarys</u>.

    13. beneficiaries

14. How will this man and his abetting wife be punished for these _deedes_?

14. deeds

15. Perhaps some crimes are trade-off's in justice; a jury will have to decide.

15. trade-offs

PART B. Write the correct plural forms of the words given in parentheses, all of which are singular. Use foreign plurals whenever possible.

Example: His (stepchild) will inherit his share of the business.

_____ stepchildren _____

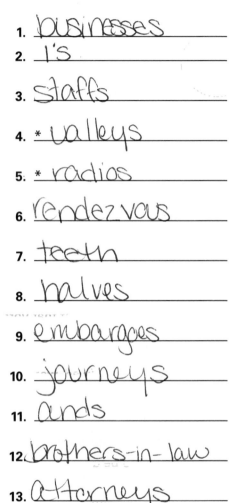

1. Several (business) in our state have paid lobbyists.

1. businesses

2. Some Welsh words have as many as six (*l*).

2. l's

3. Both daytime and nighttime (staff) must attend the meeting.

3. staffs

4. Our factories are found mostly in river (valley) with barge traffic.

4. * valleys

5. Will good coverage require three short wave (radio)?

5. * radios

6. Janeway and Carlotto have set up three (rendezvous) this week.

6. rendezvous

7. The technology award goes to a firm that makes replacement (tooth).

7. teeth

8. Please give Martin both (half) of the broken display case.

8. halves

9. That nation has suffered several serious trade (embargo).

9. embargoes

10. Our sales consultant has made four (journey) to New York this year.

10. journeys

11. Diamondes had too many (*and*) in her brief speech.

11. ands

12. How many (brother-in-law) can our C.E.O. employ?

12. brothers-in-law

13. How many (attorney) does Lawson and Palmero keep on retainer?

13. attorneys

14. Our warehouse is currently storing four (piano) from the Philharmonic.

14. pianos

15. Prices will rise dramatically if these storms affect crops of (tomato).

15. tomatoes

16. Our interns take two internship (quiz) upon which their grade is based.

16. quizzes

17. This convention draws over 3,000 (businessman) every year.

17. businessmen

18. My partner does not respond well to (don't) and (can't).

18. don'ts, can'ts

PART C. Change each of the singular nouns in parentheses in the following memo to plural nouns.

To: Floor managers, Wilson's Music Stores
Date: 9/7/99

Our fall sale on (banjo*) and (saxophone) will make us (hero) with our customers! Be sure

that they know about our willingness to take (trade-in) and to make deals on last season's

equipment. After all, we want to clear out our current inventory and not be left with great

(quantity) of merchandise on the (shelf). Invite the people in your (life) to come and shop

with us, even your distant cousins or (brother-in-law) who just love music. Finally, please

remember that during the kick-off of this sale, our owners will be dressed in (tuxedo),

strolling through the store, playing (piccolo).

1. *_____   5. _____   8. _____

2. _____   6. _____   9. _____

3. _____   7. _____   10. _____

4. _____

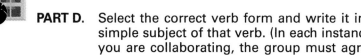

PART D. Select the correct verb form and write it in the space provided. Underscore the simple subject of that verb. (In each instance the *singular* verb form ends in *s*.) If you are collaborating, the group must agree on an answer to each item before proceeding to the next one.

Example: The <u>news</u> (was, were) alarming to some of
us.
                                                                                was
                                                           _____

1. These financial crises (is, are) exploited by the press.   1. *_____

2. Their analysis of our capabilities (leave, leaves)
   something to be desired.   2. _____

3. After all, their theories of business often (has, have)
   nothing to do with real life.   3. _____

4. Economics (is, are) a complex field.   4. _____

5. Similar series of setbacks (has, have) crushed
   lesser firms.   5. _____

6. But our leadership (is, are) strong and visionary.   6. _____

7. Politics in this corporation (work, works) well in
   the tough times.   7. _____

8. Loyal staffs (drop, drops) their individual preferences
   for the good of the group.   8. _____

9. In a cutthroat atmosphere, our thanks (go, goes) to
   our colleagues and partners.   9. _____

10. Allies (are, is) what they have always been.   10. _____

PART E. Compose ten short sentences. In each one you are to use the *plural form* of the word or numeral given in parentheses.

Example: (5) You dialed one too many 5s.

1. (trade-in) _____

_____

2. (alumna) _____

_____

_____

3. (bacterium) * _____

_____

4. (McCarthy) _____

_____

5. (diagnosis) _____

_____

THE IMPACT OF LANGUAGE

OUR STRANGE LANGUAGE

We'll begin with a box and the plural is boxes,
But the plural of ox is oxen, not oxes.
Then, one fowl is a goose but two are called geese,
Yet the plural of moose should never be meese.

You find a lone mouse or a whole set of mice,
Yet the plural of house is houses, not hice.
If the plural of man is always called men,
Why shouldn't the plural of pan be called pen?

If I speak of a foot and you show me your feet,
And I give you a boot, would a pair be called beet?
If one is a tooth and a whole set are teeth,
Why shouldn't the plural of booth be called beeth?

Then, one may be that, and three would be those,
Yet hat in the plural wouldn't be hose.
We speak of a brother and also say brethren,
But though we say Mother, we never say Methren.

Then the masculine pronouns are he, his, and him,
But imagine the feminine she, shis, and shim.
So English, I fancy you all will agree,
Is the funniest language you ever did see.

—Anonymous

The Use of Possessive Nouns

■■ POINT TO PONDER ▶

The apostrophe is actually easy to control,
but most people prefer to think otherwise.

The term **case** denotes the relation (subject, complement, modifier, object) that a noun or a pronoun bears to some other word in a sentence. There are three cases: nominative, possessive, and objective. Nouns or pronouns that serve as subjects or subject complements are in the **nominative case;** those that serve as objects of verbs or prepositions are in the **objective case.** The noun *Frank* is nominative in *Frank drove the car* but objective in *The car was driven by Frank.* Because nouns in the nominative and the objective cases are identical in form, they pose no problem for the average writer. The **possessive case,** however, requires some special study.

Many writers experience difficulty in using possessives because they do not keep in mind two important factors that are involved in the possessive relationship: the possessor and the thing possessed. The *possessor* is represented by a word that is written in the possessive case and that functions as an adjective (*Larry's* plan). The *thing possessed (plan)* is a noun modified by the possessive word.

The possessive case is frequently used to show possession, authorship, brand, kind, or origin: *John's* car, Roger *Keefe's* book, *Campbell's* soup, *dentists'* meeting, *Darwin's* theory. A noun in the possessive case generally ends in *s* and is followed by another noun. It can, as a rule, be expanded into a phrase.

today's program	the program for today
the *firm's* policy	the policy of the firm
Mr. *Caruso's* store	the store owned by Mr. Caruso
A. J. *Cronin's* book	the book written by A. J. Cronin
the *executive's* reply	the reply of the executive

When a possessive noun is needed, another noun is likely to follow (note the foregoing examples). An adjective, of course, may intervene, as in *Mr. Caruso's new store* or *today's expanded program*. The need for the possessive case is clearly established if a possessive pronoun (particularly *his, its,* or *their*) could be substituted for the word in question; for example, *Joseph Santo's recent promotion* could be changed to read *his recent promotion*.

SINGULAR POSSESSIVE FORMS

If, in writing a sentence, you have made certain that a noun should be in the possessive case, decide from the context of the sentence whether that noun is singular or plural. If it is singular, apply this rule:

> **RULE 1**   Form the possessive case of a singular noun by adding an apostrophe and *s* ('s).

Bob's notebook	the *recruiter's* patience
your *boss's* mail	a *fiduciary's* responsibility
a *month's* work	a *trustee's* background
Jess's reports	Ms. *Adams's* appointment

Some writers today apply this first rule without exception when they make singular nouns possessive. Most writers, however, prefer to deviate from the basic rule when its application would result in a word that is awkward to pronounce. As a result, we have this optional rule:

> **RULE 2**   (Optional) Form the possessive case of a singular noun that has two or more syllables and that ends in an *s* or *z* sound by adding only an apostrophe.

Mr. *Perkins'* assignment	the *witness'* manner
Ms. *Rabinowitz'* inquiry	Henry *Phillips'* new book

Many writers apply this optional rule every time they encounter such nouns. Others apply it only when they feel that the addition of '*s* would lead to an awkward pronunciation.

All the possessive forms on the following list are correct. If you pronounce each word carefully, you *may* decide that some of these forms are more acceptable than others.

Ms. *Carruthers'* report	Ms. *Carruthers's* report
Steinmetz' theory	*Steinmetz's* theory
Mr. *Fairless'* office	Mr. *Fairless's* office
Carole *Reynolds'* idea	Carole *Reynolds's* idea
Mr. *Lopez'* invention	Mr. *Lopez's* invention

Some professional writers add only an apostrophe to singular nouns of *one* syllable that end in an *s* or *z* sound (*Betz', Ross', Leads',* etc.), although few, if any, handbooks of correct English usage recommend such a practice. As you complete Worksheet 7, you will be expected to follow the more conservative practice of adding an apostrophe and *s* to any one-syllable singular noun that is to be made possessive (*Betz's, Ross's, Leeds's*, etc.).

PLURAL POSSESSIVE FORMS

Before you attempt to make a plural noun possessive, make absolutely certain that you have the correct plural form; then apply whichever of the following rules is appropriate.

> **RULE 3** Form the possessive of a regular plural noun (one ending in *s*) by adding only an apostrophe after the *s*.

the *Murphys'* indebtedness   the *attorneys'* arguments
the *Briggses'* dilemma   the *boys'* accounts
the *Calderases'* home   the *horses'* bridles

> **RULE 4** Form the possessive of an irregular plural noun (one not ending in *s*) by adding an apostrophe and *s*.

salespeople's territories   *foremen's* resistance
women's organizations   *children's* shoes

THE RIGHT QUESTIONS

Many writers find the use of possessive-case nouns challenging simply because they fail to ask the right questions. Consider this sentence:

The (jurors, juror's, jurors') votes will be counted by the foreman.

Writers who are doubtful about the proper form of the second word in the foregoing sentence would do well to ask these questions:

1. Is the word being used in the possessive case?

ANSWER: The fact that a noun *(votes)* follows the word in question suggests that the possessive case is needed. Also, this word (like all possessive-case forms) could be expanded into a phrase: the votes *of the jurors*. The possessive case, therefore, *should* be used.

2. Is the word in question singular or plural?

ANSWER: Note the use of the word *jurors* (not *juror*) in the phrase already mentioned: votes *of the jurors* (usually 12 people). The *plural* form is definitely needed.

3. How is the plural form *jurors* made possessive?

ANSWER: Form the possessive case of a regular plural noun (one ending in *s*) by adding only an apostrophe after the *s*.

The correct form, then, is *jurors'*.

SPECIAL NOTES ON THE POSSESSIVE

1. To indicate joint ownership, add the sign of the possessive to the last noun that names a possessor.

   Stacy and *Nelson's* store   Frank and *Carl's* delivery truck.

2. To indicate separate ownership, make each such noun possessive.

   buyers' and *sellers'* points of view   *Leo's* and *Tom's* voices

3. If nouns are used in apposition to name the possessor, add the sign of the possessive to the appositive itself.

   We appraised Dr. McGrath, the *dentist's,* property. (You may prefer this wording: We appraised the property of Dr. McGrath, the dentist.)

4. In compound words or phrases, place the sign of possession at the end.

   the secretary-treasurer's report   someone else's briefcase   my son-in-law's car

5. To make an abbreviation possessive, place an apostrophe and *s* after the period. If the abbreviation is plural, place an apostrophe after the *s* but not before it.

singular	*plural*
the Randall Co.'s bargains	the Ph.D.s' theses
Henry Nissen, Jr.'s market	two M.D.s' opinions

6. Do not, in most instances, use the possessive case when referring to inanimate objects. The use of an *of*-phrase is likely to be less awkward.

   the roof of the house (not *the house's roof*)

   the top of the desk (not *the desk's top*)

   If people are in some way involved, the possessive case should prove acceptable, as in *this store's policies* or *my company's pension plan*.

Common expressions that refer to time and measurement may be expressed in the possessive case.

singular	*plural*
one week's time	three weeks' time
a minute's delay	ten minutes' delay
at arm's length	five cents' worth

7. When writing the name of an organization, do not use an apostrophe unless one is used in its official name. The letterhead of an organization's stationery may tell you how a name should be written.

   California Teachers Association   Bankers Corporation

Occasionally the possessive form is not followed by the noun it modifies. In some instances that noun is not expressed; in others it appears elsewhere in the sentence.

> I met your attorney at *Morton's.* (Morton's home)

> That portfolio is *Darin's.* (Darin's portfolio)

NOUNS CLASSIFIED

Before leaving these chapters on nouns, we should acknowledge four important classifications. You encountered proper nouns and common nouns when you studied capitalization (Chapter 5). There are two other types of nouns that should be recognized and controlled by the student of business English. The first of these is the **collective noun,** which is used to name a *group* of people or objects. You will find collective nouns discussed in Chapters 10 and 12 because their use frequently influences our choice of pronouns and verbs. Also important to us are **verbal nouns,** or **gerunds,** which are verb forms that function as nouns and end in *ing.* You will find them covered, along with other verbals, in Chapter 17.

MERRY CHRISTMAS

A house on a street in my city has an attractive sign over the front door. It reads THE BANCROFT'S (fictitious name). Whenever I pass that house, I find myself wondering what message the sign is intended to convey. If the owners want us to know that *this is the Bancrofts' house,* the apostrophe should be placed at the end of the name. If they want to tell us that *the Bancrofts live here,* no apostrophe should be used. Both occupants of the house, by the way, are English teachers.

The same mistake is made again and again during the month of December when people have their names printed on Christmas cards. THE WALLICK'S (note the apostrophe) is likely to appear on a card from the Wallicks. THE CRISWELL'S may be used on a card from the Criswells. Apostrophes, it seems, are wasted on a grand scale during the holiday season.

Practice on your own name and three of your best friends' names. Write the names properly, with and without apostrophes, as simple plurals and as possessives.

A WORD TIP FROM THE REAL WORLD

Chet, a former English teacher, now a consultant on human resource issues with major corporations, makes this observation:

In the sixties, thousands of college students became English majors. They enjoyed literature and writing and were very good at it. When it came to getting jobs after college, only a fraction of them actually entered the fields of teaching or writing. Consequently we have thousands of English majors working out in industry today. They are in their forties and early fifties, in responsible positions. Doing what? A huge percentage of them work in personnel. That means that, when you apply for a job or want to be promoted within a firm, you have a very good chance of having to impress a former English major. My advice is to keep up your reading, writing, and speaking skills after college. The person who is evaluating your job application or your promotion chances will likely be impressed by strong language skills and turned off by weak ones. Give yourself every break you can.

Name _Alisha_   **Date** _2-13-02_

_____WORKSHEET 7_____

THE USE OF POSSESSIVE NOUNS

PART A. Provide the correct possessive forms.

	Singular Possessive	Plural Possessive
Example: auditor	auditor's	auditors'
1. county	1. _County's_	_counties'_
2. Claus	2. *_Claus'_	*_Clauses'_
3. Ph.D.	3. _Ph.D.'s_	_Ph.D.s'_
4. man	4. _man's_	_men's_
5. address	5. _address'_	_addresses'_

PART B. Rewrite each of the following sentence fragments by changing a phrase to a possessive-case form.

Examples: report written by Vince — Vince's report

advice given by Kendall — Kendall's advice

1. decision made by Kurilla   1. _Kurilla's decision_
2. beliefs of the board members   2. *_board members' beliefs_
3. office used by Avner   3. _Avner's office_
4. end of the day   4. _days end_
5. reply given by Jones   5. *_Jones' reply_
6. reasons cited by officers   6. _officers' reasons_
7. debts owed by the Laceys   7. _Laceys' debts_
8. timecards of the employees   8. _employees' timecards_

PART C. In the space provided, write the letter that indicates the correct choice.

Example: I overheard the (A) _guards,_ (B) _guard's,_ (C) _guards'_ answer
to your question.   B

1. Our response will be to terminate John (A) _Scannells,_ (B) _Scannell's,_
   (C) _Scannells'_ account. (the account of John Scannell)   1. _B._

2. Please speak to our donors about this proposal, especially the
   (A) _Taylors,_ (B) _Taylor's,_ (C) _Taylors'._ (donors are Larry and Donna
   Taylor)   2. _C._

3. A 4% increase in corporate taxes caused this (A) _companies,_
   (B) _company's,_ (C) _companies'_ shortfall last year.   3. *_B._

THE USE OF POSSESSIVE NOUNS (81)

4. (A) *Jones,* (B) *Jones'* and Smith's firm is jointly owned.

     4. _A._

5. The password used to access each of the accounts was Mr. (A) *Sagans,* (B) *Sagan's,* (C) *Sagans'.* (the password of Mr. Sagan)

     5. _B._

6. Did we receive the (A) *Jensens,* (B) *Jensen's,* (C) *Jensens'* last two payments.

     6. _C._

7. Customer service representatives take many (A) *clients,* (B) *client's,* (C) *clients'* questions online every afternoon.

     7. * _C._

8. Air travelers experienced several (A) *hours,* (B) *hour's,* (C) *hours'* delay this morning.

     8. _C._

9. Leave your account summaries in my box or (A) *Ms. Lewis,* (B) *Ms. Lewis's,* (C) *Ms. Lewises.*

     9. _B._

10. We read (A) *Geraldo's,* (B) *Geraldos',* (C) *Geraldo* and Levitz's annual report. (the joint report of Geraldo and Levitz)

     10. _C._

11. The (A) *Campbells,* (B) *Campbell's,* (C) *Campbells'* software setup has more option than the Rauks'.

     11. _C._

12. The team wondered about their (A) *presidents,* (B) *president's,* (C) *presidents'* tendency to stray from the topic.

     12. _B._

13. (A) *Todays,* (B) *Today's,* (C) *Todays'* meeting was far more efficient than last week's.

     13. _B._

14. Our (A) *customers,* (B) *customer's,* (C) *customers'* names are entered automatically into our data base.

     14. _C._

PART D. Underscore any error in the use of a possessive noun and then write the correct form in the answer space. If a sentence contains no error, put a C in the answer space. If you are working collaboratively, try to convince your partners that your choice is correct using chapter ideas.

Example: We must have more than one <u>persons'</u> opinion.

     person's

1. Auburn's new convention center, Riverside Place, has pulled in millions of dollars in just three <u>year's</u> time.

     1. * _years'_

2. This early success is not surprising when you look at other <u>cities'</u> convention business.

     2. _Correct_

3. More than 200 large <u>convention's</u> have come to Milltown's convention center since it opened in 1991, generating more than $600 million in total revenue.

     3. * _Conventions_

4. Clearly, conventions are big business and add to their <u>host's</u> revenue base.

     4. _____

5. Regardless of visiting <u>attendee's</u> professions, hobbies, or areas of interest, they want food shelter, transportation, entertainment, and shopping opportunities

     5. _____

6. Milltown and Auburn, like most cities, are only too happy to meet their <u>visitor's</u> expectations.

     6. _visitors'_

7. Riverside Place hosted an average of just eight conventions per year when the only adjacent space was Auburn <u>Auditoriums'</u> great hall.

     7. ~~Auditoriums~~ _Auditorium's_

8. These facilities' limited space forced many annual meetings and trade shows to forego Auburn in favor of other destinations.

8. _____

9. The Auburn Business Owner's Association began rallying around plans for improved local convention accommodations in the mid-1980s.

9. _____

10. Crews' broke ground on the addition in late 1994.

10. _____

11. One clear indication of Auburns' eagerness for profitable convention business is the number of events they booked into the new building before it was even complete.

11. _____

12. By September, 42 organizations were committed to using Riverside Places' facilities in 1999.

12. _____

13. Another 30 event's are now scheduled to take place between 2000 and 2003.

13. _____

14. To secure the new structure's first bookings, meeting planners had to act on a fair amount of faith.

14. _____

15. For example, Miller & Co.s annual convention staff arranged three future events while the facility was little more than a hole in the ground.

15. _____

16. What Riverside Places' booking staff members lacked in physical space, they made up for in persistence and personal service.

16. _____

17. Executive director Emily Fadden, on the other hand, returns some credit for Riverside Place's success to people who have convinced colleague's to come to Auburn.

17. _____

18. "Most of the national conventions that we host come as a result of local resident's willingness to work with us to bring their group here," Fadden says.

18. _____

19. "Citizen's in Auburn are proud of our city and eager to show it off."

19. _____

PART E. If you were creating signs for the following persons or businesses, using possessives, what would you print on the signs? Use the "Merry Christmas" box on p. 79 as an example.

1. the entire family of Mrs. Hansen

1. _____

2. the trucking company of Mr. D'Angelo

2. _____

3. the cabinet shop belonging to Jim Thomas

3. _____

4. the grocery store belonging to Dave and Ed

5. the summer cabin of Mike Pauli

6. the home of Mr. and Mrs. Jones and their six children

7. the pharmacy belonging to the two Moltrow siblings

8. Doris and Theodore Schmalz

9. the art studio of the Geary brothers

10. the Palace of Paris

4. _____

5. _____

6. _____

7. _____

8. _____

9. _____

10. _____

FOR CLASS DISCUSSION

(if time permits)

Note these perfectly acceptable options:

Rabinowitz's truck	Rabinowitz' truck
Watkins's dilemma	Watkins' dilemma
Fairless's notes	Fairless' notes
Davis's attitude	Davis' attitude

As you consider the foregoing options, decide which choices you would make if you were to use these expressions in your writing. Be prepared to give your reasons.

Quiz   (Chapters 5 through 7)

NAME _____   DATE _____

DIRECTIONS

Your instructor may ask you to examine any four of the sentences that follow. For each sentence chosen, you are to write the rule violated by the word or words in italics. Express the rule in your own way, but spell all words correctly. In the parentheses provided, write the correct form of the italicized word. If you are working collaboratively, your team should agree on the wording of the rules.

1. Both *attornies* seemed confident as they awaited the verdict.
2. As a graduate student he was required to write three *thesises.*
3. Six *month's* interest will become due on July 15.
4. We are hoping that *colonel* Prentiss will cooperate with us.
5. The inventory indicates that we have only three *celloes* in stock.
6. She enrolled in *marketing* 26A and a history course.
7. We did not invite the *Jones's* to our recent meeting.
8. The *mens'* faces showed evidence of their suffering.
9. Three of our *factorys* produce components for computers.
10. There are several art *studioes* in Santa Monica.

Sentence No. _____ (_____) Rule: _____

_____

_____

_____

Sentence No. _____ (_____) Rule: _____

_____

_____

_____

Sentence No. _____ (_____) Rule: _____

_____

_____

_____

Sentence No. _____ (_____) Rule: _____

_____

_____

_____

SOME GOOD ADVICE

William Lear once wrote a magazine article entitled "You Can Still Make a Million Dollars." In it he offered several valuable suggestions, the first of which appears here in the form of a puzzle. If you follow the instructions, you will be made aware of his first (and most important) recommendation for anyone who would like to become wealthy.

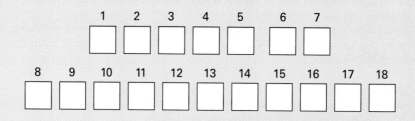

Each of the following numbered groups contains one word that typically functions as a noun. Put the first letter of that word in the square that bears the same number.

1. hesitate, since, the, liability
2. interesting, ear, concentrate, because
3. ambition, steadily, you, mine
4. foolish, readiness, with, intelligent
5. napkin, bigger, who, exceptional
6. respected, often, able, talent
7. she, coolest, truly, ornament
8. written, northern, computer, unless
9. cloudy, eastward, occasion, reluctant
10. manuscript, into, they, slowly
11. agreeable, machine, hopeful, as
12. strictly, tall, after, uncle
13. nails, scribbled, heavy, realistic
14. soft, happy, irritant, correspond
15. windy, although, calculator, serious
16. anger, costly, went, programmed
17. helped, wealthy, outstanding, television
18. from, enthusiasm, untimely, fortunately

CHAPTER 8

Comment and Review

A person's handsome features and immaculate grooming will not cover up faulty grammar.

During the twentieth century, which is rapidly drawing to a close, the world at large has enjoyed significant improvements in the field of communications. Many of those improvements have taken place since the first edition of this book was published in 1970. We have moved into an age of information, an era in which communication skills are more important than ever before. The role of computers in business and industry (as well as in the home) has been firmly established. Earlier in the century careful business writers recognized the need to eliminate trite, hackneyed expressions such as these: *your esteemed favor, pursuant to your request, be so kind as,* and *your obedient servant,* to name a few. Clear, concise, grammatical constructions are now valued by businesspeople everywhere.

Because of the number of women now employed in business, some common practices in business correspondence have come into question. Leading authorities are *still* attempting to decide what salutation to recommend for use in a letter addressed to a company that employs both women and men. One widely used handbook mentions the continuing acceptability of *Gentlemen,* but then offers five options that may be more appropriate (*Ladies and Gentlemen,* etc.). Some correspondents, of course, have chosen to use no salutation at all.

A second problem arises in referring to groups composed of both men and women. In most companies the word *salespeople* has wisely been substituted for the word *salesmen,* which inadequately identifies a mixed group. Also, most writers now try to avoid the use of constructions such as *Every employee is expected to do HIS part.* The substitution of *their* for *his,* however, is not grammatical inasmuch as *employee* is singular and *their* is plural. One option is to use the somewhat cumbersome *his or her* in place of *his.*

As our language continues to change, a text such as this one will be of real value to its readers only if it is *current,* that is, if it focuses on rules, constructions, and recommendations that are entirely acceptable in today's business world. In our attempt to keep abreast of the times, we have considered carefully the opinions of contemporary writers—grammarians, lexicographers, editors, educators, and businesspeople. Most seem to agree that our language is changing for the better. New words are being added to accommodate this new age of information, and constructions that are inadequate, imprecise, or excessively formal are being rejected by our finest writers and speakers. The student of English should profit accordingly.

A BRIEF REVIEW

Worksheet 8 will test your understanding of material contained in Chapters 1 through 7, and it should help to prepare you for an examination on this section of the text. In preparing for that examination or for Worksheet 8, you may find the following brief review helpful. It consists of 15 significant ideas contained in the chapters you have already studied.

1. Effective business writing is clear, concise, and grammatical. Sentences should not be padded with words that contribute to neither meaning nor tone.

2. There are several usable spelling rules, the most important of which is probably this one: If a two-syllable word ends in consonant-vowel-consonant and is accented on the second syllable, double the final consonant before adding a suffix that begins with a vowel (*repelled, admittance, referring,* etc.).

3. Every student of English should be able to define unhesitatingly the eight parts of speech. It would be wise to master these definitions:

   A **noun** is a name of anything. EXAMPLES: chair, George, pen, river, courage, adjective, expression

   A **pronoun** is a word used as a noun substitute. EXAMPLES: you, he, him, who, anyone, everybody, someone

   A **verb** is a word (or word group) that expresses action or state of being. EXAMPLES: communicate, are, have been, write, study, think, will be promoted

   An **adjective** is a word that modifies a noun or a pronoun. EXAMPLES: talkative, happy, small, energetic, timid, conscientious, helpful

   An **adverb** is a word that modifies a verb, an adjective, or another adverb (or any adverb-equivalent). EXAMPLES: not, well, calmly, very, hurriedly, slowly, respectfully

   A **preposition** is a word that shows the relation of its object to some other word in the sentence. EXAMPLES: to, of, with, from, on, in, under

   A **conjunction** is a connective used to join words, phrases, or clauses. EXAMPLES: but, and, or, nor, if, as, because

   An **interjection** is a word that is used solely to denote strong feeling or sudden emotion. EXAMPLES: hurray, oh, gee, wow

4. The first step in analyzing a sentence is to find the verb(s). If the verb in a particular clause is *gave,* its subject will be the answer to the question *Who* (or *what*) gave? Its object will be the answer to the question *Gave what* (or *whom*)?

5. Phrases and clauses are both groups of related words. They differ in that clauses contain subject-verb combinations and phrases do not. EXAMPLES OF PHRASES: in a few minutes, from this distance, with complete honesty, on the right side. EXAMPLES OF CLAUSES: when he arrives, while you slept, if she accepts the offer, because I had left

6. If a singular noun ends in *y* preceded by a vowel, its plural is formed by the simple addition of *s*. If a common noun ends in *y* preceded by a consonant, its plural is formed by changing the *y* to *i* and adding *es*. EXAMPLES: valleys, attorneys, parties, secretaries

7. If a singular noun ends in *o* preceded by a vowel or if it is a musical term ending in *o,* its plural is formed by the addition of *s*. EXAMPLES: radios, studios, sopranos, pianos

8. If a singular noun ends in *s, x, z, ch,* or *sh,* its plural is formed by the addition of *es*. EXAMPLES: dresses, boxes, wrenches, Joneses

9. The plurals of some foreign nouns are formed by changing the endings in these ways:

sis to *ses*	basis	bases
us to *i*	stimulus	stimuli
ex or *ix* to *ices*	index	indices
on to *a*	criterion	criteria
eau to *eaux*	bureau	bureaux

10. Any singular noun may be made possessive by the addition of an apostrophe and *s*. EXAMPLES: auditor's, Wertz's, receptionist's

11. A regular plural noun (one that ends in *s*) is made possessive by the addition of an apostrophe. An irregular plural noun is made possessive by the addition of an apostrophe and *s*. EXAMPLES: managers', Rosses', foremen's, children's

12. Joint ownership may be indicated by adding the sign of the possessive to the last noun that names a possessor. EXAMPLE: Benedict and Ferraro's new office

13. A proper noun, which indicates a specific person, place, or thing, should be capitalized. EXAMPLES: Spain, Spaniard, New York, Janet

14. Careful business writers are likely to use capital letters as they have been employed in these expressions:

The Call of the Wild	a Chrysler car
Department of Commerce	a cardigan sweater
a history course	History 12A
Jeff Matson, a lieutenant	Lieutenant Matson
my sister Loretta	Aunt Yolanda
city of Phoenix	Salt Lake City
Boston Harbor	Tanner Building
South Main Street	Waldorf and Ritz hotels

REVIEW CHART

concept	Ch. _____ page _____	first critical point to remember	example to remember	second critical point	example
effective business writing					
spelling					
parts of speech		noun pronoun verb adjective	adverb preposition conjunction interjection		
sentence analysis		finding the verb finding the subject finding the object	phrases clauses		
plural nouns					
possessive nouns					
capital- ization					

_____WORKSHEET 8_____

COMMENT AND REVIEW

PART A. Indicate whether the statement is true or false by putting a T or an F in the answer space.

1. The first step in analyzing a sentence is to find the noun(s).   **1.** * _____

2. The first word in every sentence is the subject.   **2.** * _____

3. In sentences that begin with "There are" or "Here is," the subject usually follows the verb.   **3.** * _____

4. A verb always expresses action.   **4.** _____

5. Every sentence must contain a noun and a verb.   **5.** _____

6. All adverbs that modify adjectives end in *ly*.   **6.** _____

7. The simple subject of this sentence is a single word: Some of the best athletes in town belong to Northwestern Fitness Club.   **7.** _____

8. The simple predicate of this sentence is the word *conflict*: Hendricks' opinions often conflict with those of her subordinates.   **8.** _____

9. The final letter of a root word generally is not doubled before adding the suffix *ment*.   **9.** _____

10. Mnemonic devices often help people to learn correct spelling.   **10.** _____

11. The first word in a sentence cannot be a conjunction.   **11.** _____

12. The first word in a sentence cannot be a preposition.   **12.** _____

13. Interjections are generally considered inappropriate for business writing.   **13.** _____

14. There are three prepositional phrases in this sentence: I will send the user manual to you without delay if you return your payment promptly.   **14.** _____

15. All possessive nouns require the addition of *'s*.   **15.** _____

16. Prepositions sometimes take objects; verbs always take objects.   **16.** _____

17. There are three pronouns in this sentence: Williams is still reserving the date that he set with his management team.   **17.** _____

18. All plural nouns end with the letters *s* or *es*.   **18.** _____

19. Adjectives can follow the nouns they modify.   **19.** _____

20. Words may, without changing their spelling, work as several parts of speech.   **20.** _____

21. There is a direct object in this sentence: Julliard drove to the conference instead of flying.

21. _____

22. The word *copy* acts as an object of a preposition in this sentence: I handed a copy of the novel to the customer.

22. _____

23. We can master spelling if we simply memorize all the rules.

23. _____

24. There is a conjunction in this sentence: If you complete these forms, we will process your application.

24. _____

PART B. In the space provided, write the *letter* that indicates the correct answer. Each question pertains to this sentence:

> The seminar leader quickly gave us several practical tips about meetings involving legal disputes.

1. The simple subject of the preceding sentence is
(A) seminar   (B) leader   (C) us   (D) tips

1. *_____

2. The simple predicate is
(A) gave   (B) several   (C) tips   (D) meetings

2. _____

3. The direct object of the verb is
(A) gave   (B) us   (C) tips   (D) disputes

3. _____

4. The indirect object of the verb is
(A) gave   (B) us   (C) tips   (D) meetings

4. _____

5. In this sentence the word *about* is a(an)
(A) noun   (B) verb   (C) adverb   (D) preposition

5. *_____

6. The word *gave* is modified by the word
(A) quickly   (B) leader   (C) seminar   (D) us

6. _____

7. *The seminar leader* is the
(A) simple subject   (C) complete subject
(B) simple predicate   (D) complete predicate

7. _____

8. *quickly gave us several practical tips about meetings involving legal disputes* is the
(A) modifying phrase   (C) complete subject
(C) complement clause   (D) complete predicate

8. _____

PART C. Write only the *letter* that indicates the correct choice.

1. Place both reports on the (A) *boss's,* (B) *bosses,* (C) *bosse's* desk before closing.

1. _____

2. We are considering installing a separate (A) *mens',* (B) *men's,* (C) *mens* locker room.

2. *_____

3. What is your seniority with (A) *this firm,* (B) *This Firm,* (C) *this Firm?*

3. _____

4. She believes that her task force members will be honored for their (A) *efforts',* (B) *effort's,* (C) *efforts.*

4. *_____

5. No one could have foreseen the (A) *Thompsons,* (B) *Thompson's,* (C) *Thompsons'* error.

5. _____

6. The corporate retreat is scheduled the weekend before (A) *memorial day,* (B) *Memorial day,* (C) *Memorial Day.*

6. *_____

7. Did you contact either of the (A) *Rabinowitzes,* (B) *Rabinowitz's,* (C) *Rabinowitzes'* about their travel plans? (the plans of Ira and Doris Rabinowitz)

7. * _____

8. The most volatile stock was (A) *Price,* (B) *Prices,* (C) *Price's* and Waterhouse's predicted favorite.

8. _____

9. Perry has several (A) *crisis,* (B) *crises,* (C) *crisises* every week.

9. _____

10. Corporate headhunters have been watching (A) *Gallaghers,* (B) *Gallaghers',* (C) *Gallagher's* career for the past five years.

10. _____

11. Flight (A) *ETAs,* (B) *ETA's,* (C) *ETAs'* vary according to weather conditions.

11. _____

12. The (A) *supreme court,* (B) *Supreme court,* (C) *Supreme Court* will hear his final appeal.

12. _____

13. Although (A) *Cook County,* (B) *Cook county,* (C) *cook county* has high traffic volume, the highway funding has been designated for another area.

13. _____

14. Mrs. Jones, Hubert's widow, controls all of (A) *Jones's,* (B) *Joneses,* (C) *Jonese's* estate.

14. _____

15. Our troubleshooter will need to make (A) *diagnosis,* (B) *diagnoses,* (C) *diagnosises* on all three of our linked systems.

15. _____

16. The budget committee used Patrick's (A) *agencies,* (B) *agencys,* (C) *agency's* report to justify these layoffs.

16. _____

17. This magazine has had four (A) *editor in chiefs,* (B) *editor in chieves,* (C) *editors in chief* since its start in 1990.

17. _____

18. When the (A) *DiCaprio's,* (B) *DiCaprioes,* (C) *DiCaprios* expand, we will expand.

18. _____

19. Two of Jeanette's (A) *sons-in-law,* (B) *son's-in-law,* (C) *son-in-laws* work in the family business.

19. _____

20. When we voted, the number of (A) *yes's,* (B) *yeses,* (C) *yeses'* was astonishing.

20. _____

PART D. In the answer space provided, write the *letter* identifying the sentence that would be most acceptable in a business communication. Pay particular attention to the words in italics. If you are working collaboratively, make your selection and then argue for your choice using chapter ideas.

1. (A) We wanted *Commissioner Hansby* to see our acknowledgments on *Page 5.*
   (B) We wanted *commissioner Hansby* to see our acknowledgments on *Page 5.*
   (C) We wanted *Commissioner Hansby* to see our acknowledgments on *page 5.*

1. _____

2. (A) Prerequisite courses for the Hannover job are *german and international business.*
   (B) Prerequisite courses for the Hannover job are *German and international business.*
   (C) Prerequisite courses for the Hannover job are *German and International Business.*

2. _____

3. (A) The book *The Ten Ways To Create Success* will be released in July.
   (B) The book *the Ten Ways to Create Success* will be released in July.
   (C) The book *The Ten Ways to Create Success* will be released in July.

   3. _____

4. (A) *Peter Dix's* clients often feel shortchanged.
   (B) *Peter Dixes* clients often feel shortchanged.
   (C) *Peter Dixes'* clients often feel shortchanged.

   4. _____

5. (A) *The Harveyes* have two restaurants, one across *the Bay Bridge* from the other.
   (B) *The Harvey's* have two restaurants, one across *The Bay Bridge* from the other.
   (C) *The Harveys* have two restaurants, one across *the Bay Bridge* from the other.

   5. _____

6. (A) I didn't understand the *auditors* when they spoke about value and depreciation.
   (B) I didn't understand the *auditor's* when they spoke about value and depreciation.
   (C) I didn't understand the *auditors'* when they spoke about value and depreciation.

   6. _____

7. (A) The *New England Tax Base* is not growing fast enough to support our move.
   (B) The *New England tax base* is not growing fast enough to support our move.
   (C) The *new england tax base* is not growing fast enough to support our move.

   7. *_____

8. (A) *Jerry's coffee houses* profitability is an enigma to Progress Company, its owner.
   (B) *Jerry's Coffee House's* profitability is an enigma to Progress Company, its owner.
   (C) *Jerry's Coffee Houses'* profitability is an enigma to Progress Company, its owner.

   8. _____

9. (A) Next year on *Martin Luther King Day* we will announce our *endowment* plans.
   (B) Next year on *Martin Luther King day* we will announce our *endowment* plans.
   (C) Next year on *Martin Luther King Day* we will announce our *Endowment* plans.

   9. _____

10. (A) Jeffrey is an *alumni* of Harvard and Alice is an *alumni* of Yale.
    (B) Jeffrey is an *alumnae* of Harvard and Alice is an *alumnus* of Yale.
    (C) Jeffrey is an *alumnus* of Harvard and Alice is an *alumna* of Yale.

    10. *_____

Choose the one true statement in each group.

11. (A) Some abridged dictionaries do not list the word *workers.*
    (B) Some abridged dictionaries do not list the word *gentlemen.*
    (C) The best abridged dictionaries list every word in our language.

    11. _____

12. (A) In your dictionary the entry for *commerce* is most likely to have a dot between the two syllables.
    (B) In your dictionary the entry for *commerce* is most likely to have a hyphen between syllables.
    (C) In your dictionary the entry for *commerce* is most likely to have a dash between syllables.

    12. _____

13. (A) Dictionaries do not generally list prefixes.
    (B) Many words in our language have more than one spelling.
    (C) Definitions for a given word, such as *college,* are identical in all
        good dictionaries.   13. _____

14. (A) An entry word in a dictionary is usually followed by the word's
        phonetic spelling.
    (B) Prepositions are seldom included in abridged dictionaries.
    (C) An etymology is a part of every dictionary entry.   14. _____

PART E.   Find and underscore ten errors in this cover letter for a resume.

8621 e. 62nd St.

Pitsburg, PA 71903

February 12, 1999

Mr. Nelson J. Catzberg

Director of Personnal

Command Company

483 Bridge Road

Cincinatti, Ohio

Dear Mr. Catzberg,

I am enclosing herewith my resume for your consideration. I hope you recieve it before

your hiring decisions must be completed. Because I very much want to be one of your

candidates. Once you have reviewed my qualifications, you will see that noone is more

suited to the position than I am. I will be awaiting your esteamed reply.

Your obedient servant,

Dennis Treattle

FOR CLASS DISCUSSION

(if time permits)

Two professional people were discussing the value of apostrophes. One of them admitted that he never uses apostrophes because he has no idea where they belong. "Besides," he added, "I'm sure that anyone who reads my reports won't even notice that the apostrophes are missing."

Is he likely to be right or wrong? Why? How important is the correct use of apostrophes to a professional man or woman?

THE IMPACT OF LANGUAGE

IDIOMS

English must be extremely confusing to anyone attempting to learn it as a second language. Perhaps most confusing of all is the type of word combination that suggests a meaning considerably different from the literal meaning of the words involved. Such combinations, known as *idioms,* occasionally pose problems for grammarians who attempt to analyze them in conventional ways.

Consider the usual meanings of the words *give* and *up;* then try to justify their usage in this sentence: *He will never give up.* Here are several other common idioms with which you are undoubtedly familiar:

1. How do you do? (a greeting)
2. I'll be tied up on Friday morning.
3. We want a meeting of the minds.
4. Do you feel like a cup of tea?
5. He's on another line right now.

Some years ago an American traveling in China agreed to address a group of Chinese businessmen, one of whom spoke English and volunteered to act as interpreter. When the American began, "I am tickled to death to be here," the interpreter looked thoroughly nonplused. After a long pause he said slowly in Chinese, "This poor fellow scratches himself until he dies, only to be with you."

—————————————— FOR CLASS DISCUSSION ——————————————

Can you think of other common expressions that would be considered idioms?

---

wWWw ══════════ Watching the Web ══════════

| Back | Forward | Home | Reload | Images | Open |

CD-ROM Encyclopedia of Cooking
This is the last cookbook you'll ever need. The reason you'll love it is because, on one CD, we have included over 7,000 recipes, many with full-color photographs, for your family's enjoyment! You'll be glad you ordered it. You have our guarantee.

| order now | | no thanks |

CHAPTER

9

Personal Pronouns

■ POINT TO PONDER

A surprisingly large number of common grammatical errors involve pronouns.

Of the eight parts of speech, pronouns may be the most difficult to control, primarily because they assume so many forms. Two of the most common are *I* and *me,* which obviously refer to the same person. The rules of grammar, however, do not allow us to use those two words interchangeably. The rules, in fact, restrict the use of every personal pronoun to particular functions, each of which will be covered in this chapter.

A **pronoun,** you will recall, is a *noun substitute;* therefore, it may be used as a subject, an object, or a complement. In its possessive form it is generally employed as a modifier. A word, phrase, or clause that a pronoun replaces is known as its **antecedent.** An antecedent is most likely to be a noun. In *Harry felt that he was right, Harry* is the antecedent of the pronoun *he.* In *Rita left her pen on the table,* the noun *Rita* serves as antecedent for the pronoun *her.* The clause *Mr. Rice is in Akron* would be considered the antecedent of *it* in the sentence *Mr. Rice is in Akron, but his secretary doesn't know it.* A clause or a phrase should never be used as an antecedent for a pronoun unless the reference is perfectly clear.

Pronouns differ from nouns in that they change form in order to perform as subjects, objects, or complements, and they also change form according to person, number, and gender.

Personal Pronouns

Personal pronouns stand for persons or things. The chart that follows shows the **declension** of personal pronouns, that is, the changes that are made in such pronouns in order to express correctly their relations of case, number, person, and gender. A pronoun that denotes the speaker(s) is in the **first person,** while one that denotes the person(s) spoken to is in the **second person.** When we talk *about* people and things, we use pronouns in the **third person.** Pronouns of this type may refer to males (masculine gender), females (feminine gender), or neither one (neuter gender). A pronoun is singular in number if it refers to only one person or thing; otherwise, it is plural in number. If you have not already mastered the use of personal pronouns, you can improve your ability to communicate by studying the following chart and memorizing the case forms.

	Nominative Case		Possessive Case		Objective Case	
	Singular	*Plural*	*Singular*	*Plural*	*Singular*	*Plural*
First person	I	we	my mine	our ours	me	us
Second person	you	you	your yours	your yours	you	you
Third person						
Masculine gender	he	they	his	their theirs	him	them
Feminine gender	she	they	her hers	their theirs	her	them
Neuter gender	it	they	its	their theirs	it	them

Uses of Case Forms

Case indicates the relation of a pronoun to other words in a sentence. Like nouns, pronouns are used in the *nominative, objective,* and *possessive* cases, but unlike nouns, pronouns have different forms to indicate the different cases. When a pronoun functions as the subject of a verb or as a subject complement, the nominative-case form should be used; when it functions as the object of a verb or a preposition, the objective-case form should be used. It is especially important that a writer or speaker be able to recognize these case forms:

> NOMINATIVE: I, we, he, she, they
> OBJECTIVE: me, us, him, her, them

Because most people never take the time to understand the use of personal pronouns, they too often find themselves involved in time-consuming guessing games: *I* or *me? He* or *him? She* or *her?* Anyone who wants to eliminate such guesswork will become familiar with the following rules. Chapter 4 (p. 41) may be helpful as you think through standard sentence patterns.

1. USE THE NOMINATIVE-CASE FORM
   a. when the pronoun is the subject of a verb. (sentence pattern No. 1)

   We should have a cellular telephone.

   The contractor and *he* will look over the plans.

   Grace told me that *she* and Susan had read the printouts.

   We surveyors were not in complete agreement. (A pronoun and a noun are used in apposition as the subject of the verb.)

   b. when *than* or *as* precedes the pronoun and a following verb is implied.

   No employee could be more conscientious than *he.* (Meaning *he is*)

   Lazlo is about as tall as *I.* (Meaning *I am*)

c. when the pronoun is used as a subject complement, that is, after a linking verb. The most common linking verb, *to be,* has these variant forms: *am, is, are, was, were,* and all verb phrases that end in *be, been,* or *being.* (sentence pattern No. 4)

We found ourselves wishing that we were *they.*

It may be *she* who is causing the disturbance.

Is it *he* who first raised the question?

Ms. Davidson was thought to be *she.* (When it is preceded by a verb, the infinitive *to be* has no subject, and a pronoun that follows *to be* is expressed in the nominative case to agree with the subject of the clause. The subject of infinitives is covered in Chapter 17.)

d. when the pronoun functions as an appositive following a subject or a subject complement.

The two survivors, Albert and *I,* were questioned by the press. (The noun *Albert* and the pronoun *I* are identical with the subject, *survivors,* and need to be in the same case.)

The only dissenters were my fellow employees, *you* and *he.* (The pronouns *you* and *he* are identical with the subject complement, *employees,* and need to be in the same case.)

2. USE THE OBJECTIVE-CASE FORM
   a. when the pronoun is the direct object of a verb. (sentence pattern No. 2)

Several of our members congratulated *her.*

A committee of five selected *us.*

He questioned Mr. Hoffman and *me* about the copyright. (As you attempt to choose the correct pronoun, disregard any other direct object. Read only these words: *He questioned me about the copyright.*)

b. when the pronoun is the indirect object of a verb. (sentence pattern No. 3)

We gave *him* an unusually large order. (Like all indirect objects, this one can be expanded into a prepositional phrase: *We gave an unusually large order* TO HIM.)

c. when a pronoun is the object of a preposition.

Mr. Whelan gave copies to Morgan and *me.*

Ms. Gage talked with *him* about the mortgage.

Most of the work was done by *us* carpenters. (The word *carpenters* is in apposition with *us.*)

d. when a pronoun follows an infinitive that has a subject.

I am surprised that you thought him to be *me.* (A noun or a pronoun that precedes the infinitive *to be* is considered its subject. That subject and any pronoun that follows the infinitive must both be in the objective case.)

e. when the pronoun functions as an appositive following a direct object, an indirect object, or an object of a preposition.

He resented his benefactors, Walter and *me.* (The direct object is *benefactors;* the appositives are *Walter* and *me.*)

I spoke with the authors, Mark Chapman and *her.* (*Authors* serves as the object of a preposition; therefore, the appositives that follow it must be in the objective case.)

3. USE THE POSSESSIVE-CASE FORM to show possession, authorship, brand, kind, origin, or any similar relation. Possessive forms of personal pronouns such as *hers, its, yours, ours,* and *theirs* are always written without apostrophes.

The final decision will be *yours.*

The portfolio with the blue cover is *mine.*

The Merton Company may lose *its* best customer. (There is a tendency to write the possessive form of *it* with an apostrophe. Bear in mind that *it's* is always a contraction of *it is.*)

Mr. Stein is unaware of *their* new policy. (Pronouns used to modify nouns are sometimes referred to as **pronominal adjectives.**)

Compound Personal Pronouns

A few of the personal pronouns are made compound by the addition of *self* (singular) or *selves* (plural) to the simple form.

Person	Singular	Plural
First	myself	ourselves
Second	yourself	yourselves
Third	himself, herself, itself	themselves

These **compound personal pronouns,** which have the properties of person, number, and sometimes gender, serve two main purposes:

1. They *intensify,* or *add emphasis.* In this function they are often used in apposition with a noun or a pronoun.

I will install the equipment *myself.*

The distributor *himself* commented upon a possible shortage.

2. They *reflect* the action of the verb back upon the subject.

She worried *herself* into a state of frenzy.

He knew at the time that he was endangering *himself.*

Do not use a compound personal pronoun if the shorter (simple) form of the pronoun could be used without awkwardness.

DON'T USE: Rogers expected help from Busby and *myself.*
USE: Rogers expected help from Busby and *me.*
DON'T USE: Clayton and *myself* will deliver the furniture.
USE: Clayton and *I* will deliver the furniture.

Executives' Choice

Many of the chapters in this text include a section headed "Executives' Choice." Here you will find valuable information concerning the precise meanings of words often used in business writing. The executive of today must use words skillfully. Employees who lack the ability to communicate effectively are not likely to be considered for positions in management. You can improve your chances for success on the job by recognizing the word distinctions and language refinements discussed in these sections. "Executives' Choice" will be concerned with those words that require special attention. Here are just a few:

A Half A   The use of two articles in this expression is excessive. Use *a half* or *half a.*

> The advertisement will cover *a half* (OR *half a*) page.

And Etc.   Because *etc.* means "and other things," it is illogical to use *and etc.* Avoid the use of *etc.* in business writing that has not been enclosed in parentheses. Never use *etc.* after a series introduced with *such as* or *for example.*

> We have ordered the items (shirts, ties, hosiery, *etc.*).
> We have ordered shirts, ties, hosiery, *and so forth* (not *etc.*).
> We are short of several items; for example, shirts, ties, and hosiery.

Angry   Do not use *mad,* which means "mentally ill, deranged," in place of *angry,* which means "indignant" or "wrathful."

> Ms. Leeds became *angry* when she heard the news.
> If he is really *mad,* he should be confined.

Assistance   This word refers to "the act of assisting; aid; help." *Assistants* is the plural form of *assistant,* "one who assists, an aide."

> To complete the project, he may need financial *assistance.*
> Two *assistants* will do most of the research.

Bank On   This expression is too informal for use in business writing. Substitute *depend on.*

> You can *depend* (not *bank*) on us for an early delivery.

Being That/As   Both *being that* and *being as* are nonstandard and should be avoided. Use *because.*

> *Because* (not *Being that*) the position has been filled, we will discontinue the advertisement.

Bet   It is unbusinesslike to use this term unless an actual wager is involved. Do not use *bet* if *suppose* or *believe* would be appropriate.

> He *bet* on the winning team.
> I *believe* (not *bet*) that you will enjoy the new word-processing system.

Corporation   This word refers to a common type of business organization. *Cooperation* refers to "the act of cooperating; working together toward a common end or purpose."

> Pembroke works for a major *corporation* in Cincinnati.
> To succeed, you will need the *cooperation* of everyone involved.

Forth   This adverb means "forward in time, place, or order; onward; out into view." The noun *fourth* is the ordinal number that follows *third.* It also means "one of four equal parts."

> We will use the new equipment from this day *forth.*
> This is the *fourth* day of our sales campaign.
> About a *fourth* of the women expressed their views.

THE IMPACT OF LANGUAGE

GRAMMAR AND THE VERY YOUNG

An English professor and his young daughter engaged in a bit of dialogue that suggests how frustrating grammar can be. The five-year-old girl was accompanied by a young friend when she ran up to her father and announced, "Daddy, me and Kathy want some ice cream." The father offered this annoying response: "You should have said *Kathy and I want some ice cream.*" The little girl waited several minutes while her father read his newspaper. Finally, in a genuine effort to express herself correctly, she asked, "Daddy, are you going to buy some ice cream for Kathy and I?" The English professor put his newspaper aside and said, "Honey, you should have used *Kathy and me.*" At that point the youngster's eyes filled with tears of frustration as she cried, "A few minutes ago you told me to use *Kathy and I.*"

———————————————— FOR CLASS DISCUSSION ————————————————

At what age should a child be expected to understand the functions of nominative- and objective-case pronouns?

---

wWWw ═══════════════ **Watching the Web** ═══════════════

Back	Forward	Home	Reload	Images	Open

Visit the website voted "most interesting" by TAO: Travel Agents Online. See our special offers for travel in and out of Europe for this summer. Order air, hotel, car, or rail coupons online.

If you need assistants in accessing the hyperlinks on this site, click here: | help |

Name Alisha H...

Name Alisha Hicks   **Date** 2-15-02

— WORKSHEET 9 —

PERSONAL PRONOUNS

Left page (Part D, partially cut off):

Name Alisha H...

PART D. Select the correct pr...
collaborating, teach y...
ideas and examples.

Example: The agent asked Thom...
present our problem.

1. When we arrive at the conver...
will set up our display booth.

2. When the sales team arrives...
should report to (he and I, him...

3. Habib will inform the team of...
by (me, myself, I).

4. Then they will greet clients w...
speak to Habib and (I, me).

5. This year Habib and Wilson h...
promotional logo key rings so...
remind (them, themselves) of...
convention.

6. Wilson designed the rings, an...
(he, him) has seen them yet.

7. Both Habib and (he, him) decl...
be the best promotional item...

8. If there is a prize for best mar...
believes the winner will be (he, ...
though he will not be attending...

9. Last year, neither Habib nor (h...
much about "walk-around" m...

10. However, after attending four...
understands what works to he...
remember (he, him) and his c...

11. The secret, according to Wilso...
sales team members an appea...
home with customers.

12. Apparently the key ring is col...
something that seems friendly...
touch, according to Habib and...

13. No one in our company knows...
tools as (he, him).

14. Given the huge numbers of at...
convention, I hope that Habib...
ordered at least a thousand ke...

15. I shouldn't worry; given Wilso...
can predict numbers and resul...

16. My job is to see that the displa...
a duty which Habib and (I, me, ...
easily.

PART A. In this exercise you are to (1) underscore each nominative or objective case personal pronoun and (2) indicate its function by writing the appropriate *letter* in the answer space.

A. subject   C. object of a preposition
B. object of verb   D. subject complement

Example: Proxies were not sent to Stroud and me. (Because *me* is objective, the answer must be either B or C.)   _____c_____

A 1. Sherrill and I will soon be finalizing the annual budget proposal.   1. * A. subject

C 2. Each manager must complete the on-line budget projection sheet and e-mail the form to either Sherrill or me by Wednesday at 5:00 P.M.   2. * B. obj. of verb

B 3. At that time, Sherrill will analyze all requests and add them into the total budget proposal.   3. * B. obj. of verb

C 4. After six working days the final proposal will be submitted to you.   4. C. obj. of prep

D 5. At that time the most weary two persons in the company will be we, the proposal writers.   5. D.S.C.

A 6. However, when the proposal draft is done, you will begin to participate in the work.   6. A. subject

C 7. All additions and corrections must come back to us in final form by the following Wednesday.   7. B. obj. of verb

A 8. If they have not arrived by that date, they will not be considered in this year's budget.   8. A. subject

B 9. The real fun will begin on the 15th, when each manager will attend a meeting to resolve discrepancies and make decisions about the items that concern him or her.   9. B.

D 10. Then the spectators will be Sherrill and I; the active particpants will be the managers.   10. A.

D 11. The beneficiaries of all of this work will be we, the full staff of Enterprise, Inc.   11. D.

C 12. Support your manager in this effort by bringing to her or him all relevant budget requests this week.   12. C.

A 13. Then assist in proofreading the line items that pertain to the work that you do.   13. D.

A 14. Lastly, cover for your manager during the day of the budget resolution meeting so that he or she is free to concentrate solely on these matters.   14. A.

15. In this way, our entir
our work forward, be
customers as well.

PART B. In the space p
word(s) in italic

Example: Mr. Baumholz
Mr. Baumholz

1. Sara Belize felt that *S*
watched.

2. All of the accountants

3. E-mail accounts will b
accounts.

4. The designees, accor
Manuel.

5. Senator Agee says th
examined the docum

6. Mr. Sanchez has aske
either Mrs. Tregallis o

7. We have kept the sec
Maureen are to be ho

8. Griffin Enterprises cla
Enterprises'.

9. Henley's exact words
my staff and *Henley.*"

10. Jackson agrees that I
than *Jackson.*

PART C. Find and under
brief memo.

To: Account executives
From: Sheila Hawkins, Su
Date: October 12, 2000
Subject: Upcoming repor

Being that Roger Corbin

next week, I wanted to re

1. Its important that mor

2. Reports need to be su

While we are out of town

not wait until we return. I

Marjorie DeKordhi should

always given your superv

for that to change. When

You will have earned our

ment. If you have questio

---

17. Habib's job is to keep encouraging the sales team, a duty which has fallen to either (he or I, him or me) for the past three years.

17. ___him or me___

18. I enjoy the contact with customers more than (he, him), and he enjoys contact with the sales team members more than (I, me).

18. ___he, I___

19. Habib, Wilson, and (I, me, myself) may become our own department next year.

19. ___I___

20. We will no longer be called sales team members but instead be known as Convention Marketing, a designation that appeals to Habib, Wilson, and (I, me) very much.

20. ___me___

PART E. Write the correct word or expression in the answer space.

1. Our attorney became (angry, mad) when the witness refused to answer.

1. * _____

2. (Because, Being as) we do not have a quorum, no vote will be taken today.

2. _____

3. Pearl, with the (assistants, assistance) of a computer, was able to finish by 3 P.M.

3. _____

4. I (bet, suppose) that Ferguson will refuse to accept our findings.

4. _____

5. To reach our goal, we will need the (cooperation, corporation) of everyone in this office.

5. _____

6. More than a (forth, fourth) of the grain in the large silo has spoiled.

6. _____

7. The directors will (bank, depend) on your being there.

7. _____

8. We wasted more than a (half, half a) day in getting organized.

8. _____

9. He was too polite to comment upon the misspelled word, uneven margins, poor punctuation (and etc., and so forth).

9. _____

10. He will probably buy used equipment (because, being that) the new models are very expensive.

10. _____

OPTIONAL EXERCISES

OPTION 1 In the answer space write the word that would make the sentence correct.

1. The pronoun *we* is in the _____ person.
2. The pronoun *it* is in the _____ gender.
3. The pronoun *I* is in the _____ case.
4. The pronoun *us* is _____ in number.
5. The pronoun *him* is in the _____ case.
6. The pronoun *they* is in the _____ person.
7. The pronoun *you* is in the _____ person.
8. The pronoun *our* is in the _____ case.
9. The plural form of *him* or *her* is _____.
10. The word *it's* always means _____.

1. *_____
2. *_____
3. _____
4. _____
5. _____
6. _____
7. _____
8. _____
9. _____
10. _____

OPTION 2 Write sentences. In each one you are to make use of the word in parentheses. If you are collaborating, each person should complete the sentences individually, and then all should share their work.

1. (its)   *_____
   _____

2. (it's)   _____
   _____

3. (ourselves)   _____
   _____

4. (himself)   _____
   _____

5. (their)   _____
   _____

OPTION 3 Write at least one paragraph on the subject of "Job Hunting." Make certain that all sentences are complete and that your work contains at least one personal pronoun in each case (nominative, possessive, objective). Underscore each pronoun and indicate its case by printing N, P, or O above it.

_____

_____

Agreement of Antecedents and Pronouns

■ POINT TO PONDER

The person who fails to recognize antecedents is almost certain to misuse pronouns.

Rules regarding the agreement of antecedents and pronouns are not as precise today as they were several years ago. Pronouns that are generally considered plural tend to appear more and more frequently with singular antecedents. Conscientious business writers have good reason to be at least slightly confused. Has our language changed enough so that we may accept as correct sentences such as this: *Every employee will please submit their suggestions in writing?* Although some professional writers now employ such constructions, it would be wise for a business executive to use grammar that cannot be questioned. In this chapter you will be encouraged to employ a plural pronoun only when its antecedent is a plural form; for example, *All employees will please submit their suggestions in writing.* That kind of consistency will never be questioned by any employer or by a correspondent. Because the following rules reflect the thinking of careful writers, they should prove helpful to you in your use of pronouns.

1. A pronoun and its antecedent must agree in *number.*

    SINGULAR: Our local *druggist* would do a good deal more business if *he* remained open during the evening hours.
    PLURAL: The *merchants* are concerned about decreasing sales, but *they* do not know what steps should be taken.

    a. When two or more antecedents connected by *and* refer to different persons or things, the pronoun must be plural.

Mr. Odom and *Mr. Grazzo* decided that *they* would combine *their* resources.

The assistant *cashier* and the chief *appraiser* have just submitted *their* resignations. (The word *the* is repeated to show clearly that two persons are involved.)

b. When two or more singular antecedents connected by *and* refer to only *one* person or thing, the pronoun must be *singular.* You will note that the word *my* has been used only once in the following sentence.

My confidante and business associate is always here when I need *her.* (If two people were being discussed, *my* would be repeated after *and.*)

The president and district superintendent budgets *his* time carefully. (If the subject referred to two people, the word *the* would be repeated before *district.*)

If a subject is obviously plural, the modifier (*my, the,* etc.) need not be repeated. Note this wording: My mother and dad own their own business.

c. Antecedents preceded by *each, every,* or *many a* are always singular. A singular pronoun should be used even when two such antecedents are joined by *and.*

Every man at the meeting hoped that *he* would be chosen.

Every woman and girl present expressed *her* opinion.

Every father and every son must pay *his* own expenses.

Many a young man has placed *his* trust in this product.

d. Singular antecedents connected by *or* or *nor* require singular pronouns.

Ms. Barbetti or Ms. Shimoto must put *her* signature on this bill of lading.

Neither Ron nor Cleve could find *his* copy of the minutes.

e. If the antecedents consist of a singular noun and a plural noun connected by *or* or *nor,* the singular noun should be written first. The pronoun should be plural to agree with the second (nearer) antecedent.

Neither Mr. Foster nor his *colleagues* would admit that *they* had overheard the conversation.

The president or his *advisors* should devote part of *their* time to the proposed merger.

f. A parenthetical expression that appears between an antecedent and a pronoun does not influence the form of the pronoun that should be employed. Do not be misled by expressions beginning with *rather than, as well as, in addition to, together with,* or similar words. Such expressions are generally set off with commas. (See page 306 for a discussion of parenthetical elements.)

The accountant, rather than any of the other officers, will be asked for *her* opinion of this venture. (The antecedent of *her* is *accountant,* the simple subject.)

Theresa Folsom and Mary Folsom, as well as their mother, promised to purchase *their* dresses from our shop.

Mr. Norman Brett, in addition to several other members of the organization, has offered *his* unqualified support.

g. If the antecedent is a collective noun that refers to a group as a single unit, a singular pronoun should be used. A noun is collective if, in its singular form, it names a group of people or objects; for example, *jury, audience, faculty, board, committee, number, flock, family.* Company names are generally considered to be collective nouns.

The audience expressed *its* pleasure with resounding applause.

The jury has reached *its* decision.

Stein & Grayson, Inc., has sold *its* Chicago properties.

h. If the antecedent is a collective noun that refers to individuals who are acting separately or independently of one another, a plural pronoun should be used.

The audience are going *their* separate ways.

The crew continued to argue among *themselves.*

Even though such sentences are grammatically acceptable, many people consider them to be awkward. In such situations the careful business writer is likely to eliminate any possibility of awkwardness by using a subject that is obviously plural, as in these sentences:

Members of the audience are going their separate ways.

Crew members continued to argue among themselves. (The subject *members* is obviously plural.)

You will have little difficulty in using the collective noun *number* as a subject if you remember that *the number* is always singular and *a number* is always plural.

The number of men in attendance was as small as *it* could be.

A number of the workers have changed *their* minds.

2. A pronoun, as a rule, should refer clearly to a *definite* person, place, or thing.

DON'T USE: The purchasing agent told Quigley that he does not understand our problem. (*Who* does not understand our problem?)

USE: In his conversation with Quigley, the purchasing agent admitted that he does not understand our problem.

DON'T USE: Tracy and Polson met with reporters, but he refused to discuss the appointment.

USE: When he and Polson met with reporters, Tracy refused to discuss the appointment.

DON'T USE: To appreciate the wonders of that city, you really have to live there.

USE: To appreciate the wonders of that city, a person really has to live there.

3. A pronoun should agree with its antecedent in gender.

Roger Weiskof plans to open *his* own office in New Orleans. (Pronoun *his* is in the masculine gender.)

Louise Handley will be given considerable authority if *she* accepts the new position. (Pronoun *she* is in the feminine gender.)

Our new product has many fine features, but *it* has not been well accepted by the public. (Pronoun *it* is in the neuter gender.)

a. Traditional grammar books have taught that when a singular antecedent refers to individuals of both sexes, a masculine pronoun should be employed.

A person must be aware of *his* strengths and *his* deficiencies.

Each citizen is asked to assume *his* share of the tax burden.

If anyone has additional questions, *he* may meet with me in my office.

In recent years, however, the use of masculine pronouns in such sentences has been challenged as inaccurate and offensive to women. The foregoing sentences could easily be recast to make them acceptable to all readers. Here are some possibilities:

People must be aware of their strengths and their deficiencies.

All citizens are asked to share the tax burden.

Anyone with additional questions may meet with me in my office.

b. A writer who wants to be very precise may use both masculine and feminine pronouns.

Every employee will be expected to punch *his* or *her* time card.

Each person must present *his* or *her* request in writing.

c. If two singular antecedents of different genders are used, two pronouns of different genders must be used.

No college man or college woman can afford to gamble with *his* or *her* future by regarding English lightly.

Although the foregoing sentence is grammatically acceptable, it is somewhat awkward and, therefore, should be avoided. A smoother wording would be *College students cannot afford to gamble with their futures by regarding English lightly.* Remember that grammatical correctness is only one test of good writing or speaking. We should attempt to express every thought just as effectively as the English language permits.

About Company Names

Because a company is made up of individuals, a writer might well have those individuals in mind when using the company's name. In business writing we occasionally find sentences like this one:

I wrote to the Kingston Company and told *them* to expect an early delivery. (A collective noun, *Kingston Company,* is used here with a plural pronoun, *them.*)

Such sentences are acceptable provided there is no awkwardness. The foregoing sentence would sound strange if we had employed the singular pronoun *it* instead of *them.* Remember that company names are *usually* considered singular. None of those that you find on worksheets in this text are to be thought of as plural. Use singular verbs and pronouns, therefore, when you encounter subjects of this type.

Here are the rules you've just learned about pronoun antecedent agreement, this time in a chart.

Rule 1: pronouns must agree with their antecedents in number	Rule 2: pronouns should refer to definite persons, places or things	Rule 3: pronouns must agree with their antecedents in gender
singular subject: **singular pronoun** plural subject: **plural pronoun**	do not make the reader ask "who?"	masculine subject: **masculine pronoun**
two antecedents referring to two persons/things connected by *and:* **plural pronoun**	rename an antecedent rather than leaving a pronoun with an unclear referent	feminine subject: **feminine pronoun**
two antecedents referring to the same person/thing connected by *and:* **singular**	rework sentence order to avoid awkwardness	neuter subject: **neuter pronoun**
antecedents preceded by *each, every, many a:* **singular**	avoid using the informal and general "you"	singular antecedents: **appropriate masculine or feminine pronoun**
singular antecedents connected by *or* or *nor:* **singular**	avoid referring to experts of society in general as "they"	the gender of the singular antecedent is unclear: **singular pronouns of both genders (*he or she, his or her*)**
if antecedents include both singular and plural nouns: **write singular one first and choose plural pronoun to match nearer (the latter) antecedent**		singular antecedents of different genders: **pronouns of both genders**
ignore parenthetical elements: **match pronoun to true antecedent**		
collective noun antecedents acting together: **singular**		
collective noun antecedents acting separately: **plural**		

Executives' Choice

Adapt   *Adapt* means "to change so as to make suitable." Don't confuse this word with *adopt,* which means "to take without change," or *adept,* which means "skillful."

> Perhaps we can *adapt* these blueprints to our own use.
> We intend to *adopt* a new hiring policy.
> He is *adept* at dictating.

Allowed   The most common meaning of this word is *"permitted."* It is pronounced the same as *aloud,* which means "with the voice; orally," or "in a loud tone."

> We were not *allowed* in the conference room.
> Read the letter *aloud* so that we can all enjoy it.

Altogether   This means "entirely, completely." The expression *all together* (two words) means "collectively, in a group."

> The new regulation seems *altogether* unnecessary.
>
> We were *all together* when the president gave the order.

Amount   The word *amount* refers to things in bulk or mass. *Number* should be used to refer to countable items or people.

> She offered the editor a large *amount* of money.
>
> The *amount* of work accomplished was negligible.
>
> A large *number* (not *amount*) of employees signed the petition. (*Number* often refers to a plural noun, such as *employees*.)

Everyday   This adjective means "commonplace; ordinary; suitable for routine occasions." The expression *every day*, of course, refers to all days for a period of time.

> Roscoe wore his *everyday* suit to the formal ceremony.
>
> I work with these people *every day* of the week.

TOO MANY WORDS

If you have ever taken a writing course, you are likely to be familiar with the word *redundant,* which means "using more words than are needed; unnecessary to the meaning." Careful writers and speakers, of course, avoid the use of redundancies. Each of the following sentences contains one or more words that should be eliminated. Can you find them?

1. The director generally opposes any new innovation.
2. The machine that we are offering for sale is gray in color.
3. The consensus of opinion is that Tomsic will resign in June.
4. When the verdict had been announced, the reporters quickly hurried from the courtroom.
5. The weather in Seattle, according to Zelda, is more worse than the weather here.

REDUNDANCIES: new, in color, of opinion, quickly, more

A WORD TIP FROM THE REAL WORLD

When most of today's corporate executives, upper level managers, and small business owners were very young, their teachers taught them that the "default" gender for a singular pronoun is masculine. Thus, when one began a sentence in this way: "*Everyone* needs to bring," one ended it in this way: "*his* materials to class," even if there were more girls in the class than boys.

John, a radio station manager in Nebraska, claims that such usage is obsolete. "We now realize that defaulting to masculine words created a reality for people that simply wasn't fair, or even true! Gender-fair language, or inclusive language, is better for everyone. I insist that it be used at my station, not only in written work but also on the air. If an entire generation like mine can get used to that change, we have every reason to expect the next generation to speak and write that way naturally."

_____ **WORKSHEET 10** _____

AGREEMENT OF ANTECEDENTS AND PRONOUNS

PART A. Assume that each of these word groups is the complete subject of a sentence. By checking the appropriate column, indicate whether you would use a singular pronoun or a plural pronoun to refer to such a subject.

		Singular	Plural
1.	Every signatory of this contract	X	
2.	Many an assistant manager	X	⬤
3.	Each programmer and systems analyst	X	
4.	Our C.E.O. and her administrative assistant		X
5.	Any accountant or broker	X	
6.	Our team leader, as well as our consultant,	X	
7.	My partner and friend	X	
8.	The developmental editor and the outside publisher		X
9.	No employee or relative	X	
10.	The shop foreman and the plant engineer		X ⬤
11.	A member of three advisory boards	X ⬤	⬤
12.	Neither the director nor her assistants	⬤	⬤ X
13.	Every designer and CAD instructor present	X	⬤
14.	Either Helena or the three drafting associates		X
15.	Not a single customer or client	X	

PART B. Write the antecedent of the pronoun in italics. If you are collaborating, make a good case for your selection to your teammates. When the group agrees on the best choice, move to the next item.

Example: Klinger will call you as soon as _he_ can.

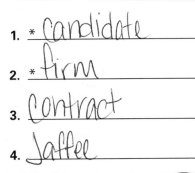
Klinger

1. The candidate has an abundance of enthusiasm, but _he_ lacks experience in this field.

   1. * _candidate_

2. The plan would benefit this firm and certain of _its_ subsidiaries.

   2. * _firm_

3. Her contract is perfectly clear, but _it_ contains too liberal a severance clause.

   3. _contract_

4. Jaffee may lose the rental property if _he_ cannot make the balloon payment.

   4. _Jaffee_

5. Department managers have cited *their* need for more computer programmers.

6. Our old 386 DX does not have an internal fax modem, but *it* does have an HR monitor.

7. The environmental specialist will have *her* own office in this building.

8. Chet's shyness should have been a handicap; instead, *it* helped to disarm his clients.

9. Kincaid offered $2.1 million for the client base, but evidently *that* wasn't enough.

10. Petrie's partners moved *their* staffs to the Griggs building.

11. Desmond smiled as *she* read the message on the display screen.

12. Neither the marketing director nor the trainees lost *their* patience.

13. Du Bois, as well as the security officers, expressed *his* willingness to help.

14. The booklets were sent from our store to *its* many credit account customers.

15. The loan processor, after she had met with Mr. Hirst, gave *her* unqualified approval.

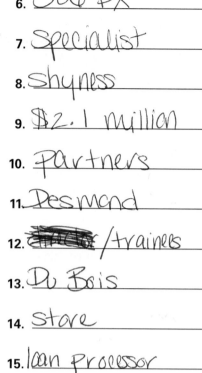

5. managers
6. 386 DX
7. Specialist
8. shyness
9. $2.1 million
10. Partners
11. Desmond
12. ~~director~~/trainees
13. Du Bois
14. store
15. loan processor

PART C. In the space provided, write the pronoun that would make the sentence correct.

1. A new idea is taking hold among many a successful business person, catching (his or her, their) imagination.

2. This new idea is the One Percent Club, begun by two brokers who wanted (his, their) wealth to make a difference in society.

3. They offer membership in the club to every client who saw (his or her, their) investments grow by more than 20% last year.

4. To join, anyone can promise to give 1% of (his or her, their) net worth to charity.

5. The member supplies no dollar figures for (his or her, their) donation.

6. No one says where (his or her, their) donations go; no clues are given as to income or net worth.

7. The member just gives (his or her, their) word that they will donate.

8. Can people agree to do this and then change (his or her, their) intentions?

9. Yes, anyone can change (his or her, their) mind the next day or the next year.

10. Whenever club members want to stop, (he or she is, they are) allowed to stop.

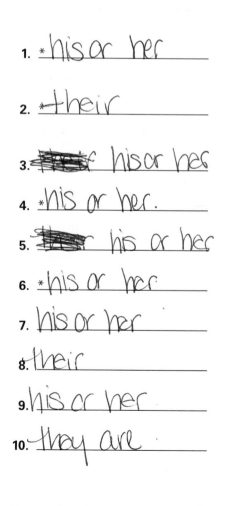

1. *his or her
2. *their
3. ~~their~~ his or her
4. *his or her.
5. ~~their~~ his or her
6. *his or her
7. his or her
8. their
9. his or her
10. they are

11. Since no one audits members' contributions, members are the only ones who know the amount of (his or her, their) giving.

12. If more people joined the One Percent Club, society could see an enormous increase in charitable giving, traceable to each member and (his or her, their) generosity.

13. All nonprofit companies would get (his or her, their) share of the increase.

14. Many a current member points out that (his or her, their) favorite social service organizations receive more money, as do the arts.

15. If those persons who already give generously want to do even more for the world, perhaps (he or she, they) will consider joining the One Percent Club.

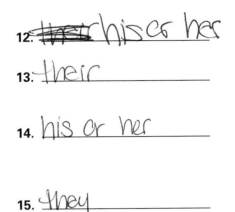

11. ~~his or her~~ their

12. ~~their~~ his or her

13. their

14. his or her

15. they

PART D. Find and underscore the pronoun and other word choice errors in this paragraph from a memo. Then discuss and together construct a response to the question that follows it.

No one in this company has the right to impose their opinions or language on anyone else. Humor in questionable taste is unwelcome, no matter what amount of people think its funny. We work with each other everyday, and its very important to agree on some standards for conduct altogether as a group. Every employee needs to watch their behavior if we are going to create an atmosphere in which everyone feels themself to be safe and welcome.

The memo is clearly addressing a serious issue in business. When you read a memo about something important and it contains many grammatical errors, what do you think? Draw two conclusions.

_____

_____

_____

_____

PART E. In each of these sentences at least one pronoun is employed vaguely. You are to rewrite each sentence so that the thought is clearly and precisely expressed. You may add or delete words.

Example: They say that you have to understand accounting to qualify for that kind of work.
I have been told that a person must understand accounting to qualify for that kind of work.

1. When you're going to Macy's personnel division, you have to walk through the store.

* _____

_____

2. Jeffers told Renquist that she couldn't solve the problem alone.

_____

_____

3. They say that there are no appreciable differences among PC clones.

_____

_____

4. To understand any systems approach, you must recognize your role in the system.

_____

_____

5. Neither Polini nor Bachrach were sure what she would say to her assistant.

_____

_____

6. At a job interview, be sure you have a clean copy of your resume.

_____

_____

PART F.   Write the word(s) that would make the sentence correct.

1. Every job ticket must show the (amount, number)
of hours estimated for completion.   **1.** _____

2. WonderSystems, Inc., is about to (adapt, adopt,
adept) its old building to new uses.   **2.** _____

3. According to the manager's guide, we are not
(allowed, aloud) to bring supplies home.   **3.** _____

4. Should we use the (everyday, every day)
letterhead or a promotional version?   **4.** _____

5. Our complex schedules make being (altogether,
all together) for meetings very difficult.   **5.** _____

FOR CLASS DISCUSSION

(if time permits)

Traditional grammar books taught that *he, his,* and *him* are common-gender pronouns in sentences like these:

Every taxpayer must file *his* return by April 15.
Someone parked *his* new Buick in my space.

The trend in modern business writing is to avoid the use of common-gender pronouns, which are basically masculine forms. How would you change the two sentences to make them more acceptable?

CHAPTER 11

Miscellaneous Pronouns at Work

■ POINT TO PONDER

If you use *he* and *him* or *she* and *her* correctly, you can master *who* and *whom*.

Grammarians ordinarily divide pronouns into six or more classes and provide an appropriate name for each. Most people who work daily with language, however, would probably experience difficulty in naming even two of these classes. Because the study of such terminology would have little practical value, this text will concentrate on how pronouns should be used rather than how they should be classified. Chapter 9 dealt with *personal pronouns,* which have the properties of person, case, number, and (sometimes) gender. This chapter will be concerned with all other pronouns that tend to challenge the communicator.

A Few Singular Pronouns

The English language has many words that may function as noun substitutes even though they do not possess the properties of personal pronouns. Some may be used only as pronouns; others are employed also as adjectives. The pronouns on the following list are **singular.** When used as subjects, they take singular verbs, and they often function as singular antecedents for other pronouns.

anybody	either	much	one
anyone	everybody	neither	somebody
anything	everyone	nobody	someone
each	everything	nothing	something

Observe that singular pronouns and verbs have been italicized in these sentences:

Each of these documents *is* to be microfilmed before *it is* destroyed.
Neither of the salesmen *has reached his* quota.
Everyone has been offered a choice of brands.
Anyone in this position *must be* careful about *his or her* appearance.
Either of Donna's essays *is* usable in *its* present form.

Write *some one, any one,* or *every one* as two words only when an *of*-phrase follows.

Any one of these floppy disks should prove satisfactory.
Every one of our engineers has a bachelor's degree.

A Few Plural Pronouns

The pronouns that follow are always plural. When used as subjects, they take plural verbs. Other pronouns that refer to them must also be plural.

both   few   many   several   others

Both of New Jersey's major networks *have changed their* program schedules for Tuesday.
Few of the newer motels *are located* that far from the freeway.
Several of the jobbers expressed *their* opinions concerning excessive discounts.

Pronouns That May Be Singular or Plural

The pronouns *all, any, more, most, none,* and *some* may be used either as singular or as plural subjects. The word to which the pronoun refers is the determining factor. If an *of*-phrase follows one of these pronouns, the object of that phrase will determine whether the pronoun should be considered singular or plural. *Most of the representatives* would function as a plural subject because the pronoun *most* (simple subject) refers to a plural noun *(representatives)*. Observe the pronoun and verbs in these sentences:

SINGULAR: *Most* of the money *is deposited* in a local bank.
PLURAL: *Most* of us *are hoping* that Flanders will be exonerated.
SINGULAR: *Some* of the surplus *is* to be used for expansion purposes.
PLURAL: *Some* of our clients *are* slow about paying for services rendered.
SINGULAR: *None* of the wheat *is* to be shipped until Friday.
PLURAL: *None* of the retailers on your list *are reordering* our products.
EXCEPTIONS: *None* of the applicants *is qualified.* (The pronoun *none* is singular whenever its meaning is clearly *not one.*) *Any* of the smaller lamps *is* satisfactory. (*Any* is singular whenever its meaning is clearly *any one.*)

Although some authorities consider the pronoun *none* to be singular in all constructions, a clear majority prefer to use it with a plural verb if *no persons* or *not any of a group of persons or things* could be substituted. The intent of the writer or speaker may be a determining factor. The editors of *The American Heritage Dictionary* have included interesting usage notes at their entries for both *none* and *any.*

The Case of Who Versus Whom

If *The Case of Who Versus Whom* suggests an element of mystery, you may be assured that the phrase was chosen with that thought in mind. Consider the millions of Americans—and English-speaking people everywhere—who have struggled for years to put *who* and *whom* in their rightful places. Some authorities have suggested abandoning the use of *whom* on the grounds that our language would be more manageable and no less efficient without it. Despite all the protests, however, *whom* is still a part of our language, and employees who use it appropriately can set themselves apart from their associates. Attempt to use it correctly when you speak; make certain that you use it correctly when you write. Here are a few ideas to help you control *who, whose,* and *whom:*

1. Because the word *who* is in the nominative case, it should be employed as the subject of a verb or as a subject complement.

   Who requested the information? (*Who* is the subject of *requested.*)

   Who placed this order for 50 bags of cement? (*Who* is the subject of *placed.*)

   Mr. Maxwell is the salesperson *who spoke with you on the telephone.* (*Who* is the subject of *spoke.* The adjective clause modifying *salesperson* has been printed in italics.)

   Mr. Maxwell, *who spoke with you on the telephone,* is in Hartford today. (Note the placement of the adjective clause and the use of *who* as its subject.)

   He is the man *who* some people feel will be our next vice president. (In this sentence *some people feel* is a parenthetical expression. Can you recognize *who* as the subject of *will be?* Try rewording the adjective clause in this way: *Some people feel that who will be our next vice president.*)

   Who would you guess has seniority in this office? (*Who* is the subject of *has.* Did you recognize *would you guess* as a parenthetical expression? Expressions of this type tend to interrupt the natural flow of a sentence.)

   I have no way of knowing *who* it is. (In the noun clause *who it is, it* is the subject and *who* is a subject complement.)

2. The word *whose* is a possessive-case form. Do not confuse it with the contraction *who's,* meaning *who is.*

   Whose typewriter is in need of repair?

   We need more people like Dodson, *whose* work is always neat and well organized.

   Who's the new advertising executive for the Acme Agency?

3. Because the word *whom* is in the objective case, it should be employed as the object of a verb or a preposition.

   The job was given to the applicant *whom* you recommended. (The adjective clause *whom you recommended* modifies *applicant.* The subject of *recommended* is *you;* the direct object is *whom*).

   We were surprised to hear about Lonberg, *whom* Mr. Cassady trusted completely. (*Whom* is the direct object of *trusted.*)

   Whom did you have in mind? (You might try this wording: *You did have whom in mind.*)

   Whom were you with on Thursday afternoon? (*Whom* is the object of the preposition *with.* Try this wording: *You were with whom on Thursday afternoon.*)

   To *whom* should this letter be addressed? (*To whom,* of course, is a prepositional phrase.)

Compound Forms

If you can control *who* and *whom*, you are prepared to control their compound forms, *whoever* and *whomever*. *Whoever*, like *who*, is in the nominative case; *whomever* is in the objective case. Observe their roles in these sentences:

> *Whoever* volunteers will serve a worthy cause. (The noun clause *whoever volunteers* is the subject of *will serve*. *Whoever* is the subject of the verb *volunteers*.)
>
> Ms. Goddard wants to meet *whoever* wrote the article about Tennessee. (*Whoever*, which introduces a noun clause, is the subject of *wrote*.)
>
> We will need the name of *whomever* you select. (The noun clause *whomever you select* is the object of a preposition. *Whomever* is the direct object of *select*.)

Who, Which, and That

The word *who* (or *whom*) is used to refer to persons. *That* may be used to refer to animals or inanimate objects; it may also refer to people spoken of as a class or type (see third sentence of those following). *Which* may be used to refer to animals or inanimate objects.

> Maznicki is the agent *who* conducted the investigation.
>
> We have not yet received the machine *that* we ordered.
>
> He is not the kind of leader *that* our department needs.
>
> Please work on the Agee account, *which* must be ready by tomorrow.
>
> She works for a company *that* has been in business since 1875.

A Troublesome Construction

Be careful of sentences that contain expressions such as *one of the people who*. Note this sentence carefully:

> She is one of the employees who seem happy with their work. (*Who seem happy with their work* is an adjective clause modifying *employees*. Its subject, *who*, is plural because the antecedent of *who*, *employees*, is plural; therefore, a plural verb, *seem*, has been used. *Their* agrees in number with its antecedent, *employees*.)

A WORD TIP FROM THE REAL WORLD

Phyllis, a corporate head-hunter, formerly the director of a large employment agency, tells the story of making a call to a very qualified applicant to set up an interview for her. The job involved dealing with wealthy art patrons at a gallery. When Phyllis called and asked for Suzanne, the applicant answered, "This is her." Phyllis made a split-second decision, created some noise that sounded like a bad connection, and hung up. She knew that Suzanne's poor grammar habits, evident as she answered the phone, would create trouble with her well-educated clients at the gallery.

Fortunately, she took the time later on to explain this difficulty to Suzanne instead of simply ignoring the problem. Suzanne was angry about Phyllis's decision not to recommend her for the position and became determined to do better. She kept her file at the agency, worked on learning good habits, and a short time later proved to Phyllis that, even under unexpected circumstances, her grammar was reliable. She has been working rewardingly for several years now in a leading Southern California gallery, in a position Phyllis helped her to find.

_____WORKSHEET 11_____

MISCELLANEOUS PRONOUNS AT WORK

PART A. Identify the word that may be used as a singular pronoun but never as a plural pronoun.

Example: (A) someone, (B) several, (C) they, (D) most

1. (A) few, (B) many, (C) everybody, (D) yours
2. (A) some, (B) each, (C) any, (D) others
3. (A) both, (B) pronoun, (C) none, (D) nobody
4. (A) time, (B) all, (C) anything, (D) you
5. (A) either, (B) more, (C) who, (D) single

A

1. _C_
2. _B_
3. _D_
4. _C_
5. _A_

PART B. Select the correct word and write it in the answer space.

1. Each of our conference managers has been working out (his or her, their) conference accommodation package.

2. Whenever people convene in this city, everyone has (her or his, their) expectations.

3. Most of our guests are quite flexible; meeting (his or her, their) needs is easy.

4. Now and then, of course, we encounter a person who dislikes (everyone, every one) of our suggested hotel packages.

5. A few people last year gave us very poor ratings, yet (his or her, their) intentions are to return this year.

6. We tell (anyone, any one) who wants to stay downtown to select a hotel connected by skyway to the convention center.

7. Using (anyone, any one) of the skyway connections makes walking through downtown pleasant, even in the worst weather.

8. Sometimes none of our guests use (his or her, their) free shuttle bus access at all, preferring to walk the skyways.

9. More people seem to prefer having (their, his or her) rooms at the Halifax.

10. We attribute this trend to the fact that (everyone, every one) loves The Halifax's chef.

11. Some of our gourmet guests telephone us directly to ask where (he or she, they) ought to eat.

1. *his or her
2. *his or her
3. their
4. every one
5. their
6. *anyone
7. any one   their
8. ~~his or her~~
9. their
10. everyone
11. they

12. That sort of inquiry is something each conference manager must handle in (her or his, their) own positive style.

13. While these managers seek (their, her or his) answers, at least four new questions arise each day.

14. In fact, as a conference date draws nearer, some of our conference managers find (their, his or her) telephone work doubling.

15. For this reason, each manager is asked to select (their, her or his) favorite two assistants who will be assigned to the project for six months.

16. Together this conference team of three plans the event from the start, each giving (his or her, their) best wisdom on agenda, accommodations, and entertainment options.

17. After an initial meeting, months in advance, each team member works separately on (their, her or his) part of the conference.

18. About a month ahead of the actual conference date, all of the team members bring (his or her, their) work together to finish the plan.

19. If either of the assistants cannot answer an incoming question, (he or she, they) can ask the team as a whole to solve the problem.

20. After a conference is finished, each of the team members knows that (they, she or he) can count on the others.

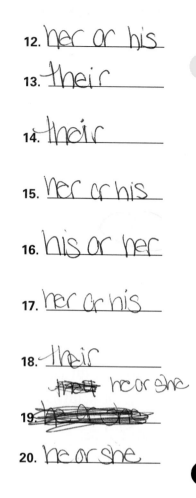

12. her or his

13. their

14. their

15. her or his

16. his or her

17. her or his

18. their

19. ~~their~~ he or she

20. he or she

PART C. Find and underscore ten errors in pronoun and other word choice in this selection from the body of a letter. Agree on improved word choice and list the error and its correction in the blanks that follow the paragraph.

At the market research conference, try to learn why either of the two leading advertising executives has doubled their business this year. Anyone of their strategies might help us next season. If we can achieve the goals we have set for next year, every one will share in the profits. Both of our competitors will be attending that conference, but neither of them knows whether they will have enough business next year. Your colleagues back at the office, like Sarah Leiberwitz, will support your accounts while you are away, regardless of her own schedule. We want you to know that we value the important work you will be doing for everyone of us. Even if someone should try to discourage you, don't let their remarks bother you. Don't worry about anything anyone says out of their envy over your work. Its your loyalty to everyone of us that makes you the right person to go to the conference for our benefit. We are counting on you.

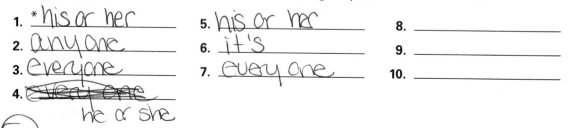

1. *his or her
2. anyone
3. everyone
4. ~~~~ he or she
5. his or her
6. it's
7. every one
8. _____
9. _____
10. _____

(124) MISCELLANEOUS PRONOUNS AT WORK

A FOUR-STEP ANALYSIS

Ed Post, who(m) we just promoted, is an excellent writer.

In choosing between *who* and *whom,* follow these steps:

1. Isolate the clause: *who(m) we just promoted.* (Can you see that this is an adjective clause modifying *Ed Post?*)
2. Find the verb: *promoted.* (This word shows action.)
3. Determine its subject: *we.* (This word answers the question *Who promoted?*)
4. Determine its object: *whom.* (This word answers the question *Promoted whom?* Because *who* is nominative, it cannot function as an object.)

PART D. Choose the correct word and write it in the answer space. If you are working collaboratively, split the items among the group members. Each member should use the four-step analysis above to teach the other members how to figure out each item.

1. (Whoever, Whomever) is hired by the marketing department will have fine qualifications.

   1. _Whoever_

2. Dr. Picard, (who, whom) we have seen as a consultant for years, is leaving.

   2. _Whom_

3. The vacancy will be filled by (whoever, whomever) the search committee recommends.

   3. _Whomever_

4. The top sales executive (who, whom) won last year's trip will not compete this year.

   4. _Who_

5. (Who, Whom) are we expecting to attend the board meeting in March?

   5. _Whom_

6. Spiridelis is the M.I.S. in-service trainer to (who, whom) our office has been assigned.

   6. * _Whom_

7. Lauber sent a duplicate invoice to the man (who, whom) ordered the software package.

   7. * _Who_

8. The human resources specialist (who, whom) Peterson met in Chicago is arriving today.

   8. _Whom_

9. With (who, whom) did you make the service call appointment?

   9. _Whom_

10. She is the graphic image designer (who, whom) was given the Purdy Award.

    10. _Who_

11. (Whoever, Whomever) controls the budget controls the power of decision.

    11. * _Whoever_

12. The commission seeks advice from experienced persons (who, whom) they can trust.

    12. _Whom_

13. The frayed computer cables are evidence of the squirrel (who, that) Darius thought she saw in the storage room.

    13. _that_

14. Our task force wants to discover (who, whom) organized the banquet last year.

    14. _Who_

15. That is the company with (who, whom) Allied Electronics does all of its foreign business.

15. _____

16. Our own Hannah Seinfeldt, (who, whom) *The Times* praised, will be promoted.

16. _____

17. Jay Cremonini is the man (who, whom), I am told, can be trusted with the documents.

17. _____

18. Gallagher Enterprises will not hire persons (who, whom) are not computer literate.

18. _____

19. Can we find out (who, whom) distributes the video version of the training material?

19. _____

20. You work for the firm (who, that) rose to Fortune 500 status in three years time.

20. _____

PART E. The following sentences would be unacceptable in business. Tell, in complete sentences, what is wrong with each one.

Example: Neither of the women did their own typing.
Comment: A plural pronoun *(their)* has a singular antecedent *(Neither)*.

1. Each of the new programmers has their company manual.

Comment: _____

_____

_____

_____

2. Who did you want to invite to the recognition dinner?

Comment: _____

_____

_____

_____

3. Who's van is parked in the handicapped-accessible spot again this morning?

Comment: * _____

_____

_____

_____

4. Our marketing research department talks with whomever wants to participate.

Comment: _____

_____

_____

_____

OPTIONAL EXERCISES

OPTION 1 Select the correct word and write it in the answer space. If you are collaborating, work through the items together, showing each other chapter material that supports your choice.

1. When you process applications, be certain that each employee enters (her, their) social security number clearly at the top.

   1. _____

2. Those numbers are used as employee access codes that permit each employee to enter (their, his) locked office without using a key.

   2. _____

3. All employees learn to enter (his, their) social security code onto a keypad.

   3. _____

4. With that number as identification, every worker can enter (her, their) office space at any time, day or night.

   4. _____

5. Of course, certain security precautions are taken so that employees are limited to (his, their) particular work areas.

   5. _____

6. Everyone keeps (her, their) access code to (herself, themselves).

   6. _____

7. Since we have begun to use the social security code access system, random office thefts have decreased, and everyone still has access to each of (his, their) own work areas.

   7. _____

8. We had a few complaints from people (who, whom) believed (his or her, their) movement was being unnecessarily restricted.

   8. _____

9. (Everyone, Every one) of these complaints was answered personally by a manager.

   9. _____

10. Each manager met with all persons from (her, their) department.

   10. _____

11. If (anyone, any one) remained unsatisfied after those meetings, further conversations took place with officers in the security division.

   11. _____

12. What security officers hesitated to say openly at first was that (his, their) new security precautions came about because of several serious office break-ins.

   12. _____

13. Company files were stolen, (anyone, any one) of (whom, which) could have given our competition an important edge and seriously hindered our success.

   13. _____

14. Worse than that, last fall security officers noted in several of (her, their) reports that nonemployees had been walking in hallways after the offices had closed.

14. _____

15. When questioned, each of these people had said that an employee friend had let (her, them) in through the buzzer-controlled door.

15. * _____

16. Yet, the friend was not in (his, their) office.

16. _____

17. With suspicious incidents on the rise, any head of security would propose that (her, their) department be allowed to implement a better system.

17. _____

18. Our security officers investigated (everyone, every one) of the affordable systems.

18. _____

19. Even the employees (who, whom) were at first most upset by these new measures soon understood the reasons for them and promised (her, their) full cooperation.

19. _____

20. In the end, we hope that the social security code system will make it possible for all our employees to feel that (his or her, their) work, possessions, and selves are protected.

20. _____

OPTION 2 Some people have suggested that we eliminate *whom* from our language. In a short paragraph, give at least one reason for keeping the word and at least one for eliminating it.

_____

_____

_____

_____

_____

_____

_____

_____

_____

_____

_____

_____

_____

_____

_____

_____

CHAPTER 12

Verbs: Agreement and Mood

■ POINT TO PONDER

There is no such thing as a sentence without a verb.

This chapter is the first of four that pertain to the very important subject of verbs. Your understanding of this material is basic to your understanding of English grammar; consequently, you will want to study it carefully.

You will recall from your reading of Chapter 3 that every sentence must have a verb. You know that verbs are words that express *action* or *state of being*. They are used to make statements, ask questions, give commands, and make requests. The main verb in a clause is referred to as the **simple predicate**. The **complete predicate** consists of the verb together with its complements and modifiers. Let's review a few basic terms as we consider this sentence:

The new owner of the clothing store purchased his fixtures from us.

SIMPLE SUBJECT:	owner (Answers the question *Who purchased?*)
COMPLETE SUBJECT:	The new owner of the clothing store
SIMPLE PREDICATE:	purchased
COMPLETE PREDICATE:	purchased his fixtures from us
DIRECT OBJECT:	fixtures (Answers the question *Purchased what?*)

AGREEMENT OF SUBJECT AND VERB

Perhaps the most basic rule of grammar is that a verb must agree with its subject in number. If the subject is singular, the verb must be singular. If the subject is plural, the verb must also be plural. In previous lessons attention has been given to the types of subjects that tend to prove troublesome. Perhaps we should consider a few of them again as we begin the study of verbs.

1. A verb should agree in number with its simple subject. Do not be misled by intervening phrases or clauses. In each of the following sentences, the verb and its simple subject have been printed in italics.

SINGULAR: The young *woman* with five excellent recommendations *is being considered* for the position.
PLURAL: Two young *women* with excellent recommendations *are being considered* for the position.
SINGULAR: *Mr. Lowe,* as well as his staff members, *has been informed.* (In determining whether a subject is singular or plural, ignore phrases that begin with expressions such as *together with, in addition to, rather than, as well as, along with, including,* or *accompanied by.*)
PLURAL: The staff *members,* as well as Mr. Lowe, *have been informed.* (The simple subject is *members;* therefore, a plural verb was used.)

2. If *many a, each,* or *every* is used to modify a subject, that subject is singular even though it may have more than one part.

SINGULAR: Every *man* and *woman has* the opportunity to give.
PLURAL: All *men* and *women have* the opportunity to give.
SINGULAR: Many a *person is* likely to be disappointed.
PLURAL: Many *people are* likely to be disappointed.

3. The subjects *none, some, any, all, more, most,* and fractions, such as *half,* may be singular or plural. The noun or pronoun to which the subject refers will determine its number. If a prepositional phrase with a plural object follows the subject, the subject will be considered plural. (Exceptions: *None* may be used to mean *not one; any* may be used to mean *any one.*)

SINGULAR: A *third* of the shipment *has been stolen.* (The subject refers to *shipment,* which is singular.)
PLURAL: A *third* of the boxes *have been stolen.* (The subject refers to *boxes,* which is plural.)
SINGULAR: *Most* of the building *is made* of brick.
PLURAL: *Most* of the offices *are painted* gray.

4. The name of one book, song, magazine article, or company is singular even though the name itself may be compound or plural in form.

SINGULAR: *Three Angry Men is* a fine novel.
PLURAL: Three angry *men are waiting* to see you.
SINGULAR: *Tustin, Fox and Benson, Inc., has submitted* a bid.
PLURAL: *Tustin* and *Fox are* fine executives.

5. An amount (money, distance, time, etc.) is singular when it is expressed as a single unit.

SINGULAR: Four hundred *dollars is* a fair price.
PLURAL: Four hundred *chairs have been ordered.*
SINGULAR: Forty *feet* of cord *is* still on the shelf.
SINGULAR: Thirty *minutes is* more time than we need.

6. Collective nouns may be singular or plural. If the noun refers to a group as a single unit, a singular verb should be used. If the sentence suggests that members of the group are acting independently of one another, a plural verb should be used.

SINGULAR: The *audience is* quiet and attentive.
PLURAL: The *audience* (or *Members of the audience*) *are going* their separate ways.

7. If *or* or *nor* is used to join two singular subjects, a singular verb should be used. If a singular subject and a plural subject are joined by *or* or *nor*, the plural form should be placed closer to the verb and a plural verb used.

SINGULAR: Neither *Martin* nor his *brother is* willing to cooperate.
PLURAL: Neither *Martin* nor his *brothers are* willing to cooperate.
SINGULAR: *Bob* or *Paul is* probably responsible.
PLURAL: *Bob* or his two *associates are* probably responsible.

8. When used as subjects, these pronouns are singular: *anyone, anybody, everyone, everybody, someone, somebody, one, nobody, either, neither, each.* Use them with singular verbs.

SINGULAR: *Nobody has seen* Whelan for several days.
SINGULAR: *Everybody seems* pleased with the results.
SINGULAR: *Each* of our products *has been accepted* by the public.
SINGULAR: *Neither* of his comments *was overheard.*

9. Some singular subjects end in *s.* Be careful to use them with singular verbs.

SINGULAR: *Mathematics is* an intriguing subject.
SINGULAR: *Politics has played* an important role in her life.

10. Occasionally two nouns are used to name a single unit or idea. Use them with a singular verb.

SINGULAR: The *horse* and *buggy was* popular in 1890.
PLURAL: The *automobile* and the *buggy have served* the same basic purpose.

Remember that in some sentences, such as most of those beginning with *There* or *Here,* the subject will be placed after the verb. Note the underscored subjects in these sentences: *There are several items to be considered. There was no time for delay. Onto the stage walked Mr. Babson. Here are two copies of the Toshiba manual.*

MOOD

The **mood** (or **mode**) of a verb indicates the manner in which an action or a state is conceived. There are three moods, and the only one that ordinarily proves challenging (the subjunctive) has far fewer uses now than it had in former years.

A verb is said to be in the **indicative mood** if it is used to make a statement or ask a question. A verb is in the **imperative mood** if it is used to issue a command or make a request. Ordinarily the subject (you) is omitted. Because your understanding of these two moods will not help you to communicate more effectively, they will not be mentioned in the worksheets that follow this chapter. Your mastery of the **subjunctive mood,** however, may help you to avoid some common grammatical errors.

Subjunctive Mood

One hundred years ago writers made extensive use of the subjunctive mood. A significant change in our language in recent years has been our deemphasis of the subjunctive in favor of the indicative mood. Many uses of the subjunctive have proved just too formal and cumbersome for modern business writers. Its use is virtually nonexistent in much informal writing. Authorities disagree slightly concerning its importance in more formal business writing, but all seem to agree that the two uses described here should be thoroughly understood by careful speakers and writers.

1. Use the subjunctive mood to express an idea that is clearly *contrary to fact.* In the past tense, which actually expresses present time, the sign of the subjunctive is *were.* Use this verb with *all* subjects, as in these sentences:

    If Mr. Wiley *were* here, he would suggest a solution.

    If the story *were* true, Johnson would not have resigned.

    I wish it *were* possible for me to go with you.

Even though the last of the foregoing sentences is expressed as a wish, the idea conveyed by the subjunctive is clearly contrary to fact.

2. Use the subjunctive (*be*) to express a desire, a recommendation, a demand, a motion, a suggestion, a request, a necessity, or a resolution, as in these sentences:

    It is recommended that all overtime work *be* eliminated.

    I demand that the damage *be* repaired immediately.

    He moved that the meeting *be* adjourned.

    It is my wish that Lassen *be* promoted.

    She requested that the information *be* stored on a hard disk.

Writers are not likely to have difficulty with such constructions when verbs other than *be* are used. Note how smoothly the italicized verbs (in the subjunctive mood) are employed in these sentences: It is my wish that she *go* to the convention. It is necessary that he *finish* the project by Friday.

Other uses of the subjunctive mood have been replaced by the indicative in most business writing today. Because neither of the foregoing rules pertains, the indicative mood would be used in these sentences:

    If Mr. Hodges *was* ill on Tuesday, the disbursements may not have been made.

    If Craig *was* on television, he probably appeared in a commercial.

Neither of the foregoing sentences expresses an idea that is clearly *contrary to fact.* Mr. Hodges may have been ill on Tuesday, and Craig may have appeared on television. Contrast the sentences under discussion with one that *does* require the subjunctive mood: *If Mr. Hodges were really ill, he would not be playing golf today.* The idea expressed in this sentence is contrary to fact because Mr. Hodges is *not* really ill.

As you complete Part C of Worksheet 12, bear in mind that verb forms ending in *s* (*seems, informs, tells,* etc.) are generally singular.

Accept   This verb means "to take" or "to agree to." It is often confused with *except,* which usually functions as a preposition meaning "with the exclusion of." *Except* may also be used as a verb meaning "to exclude from consideration."

> We cannot *accept* the shipment.
>
> Everyone *except* Virginia Thomas seemed pleased with the results.
>
> The report is very satisfactory, if you *except* a few typographical errors.

Affect   This verb means "to influence." The verb *effect* means "to bring about." *Effect* is more frequently employed as a noun to mean "the result."

> The new law may *affect* our expansion program.
>
> We are hoping to *effect* a few minor changes.
>
> They could not foretell what the *effect* would be.

Appraise   Do not confuse this word with *apprise,* which means "to notify" or "to inform." *Appraise* means "to make an official valuation of."

> The bank will *appraise* our property on Sycamore Street.
>
> We did not *apprise* them of our decision.

Can   Careful writers use this word to suggest the power or ability to do something. *May* suggests permission or allowance. Other uses of these words are easily controlled by most writers.

> *Can* you make delivery by August 20?
>
> *May* I accompany you on your trip?
>
> *May* I please have your name?

Canvass   This verb, which means "to go about seeking votes, opinions, or orders for goods," should not be confused with *canvas,* which refers to a heavy, coarse cloth.

> Hale will *canvass* the entire district on Thursday.
>
> This piece of *canvas* may be too small to cover the equipment.

19. If Sharon (A was, B were) in the building today, she may have
returned the call.

19. _____

20. Neither the truckers nor their managing director (A has, B have)
resigned.

20. _____

OPTION 2 Write one or more paragraphs on the subject of "Business Travel." Make
certain that it contains at least one verb in the subjunctive mood and that you
underscore any such verb.

_____

_____

_____

_____

_____

_____

_____

_____

_____

_____

_____

_____

_____

OPTION 3 (CLASS DISCUSSION)   In several of this country's colleges, grammar is a part
of every academic course. Papers submitted for all courses, not just English,
are penalized for errors in grammar and punctuation.

Is grading of this type a fair and logical inducement to help students improve
their communicating skills? Give reasons for your answer. If you are completing this option collaboratively, your small work group should determine its
position on this question and present its reasons to the class.

CHAPTER 13

Verbs in Sentences

Dictionary entries indicate whether a verb
is transitive or intransitive.

A s already indicated, business writers who want to control verbs must be concerned
with agreement and with mood. They must also understand several other characteristics of this important part of speech.

VOICE

The main verb in a clause may be in either the active voice or the passive voice. If it is in
the **active voice,** the subject is the *doer* of the action. If it is in the **passive voice,** the subject is
acted upon. The active voice is considered to be the stronger of the two and is recommended for
most business writing. Certainly it has the directness favored by most executives today. Consider
these sentences:

ACTIVE VOICE: We *received* your order on January 16.
PASSIVE VOICE: Your order *was received* by us on January 16.
ACTIVE VOICE: Paulson *has made* five excellent sales this morning.
PASSIVE VOICE: Five excellent sales *have been made* by Paulson this morning. (A verb
phrase in the passive voice always contains a form of the verb *be* as a
helping verb.)

Even though the passive voice is not generally favored, it has its place in business writing. The occasional use of verbs in the passive voice lends variety to one's writing. Also, there are

PART B. By writing the appropriate *letter* in the answer space, indicate whether the verb (in italics) is *transitive* (T) or *intransitive* (I).

Example: This country's first locomotive *traveled* at a speed of ten miles an hour.   I

1. A recent focus group *considered* several interesting topics.   1. _____

2. Today's entry-level workers *seem* unprepared to work, both in skill and attitude.   2. *_____

3. Is this a Generation-X phenomenon, or is it the fault of a system of education that *doesn't understand* the needs of business.   3. _____

4. Economic development policy at every level of government still *pursues* job creation as a top priority.   4. _____

5. Why *should* they not *consider* worker creation?   5. _____

6. If more attention were paid to worker creation, the relocation of displaced workers *would* not *be* so difficult.   6. _____

7. This year's research *was expanded* to include two new groups.   7. *_____

8. One group *represented* the public affairs community, mostly lobbyists and political professionals.   8. _____

9. The other group *talked* with people from outside of metropolitan areas.   9. *_____

10. These focus discussions *happened* because Chamber of Commerce presidents were interested in the opinions of persons not often included in business dialogues.   10. _____

PART C. Convert the following brief memo from passive voice to active voice. Comment on the difference that conversion makes in the memo's tone.

Employees will be given five working days to respond to the new contract. After that period, the contract will be signed and submitted for ratification. Because of this brief timeframe, no company-wide discussion will be held. It is hoped that the need for swift ratification of the contract and swift return to work is understood by all employees, whose cooperation is greatly appreciated.

*_____

_____

_____

_____

_____

_____

PART D. Underscore the verb in each sentence; then write, in the answer space, any direct object or subject complement that you find. Label each one DO or SC, as in the example. If you are collaborating on this exercise, all collaborators must agree on a final answer.

Example: Vandermeer <u>gave</u> us the benefit of his advice.   _____benefit (DO)_____

1. Investor confidence today has something to do with the volume and quality of investing information.

    1. _____

2. Never before have investors had such extensive information on such a broad array of investments choices.

    2. * _____

3. In the days before 1990, the primary distribution outlets for information were the telephone, the newspaper, and weekly journals.

    3. _____

4. In contrast, traders today can make better decisions, thanks to internet charting which is immediate and inexpensive for a much broader clientele.

    4. _____

5. Analysts are busy around the clock and around the globe.

    5. * _____

6. CNBC, MSNBC, FNN, and other business-news networks beam local currency, stock, and commodities quotes to audiences 24 hours a day.

    6. _____

7. Powerful home computers were unimaginable a few years ago.

    7. _____

8. Yet now those computers scan and analyze data at accelerated speed.

    8. _____

9. Special phone line internet access allows trading 24 hours a day.

    9. _____

10. Investors are eager to trade without brokerage firm involvement.

    10. _____

PART E. Because the active voice is stronger and more direct than the passive, it is generally considered more suitable for business. Rewrite the following sentences so that each verb (in italics) is in the active voice. Collaborate to enhance your best rewrites.

Example: A detailed report *will be submitted* by us on Friday.
We will submit a detailed report on Friday.

1. The necessary papers *were signed* by Mr. Lindstrom on March 10.

_____

_____

2. Your questions concerning personal computers *will be answered* by Mr. Ramirez at our meeting this afternoon.

* _____

_____

3. Work on the Walker Building *has been completed* by a local contractor.

_____

_____

4. No more furniture *will be manufactured* by this firm until next year.

_____

_____

5. The will *was signed* by the testator, Henry P. Hallstrom.

_____

_____

6. This type of optical scanner *has been ordered* by Ms. Alvarado.

_____

_____

7. I *was told* by Stanislaus that no action *will be taken* by his client.

_____

_____

8. The loan *will be made* by Citibank only if adequate collateral *can be furnished* by the borrower.

_____

_____

_____ FOR CLASS DISCUSSION _____

(if time permits)

There are many common verbs that may be used with or without objects. For example, *The American Heritage Dictionary* provides ten definitions for the transitive verb *write* and three definitions for the intransitive verb *write*. Note how the word is used in these two sentences:

INTRANSITIVE: Most of our executives write extremely well.
TRANSITIVE: Wicker writes a weekly column for *The New York Times*.

Name at least five other verbs that may be used smoothly with or without an object. Suggest pairs of sentences to illustrate such usage.

HE SPOKE ABOUT WHAT?

The possessive case should be avoided if its use results in an ambiguous construction. A sentence such as *He spoke at length about Jeff Zale and Ron Nimmo's new car* has more than one possible meaning. Here is one perfectly clear version: *He spoke at length about the new car purchased by Jeff Zale and Ron Nimmo*. (Another possibility: *He spoke at length about Jeff Zale and also about Ron Nimmo's new car*.)

Most careful writers avoid the use of pronouns to indicate joint possession. Note that more than one word must be made possessive in sentences like these: (1) *His and my report should be ready by Friday*. (2) *Austin's and her quarrel did not surprise any of us*. Although grammatically correct, such constructions are considered somewhat awkward by most readers.

Tenses of Verbs

■■ POINT TO PONDER

Most people, in telling stories, find it especially difficult to use appropriate verb tenses.

O f the eight parts of speech, verbs have the largest number of variant forms. The need for many verb forms becomes apparent when we realize that verbs express *time* as well as action. **Tense** refers to time. English verbs may be expressed in several tenses, and each tense has its purpose. In the material that follows, verbs are shown first in the active voice. If there is a passive-voice form, you will find it enclosed in parentheses.

PRESENT TENSE

Simple

I drive (am driven)   We drive (are driven)
You drive (are driven)   You drive (are driven)
He, she, *or* it drives (is driven)   They drive (are driven)

Progressive

I am driving (am being driven)   We are driving (are being driven)
You are driving (are being driven)   You are driving (are being driven)
He, she, *or* it is driving (is being driven)   They are driving (are being driven)

Emphatic

I do drive   We do drive
You do drive   You do drive
He, she, *or* it does drive   They do drive

The **present tense** is used to state general truth, as in these sentences:

He *helps* me with my work.
Mr. Reilly *visits* New York every month.
She *answers* letters promptly.

The present tense of a verb should also be used to express action in progress.

I *am enjoying* my new work.
You *are driving* too fast.

The present tense may even be employed to express future action.

I hope he *arrives* before the meeting *ends*.

Most of us have little difficulty in our use of the present tense. Two kinds of errors, however, are made often enough to warrant these words of caution:

1. Remember that, unlike nouns, the verb form ending in *s* is likely to be *singular*. Note carefully the endings of verbs that have third-person subjects.

Singular	*Plural*
He knows	They know
She hesitates	They hesitate
Benson writes	They write

2. Do not put a verb in the past tense simply because another verb in the same sentence happens to be in the past tense. Use the present tense to express an idea that continues to be true.

DON'T USE:	What did you say your name *was?*
USE:	What did you say your name *is?*
DON'T USE:	He told me that he *didn't* like this brand.
USE:	He told me that he *doesn't* like this brand.

PAST TENSE

Simple

I drove (was driven)	We drove (were driven)
You drove (were driven)	You drove (were driven)
He, she, *or* it drove (was driven)	They drove (were driven)

Progressive

I was driving (was being driven)	We were driving (were being driven)
You were driving (were being driven)	You were driving (were being driven)
He, she, *or* it was driving (was being driven)	They were driving (were being driven)

Emphatic

I did drive	We did drive
You did drive	You did drive
He, she, *or* it did drive	They did drive

The **past tense** is used to express action that was started and completed before the present time. The average person uses past-tense verbs with ease. If the spelling of past-tense forms such as *occurred* and *compelled* proves to be a problem, refer again to Rule 2 in Chapter 2, "A Few Spelling Rules."

FUTURE TENSE

Simple

I will drive (will be driven)   We will drive (will be driven)
You will drive (will be driven)   You will drive (will be driven)
He, she, *or* it will drive (will be driven)   They will drive (will be driven)

Progressive

I will be driving   We will be driving
You will be driving   You will be driving
He, she, *or* it will be driving   They will be driving

The **future tense** is used to express an action or condition that has not yet taken place. It is formed, as a general rule, by the use of *will* as a helping verb. Although *shall* is occasionally employed in formal usage, recent surveys suggest strongly that the great majority of today's writers and speakers find it more natural to use *will.*

A few grammarians recommend the use of *shall* with first-person subjects *(I, we)* and *will* with all other subjects. They suggest, however, that we reverse this procedure when we want to express determination, emphasis, or promise. *Will,* they tell us, should then be used with first-person subjects and *shall* with all other subjects. Sentences like *I will post the bulletin* and *He shall tell the truth* should, according to them, be used to suggest determination or promise. Most business writers find such distinctions to be impractical; they tend, therefore, to use *will* with all subjects, whether emphasis is intended or not.

When the word *shall* appears in a legal document, such as an employment contract or a lease, it generally means that a particular action is mandatory, or imperative. Here is an example of such usage: *The lessee, James T. Santiago, shall pay the lessor, Joseph P. Velasco, on or before April 1, 1995, the sum of Nine Hundred Fifty Dollars ($950).*

PRESENT PERFECT TENSE

Note the helping verbs that may be used to form this tense: *have, have been, has,* and *has been.*

Simple

I have driven (have been driven)   We have driven (have been driven)
You have driven (have been driven)   You have driven (have been driven)
He, she, *or* it has driven (has been driven)   They have driven (have been driven)

Progressive

I have been driving   We have been driving
You have been driving   You have been driving
He, she, *or* it has been driving   They have been driving

1. The **present perfect tense** may be used to indicate that an act has just been completed.

    I *have* just *finished* reading the instructions.
    He *has discovered* the real meaning.
    The computer in my office *has been repaired.* (passive voice)

2. This tense may also indicate an action beginning in the past and continuing into the future.

    We *have worked* for this firm for seven years.
    He *has been helping* with the book work.

3. It can be used to indicate past actions that may occur again.

    I *have helped* Harry on three occasions.
    She *has had* three promotions since the companies merged.

PAST PERFECT TENSE
Note the helping verbs that may be used to form this tense: *had* and *had been.*

Simple

I had driven (had been driven)	We had driven (had been driven)
You had driven (had been driven)	You had driven (had been driven)
He, she, *or* it had driven (had been driven)	They had driven (had been driven)

Progressive

I had been driving	We had been driving
You had been driving	You had been driving
He, she, *or* it had been driving	They had been driving

The **past perfect tense** is used to indicate an action that was completed prior to either another past action or a past time, which may be specified or simply implied.

I tried to telephone Wayne, but he *had left* his office by that time. (Wayne's leaving occurred *prior to* my trying.)
Although it was only 3 P.M., we *had sold* every camera in stock.
It *had been raining* for several days when disaster struck.
Jim told us that he *had signed* the contract.
By midnight the rain *had stopped.*

FUTURE PERFECT TENSE
Note the helping verbs that are generally employed to form this tense: *will have* and *will have been.*

Simple

I will have driven (will have been driven)	We will have driven (will have been driven)
You will have driven (will have been driven)	You will have driven (will have been driven)
He, she, *or* it will have driven (will have been driven)	They will have driven (will have been driven)

Progressive

I will have been driving	We will have been driving
You will have been driving	You will have been driving
He, she, *or* it will have been driving	They will have been driving

The **future perfect tense** is used to indicate an action that will be completed (1) before another future action or (2) by a specified future time.

By 9:30 P.M. the program *will have ended.*

The auditor *will have examined* the books by the time you return from your vacation.

A Final Look

Let's take a final look at all six tenses. The following verb forms (in italics) are all in the active voice. Note that emphatic and progressive *(ing)* forms have been added where appropriate.

PRESENT TENSE:	I *work,* I *do work,* I *am working*
PAST TENSE:	I *worked,* I *did work,* I *was working*
FUTURE TENSE:	I *will work,* I *will be working*
PRESENT PERFECT TENSE:	I *have worked,* I *have been working*
PAST PERFECT TENSE:	I *had worked,* I *had been working*
FUTURE PERFECT TENSE:	I *will have worked,* I *will have been working*

If you are thoroughly familiar with all six of these tense forms, you should find the worksheet that follows relatively easy.

Executives' Choice

Advice This word is a noun. Don't confuse it with *advise,* the verb.

Mr. Markowitz offered her some excellent *advice.* What would you *advise* me to do?

Break In business this word may refer to "a pause or interval, as from work" or "a fracture or crack." A *brake* is "something that slows down a vehicle, an activity, or a movement."

Before continuing, we should take a short *break.*

Set the emergency *brake* before you leave the truck.

Capitol Keep in mind that this noun always refers to a building—one in which the U.S. Congress or a state legislature convenes. Do not confuse it with *capital,* which has several meanings.

We may visit the *Capitol* while we are in Washington.

Barnes will be in Springfield, the state *capital,* on March 7.

We could not raise the *capital* needed to meet his terms.

Several states still practice *capital* punishment.

Confidant This noun, which has the feminine form *confidante,* names "one with whom secrets are shared; a trusted friend." *Confident,* the adjective, means "assured, certain, trusting."

During that critical period Max was my only *confidant.*

She is *confident* that the public will respond to our plea.

Consensus   This word means "general agreement, a collective opinion." *Consensus of opinion,* therefore, is somewhat redundant.

> The *consensus* (not *consensus of opinion*) is that we should leave now.

Counsel   This word may be used as a noun meaning either "one who gives advice, as an attorney," or "the advice given." It may also be used as a verb meaning "to advise." A *council* is a "legislative or consulting body."

> Ms. Aiken *counseled* me during the recent controversy.
>
> The *counsel* for Mr. Olsen presented her case in brilliant fashion.
>
> One member of the *council* was not present when the meeting began.

Data   This is the plural form of *datum,* which is used infrequently. Although some dictionaries indicate that *data* (as a subject) is sometimes used with a singular verb, a significant number of professional writers object to such a practice. The use of *data* with a plural verb is always acceptable.

> The *data* are contained in our annual report.

Deal   This word is somewhat informal for business when it is used in place of *sale, transaction, agreement, merger, trade, plan, offer,* or *proposal.*

> This proposal (not *deal*) is likely to be accepted.
>
> We are hoping that your company agrees to the trade (not *deal*).

Either   Use *either* or *neither* in referring to only two; use *any* in referring to more than two.

> *Either* (of these two) desk lamp(s) will provide enough light.
>
> *Neither* (of the two) cabinet(s) is large enough.
>
> *Any* of these four bookcases should prove satisfactory.

---

wWWw ═══ Watching the Web ═══

Back	**Forward**	**Home**	**Reload**	**Images**	**Open**

```
Enroll in our on-line investment club today. You will re-
ceive the most up-to-the-minute market information daily.
You will discover market patterns that have until now been
known and understood only by investment professionals. You
will also read expert advise from top brokerage firms in
our new commentary section. Interested?        Click here.
```

[no thanks]   [more info]

_____WORKSHEET 14_____

TENSES OF VERBS

PART A. By writing the appropriate *letter,* indicate the tense in which the listed helping verb(s) would be used.

A. present   C. future   E. past perfect
B. past   D. present perfect F. future perfect

1. have   1. _____   5. had   5. *_____
2. do   2. _____   6. will   6. *_____
3. does   3. _____   7. has   7. _____
4. will have   4. _____   8. did   8. _____

PART B. Two verb forms are given in parentheses. Write the correct one in the answer space.

1. Underwood returned from the trade show today, and
   he (is, was) very excited about what he saw.   1. *_____

2. During the three-day show, several of our competitors
   (have demonstrated, were demonstrating) their newest
   products while Underwood took careful notes,   *
   undetected.   2. _____

3. By the last day of such shows, he always (has, had)
   enough information to test our own products against
   theirs.   3. _____

4. He is convinced that by this time next year we
   (will work, will have worked) all the flaws out of our
   prototype model.   4. _____

5. He also says that we (are, were) able to begin
   production of Models T-9 and T-10 at this time.   5. _____

6. As a result, we should (be, have been) one step ahead
   of competition by next May.   6. _____

7. Because of what Underwood usually (learns, learned)
   at trade shows, morale goes up and designers are
   pleased.   7. _____

8. Our production boss (is thinking, thinks) that his notes
   and sketches will be helpful.   8. _____

9. Underwood is proud of his industrial espionage work and
   (has planned, is planning) to continue it at other shows.   9. _____

10. This scheme will work only if he (is, will be) able to
    keep his identity a secret.   10. _____

PART C. In the answer space write the correct tense form of the verb in parentheses. Use the active voice; do not use emphatic or progressive forms. (After each of the first six sentences, the correct tense form has been named.)

Example: Delano always (come) to work on time   <u>came</u>
when he worked for this firm. (past)

1. Ms. Gaines (want) to receive a degree in business
administration. (present)   1. _____

2. By the time we found the missing affidavit,
Craig's attorney already (go). (past perfect)   2. * _____

3. During the past hour Nelson (place) four personal
telephone calls. (present perfect)   3. _____

4. The project manager (arrive) while you were out
to lunch. (past)   4. _____

5. By the time we reach Paris, the trade talks
(begin). (future perfect)   5. * _____

6. Sometime during the next year this company
(expand) its human resources department. (future)   6. _____

7. By 5 P.M. yesterday our group (complete) its work. 7. _____

8. Seigel (return) several cellular telephones about
two weeks ago.   8. _____

9. The Bethlehem Steel representative (visit) us
whenever he visits Omaha.   9. _____

10. If you type the letter now, I (proofread) it before
leaving the office.   10. _____

11. Our senior tax accountant (be) with this company
for more than 30 years.   11. _____

12. By noon tomorrow the claims processor already
(submit) his paperwork.   12. _____

13. If there is enough money available, we (acquire)
another letter-quality printer next month.   13. _____

14. The director of personnel (dismiss) more
employees than she cares to admit.   14. _____

15. We reached the office at 9 A.M. to discover that the
auditor (begin) work an hour earlier.   15. _____

PART D. In the space provided, indicate the tense of the verb in italics; then write *progressive* or *emphatic* if either of those forms has been used.

Example: Shannon *is talking* on the telephone.   <u>present (progressive)</u>

1. During in-service workshops, many employees
have complained about shop hours.   1. * _____

2. This issue comes up time after time, especially
when employees *are given* the opportunity to raise
questions and concerns.   2. _____

3. Every time we believe that we have solved the
problem, we discover that they *are* still
complaining about shifts and hours of operation.   3. _____

4. We *do ask* our workers to put in long hours.

4. *_____

5. We *will be asking* them to continue to put in long hours during the high season.

5. _____

6. But our wages are fair and we *have been known* to be generous with overtime pay.

6. _____

7. Our firm *will have been operating* continuously for 53 years next September.

7. _____

8. We *have* not *come* this far without knowing what constitutes a fair wage for fair labor.

8. _____

9. We *are asking* for employee feedback to help us solve this perennial complaint.

9. _____

10. We hope that by next month's in-service workshop, a team of employees *will have created* a true solution for the good of us all.

10. _____

PART E. Verbs in the following sentences are in italics. You are to provide the tense forms indicated. If you are working collaboratively, teach the others why you favor your particular selections.

Example: He *will use* a new picture book computer.

PAST _____used_____ PRESENT PERFECT _____has used_____

1. She *appreciates* your prompt and courteous service.

PAST *_____ FUTURE *_____

2. The telemarketers *will know* within seconds that a power outage has occurred.

PRESENT _____ PRESENT PERFECT _____

3. I *manage* the New York office of TelComp.

PRESENT PERFECT _____ FUTURE _____

4. The new software upgrade *is* far more efficient than its predecessor.

PAST _____ PRESENT PERFECT _____

5. The enlargement button on the copier *was jammed.*

PAST PERFECT _____ PRESENT PERFECT _____

6. We *have waited* here for five minutes.

FUTURE _____ FUTURE PERFECT _____

PART F. Write four sentences. In each one you are to use the indicated verb.

1. (Present perfect tense of *learn*) *_____

_____

_____

2. (Past tense, emphatic form of *suggest*) _____

_____

_____

3. (Future tense of *build*) _____

_____

_____

4. (Past perfect tense of *leave*) _____

_____

_____

PART G. Work collaboratively to decide whether each underscored word in this paragraph from a business letter is the correct choice or whether a change needs to be made. For those words which need to be changed, supply the correct word in the blanks below.

When the problem first arose, I asked Mr. Verzella to <u>counsel</u> me. He represented the Board of Directors, whose <u>consensus of opinion</u> was that our office couldn't raise enough <u>capitol</u> for the project. In fact, no one on the board seemed <u>confidant</u> that the funds could be raised. Mr. Verzella's <u>advice</u> was to confer with one of his <u>confidants</u> whose job it is to help state politicians with funding. We went to his office on the second floor of the <u>capital</u> building, and during a legislative <u>brake</u>, Mr. Verzella's friend <u>councilled</u> us to speak with one of three investors to raise our needed <u>capitol</u>.

1. *_____   5. _____   8. _____

2. *_____   6. _____   9. _____

3. _____   7. _____   10. _____

4. _____

15

Regular and Irregular Verbs

English, as mentioned in Chapter 2, is made up of words borrowed from a surprisingly large number of foreign languages. The resulting odd mixture poses a serious spelling challenge for all of us; furthermore, this blending gives us several hundred plural forms that require special attention. The lack of pattern, of course, is found also among the many variant forms of verbs, particularly those that are classified as *irregular.* To cope most effectively with this important part of speech, a business communicator should understand the distinction between *regular* and *irregular* verbs.

REGULAR VERBS

The **principal parts** of a verb are the present tense, the past tense, and the past participle, which is used with helping verbs to form verb phrases. The present participle, which always ends in *ing,* is sometimes included. In the phrase *will have written, will* and *have* are helping verbs; *written* is a past participle. We classify as **regular** those verbs that form the past tense and the past participle by the simple addition of *ed* (or *d*).

Present Tense	Past Tense	Past Participle
look	looked	looked
listen	listened	listened
hope	hoped	hoped
walk	walked	walked

Many dictionaries do not show the past tense or the past participle of a regular verb. When such forms are not given, we assume that *ed* should be added to the present tense of the verb to form both the past tense and the past participle.

IRREGULAR VERBS

An **irregular verb** is one that does not form its past tense and its past participle by the addition of *ed*. In most cases, a vowel change is involved. Such verbs represent at least a minor problem for most of us. Their mastery is strictly a matter of memorization. If a verb is irregular, all its principal parts will be shown in the dictionary. For example, the entry for the verb *do* in most good dictionaries begins something like this: DO (DOO) v.t. [DID, DONE, DOING]. Shown in brackets are the past tense, past participle, and present participle.

The entry for *feel* begins in this way: FEEL (FĒL) v.t. [FELT, FEELING]. . . . The inclusion of only two forms within the brackets tells us that *felt* is both the past tense and the past participle of this verb; *feeling* is the present participle.

The following list is not complete, but it does contain most irregular verbs that are reasonably common. The forms shown are those that careful writers consider most acceptable.

Present	Past	Past Participle
be (am, is, are)	was *or* were	been
bear	bore	borne
beat	beat	beaten
begin	began	begun
bid (offer a price)	bid	bid
bite	bit	bitten
blow	blew	blown
bring	brought	brought
build	built	built
burst	burst	burst
choose	chose	chosen
cling	clung	clung
come	came	come
cost	cost	cost
deal	dealt	dealt
dig	dug	dug
drink	drank	drunk
drive	drove	driven
do	did	done
draw	drew	drawn
eat	ate	eaten
fall	fell	fallen
fight	fought	fought
fly	flew	flown
forecast	forecast	forecast
forget	forgot	forgotten
freeze	froze	frozen
get	got	got (gotten)

Present	Past	Past Participle
give	gave	given
go	went	gone
grind	ground	ground
grow	grew	grown
hang (an object)	hung	hung
hide	hid	hidden
hit	hit	hit
hurt	hurt	hurt
know	knew	known
lead	led	led
mean	meant	meant
meet	met	met
pay	paid	paid
put	put	put
quit	quit	quit
ring	rang	rung
rise	rose	risen
run	ran	run
see	saw	seen
seek	sought	sought
set	set	set
shake	shook	shaken
shine	shone (shined)	shone (shined)
shrink	shrank (shrunk)	shrunk
sing	sang	sung
sink	sank	sunk
sit	sat	sat
speak	spoke	spoken
spend	spent	spent
spring	sprang	sprung
sting	stung	stung
strike	struck	struck (stricken)
swear	swore	sworn
swim	swam	swum
swing	swung	swung
take	took	taken
teach	taught	taught
tear	tore	torn
tell	told	told
throw	threw	thrown
wear	wore	worn
win	won	won
wring	wrung	wrung
write	wrote	written

A number of verbs are both regular and irregular, depending upon the meaning intended. In the sentences that follow, the verbs *fly, shine,* and *hang* have been used correctly in the past tense. Note the variant forms.

The pilot *flew* the new plane.   The batter *flied* out to the left fielder.
The sun *shone* brilliantly.   The salesman *shined* his shoes.
I *hung* the picture in my office.   We *hanged* the man for killing his employer.

CAUSE FOR CONFUSION

LIE, LAY   Because the verb *lie* is intransitive, it should never be used with an object. When used in the active voice, the transitive verb *lay* must be followed by an object. Note the definitions of these words:

> *Lie* (v.i.) To put oneself in a reclining position; to rest or recline; to remain in a specified place or condition. Principal parts: LIE LAY LAIN LYING

> *Lay* (v.t.) To place; put; set; deposit; to cause to lie.
> Principal parts: LAY LAID LAID LAYING

These verbs may prove confusing to some of us because the present tense of *lay* is identical with the past tense of the intransitive verb *lie*. A careful study of the definitions and the principal parts of these verbs may be helpful. Note these correct usages:

> He seldom *lies* down during the day. (He seldom *rests* or *reclines.*)
> He *lay* down for several minutes this morning. (He *rested.* Verb *lay* is in past tense.)
> He *was lying* on the couch when the telephone rang.
> The report *is lying* on my desk.
> He *will* not *lie* down during working hours.
> He *has* not *lain* down today.
> He *lays* bricks expertly. (He *places* or *sets* bricks. Transitive verb *lays* is in the present tense.)
> He *laid* the specifications on Mr. Ware's desk.
> He *was laying* bricks at 8 A.M.
> He *will lay* his tools aside.

Executives' Choice

Cite   This verb means "to quote" or "to refer to." Do not confuse it with the noun *site,* which means "a location or plot of ground, usually for building," or the more common *sight,* which refers to vision.

> Mr. Theiss will *cite* several cases from California law.
> We could not find a suitable building *site.*
> Kay Haver's *sight* is failing.

Contact   This verb is too frequently used in place of something more precise, such as *telephone, consult,* or *write to.* (It may be used by one who prefers *not* to be specific.)

> Please *write to* (not *contact*) our Seattle office concerning the new plans.

Could Of   Careful business writers do not use *could of* to mean *could have.*

> With little effort Briggs *could have* (not *could of*) raised the money.

Due To   When this expression appears after a linking verb, *due* functions correctly as an adjective. Careful writers tend to employ *because of,* not *due to,* as a preposition.

> The success of our project was *due to* your fine cooperation.
> Classes were canceled *because of* the storm.
> *Because of* the pending merger, my job is in jeopardy.

Enthuse   This word is too informal for business use.

> We were enthusiastic (not *enthused*) about the compact disc.

Expect   This word, which means "to anticipate" or "to look for as right and proper," should not be used as a substitute for *suppose*, which may be used to mean "believe" or "assume."

> I *suppose* (not *expect*) you had some difficulty in collecting the money.
> We *expect* our employees to dress conservatively.
> I *suppose* (not *expect*) you have spoken with the lender.

Got   The word *got* tends to be overused. Frequently a more businesslike term can be substituted.

> I *received* (not *got*) your message on January 9.
> Paul *was given* (not *got*) a well-deserved promotion.
> The bookkeeper *has* (not *has got*) a new automobile.

Guess   It is not businesslike to substitute this verb for one that is more specific.

> I *believe* (not *guess*) that business will improve in the spring.
> I *am convinced* (not *guess*) that Hayes will cooperate in this matter.

Had Ought   Both *had ought* and *had of* are nonstandard. Use *should* or *had* or *ought* in their places.

> The firm *should* (not *had ought to*) remain open on Friday evening.
> If you *had* (not *had of*) stayed, you would have met our president.

Imply   Careful business writers distinguish between *imply* and *infer.* Only a speaker or writer may *imply* something, for this word means "to suggest or intimate without stating." The listener or reader may *infer* an idea from what was said or written, since this verb means "to conclude or derive from reasoning."

> Mr. Vangalis *implied* that the firm would not purchase a new computer.
> I *infer* from your remark that you had hoped the firm would buy one.

A WORD TIP FROM THE REAL WORLD

Lynda is the head of the sales division of a national automotive supply corporation. She began her sales career as a part-time telemarketer. She has this to say about working on good grammar habits:

I have dealt with people in person and on the phone day in and day out, ever since my first telemarketing phone call. Although my first employers had us use a script for our calls, I was often asked questions by customers that required me to depart from that script. I experienced fewer hangups when I responded carefully to their questions. I used the best language skills I had in order to sound intelligent and worth conversing with. I believe that's at the heart of an excellent sales pitch: having a fine product to talk about and knowing you're worth talking to. It surely has much to do with my success in this business.

_____**WORSHEET 15**_____

REGULAR AND IRREGULAR VERBS

PART A. Put a T or an F in the answer space to indicate whether the statement is true or false.

1. Many dictionaries do not show the principal parts of regular verbs. 1. *_____

2. The *present participle* of a verb always ends in *ing.* 2. *_____

3. A verb is considered *irregular* if it has no past participle. 3. _____

4. *Regular* verbs are those that we use in familiar conversation (*do, go, tell,* etc.). 4. _____

5. Every verb has only one past-tense form. 5. _____

6. If a dictionary shows a past-tense form but no past participle, we may assume that the two are identical. 6. _____

7. It is always correct to use *hanged* as the past tense of *hang.* 7. _____

8. The word *cite* is a verb; the word *site* is a noun. 8. _____

9. The word *lay* may be used in the past tense. 9. _____

10. The transitive verb *lay* means "to rest or recline." 10. _____

PART B. A form of *lie* or *lay* is needed to complete each of the following sentences. Write the *one word* that would make the sentence correct.

Example: The chief engineer _____ the specifications on my desk. laid
_____

1. I saw the affidavit _____ on the filing cabinet. 1. _____

2. When a migraine begins, it is usually best to _____ down immediately. 2. _____

3. This book will _____ the groundwork for several new product lines. 3. *_____

4. When you set up the room for the keynote speaker, _____ several copies of her handout near the lectern. 4. _____

5. When the vice president _____ plans for the new division, she anticipated a considerable increase in revenue. 5. *_____

6. After Simpson had _____ down for awhile, his pain subsided. 6. _____

7. The envelope _____ unopened in the mail slot for three days. 7. _____

8. He believes that his new assistant left the laptop _____ on the seat. 8. _____

9. The workers will be _____ the paving stone on Monday.

9. _____

10. The ceremonial pens are _____ next to the official certificates.

10. _____

PART C. In the space provided, write the correct form of the verb enclosed in parentheses. If you are collaborating, convince one another of the best choice.

Example: The tires on the Mack truck are badly (wear).

_____worn_____

1. Insurance fraud is (rise) in frequency.

1. _____

2. Investigators' efforts are (spend) trying to curb this type of crime.

2. *_____

3. However, the vast majority of fraudulent claim filers have never (see) a courtroom, let alone a jail cell.

3. _____

4. Of course, some egregious scams involving thousands of dollars have been vigorously prosecuted because they have (shake) the public into awareness.

4. *_____

5. But such high-profile cases (tell) only a tiny portion of the $2 billion story of false insurance claims filed in every state every year.

5. _____

6. More than 90 percent of insurance-fraud cases reported to law enforcement are never (fight).

6. _____

7. Murderers, rapists, and muggers have (take) much of the blame for lax prosecution of insurance fraud.

7. _____

8. Most police forces and county attorney groups have been (strike) by waves of violent crime.

8. *_____

9. They have (spend) their limited time and resources on crimes against people, not against insurance companies.

9. _____

10. "Often violent crime has been (give) a higher priority than a faked auto accident or fire loss," says the vice president of the National Insurance Federation.

10. _____

11. Pursuing a criminal case has (begin) to be so difficult that many insurers don't even bother to do so.

11. _____

12. They have (choose) to focus their energies on prevention and civil remedies.

12. _____

13. Other factors have also (contribute) to the halfhearted enforcement of fraud statutes.

13. _____

14. Complaints filed by insurance companies often (sink) into a sea of overlapping law-enforcement jurisdictions.

14. _____

15. Prosecutors say that insurance investigators over the years (do) a poor job of gathering evidence, and as a result, that evidence has not stood up in criminal court.

15. _____

16. Police, attorneys, and insurance executives have (build) consensus on one thing.

16. _____

17. In places where insurance fraud was aggressively, consistently prosecuted, fraud rates (fall) dramatically, catching con artists and casual claim-padders alike.

17. _____

18. Thousands of people (choose) to commit insurance fraud every day in America.

18. _____

19. They have exaggerated injuries in order to collect disability benefits, billed for phantom medical procedures, (dump) their cars in lakes, or faked their own deaths.

19. _____

20. All those thefts (cost) a staggering *$85.3* billion in the United States in one year.

20. _____

21. Every cent was (pass) on to businesses, government, and individuals in the form of higher premiums, taxes, and increases in the cost of goods and services.

21. _____

22. Determined to stop the hemorrhaging, insurance companies have (pay) more to improve their investigative efforts.

22. _____

23. "However, the justice system just hasn't (deal) with property crimes," says prosecutor James Wilbur.

23. _____

24. Detectives in most police departments have (fall) prey to the same realities.

24. _____

25. Even when the property-crimes detectives believe that there is probable cause to charge a person with a crime, county assistant attorneys (draw) the case to a close, citing a lack of conclusive evidence.

25. _____

PART D. Find the nine word choice errors in this sample memo paragraph and correct them in the blanks below.

This fall our company budget remains tight due to slim profits. The finance office sites several divisions which could of improved our standing this year but which were unable to do so. As a result, plans for opening an office on the Plainsview cite have been postponed until after the first of the year, when the site of year-end profits typically appears on our balance sheet. We don't mean to infer that we can relax our efforts as the year draws to a close; rather, every one of us had ought to make sure that all account materials are completed within two hours of receiving them, that every one of us contact our customers regularly, and that we all remain enthused and hopeful about our great products.

1. _____ **4.** _____ **7.** _____

2. _____ **5.** _____ **8.** _____

3. _____ **6.** _____ **9.** _____

PART E. Supply the past tense and the past participle for each of these verbs. Use your dictionary when necessary.

Present Tense	Past Tense	Past Participle
1. dig	*_____	*_____
2. freeze	*_____	*_____
3. write	_____	_____
4. swim	*_____	*_____
5. speak	_____	_____
6. teach	_____	_____
7. grow	_____	_____
8. go	_____	_____
9. sink	_____	_____
10. swear	_____	_____

PART F. Write four sentences as indicated.

1. (Use the past participle of the verb *ban*.) *_____

_____

2. (Use the verb *catch* in the past tense.) _____

_____

3. (Use the present participle of the verb *try*.) _____

_____

4. (Use the past participle of the verb *give*.) _____

_____

FOR CLASS DISCUSSION

(if time permits)

A four-year-old friend of mine has a habit of using constructions such as these: *He throwed me the ball. She teached me how to swim. I buyed some candy at the store.*

How would you account for the fact that young children tend to use such strange-sounding verbs? Look again at the irregular verbs listed in Chapter 15 and choose five that you think are especially troublesome for adults. Give your reason for each choice.

Quiz   (Chapters 12 through 15)

NAME _____   DATE _____

DIRECTIONS

Your instructor may ask you to examine any four of the sentences that follow. For each sentence chosen, you are to write the rule violated by the word in italics. Express the rule in your own way, but spell all words correctly. In the parentheses provided, write the correct form of the italicized word. If you are collaborating, divide the sentences among your group members and teach one another the rules.

1. Neither of your candidates *appear* to be qualified.
2. The members who most deserve recognition are Mr. Blair and *her*.
3. The new medical plan will not help Wilkens and *I*.
4. The air smells *pleasantly* because of the incense.
5. She said that San Diego *was* in the southern part of this state.
6. I turned the radio on, but the program already *ended.*
7. By the time you see him, Dwight already *will graduate.*
8. If you *lay* on one of our orthopedic mattresses, you will want to buy it.
9. Don turned pale after he had *drank* six glasses of punch.
10. Mr. Tasby would disagree with you if he *was* here now.
11. Neither Marge nor Paula *seem* pleased with the idea.
12. In his speech Mark *inferred* that he enjoys walking.

Sentence No. _____ (_____) Rule: _____
_____
_____
_____

Sentence No. _____ (_____) Rule: _____
_____
_____
_____

Sentence No. _____ (_____) Rule: _____
_____
_____
_____

Sentence No. _____ (_____) Rule: _____
_____
_____
_____

KEEPING LATIN ALIVE

Business writers occasionally make use of abbreviations borrowed from Latin. The five that are italicized in the following sentences are extremely common.

We invited O'Neil, Gretsky, Bierbaum, *et al.* (The abbreviation *et al* generally means *et alii,* Latin for "and others.")

He ignored our most important financial statement, *i.e.,* the balance sheet. (The Latin words *id est* mean "that is.")

Several pieces of office equipment should be replaced, *e.g.,* this old Underwood typewriter. (The Latin words *exempli gratia* mean "for example.")

The supplies (memo pads, binders, blank tapes, *etc.*) arrived this morning. (The Latin words *et cetera* mean "and so forth.")

At the banquet we will honor three outstanding employees, *viz.,* Callahan, Lozano, and Nordhoff. (Strange though it may seem, the abbreviation stands for *videlicet,* a Latin word meaning "that is; namely.")

CHAPTER

16

Review of Pronouns and Verbs

■ POINT TO PONDER ➤

Because pronouns and verbs have variant forms they challenge *every* English speaker.

B ecause Chapters 9 through 15 are concerned with pronouns and verbs, they are especially important to us. Anyone who can master the principles and rules presented in that portion of the text should have little difficulty with the chapters that follow. A significant percentage of the grammatical errors that people make involve the misuse of pronouns and verbs.

HIGHLIGHTS

The preceding seven chapters contain more rules and recommendations than we can hope to review here. There are, however, a number of items that should be mentioned again because they have significant practical value for the business communicator.

1. The pronouns *I, we, he, she,* and *they* are in the nominative case and should never be used as objects of verbs or prepositions.
2. The pronouns *me, us, him, her,* and *them* are in the objective case and should never be used as subjects or subject complements.
3. Compound elements often prove to be confusing. In a sentence such as *Sacco and (I, me) will help you,* the correct pronoun may become obvious if part of the compound element is ignored *(I will help you).*
4. Pronouns in the possessive case *(its, hers, ours, theirs, yours,* etc.) do not take apostrophes.
5. A compound personal pronoun such as *myself* should not be used if a shorter pronoun such as *I* or *me* could be used smoothly.

6. These are singular subjects: *each person, every man and woman, many a girl, neither he nor I, either Lasky or Baumholz.*

7. Expressions that begin with *rather than, as well as, in addition to,* or *together with* should be ignored when one attempts to determine whether a subject is singular or plural.

8. When used as subjects, the following pronouns take singular verbs: *anyone, anybody, either, everybody, neither, one, someone.*

9. An amount (money, distance, time, etc.) is singular when it is expressed as a single unit. Example: Twenty years *is* a long time.

10. Ideas that are contrary to fact should be expressed in the subjunctive mood. Example: If she *were* here, she would agree with us.

11. Transitive verbs in the active voice take objects; intransitive verbs *do not* take objects. Linking verbs, which are intransitive, are followed by subject complements.

12. Business writers generally favor active-voice verbs, which tend to be more direct and more forceful than passive-voice verbs.

13. These are the principal parts of a verb: present tense, past tense, past participle, and present participle. Examples: *see, saw, seen, seeing.*

14. The past participle of a verb is always used with one or more helping verbs, as in these verb phrases: have *seen,* will have *gone,* has *known.*

15. The word *lie,* which means *to rest or recline,* is often confused with *lay,* which means *to place or put.*

FREQUENTLY MADE ERRORS

Each of the numbered sentences that follow would be considered unacceptable by the average business executive. Before reading the explanation that follows each sentence, attempt to determine to your own satisfaction the precise error that was made. If you have been conscientious in your study of these chapters, the errors should be obvious to you.

1. The bookkeeper thought that you and him would get the same answer.

In your reading of the foregoing sentence, did you detect an error? The pronoun *him,* as you know, must always be used in the objective case. Because the pronouns in this sentence serve as subjects of the verb *would get,* the nominative-case forms *you* and *he* should have been employed. Did you recognize the dependent (noun) clause that serves as the object of *thought?*

2. Mr. Symes discussed the problem with Ted and I.

In this sentence the pronoun *I,* which is nominative, has been used, along with the noun *Ted,* as an object of the preposition *with.* Because all objects are in the objective case, the pronoun *me* should have been utilized.

3. Neither Ruth nor Diana expressed their opinions.

In this sentence the plural pronoun *their* has been used to refer to a singular antecedent. You may recall that a subject is considered singular if, as in our sentence, it contains *or* or *nor* followed by a singular noun or pronoun. The expression *their opinions* should be changed to *her opinion.* You might compare our sentence with this one: *Neither Ruth nor her friends expressed their opinions.*

4. Mr. Belikoff, as well as his two partners, have built their homes in the suburbs.

In this sentence the simple subject is Mr. Belikoff, and it is singular even though the parenthetical expression that follows it contains the plural noun *partners*. When looking for a simple subject, don't forget to ignore expressions that begin with *as well as, in addition to, together with,* and similar intervening words. The sentence in question should end with these words: *has built his home in the suburbs.*

5. Someone left their notebook on my desk.

In this sentence a plural pronoun *(their)* has a singular antecedent *(someone)*. The word *their*, of course, should be changed to *his or her.* Many writers would prefer this wording: *Someone left a notebook on my desk.*

6. Who did you telephone just now?

You should have no difficulty in recognizing *did telephone* as the verb in this sentence. You can find its subject, *you,* by asking the question *Who did telephone?* Because *you* is the subject, the first word in the sentence must serve as the direct object of the verb. Its function as an object is clear when you reword the sentence in this way: *You did telephone whom just now.* Because *whom,* not *who,* is in the objective case, it should be employed as the object.

7. Barok & Sons, Inc., have gone out of business.

Because the subject of this sentence (Barok & Sons, Inc.) is the name of one company, it is singular and should be used with a singular verb. The word *have,* therefore, should be changed to *has.*

8. If Grant was here now, he would object to your plan.

The first clause of this sentence refers to an idea that is clearly contrary to fact; that is, Grant is obviously not here. When expressing such ideas, use *were,* the sign of the subjunctive mood, with all subjects. The sentence should begin with these words: *If Grant were here now.*

9. What did you say your son's name was?

Because the verb form *did say* is in the past tense, we may be tempted to use the past-tense form of any other verb in the sentence. We should, however, use the present tense to express an idea that continues to be true. Because the son's name has not changed, the verb *was* (past tense) should be changed to *is* (present tense).

10. By 11 P.M. last night we counted all the votes.

Because the votes were counted before a specified past time (11 P.M.), the past perfect tense *(had counted)* should have been used in this sentence.

11. The only unwelcome guests were his competitors, Marion and me.

The word *competitors,* which follows a linking verb *(were)* and completes the meaning of the subject, is a subject complement. Because it is nominative, the appositives that follow it *(Marion* and *I)* must also be nominative.

12. Their annual report is considerably more elaborate than our's.

The mistake made in this sentence should be easy to detect. Personal pronouns are not written with apostrophes; therefore, the final word should be spelled *ours*.

13. The final paragraph of the report referred to you and myself.

A compound personal pronoun, such as *myself,* should be used only if the shorter form of the pronoun would sound awkward. Because the sentence in question does not need a compound pronoun to *reflect* or to *intensify,* it should be ended smoothly with *you* and *me*.

14. Every contractor involved has their own tools.

Did you react negatively to the use of *their* in this sentence? Because the word *Every* makes our subject singular, we must refer to it with a singular pronoun. The sentence, therefore, should end with *his or her own tools* or *his own tools.*

15. They should increase our social security payments.

The only questionable word in this sentence is the pronoun *They*. Too often it is used in this kind of construction with no antecedent whatsoever. A more acceptable subject would be *Congress.*

Executives' Choice

Before you begin the worksheet that follows, you should review briefly the preceding seven chapters. Look again at the sections headed "Executives' Choice" and note the precise meanings of easily confused words such as *angry* and *mad, accept* and *except, affect* and *effect, apprise* and *appraise.* Note again that these chapters contain a number of expressions that careful business writers should avoid using. Here are several:

adopt the text to my use	my loyal confident
all together unnecessary	amount of parcels
words of advise	raise the capitol needed
consensus of opinion	council for the defense
this data	a business deal
either of the three	enthused about the program
got your telegram	take a short brake
a half a day's pay	stocks, bonds, and etc.
bank on this company	being that/as he knows
had ought to go now	an every day occurrence
the forth of June	gave his corporation

REVIEW CHART

concept	Ch. ____ page ____	first critical point to remember	example	second critical point to remember	example
nominative case pronouns					
objective case pronouns					
compound personal pronouns					
determining whether subjects are singular or plural		always singular: always plural:		ignore these:	
verbs in the subjunctive mood					
transitive and intransitive verbs					
active and passive voice					
principal parts of verbs					

| Back | Forward | Home | Reload | Images | Open |

```
CIGN Search Engine for Windows 97
"The best engine you can get for the money!" CyberWeekly

Every web user needs to check out this great offer, get
out their MasterCard or Visa number, and order today.
```

| order now | | no thanks |

_____WORKSHEET 16_____

REVIEW OF PRONOUNS AND VERBS

PART A. In the answer space write the personal pronoun that has been described.

Example: Singular pronoun in first person, nominative case _____I_____

1. Plural pronoun in first person, nominative case **1.** *_____

2. Plural pronoun in third person, objective case **2.** _____

3. Singular pronoun in third person, objective case, masculine gender **3.** _____

4. Singular pronoun in third person, nominative case, feminine gender **4.** _____

5. Singular pronoun in third person, possessive case, neuter gender **5.** _____

PART B. Underscore the verb; then write active (A) or passive (P) to indicate its voice. If you are collaborating, teach one another why you make the selections you do.

Example: This company manufactures a variety of steel products. _____A_____

1. We have purchased a new HJ Model 600 copier, fax, scanner, and printer. **1.** _____

2. The peripheral phone connector was sold to us as well. **2.** *_____

3. Its capabilities were shown to us in an on-site sales demonstration. **3.** _____

4. The Model 600 has been designed to give high quality scanning results. **4.** _____

5. Its copying speed has been timed at 2 seconds per page. **5.** _____

6. We have put this machine to the test on several occasions. **6.** *_____

7. It has been found to be flawless in its performance. **7.** _____

8. Legible faxes and photocopies are delivered daily. **8.** _____

9. Printing can be done in color or black and white with the same cartridge. **9.** _____

10. We can recommend the Model 600 to anyone. **10.** _____

PART C. Indicate whether the italicized verb is intransitive (I) or transitive (T) by writing the appropriate letter.

Example: On Monday Mr. Phillips *will post* the vacation schedule. _____T_____

1. When job hunting, always *give* some thought to past employment.   1. _____

2. You *should think* about reasons for previous positive and negative experiences.   2. *_____

3. You *must consider* your own preferences.   3. _____

4. Your resume *can include* a section on your preferred work environment.   4. _____

5. You *can* also *talk* about environment during an interview.   5. _____

6. Think about whether you *work* best alone or on a team.   6. _____

7. Does your creativity *rise* or *sink* when using computers?   7. _____

8. *Discover* and *describe* your best performances in previous work.   8. _____

9. Then you *can make* a good case for your best environment.   9. *_____

10. You *will be* the choice of many employers if you know yourself.   10. _____

PART D. Write the *letter* preceding the sentence that would be most acceptable in a business communication. Pay particular attention to the words in italics. Convince your fellow collaborators why your suggestion is a better alternative.

1. (A) We were *appraised* that the boiler had *burst.*
   (B) We were *apprised* that the boiler had *burst.*
   (C) We were *appraised* that the boiler had *bursted.*   1. *_____

2. (A) We are *allowed* to take a short *brake.*
   (B) We are *aloud* to take a short *break.*
   (C) We are *allowed* to take a short *break.*   2. _____

3. (A) I am *confident* that the data *are* accurate.
   (B) I am *confident* that the data *is* accurate.
   (C) I am *confidant* that the data *is* accurate.   3. _____

4. (A) I *bet* you know where the Board of Directors *meet.*
   (B) I *suppose* you know where the Board of Directors *meet.*
   (C) I *suppose* you know where the Board of Directors *meets.*   4. _____

5. (A) His *counsel* gave him some strange *advise.*
   (B) His *counsel* gave him some strange *advice.*
   (C) His *council* gave him some strange *advise.*   5. _____

6. (A) About a third of the men *was angry with* the foreman.
   (B) About a third of the men *were mad at* the foreman.
   (C) About a third of the men *were angry with* the foreman.   6. _____

7. (A) The group *meets* at 4 P.M. *due to* work schedules.
   (B) The group *meets* at 4 P.M. *because of* work schedules.
   (C) The group *meet* at 4 P.M. *because of* work schedules.   7. _____

8. (A) Kuhn *implied* that he would *accept* my revised report.
   (B) Kuhn *implied* that he would *except* my revised report.
   (C) Kuhn *inferred* that he would *accept* my revised report.   8. _____

9. (A) You *should of payed* this bill by the 10th of May.
   (B) You *should have paid* this bill by the 10th of May.
   (C) You *should have payed* this bill by the 10th of May.   9. _____

10. (A) A *half* page of notes was *hidden* behind the computer.
    (B) A *half a* page of notes was *hidden* behind the computer.
    (C) A *half a* page of notes was *hid* behind the computer.   10. _____

PART E.   Indicate the preferred choice by writing the appropriate *letter.*

1. Location, low rental rates, and architecture (A) *are,* (B) *is* what
   fuels growth in the warehouse district.   1. *_____

2. The effort to renew many of the historic buildings (A) *are,* (B) *is*
   not new.   2. *_____

3. Building owners have been redeveloping (A) *his,* (B) *their*
   properties for twenty years.   3. _____

4. But projects that have lagged for years have now (A) *begun,*
   (B) *began* to hasten their pace.   4. _____

5. The push to redevelop this area started in 1974 when (A) *Winters
   and I,* (B) *Winters and me* began the remodeling of Pangrove
   Square.   5. _____

6. Renovation of an old railroad depot and several warehouses
   (A) *were,* (B) *was* the catalyst for widespread redevelopment.   6. _____

7. Large-scale redevelopment, however, has been gradual,
   especially for (A) *Winters and I,* (B) *Winters and me.*   7. _____

8. Of 150 buildings in the 30-block warehouse district, only about
   20 have been converted to multi-tenant office (A) *cites,* (B) *sights,*
   (C) *sites.*   8. _____

9. But now, (A) *except,* (B) *accept* in certain blocks, redevelopment
   is on the rise.   9. _____

10. Artists and arts-related tenants (A) *who,* (B) *whom* once
    populated the small, inexpensive studios and lofts have given
    way to a new type of tenant.   10. _____

11. This new group of tenants (A) *are,* (B) *is* willing to pay higher
    rates.   11. _____

12. Software, legal, and architectural firms are the ones (A) *Winters
    and I,* (B) *Winters and me* predict will take over the district.   12. _____

13. NJP, a legal consulting firm, (A) *apprised,* (B) *appraised* space
    in the warehouse district 13 years ago.   13. _____

14. Jane Conroy, NJP's director, says no one but (A) *she,* (B) *her*
    originally wanted to move there.   14. _____

15. She made a case to colleagues (A) *who,* (B) *whom* she'd
    worked with for years.   15. _____

16. She told them that she wished the firm (A) *were,* (B) *was*
    wealthy enough to get center city office space.   16. _____

17. But she knew that neither the Campbell Building nor McDonald Towers (A) *was,* (B) *were* affordable.

17. _____

18. She then asked everyone to express (A) *their,* (B) *an* opinion about moving.

18. _____

19. The number of persons remaining negative about the move (A) *were,* (B) *was* small.

19. *_____

20. The group members expressed some conflicting ideas, however, as (A) *they,* (B) *it* met.

20. _____

21. In the end, Jane offered testimony from a man (A) *who,* (B) *whom* the Warehouse District Council had sent to their meeting.

21. _____

22. This man made such a compelling argument that not one man or woman present (A) *was,* (B) *were* able to resist being persuaded.

22. _____

23. He argued that the firm would be able to move into larger office space in the building as (A) *they,* (B) *it* grew.

23. _____

24. Currently, the firm occupies an entire floor in Pangrove Square, something none of them would have (A) *forecasted,* (B) *forecast.*

24. _____

25. Many a client, when asked (A) *his or her,* (B) *their* opinion, praises the space.

25. _____

26. "We love it here. Our offices have the desire (A) *affect,* (B) *effect,*" Conroy says.

26. _____

27. "If I (A) *was,* (B) *were* working in the old place, I would be hopelessly cramped."

27. *_____

28. Every one of the converted buildings in the district (A) *are,* (B) *is* nearly full.

28. _____

29. Realtors recommend that space (A) *be,* (B) *ought to be* reserved as soon as it becomes available.

29. _____

30. "Our $3,000 (for reserving a future suite) (A) *has,* (B) *have been* well spent," says Ken Dougherty of KRM Designs.

30. _____

31. "If either the third floor or the plaza level (A) *becomes,* (B) *become* available, I'll be thrilled."

31. _____

32. Building owners could (A) *of,* (B) *have* predicted this trend by looking at other cities.

32. _____

33. Many cities have seen conversion of a great (A) *amount,* (B) *number* of sagging derelict blocks into vital commercial space.

33. _____

34. This historic district in many cities (A) *are,* (B) *is* sandwiched between the downtown business core and a river or another old transportation route.

34. _____

35. Most communities (A) *accept,* (B) *except* that when a district is revitalized, activity thrives on both ends.

35. _____

36. It can be said that a booming warehouse district is a gift to (A) *it's,* (B) *its* neighbors.

36. _____

PART F. Look through this actual interoffice memo and find the errors in word choice. Underscore ten problems and substitute better words in the blanks below the memo.

To: All employees

From: Michelle Yarr, President of Stores

Date: October 1

Subject: Annual Community Charity Fund Drive

I am enthused about coming to you once again to consider contributing to our annual Community Charity Fund. As you know, our store has been a leader in past years among local businesses who participate in the drive. Neither our main store nor our many smaller outlets has any intention of being outdone by any of our competitors. So Janet Vitek of the marketing office, this year's chairperson for charity, suggests the following actions:

Everyone considers raising their pledge above last year's amount.

Everyone turns in a new pledge or contribution before November 1.

The contributions and pledges are tallied weekly and a comparison with our competitor stores are posted at First National Bank downtown each Friday.

After being tallied, each pledge or contribution is placed into the glass fishbowl at the main office.

On November 1, a drawing is held at the main office.

The contribution or pledge drawn out of the fishbowl gets a $100 shopping spree at any of our stores or outlets.

The competitor store with the highest giving level is featured on a billboard downtown paid for by the other stores.

Our contributions to the Community Charity Fund are quite important. Of course, each employee can make contributions to whoever they choose, but I am asking that we all try to make this year's charity campaign a big success. We can do more together than anyone of us can do alone, and when we see our store's name on that downtown billboard, each of us will feel a great deal of pride in our heart that we have given our best effort for our community.

_____   _____   _____

_____   _____   _____

_____   _____   _____

_____

PART G. Expand each of the following subjects into a complete sentence. What you add, in each instance, should begin with either *is* or *are.*

Example: Several of his colleagues   _are willing to work on Saturday._

One of my books   _is missing._

1. Each of my colleagues _____

2. Neither my partner nor my spouse _____

3. Both of the delivery services _____

4. Some of the money _____

5. Every one of our competitors _____

6. Neither of the buildings _____

7. Either Old Main or the two sports arenas _____

8. Several or our books _____

9. No one in our office _____

10. Neither the teamsters nor the executive director _____

———— FOR CLASS DISCUSSION ————

(if time permits)

Do you feel that grammatical errors are made often because people fail to recognize *antecedents* and *simple subjects?* How important are the terms themselves? Can the person who pays no attention to either of those elements communicate with genuine confidence? Give reasons for your answers.

CHAPTER 17

Verbals

■■ **POINT TO PONDER**

Verb forms occasionally pose as other parts of speech.

A verbal is a verb form used as a noun, an adjective, or an adverb. The English language has three verbals: the infinitive, the gerund, and the participle. Although all three are mentioned briefly in other parts of this text, a complete discussion of their uses and peculiarities is presented in this chapter.

THE INFINITIVE

Many authorities consider the **infinitive** to be the most basic form of a verb. We frequently refer to a verb by its infinitive form: *to be, to study, to give, to understand.* The word *to* is generally present, although it may be omitted in certain constructions; for example, *He helped me choose a secretary* or *Lomax let me use his drill.* The infinitive is more versatile than either of the other verbals. You have undoubtedly employed infinitives in several ways:

> As a subject (*To fail* is not a calamity.)
> As an object (Mary was asked *to help.*)
> As a modifier of a noun (Now is the time *to go.*)
> As a modifier of an adjective (Markquart is difficult *to please.*)

The infinitive, like the gerund and the participle, may take objects, complements, and modifiers. Its use is easily controlled by most writers and speakers. These two suggestions, however, may prove helpful:

1. Avoid awkward split infinitives. The placing of one or more words between *to* and the verb form will frequently result in an awkward construction.

DON'T USE: I want you *to, as quickly as possible, finish* this project.
     USE: I want you *to finish* this project *as quickly as possible.*
DON'T USE: No one in the room was able *to perfectly complete* the test.
     USE: No one in the room was able *to complete* the test *perfectly.*

Many of our finest writers occasionally split an infinitive if the resulting construction is sufficiently smooth. More often than not, however, they avoid the use of split infinitives.

2. Use the present infinitive (*to do, to say, to go,* etc.) except on those rare occasions when the action expressed by the infinitive is prior to that of the governing verb. On those occasions the perfect infinitive (*to have done, to have said, to have gone,* etc.) should be employed. Both the present and the perfect infinitive may be used in the passive voice.

PRESENT TENSE: to tell, to be told
PERFECT TENSE: to have told, to have been told

Some people like *to write* letters. (Present infinitive, active voice)

The file is known *to be corrupted.* (Present infinitive, passive voice)

Proxmire is said *to have stolen* from the firm. (The perfect infinitive is used because the stealing preceded the action of the main verb.)

The file is known *to have been corrupted* on the disk. (Note the use of the perfect infinitive in the passive voice. The file is known *now* to have been corrupted *earlier.*)

THE GERUND

The **gerund** was defined in Chapter 7 as a verb form that ends in *ing* and functions as a noun. Because it is a verbal *noun,* it may be used as a subject, an object, or a complement. Unlike other nouns, however, it may take an object. The gerund gives us no difficulty in sentences such as these:

Writing can become tiresome. (Gerund is used as subject.)

The new accountant is slow in his *thinking.* (Gerund is used as object of preposition.)

Edmond's favorite pastime is *hiking.* (Gerund is used as subject complement.)

Gerund phrases, which are frequently misplaced in sentences, will be discussed later in this chapter. In our day-to-day use of gerunds we should be especially careful to observe this rule: Make certain that a noun or pronoun used to modify a gerund is in the possessive case. The possessive-case form, of course, does the work of an adjective.

DON'T USE: I heard about *Graham* getting the order.
     USE: I heard about *Graham's* getting the order (The word *getting* is a gerund because it is the *ing* form of the verb *get* and it serves as the object of the preposition *about;* thus it functions as a *noun.* The noun *order,* you will note, serves as the object of the gerund.)

DON'T USE: We were not aware of *him* leaving the firm.
      USE: We were not aware of *his* leaving the firm.
DON'T USE: Did *Clyde* winning the contest surprise you?
      USE: Did *Clyde's* winning the contest surprise you? (The surprise was not *Clyde;* it was *his winning.*)

As you study the foregoing sentences, observe that in each of the preferred versions a noun or pronoun in the *possessive case* has been used to modify a gerund. Remember that a gerund, which itself may take an object, will always serve as a subject, an object, or a complement.

THE PARTICIPLE

As used here, the term **participle** refers to a verb form that functions as an adjective. In the sentence *The boy waiting by the door is my son, waiting* is a participle. It is a form of the verb *to wait,* and it is used here to modify the noun *boy.* If the sentence read *The waiting boy is my son, waiting* would be readily recognized as an adjective. The participle may appear in any of several forms:

	Present	*Past*	*Perfect*
Active	finding	found	having found
Passive	being found	found	having been found

Dangling participial phrases will be discussed in the following section of this chapter. Before you consider such phrases, you will want to master these two basic rules:

1. Use the present participle if the action expressed is concurrent with the action of the main verb. Use the past participle or the perfect participle, whichever is suitable, if the action expressed is prior to the action of the main verb.

    Reading rapidly, Haynes made excellent progress.
    Hoping for a promotion, Colburne accepted every difficult assignment.
    The report *read* by Haynes has 50 pages. (Note the use of the *past participle* to indicate a completed action.)
    Having worked rapidly for an hour, Haynes looked exhausted. (Perfect participle is used to express action prior to that of the main verb.)
    Having failed to get the promotion, Colburne was bitter. (*First,* he failed; *then,* he was bitter.)

2. Avoid the awkward use of absolute phrases. An absolute phrase consists of a noun or pronoun and a participle. It is used to modify the predicate of a sentence.

DON'T USE: *Wednesday being a holiday,* we were not required to work.
      USE: *Because Wednesday was a holiday,* we were not required to work.

DANGLING VERBAL PHRASES

Verbals (infinitives, gerunds, and participles) appear frequently in phrases that function as modifiers, and such phrases are often used to introduce sentences. It is not important that you be able to distinguish an infinitive phrase from a gerund phrase or a participial phrase. It is important, however, that you place a verbal phrase properly when you use it in a sentence. If a phrase of this type relates to another word in the sentence, it should be placed so that its relation to that word is perfectly clear. If it is not so placed, it is said to dangle. Some grammarians consider a verbal phrase to be *misplaced* if it is too far removed from the word(s) to which it relates and to be *dangling* if it relates to no other word in the sentence. Most modern handbooks, however, do not make that distinction.

If a sentence begins with *Having left Seattle in March,* the next word(s) should tell *who* left Seattle in March. If a sentence begins with *In correcting the mistake,* the next word(s) should tell *who* corrected the mistake. Following are ten sentences that begin with verbal phrases. Note that in each acceptable version the introductory phrase is followed immediately by the word to which it is related (in italics).

CONFUSING:	Reading very rapidly, the manuscript took only 45 minutes.
LOGICAL:	Reading very rapidly, *she* finished the manuscript in only 45 minutes.
CONFUSING:	Having retired early, the years ahead looked bright.
LOGICAL:	Having retired early, *Sam* looked forward to the years ahead.
CONFUSING:	By using this new technique, ten minutes will be saved.
LOGICAL:	By using this new technique, *you* will save ten minutes.
CONFUSING:	While writing the letter, her telephone rang four times.
LOGICAL:	While writing the letter, *Lois* received four telephone calls.
CONFUSING:	To determine its value, the property was appraised.
LOGICAL:	To determine its value, *we* appraised the property. (Although the infinitive phrase modifies *appraised,* it relates to the pronoun *we,* which some grammarians would refer to as its subject.)

It is possible, of course, for a verbal phrase to be misplaced at the end of a sentence. It is also possible for an elliptical phrase or clause (one from which words have been omitted) to be placed illogically at the beginning of a sentence. Don't be concerned with terminology. Simply observe the logical placement of parts in all such sentences.

CONFUSING:	The witness hesitated before answering the attorney, looking somewhat bewildered.
LOGICAL:	The witness, looking somewhat bewildered, hesitated before answering the attorney.
CONFUSING:	While president of the firm, I am sure that Moretti made many important decisions.
LOGICAL:	While president of the firm, Moretti undoubtedly made many important decisions.

Because *you* (understood) is the subject of a command or request, verbal phrases are easily controlled in grammatical constructions such as these: *To save time, use the new computer. In addressing Mr. Pulaski, don't mispronounce his name.*

A WORD ABOUT PUNCTUATION

An introductory verbal phrase that functions as a modifier is generally considered nonrestrictive and should, therefore, be followed by a comma.

To succeed, a person must work hard.

By telling the truth, he made a fine impression.

Having told his story, he left the room.

Use commas to set off a **nonrestrictive** phrase within a sentence. If a phrase is needed to identify the word it modifies, it is **restrictive** and should *not* be set off. A nonrestrictive phrase is not necessary to the meaning of the main clause. Although it does provide additional information, it could be omitted. Observe the punctuation of these sentences:

RESTRICTIVE PHRASES: The person *to put in charge* is Ken Akens.
         The woman *talking on the telephone* is Ms. Tulley.
         His reason *for being late* is a poor one.
         (Because the italicized phrases in these first three sentences are restrictive, no commas have been used.)

NONRESTRICTIVE PHRASES: The bookkeeper, *to expedite her work,* used a calculator.
         Bigelow, *noting my look of concern,* said nothing.
         Mr. Coffey, *in making his selection,* seemed somewhat confused.

Read each of the foregoing sentences *without* the italicized phrase. Note the essential nature of the three restrictive phrases; observe that they are needed to identify the nouns they modify. The nonrestrictive phrases, although they are informative, could be omitted without seriously changing the meaning of the main clauses.

VERBAL REVIEW CHART

verbal	how it looks	it can be used as
infinitive My doctor advises me **to swim** ten laps every day.	*to + verb* (rarely, the *to* can be omitted) to swim to walk	a subject an object a modifier of a noun a modifier of an adjective
gerund Perez really loves **working** on his portfolio.	*verb + ing* ending working joking	a noun: that is, as an object a complement
participle The **broken** bicycle lay on the **cracked** pavement.	*verb* + any standard ending such as *ing, ed, en,* and so on whining broken cracked	an adjective: that is, placed near the noun or pronoun it modifies, or following a linking verb as a complement

10. If you were (to learn, to have learned) from anyone in that department during the next year, I would suggest learning from Jenkins.

10. _____

PART C. In the space provided, write the correct form of the infinitive. Do not use any progressive forms.

Example: The laboratory technician seems (leave).

to have left
_____

1. Desmond tried (gain) access to my file.

1. * _____

2. The chairman wants (choose) his own successor.

2. _____

3. The idea is believed (originate) with the early Romans.

3. * _____

4. Our financial analyst is said (be) a child prodigy.

4. _____

5. Our marketing director is known (vote) in favor of a strike in 1990.

5. _____

PART D. Underscore an infinitive in each of these ten sentences; then write the letter that indicates the correct response.

    A. This sentence contains no errors.
    B. This sentence has an awkward split infinitive.

Example: You will want to, of course, read every clause carefully.

B
_____

1. When you plan your trip to the Baltimore Sales Conference, be sure to visit our travel desk.

1. * _____

2. This service was set up to more effectively plan business travel.

2. * _____

3. Agents there can help you to take advantage of special rates.

3. _____

4. They are able to very quickly contact airline agents and find low fares.

4. _____

5. In the long run, to visit the travel desk means saving money for the firm.

5. * _____

6. If it is possible for you to just as conveniently make travel arrangements about a month in advance of your trip, everyone will save even more money.

6. _____

7. No one is able to make sense out of advance purchase requirements better than the two agents at our travel desk.

7. _____

8. They will ask for your dates, and you will tell them where you need to go.

8. _____

9. They will find a way for you to, simply and comfortably, arrive at your destination.

9. _____

10. Be sure to keep them updated, especially if your travel plans change.

10. _____

PART E. Each of the following sentences either begins or ends with a verbal phrase (in italics). In the answer space write A or B to indicate whether the sentence is properly constructed. If you are collaborating, persuade one another of your answer using chapter ideas.

    A. This sentence has a *misplaced* or a *dangling* verbal phrase.
    B. This sentence is properly constructed.

1. *Looking for a bargain,* some people may overlook the stability of an insurance company.

1. * _____

2. *To get the most for your money,* premiums and policies should be
closely compared.

2. * _____

3. *In purchasing medical insurance,* a big mistake is to ignore
deductible features.

3. _____

4. There are several important exclusions *listed on page 4,* as I
explained yesterday.

4. _____

5. *In computing the premium,* the actuary made a minor error
yesterday.

5. _____

6. *To avoid any undue risk,* Mr. Janick bought a comprehensive
policy.

6. _____

7. *Working quickly,* we completed the paperwork in only a few
minutes.

7. _____

8. *Speaking very rapidly,* the agent insisted that I make an immediate
decision.

8. _____

9. *To satisfy myself,* I compared three insurance programs.

9. _____

10. *Before signing a contract,* every clause should be read carefully.

10. _____

11. *Realizing that I was not ready to make a decision,* the unsigned
contract simply lay on my desk as the agent left.

11. _____

12. *After leaving my office,* the agent stopped to talk with Billingham.

12. _____

13. *Talking with me last week,* I heard Billingham say that she was
looking for additional insurance.

13. _____

14. All providers today carry plans, as any agent can tell you, *designed
for single parents.*

14. _____

15. *In selecting a plan to fill her needs,* she should consider both costs
and benefits.

15. _____

PART F. Rewrite each of the following sentences in a more acceptable way. Use the
verbal phrase given, but supply a logical subject so that the phrase does not
dangle. Add or delete words as necessary. If you are collaborating, come to an
agreement about this editing.

1. To do the job properly, a power drill should be used.

* _____

_____

2. Having used this RCA camcorder, it seems to me that it would be perfect for your line
of work.

_____

_____

3. While giving his demonstration, I am pleased that Ziegler used several graphs.

_____

_____

4. Working six days a week, the project should be finished by December 8.

_____

_____

5. In completing the research, a few startling facts were uncovered.

_____

_____

PART G. In the following paragraph, insert the ten commas needed to set off nonrestrictive phrases.

Paul Ralston representing the Redding Corporation met with Alan Reed on Tuesday. Mr. Reed was authorized to speak in behalf of his company. The two men in discussing the proposed merger agreed on most major points. To be perfectly fair Reed offered to have cumulative preferred stock issued to Redding's present stockholders. Ralston in accepting the offer praised Reed for his fairness. The firms planning this merger are both producers of industrial chemicals. Redding's stockholders hoping that the move results in increased earnings are enthusiastic about the consolidation. To expedite matters each company will call a stockholders' meeting in July.

FOR CLASS DISCUSSION

(if time permits)

A friend of mine, an attorney, was writing a personal letter when he turned to me and asked for my opinion concerning this sentence: "Did you hear about _me_ (or _my_) going overseas?" When I told him to use the possessive case with a gerund, he seemed genuinely amazed. He couldn't understand how anyone could remember the rules of grammar several years after studying them in high school or college. On the other hand, I can't understand how a serious student can ever _forget_ those rules. They are not easy to learn but, once learned, almost impossible to forget. Comment. Why _should_ the rules be difficult to forget?

Modifiers of Nouns and Pronouns

■■ POINT TO PONDER

Most people use only a handful of the many colorful adjectives our language has to offer.

I recall conversing at length with a young man who was enrolled at one of America's most prestigious universities. He proved to be highly intelligent, ambitious, innovative, and personable, but he was also dull—dull as a conversationalist because of his continual (and generally inappropriate) use of the adjective *fabulous*. He used that word again and again to describe virtually everything in his life that he found to be even remotely desirable.

The effective use of descriptive language, while important to all of us, is of special value to those people in business who must paint vivid word pictures of the products or services they have to offer. Consider the plight of the salesperson whose language limitations will not permit him or her to describe adequately a product that would serve the prospect's needs. Pity the poor executive who must struggle to write a simple letter of recommendation because the right descriptive words will not come to mind.

Skill in the use of **modifiers** (descriptive words, phrases, or clauses) is especially important to the men and women who write advertising copy for today's newspapers, magazines, radio, television, and billboards. They attempt to whet the public's appetite for their products with words like these: "bold architectural lines, enriched by glowing woods, vigorous carvings, and burnished brass hardware . . . superbly crafted from six lively woods, in four distinctive finishes." Copywriters for advertising firms obviously must control an arsenal of colorful adjectives and adverbs. Whether we work in advertising or not, however, it is important for us to understand what modifiers are and how they should be employed.

Adjective Defined

Words that describe, limit, or restrict nouns or pronouns are called adjectives. They answer questions such as *What kind? Which one?* and *How much (many)?*

> WHAT KIND? *Credit* accounts are beneficial to both retailers and customers.
> WHICH ONE? *That* system is too complicated.
> HOW MANY? *Six* members of the committee attended the preview.

Pronouns and nouns in the possessive case often function as adjectives to identify nouns.

> Mr. Stimson is carrying *his* briefcase.
> No one seemed interested in *Langer's* problem.

The Placement of Adjectives

Adjectives usually precede the words they modify. To achieve greater emphasis or variation, however, a writer may occasionally place adjectives *after* the word modified.

> Current records, *routine* or *special,* are easily located in our files.
> The building, *old* and *unpainted,* was finally demolished.

An adjective used as a subject complement is written after a linking verb.

> The new format will be *satisfactory.* (satisfactory format)
> The information is *confidential.* (confidential information)

The Use of Adjectives

Adjectives should be chosen carefully to add exactness or color to an explanation or to a description. The expression *salty ocean* tells a reader little, since all oceans are salty. General adjectives such as *good, beautiful, nice,* and *fine* usually add little to an idea and may even detract from the strength of a statement. *I recently read a good book* is a comment that reveals virtually nothing about the book in question. A book may be *inspiring* or *thought provoking* or *suspenseful* or *exciting* or *humorous* or *educational* or *profound* or *revealing* or *refreshing* or *wholesome* or *unique;* the possibilities are almost limitless.

Because some adjectives have been used too often with certain nouns, they have become trite—so overworked that they should be avoided. Skillful writers choose varied adjectives that give exact pictures, that contribute an accent, or that make an appeal to the imagination or emotions of the reader.

Adjectives That Deserve Special Mention

1. The adjectives *a* and *an* are commonly referred to as *indefinite articles,* while the adjective *the* is known as a *definite article.* In choosing between *a* and *an,* a writer should use *a* before words beginning with a consonant sound and *an* before words beginning with a vowel sound. The initial *letter* of the word following is not important. The initial *sound* of the word determines whether *a* or *an* should be used.

an hour (*h* is silent)	*an* egg	*an* envelope
a union (*u* sounds like *you*)	*an* upper berth	*a* factory

Because the article serves no purpose in expressions such as *sort of (a) person* or *kind of (a) product,* it should not be used.

AVOID: What *kind of a position* do you want?
  USE: What *kind of position* do you want?
  USE: He is the *type of leader* that this organization needs.

2. *This* and *that,* as well as their plural forms, *these* and *those,* may be used as adjectives to point out particular nouns and pronouns. Careful attention should be given to the correct use of the singular and plural forms. The pronoun *them* should never be used in place of *those.*

this kind	these kinds	this company	these companies
that type	those types	that office	those offices

3. The word *only* may be used as an adjective or as an adverb. Writers frequently misuse this word by placing it illogically in sentences. The careful business writer will always place *only* so that it clearly modifies the word(s) intended.

AVOID: We *only* have seven barrels of flour.
  USE: We have *only* seven barrels of flour.
AVOID: Varney *only* plans to be in Detroit for a month.
  USE: Varney plans to be in Detroit for *only* a month.

4. Here are four suggestions to guide you in your use of articles *(a, an, the):*
  a. When two adjectives modify the same noun, the article, if needed, is used only once.

  The old and worn gloves gave evidence of his work.
  A large and airy trailer makes a usable temporary office.

  b. When the same article identifies two different nouns, it should be repeated before each noun if there is the possibility of a misunderstanding.

  The vice president and *the* treasurer disputed our claim.
  A box and *a* carton came in the shipment.

  c. If one noun is modified by *a* and another noun is modified by *an,* each article must be expressed.

  We would like to hire *a* painter and *an* electrician.

  d. When the same article modifies two nouns that name only one person or thing, the article should not be repeated.

  The secretary and treasurer is an appointed officer. (One person serves as both secretary and treasurer.)
  The scanner and fax machine is expensive. (One machine serves both purposes.)

5. Words such as *each, one, any, many, some,* and *all* may be used as adjectives or as pronouns.

ADJECTIVE: *Each* suggestion will be seriously considered.
PRONOUN: *Each* of the men will be asked to do his own work. (*Each* is a singular subject.)

Adjective Phrases and Clauses

Phrases and clauses often function as adjectives to modify, describe, or limit nouns and pronouns. They can be classified by the work they do in sentences. Note that in the following sentences each italicized phrase or clause functions as an adjective.

PHRASES: The man *in the black suit* did not attend the rally. (The italicized phrase functions as an adjective to modify the word *man.*)
CLAUSES: The man *who answered your inquiry* is the manager. (The clause *who answered your inquiry* modifies *man.*)
Our firm's main office, *which is in Toledo,* employs 53 people.

Words, phrases, and clauses that function as adjectives can add interest, exactness, and color to the nouns and pronouns they modify. Business writers can often avoid costly misunderstandings by using them skillfully to achieve maximum clarity.

Executives' Choice

Almost This word means "nearly, approximately, all but." Do not substitute the word *most,* which functions as an adjective or a pronoun to mean "the greater number or amount."

Almost everyone (not *most everyone*) was pleased with the results.
She *almost* finished her analysis of accounts by noon.
Most bank tellers handle money skillfully.

Coarse The adjective *coarse* means "common, of inferior quality" or "rough, harsh." Do not substitute it for the noun *course,* which has several common definitions.

The *coarse* sand cut the paint on his truck.
Brannigan should take a *course* in accounting.
They will, of *course,* make delivery before Saturday.
The helmsman was ordered to steer a *course* of 270 degrees.

Continual This word, an adjective, means "frequent, often repeated." The adjective *continuous* means "unceasing, constant, without a break."

The *continual* ringing of the telephone interrupted his work.
Our decision was influenced by the ten hours of *continuous* fog.

Disinterested The word *disinterested* is an adjective that means "free from personal bias, impartial, or objective." Do not use it in place of *uninterested,* which means "without interest."

We should ask a *disinterested* expert to settle our differences.
Employees who are *uninterested* in their work do not often succeed.

Eminent This adjective means "distinguished, highly esteemed." Do not confuse it with *imminent,* which means "impending, about to happen."

> The *eminent* scientist gave a scholarly analysis of the discovery.
> Many of us fear that a hurricane is *imminent.*

Foreword This word refers to "a preface or introductory note (as in a book)." *Forward,* of course, has several meanings. The most common are these: "in the front; tending toward a position in front; in or toward the future."

> The *foreword* of his book was well written.
> He went *forward* with his plans to modernize the building.

Intelligent This adjective means "mentally acute; showing sound judgment and rationality." *Intelligible* means "capable of being understood."

> You could not have made a more *intelligent* choice.
> His confusing presentation was barely *intelligible.*

Nice Do not use *nice* as a blanket word to indicate all degrees of pleasantness. It is better to select an exact adjective to describe an agreeable situation.

> His colleagues were extremely *helpful* (not *nice*).
> The weather was *sunny* and *warm* (not *nice*).

Personal The adjective *personal,* which refers to a particular person, should not be confused with the word *personnel,* which refers to the employees of a business and often functions as a noun.

> His *personal* belongings were left untouched.
> Hartford handles problems involving *personnel.*

Raze This verb means "to tear down or demolish; level to the ground." It is pronounced the same as the word *raise,* which has several definitions. The most common are these: "to lift; to cause to move upward; to increase in size or worth."

> We will buy the property and *raze* the existing structure.
> Penworthy will leave unless we *raise* her salary.

Real This word means "genuine, actual, not imaginary." Careful business writers do not use it in place of *really* or *very.* Because it is an adjective, the word *real* should be used to modify nouns and pronouns.

> The lecture was *very* (not *real*) difficult to understand.
> The book was bound with *real* leather.

Stationary This word means "not moving, fixed, at rest." The noun *stationery* refers to writing paper and envelopes.

> It is not difficult to photograph a *stationary* object.
> Ashton wrote the letter on *stationery* of excellent quality.

Waive   This word means "to give up (a claim or right) voluntarily; to refrain from enforcing." *Wave,* as you know, means "to move back and forth in the air" or "to signal with a hand movement."

He will *waive* his rightful interest in the property.

The flag did not *wave* because there was no breeze.

MY *ONLY* COMMENT

It is doubtful that any other word in our language is misplaced in sentences as frequently as the word *only.* Even professional writers and speakers tend to use the word without proper regard for *what it modifies.* Each of the following sentences should be reworded.

1. This cat only likes one person. (a newspaper headline)
2. Some people think Bank of America only works with industrial giants. (headline of a magazine advertisement)
3. Join now! It only takes $1. (headline of a magazine advertisement)
4. Tax-free time deposits can only be opened for a few more months. (end of a radio commercial)

_____ **FOR CLASS DISCUSSION** _____

Study each sentence to determine the intended meaning; then decide where the word *only* should have been placed to convey that meaning.

———— **WORSHEET 18**————

MODIFIERS OF NOUNS AND PRONOUNS

PART A. Indicate whether each statement is true or false by writing T or F in the space provided.

1. An adjective may describe a noun or a verb.   1. _____

2. Nouns and pronouns in the possessive case often function as adjectives.   2. _____

3. Adjectives should always precede the words they modify.   3. _____

4. The words *a* and *an* are often called *articles.*   4. _____

5. *This, that, these,* and *those* are always used as adjectives.   5. _____

6. The word *only* may be used as an adjective or as an adverb.   6. _____

7. The article *an,* not *a,* should be used whenever the following word begins with a vowel.   7. _____

8. A subject complement may be an adjective.   8. _____

9. Phrases cannot be used to modify nouns.   9. _____

10. An adjective clause may be introduced with *who, which,* or *that.*   10. _____

PART B. Underscore any error and write the correct form in the space provided. If there is no error, write C. If you are collaborating, agree together on an improved choice.

1. Which kind of a colleague is Carlotti?   1. *_____

2. By using the new power tools, we completed the job in less than an hour.   2. _____

3. Ian had only two of those kind of diskettes.   3. _____

4. The kind of copier you described may be purchased for only $500.   4. _____

5. Dunn only waited one week for his software upgrade.   5. *_____

6. Peterson appears to be disinterested in this kind of work.   6. _____

7. Be real careful when entering your phone card number.   7. _____

8. Tessa's continuous complaining caused trouble.   8. _____

9. Most everyone in our department participates in the fund drive.   9. _____

10. The fax and e-mail, of coarse, may be used by anyone in the department.   10. _____

PART C. In the space provided, write *a* or *an* to indicate which of these two articles would make the sentence correct.

1. You can upgrade word processing software at (a, an) exposition this week.

   1. *_____

2. It will take place in (a, an) hall on the second floor of the convention center.

   2. *_____

3. The exposition was the brainchild of Upgrades Incorporated, (a, an) software clearinghouse.

   3. _____

4. Upgrades Incorporated president, Steven Corey, expects (a, an) increase in participants this year.

   4. _____

5. He credits excellent word-of-mouth publicity after (a, an) modest first-ever exposition last year.

   5. _____

6. "Many people just don't have time to keep up with upgrades," says (a, an) exuberant Corey.

   6. _____

7. "They simply want (a, an) expert to analyze their application and tell them the most effective ways to improve it.

   7. _____

8. Corey is surprised at the growth of his rather new company, particularly in (a, an) somewhat slow business growth season.

   8. _____

9. He believes he is providing (a, an) service that truly meets customers' needs.

   9. _____

10. "I guess that when you save (a, an) client's time, that's a service worth paying for.

   10. _____

PART D. In the space provided, write the adjective that will more exactly describe or identify the noun to which it refers. Do not choose blanket adjectives that tell the reader little. When collaborating, be sure you agree about which adjective is the better choice.

Example: Segura hopes that his (big, expanded) territory will result in improved sales.

   _____expanded_____

1. No one could have predicted Kozinski's (good, exceptional) performance last year.

   1. _____

2. As a second-year sales executive, he had set (reachable, medium) goals for his evaluation period.

   2. _____

3. He not only met those goals but also (rose above, pressed past) them.

   3. *_____

4. He (broke, shattered) two long-standing company records for most sales during a single convention.

   4. _____

5. He even managed to cut his own expenses, making a (larger, 60-percent) profit for the firm.

   5. _____

6. Sometimes salespersons like Kozinski become the victims of (vengeful, mean) practical jokes.

   6. _____

7. The jokes are the result of other salespersons' (bad feelings, resentment) toward someone successful.

   7. _____

8. In an effort to avoid negative reactions, the company has adopted a(n) (fine, equitable) incentive program.

   8. _____

9. In this (new, current-year) program, every sale is
rewarded according to its size, so there are fewer
complaints.

9. _____

10. As a result, high achievers like Kozinski can be
rewarded with kudos as well as monetary prizes and
others are less (resentful, angry).

10. _____

PART E. Write the word(s) that would make the sentence correct.

1. Chandrakis is the president (and, and the) founder of
this shipping company.

1. _____

2. (This, These) kinds of conflicts are best dealt with
openly and early.

2. _____

3. I (only have, have only) one response to your survey.

3. * _____

4. Generally, Porter prefers to order (this, these) type of
stationery for official correspondence.

4. _____

5. Our receptionist is particular about what (kind of a,
kind of) headset he uses.

5. _____

PART F. The following business letter body has eleven errors in word choice. Find them
and suggest a clearer replacement for each one in the spaces that follow the
letter.

As we look foreword to the eminent visit of imminent psychologist Dr. Taylor
Seigal, we are attempting to make some intelligible decisions about which personal should
be invited to attend the special day-long workshops given by Dr. Seigal. We want to select
our attendees wisely, since we understand from other conference hosts that, although Dr.
Seigal is a nice person, she can be easily upset by continuous questioning and real
persistent interrupters. Not all of our employees can be counted on to simply sit quietly or
even participate during her presentations; in fact, in the coarse of a department meeting
just last week I noticed some employees waiving to one another in the back of the room,
others doing paperwork instead of paying attention, and still others asking questions that
weren't even about the agenda item being discussed. Let's make our selections carefully
and then issue formal invitations on company stationary, so that those invited will
understand that they are being honored.

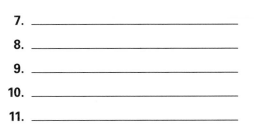

1. * _____   7. _____

2. * _____   8. _____

3. _____   9. _____

4. _____   10. _____

5. _____   11. _____

6. _____

DO YOU SPEAK GOOD?

Some grammatical errors are considerably more common than others. Each one of the numbered sentences that follow contains an error that is made with great frequency, even by well-educated people. During the past 24 hours I have heard or seen each of these statements:

1. He doesn't speak as good as he writes.
2. The new copier works really good.
3. I'm doing good. (Answer to the question *How are you doing?*)
4. He hits left-handed pitchers pretty good.

_____ **FOR CLASS DISCUSSION** _____

What error was made in each of the four sentences? What grammatical principle has been violated? How would you account for the fact that this error is extremely common?

A WORD TIP FROM THE REAL WORLD

Susan, an administrative assistant working in the executive office of a large Wisconsin manufacturing firm, has the responsibility of scanning and making first-cut decisions about various management applicants based on their resumes. "There are so many applicants for every position we advertise that we simply cannot give each candidate the in-depth time we'd like," she says. "Consequently, we scan their letters of application and their resumes rather quickly the first time through. I'm afraid the first ones to be rejected are the ones with errors in spelling, word choice, and formatting. If the applicant can't take charge of those details when putting together application paperwork, we assume that the applicant won't do any better with details on the job."

Special Uses of Adjectives

A n abridged dictionary, you will recall, does *not* contain every word in our language. There is a possibility that the dictionary you use does not list words like *fewer, fewest, taller,* or *tallest,* although such words are extremely common. You are likely to discover that words of this type have not been included in a particular dictionary because they are *regular* variations of adjectives.

COMPARISON OF ADJECTIVES

The average person makes frequent use of adjectives in three different forms, or *degrees.* It is natural for most of us to add *er* or *est* to one-syllable adjectives or to two-syllable adjectives that end in *y.* In expressing variations of other adjectives, we find it just as natural to use *more, most, less,* or *least* appropriately. The following list includes the three degrees for each of several adjectives.

Positive	Comparative	Superlative
fine	finer	finest
cold	colder	coldest
funny	funnier	funniest
careful	more (or *less*) careful	most (or *least*) careful
difficult	more (or *less*) difficult	most (or *least*) difficult

A number of adjectives have highly irregular comparative forms. Here are several:

good, well	better	best
little	less	least
much, many	more	most
far	farther, further	farthest, furthest
bad	worse	worst

Some adjectives, such as *perfect, unique,* and *universal,* do not lend themselves to comparison. Because words of this type suggest extremes, it would be illogical to use expressions like *more perfect* or *more unique.*

Use of Comparisons

1. When comparing two people, things, or ideas, use the comparative degree.

   Interest rates on personal loans are *higher* than those on business loans.
   He is interested in the *less expensive* of the two properties.
   Tomorrow may prove to be even *colder* than today.

2. When comparing a person or an object with others in the same class, use the comparative degree. In addition, use either *other* or *else* in this way:

   Bank of America has *greater* assets than any *other* California bank.
   Ms. Thurston is *more* conservative than anyone *else* on the management team.
   This new Xerox copier is *faster* than any *other* copier in the office.

3. When referring to more than two (people, objects, etc.), use the superlative degree to indicate an extreme.

   He is the *wealthiest* manufacturer in the city.
   Of all the novelty dealers John Kindel had the *highest* sales.
   The Burroughs representative proved to be the *most* persuasive of the four.

COMPOUND ADJECTIVES

When using two or more words as a single adjective *before the noun it modifies,* use a hyphen to show the close association. By combining words in this way, writers can coin their own modifiers and, even more important, clarify the intended meaning.

my worn-out notebook	Mr. Poe's get-to-work look
our much-discussed theories	a 50-foot frontage
his never-say-die attitude	a well-to-do client

A compound adjective is likely to require a hyphen only when it precedes the word it modifies. The expression *long, dull journey* refers to a journey that is long and dull. Because the adjectives modify the noun *journey* independently, they are separated with a comma. The expression *long printer cable* obviously refers to a printer cable that is long. The two adjectives, *long* and *printer*, do not function as a unit.

The expression *ten-year lease,* however, does not refer to a lease that is *ten* and *year,* nor does it refer to a *year lease* that is *ten.* The lease described, of course, would run for a period of ten years, and a writer can clearly establish that fact by inserting a hyphen in the compound adjective *ten-year.* If the words that would make up such an adjective appear *after* the word modified, a hyphen is not generally needed. Note the contrast in these sentences:

> A *coin-operated* vending machine is in the hall.
> The vending machine is *coin operated.*
> Our *steam-driven* engine is now obsolete.
> The only engine we have is *steam driven.*

The only purpose of a hyphen in a compound adjective is to make the writer's meaning perfectly clear. You should not, therefore, use a hyphen to connect an adverb ending with *ly* (*carefully, nearly,* etc.) with a following adjective inasmuch as the function of the adverb is readily understood.

> a carefully prepared statement   a fairly reliable estimate

The hyphen should also be omitted if the compound modifier consists of words that ordinarily function as an easily recognized compound noun requiring no hyphen. Here are several examples:

> New England states   post office box
> Rocky Mountain scenery   real estate broker
> high school administrator   ice cream cone

Exceptions to the Rule

In using your dictionary, you will discover that some words are written with hyphens regardless of where they are placed in sentences. Here are several examples:

1. Compound numbers from *twenty-one* to *ninety-nine*

> forty-five   sixty-one   eighty-two

2. Most fractions that must be spelled out. (If either the numerator or the denominator is hyphenated, do not place a hyphen between them.)

> one-third   eleven forty-fifths   BUT: a half
> three-fourths   thirty-one thirty-seconds   a third

Note: Some writers do not use a hyphen in a *fraction* that functions as a noun. (*Two thirds* of our members were present. BUT: A *two-thirds* vote was required.)

3. Many words that include the suffix *elect* or one of these prefixes: *self, all, ex,* or *great*

governor-elect   ex-treasurer
self-conscious   all-powerful
self-respect   great-uncle

EXCEPTIONS: selfish, selfsame, selfhood, selfless

4. Words that would be difficult to understand if a hyphen were not used to separate a prefix or suffix from a root word.

He was asked to *re-sign* the contract. (COMPARE He *resigned* from his job.)

The figure in the center of the drawing is *bell-like.*

Most of our executives are *pro-American* about plant locations. (Use a hyphen between a prefix and a proper name.)

You may have occasion to use a series of compound adjectives that require hyphens. Even though some words are only partially expressed, appropriate hyphens should be inserted, as in this example:

All four-, five-, and six-story buildings will be inspected.

FREQUENTLY MISUSED ADJECTIVES

1. LATER, LATTER   The adjective *later,* which is the comparative form of *late,* generally refers to time. *Latter,* in contrast to *former,* refers to the "second of two mentioned." It may also be used to mean "near to the end."

The debate will be continued *later.*

He praised the *latter* of the two speakers mentioned.

Most of these changes took place during the *latter* part of the century.

2. FIRST, LAST   When using either of these words with a number *(first four, last five),* write the number last.

Read the *first ten* pages of the manual.

His accounts covered the *last 45* days of the operation.

3. GOOD, WELL   When used as a modifier, *good* is always an adjective. *Well* may be used as either an adjective or an adverb. When used as an adjective, *well* refers to health.

Akamoto expresses herself *well.* (The adverb *well* modifies the verb *expresses.*)

Morehouse is not *well.* (He is not in good health.)

Wagner feels *good* about the progress we have made. (The adjective *good* modifies Wagner.)

4. LESS, FEWER   These are the comparative forms of *little* and of *few*. *Less* generally is used to modify singular nouns; *fewer* is used to modify plural nouns. *Less,* however, may be used with plural nouns that name single units of time, distance, or money.

The new Canon copying machine uses *less* paper than the old one.

The strike lasted for *less* than three weeks.

You will find *fewer* employees on the sixth floor.

There have been *fewer* complaints since the pay raise was granted.

A WORD ABOUT PUNCTUATION

Two or more consecutive adjectives may be used to modify the same noun. If they are equal in rank, or **coordinate,** they should be separated by commas. Of course, the last adjective in a series must never be separated by a comma from the noun it modifies. Often a series of such adjectives will be arranged with the shorter words first.

He is a *brusque, efficient, hard-working* bookkeeper.

If consecutive adjectives are not equal in rank, do not separate them with commas. Although the first four words in the following sentence are adjectives modifying *tables,* no commas are needed.

Several small walnut end tables are still in stock. (For a more complete discussion of adjectives in a series, see Chapter 28.)

Executives' Choice

Alter   This verb means "to change or make different; modify." The noun *altar* refers to an elevated area used for ceremonial purposes (usually in the sanctuary of a church or temple).

The auditor refused to *alter* his plans.

The young man kneeled before the *altar.*

Passed   This word serves as the past tense and past participle of the regular verb *pass.* Do not confuse it with *past,* which may be used as a noun, an adjective, a preposition, or an adverb.

Crowley recently *passed* her bar examination.

Let me know when you have driven *past* the Wrigley Building.

We have accomplished very little during the *past* hour.

Please stop talking about the *past.*

Phone   This word is informal for *telephone* and should generally be avoided in business letters and reports.

Please *telephone* (not *phone*) every member of Avnet's management team.

Proceed   This word means "to advance or go on, especially after stopping" or "to undertake and carry on some action." Do not confuse it with *precede,* which means "to be, come, or go before."

> When I had finished my research, I *proceeded* to write the report.
> The speaker from Xerox will *precede* you on the program.

Should Of   Do not use this expression in place of *should have.*

> You should *have* (not *of*) received your shipment by September 10.

Suspicion   This word is a noun. Its use as a verb to mean *suspect* is considered nonstandard.

> The detective *suspected* (not *suspicioned*) everybody who had the combination to the safe.
> Every person in the office was under *suspicion.*

Whether   This conjunction is used to introduce alternative possibilities. It is often confused with *weather,* which refers to the state of the atmosphere. As a verb, *weather* means "to pass through safely; to survive."

> Let me know *whether* he stays here or leaves for Memphis.
> We had pleasant *weather* for our sidewalk sale.
> The company managed to *weather* the storm.

Wright   This word, which generally appears in compounds, refers to a worker. Do not confuse it with the more common *write* or *right.* Less common is the word *rite,* which refers to "a formal or ceremonial act, observance, or procedure."

> George Kaufman was an excellent play*wright.*
> You were *right* in your decision to withdraw.
> Every businessperson should attempt to *write* legibly.
> The marriage *rites* lasted for less than 15 minutes.

---

wWWw ═══════════ **Watching the Web** ═══════════

| **Back** | **Forward** | **Home** | **Reload** | **Images** | **Open** |

> How's your mileage?
> If you're paying today's higher gas prices but getting less miles to the gallon, here's something you've been waiting for: MEA (mileage extender additive)

| to learn more; click here | | no thanks |

_____ WORKSHEET 19 _____

SPECIAL USES OF ADJECTIVES

PART A. Write the word(s) that would make the sentence correct.

1. The two divisions will have to (alter, altar) their display for the next trade show.

2. The (more, most) lucrative account this year has been Winkler's.

3. I am certain that I know more about the product than (any, any other) employee in my department.

4. Can you guess why the spring line designs have been so (well hidden, well-hidden)?

5. We have more to be grateful for than (anyone, anyone else) in this company.

6. They anticipate (fewer, less) traffic on the main show floor on Saturday afternoon.

7. Stiffel has produced (twenty five, twenty-five) new models in ten years.

8. She has been (past, passed) over for promotion twice.

9. The clerk does not know (whether, weather) Jonas requested a single room.

10. We understand that the (small, wooden; small wooden) stands have been shipped.

11. Of the two finalists, Ghiardi is the (better, best) qualified.

12. We believe that the speaker was too (self-conscious, self conscious) to be persuasive.

13. Is it fair to blame the (whether, weather) for a poor turnout?

14. It is critical that we return with (fewer, less) unsold items than we did last year.

15. The (well cared for, well cared-for) mahogany desk will last for years.

16. Durfee is excited about his (recently opened, recently-opened) restaurant.

1. *alter*
2. * *most*
3. * *any other*
4. * *well hidden*
5. *anyone else*
6. *less*
7. *twenty-five*
8. *passed*
9. *whether*
10. *small, wooden*
11. *better*
12. *self-conscias*
13. *weather*
14. _____
15. _____
16. *recently, opened.*

PART B. Look at this business memo and find and underline the seven errors in word choice and hyphen use. Correct these errors in the spaces that follow the memo.

Since one of our buildings is not <u>air-conditioned</u>, and since the <u>whether</u> will become hot soon, we suggest that doors and windows be kept closed during the heat of the day and opened after the sun sets. Especially during the <u>two first</u> days of every work week, after the building has been empty over the weekend, the stuffy air may be a bit uncomfortable, and people may find themselves becoming <u>crankyer</u> than usual. But I can assure you that, even if there is a breeze, the temperature will remain cooler if we open <u>less</u> windows during the daytime. The night crew will take responsibility for cooling the place down at night by operating eight window fans in the <u>two story</u> structure. These fans will move cool night air through the building. In fact, since August is the <u>hotter</u> of the three summer months, we plan to pay a crew to come in late on Sunday nights in August and operate the fans to cool the buildings for work on Monday mornings.

1. weather
2. first two
3. two-story
4. fewer

5. hottest
6. air conditioned
7. crankier

PART C. If the expression in italics is incorrect, put the correct form in the answer space. If it is correct, put a C in the space. Decide together with your partners about each sentence, using chapter logic.

1. Atherly *should of* asked every employee to participate.

1. * _____

2. The *Middle-East* is growing rapidly as a manufacturing region.

2. _____

3. *Forty-five* boxes arrived this morning.

3. _____

4. This season our repertory theater will feature local *playrights*.

4. _____

5. Larson's presidency in 1981 *proceeded* Champ's 1985 term.

5. _____

6. There are certain *rights* one must follow when being sworn in.

6. _____

7. Will Houston *whether* this latest controversy over his finances?

7. _____

8. For a university-educated person, Billings doesn't articulate very *good*.

8. _____

9. I'm afraid I have slept through the *last five* annual meetings.

9. _____

10. Our fax machine holds *less* pages in memory than yours.

10. * _____

11. Of those two presenters, I perferred the *latter*.

11. _____

12. Hillmer *past* the first three milestones of his career without incident.

12. _____

13. We must *altar* our budget to accommodate the grant
dollars we have acquired.

13. _____

14. The C.E.O. is Kendall's *great uncle.*

14. _____

15. There is considerable *anti-Carson* sentiment in this
office.

15. _____

PART D. Rewrite each word group so that a compound adjective with at least one hyphen
is needed.

Examples: a shirt stained with ink

_____an ink-stained shirt_____

a house that was constructed well

_____a well-constructed house_____

1. a video camera operated by hand

1. _a hand-operated video camera_

2. an apple, half of which has been eaten

2. _a half-eaten apple_

3. a room filled with smoke

3. _a smoke-filled room_

4. research data that are ten years old

4. _ten-year-old research data_

5. a task force that has 12 persons

5. _a 12-person task force_

6. a man who is taller than average

6. _a taller-than-average man_

PART E. Choose the correct word and write it in the answer space. Be sure your
collaborators know why you make the choices you make.

1. No one could (of, have) relaxed in that tense
environment.

1. _____

2. I will (proceed, precede) the president's wife into the
banquet hall.

2. _____

3. Seversen knows what we need to do to complete our
(copywright, copyright) forms.

3. _____

4. When hand-crafting historic wagon replicas, it pays to
hire a qualified (wheelwright, wheelwrite).

4. _____

5. The (passed, past) decade has seen dramatic changes
in inflation.

5. *_____

6. We couldn't (of, have) been more suprised to see
Maxwell.

6. _____

7. When you arrive in Washington, (telephone, phone)
the office immediately.

7. _____

8. I have (passed, past) your office many times without
seeing this painting.

8. _____

9. I will stop at the office (latter, later) in the afternoon.

9. _____

10. This program can design (three-, four-, and five-cell;
three, four, and five cell) tables.

10. _____

PART F. Write a short, smoothly worded paragraph on the subject of "Salespeople." Underscore at least two compound adjectives that contain hyphens.

_____

_____

_____

_____

_____

_____

_____

_____

_____

_____

_____

_____

_____

_____

_____

_____

_____

_____

_____

_____

_____

_____

_____

_____

_____

_____

_____

_____

_____ FOR CLASS DISCUSSION _____

(if time permits)

(A) On several occasions I have heard someone say, "He always seems to talk in superlatives." Exactly what does that statement mean?

(B) Comment on the use of the word *recreation* in the following sentence, which was taken from a magazine article.

This program allows students to go aboard the full-scale replica of Richard Henry Dana's ship for the living recreation of sailing life in the early 1800s.

Adverbs in Use

Adverbs that end in *ly* are seldom used by some people.

D on't be surprised if you cannot find a particular adverb in the main listing of your dictionary. Many words that are used as this part of speech end in the suffix *ly,* which is likely to be added to a common adjective form. If the word *quickly* does not appear as a main entry in your abridged dictionary, you may find it in small boldface at the end of the entry for the word *quick.* Adverbs handled in this way (*carefully, solemnly, briskly,* etc.) are not followed by definitions. Because the adjective is fully defined, however, the meaning of the adverb is readily apparent. (You will find one or more such entries on page 4).

Adverbs are not difficult to control, yet we hear them misused frequently. People who fail to use adverbs appropriately are often well aware of governing rules but disinclined to apply them. The employee who claims to be able to "operate this machine just *perfect*" is probably familiar with the word *perfectly.* Certainly the young woman who, after taking her college entrance examination, said, "I did real good in the grammar part" knows more about adverbs than her sentence would suggest.

POINTS TO REMEMBER

1. An adverb is a word used to modify a verb form, an adjective, another adverb, or an adverb-equivalent. Examples (in italics):

He studied the sales literature *very carefully.*

2. The typical adverb is formed by adding *ly* to an adjective.

> *completely, sadly, greatly, secretly, busily*

3. A number of common adverbs do not end in *ly*.

> *well, never, always, very, not*

4. Every adverb should be placed reasonably close to the word(s) it modifies.

> The *neatly* dressed applicant walked *hesitantly* into my office. (The adverb *neatly* modifies the adjective *dressed;* the adverb *hesitantly* modifies the verb *walked.*)

5. A common grammatical error is the use of an adjective when an adverb is needed. You will find several excellent examples in the material that follows.

SIX NONSTANDARD USES OF ADVERBS

Let's take a penetrating look at six questionable constructions, each of which involves our understanding of adverbs. A careful analysis of each should bring to light some interesting aspects of this important part of speech. Business writers should, of course, avoid the use of constructions such as these:

Did Real Good

1. I did *real good* in the grammar part.

This short sentence contains two nonstandard modifiers. The word *good,* which may properly modify a noun or a pronoun, has been used to modify *did,* a verb. The adverb *well,* of course, should have been used. (Adverbs answer questions such as *How? When? Where? How often? To what degree?*) The word *real* was identified in Chapter 18 as an adjective. As such, it should not be used to modify an adverb. Note these correct constructions:

> I did *very well* in the grammar part.
> Our new shipper has performed *extremely well.*

Do Satisfactory

2. We hope that you *do satisfactory* in the coming speed trials.

Adverbs that end with *ly* tend to be neglected. In this sentence the adjective *satisfactory* has been used to modify a verb, *do.* A careful writer would substitute the adverb *satisfactorily.* Other types of adjectives are also often misused as adverbs. The following list contains 16 words that may be employed as adverbs. In parentheses are the adjectives from which eight of these adverbs have been derived.

not	calmly (calm)
well	happily (happy)
very	accidentally (accidental)
fast	usually (usual)

early	devotedly (devoted)
late	pleadingly (pleading)
only	angrily (angry)
there	hopefully (hopeful)

Note these correct constructions:

The form letter was sent *unintentionally.*

The officer spoke *angrily* to Townsend.

Weren't Given Scarcely

3. We *weren't given scarcely* one hour to make the necessary corrections.

This construction is just about as common as it is faulty. Words like *scarcely, hardly,* and *barely* imply a negative idea when used to mean "not more than," "not quite," "not easily," or "only just." The insertion of another negative, such as *not,* is completely illogical. Note the absence of *not* in these correct sentences:

We were given scarcely one hour to make the necessary corrections.

We were barely finished when King asked for the affidavit.

You could hardly expect Stern to join such an organization.

Tastes Badly

4. Whelan agrees that the new soft drink *tastes badly.*

A surprisingly large number of people use *badly* inappropriately. Among standard English modifiers, the word *bad* is an adjective; *badly* is an adverb. In the sentence under discussion, *tastes* is a linking verb and should be followed by an adjective that can modify the noun *drink.* Such modifiers, you may remember, are known as subject complements. The adjective *bad,* which in this construction means "unpleasant, disagreeable, not good," is the logical choice to modify the noun. Observe the use of adjectives (in italics) as complements in these sentences:

The air smells *pleasant* because of the flowers on your desk.

The workers in the warehouse seem *happy.*

Crowe feels *bad* about his poor performance. (Because many people use *badly* after the linking verb *feel,* leading dictionaries now show it as an acceptable option. Grammatically, *bad* is the logical choice.)

Sure Hope

5. We *sure hope* that you recover the stolen money.

This use of the adjective *sure* as an adverb is colloquial and should be avoided in business writing. The word *surely* is an adverb that may be used to mean "assuredly, certainly, without a doubt" or "in a sure, unhesitating manner." It modifies a verb in each of these sentences:

We *surely* hope that you recover the stolen money.

He will *surely* telephone us before Friday.

You *surely* succeeded in confusing Baum.

Runs Smoother

6.   The engine in the truck *runs smoother* than the engine in the car.

Adverbs in the comparative or superlative degree are frequently neglected. The word *smoother* is an adjective in the comparative degree and, as a result, cannot logically modify the verb *runs*. *Smoothly* is an adverb. Its comparative form, *more smoothly,* should be used in the sentence under discussion. Note the italicized adverbs in these sentences:

> The engine in the truck runs *more smoothly* than the engine in the car.
>
> Of the two men Jim Cowan handled the problem *more easily.*
>
> Her colleague works *more slowly* than she does. (In informal writing, the adjective forms of *slow, quick, loud,* and *cheap* may double as adverbs. In business writing, the *ly* forms should be used.)

Following are the comparative forms of several common adverbs. Note that the first two listed may function as adjectives also.

Positive	Comparative	Superlative
fast	faster	fastest
far	farther	farthest
calmly	more (or *less*) calmly	most (or *least*) calmly
promptly	more (or *less*) promptly	most (or *least*) promptly
quietly	more (or *less*) quietly	most (or *least*) quietly
hurriedly	more (or *less*) hurriedly	most (or *least*) hurriedly

Remember: Your dictionary is not likely to show the comparative or superlative forms of adverbs that end in *ly.* If run-on entries are used, an adverb ending in *ly* (*peacefully*) will usually be added to the entry for the shorter form (the adjective *peaceful*).

ADVERB PHRASES AND CLAUSES

It is interesting to note that both phrases and clauses may function as adverbs. In the sentences that follow, two phrases and two clauses have been italicized. Each functions as an adverb in that it modifies a verb.

> Staub will telephone you *in the morning.*
>
> A stranger walked *into the room.*
>
> Check my figures *before you leave.*
>
> We sold an expensive painting *while you were out.*

Executives' Choice

Already   This adverb means "previously, before the indicated time." The expression *all ready* may mean "completely ready," or it may suggest that "everyone is ready."

> He had *already* made his decision when you arrived.
>
> We were *all ready* to adjourn by ten o'clock.

Formerly   This word means "some time ago" or "in the past." Don't confuse it with *formally*, which means "in a ceremonial or structured manner; respectfully."

> Berkowitz was *formerly* a partner in this firm.
> The new building was *formally* accepted by the board at our recent dedication ceremonies.

Kindly   This word, which may function as an adjective or an adverb, has been overused in business. Careful writers of today seldom use it as a substitute for *please*. Its use as an adjective is perfectly acceptable.

> Will you *please* (not *kindly*) mail me your decision by Friday.
> His *kindly* manner was appreciated by everyone in the office.

Maybe   This adverb means *perhaps*. Do not write it in place of the verb phrase *may be*.

> *Maybe* the paint will not meet the architect's specifications.
> You *may be* given an opportunity to submit a bid.

Respectfully   The adverb *respectfully* means "with respect or high regard" and indicates an attitude of deference. *Respectively* means "in the order designated."

> We *respectfully* request your presence at the inauguration.
> Baker, Kimball, and Sievers scored 82, 79, and 86, *respectively*.

Seldom Ever   These words make an illogical combination. Use the one word *seldom* or the expression *seldom if ever*.

> He *seldom* contributes to our discussions.
> Quimby *seldom if ever* visits this part of the city.

Too   This word is an intensifying adverb that is occasionally confused with the preposition *to* or the number *two*. *Too* may be used to mean "also."

> We cannot buy the truck because it is *too* expensive.
> The trailer is expensive *too*.
> Please buy *two* staplers if you go *to* an office supply retailer.

CLASSROOM FUN WITH ADVERBS

Take three minutes to think of ten words that end in *ly* and would ordinarily be used as adverbs. Your first word is to begin with *a*, your second word with *b*, your third word with *c*; that is, you are to suggest a word for each of the first ten letters of the alphabet. If you do this exercise in class, give yourself a pat on the back for any acceptable adverb that appears on your list but no one else's.

A _____   F _____
B _____   G _____
C _____   H _____
D _____   I _____
E _____   J _____

AN ADDED CHALLENGE: If time permits, suggest adverbs for each of the next ten letters in the alphabet *(k, l, m, n, o, p, q, r, s,* and *t)*.

A WORD TIP FROM THE REAL WORLD

Joan, vice president of a popular advertising agency, says that designing a package for a product requires skill. "Consumers buy what they trust, what appeals to them, what they value. We can use all the colors, bells, and whistles we want, but when consumers take the box off the shelf, they want to be able to read clearly (and *quickly*) what's inside. If they don't get the message at a glance, we have failed. The best standard English is critical to getting our clients' products into consumers' homes. It's that simple."

Name *Alisha Hicks* Date *2-28-08*

WORKSHEET 20

ADVERBS IN USE

PART A. By writing the appropriate *letter,* indicate whether the missing word should be an adverb or an adjective.

A. adverb   B. adjective

Example: Sales for the past quarter have been _____. (A person writing such a sentence would make use of an adjective such as *adequate* or *slow* or *satisfactory.*)

B

1. Several of our office machines are not working _____.

1. * A

2. His reply to my question was somewhat _____.

2. B

3. He may be a capable hazardous waste scientist, but he does not express himself _____.

3. A

4. The new fax machine is remarkably _____.

4. B

5. Genovese does not perform _____ under pressure.

5. A

6. When it became necessary to discharge ten workers, Mr. Maher really felt _____.

6. B

7. Paper manufacturing generally makes the surrounding atmosphere smell _____.

7. B

8. Dougan will be hired if he does _____ in the two-hour test.

8. A

9. Gates spoke _____ about her new Sony portable disc player.

9. A

10. Lawson has many fine qualities, but he does not manage money _____.

10. A

PART B. This exercise will test your ability to spell adverbs correctly. You are to write the adverb that can be derived from the word in parentheses. Use your dictionary if necessary. If you're working collaboratively, convince your partner(s) about your answers.

Example: His comments will not (necessary) concern office automation.

necessarily

1. Businesses can become partners (profitable) as large groups of convention participants invade a city.

1. * _____

2. Hotel managers are delighted to see large convention centers succeed because, as people come to meet, they also need a place to sleep (comfortable).

2. _____

3. Convention traffic creates almost (instant) a ripple effect.

3. _____

4. As rooms near a meeting site fill up, attendees know they may have to stay (inconvenient) far from the site.

4. _____

5. Retailers, entertainment venues, and restaurants also (happy) share pieces of the convention-revenue pie.

5. _____

6. Some restaurants in downtown areas (typical) serve 35 to 40 people on an average Monday night.

6. * _____

7. However, during a convention held in a downtown convention center (recent), one eatery fed 200 guests for dinner as well as another 100 for lunch.

7. _____

8. The crowds don't (usual) take local managers by surprise, however.

8. _____

9. After years in the same location, managers have good instincts about whether or not those visitors will add (significant) to their income.

9. _____

10. "We learn which conventions' participants tend to eat less (expensive) and which are going to spend more money for dinner," one says.

10. _____

11. "Visiting youth organizations, for example, are (apparent) very good for the fast food places and the shopping center.

11. _____

12. "Medical conferences (general) bring patrons that can afford more luxurious dining."

12. _____

13. (Additional), convention visitors help fill city and state tax coffers as well.

13. _____

14. Hotel bills, restaurant tabs, and retail receipts all come with taxes (dutiful) applied.

14. _____

15. (Near) every transaction by a visitor sends the state 6.5 percent in sales tax.

15. _____

PART C. Choose the correct word and write it in the space provided. Underscore the word it modifies.

Example: He <u>writes</u> extremely (good, well).

well
_____

1. You (sure, surely) don't intend to miss the plenary session of the convention.

1. surely

2. That session features the author of *The Six Key Principles,* the book that was (real, really) helpful in focusing our mission statement.

2. really

3. The last time I heard her speak, I thought she was (extremely, extreme) persuasive.

3. extremely

4. Her books makes its points (clearer, more clearly) than any other management text.

4. more clearly

5. Did you know that she completed her degree (more quickly, quicker) than any other business graduate in her class?

5. more quickly

6. Some of her audience is (real, really) surprised to hear her speak positively about company discipline and rules.

6. really

7. In her principle-based system, however, rules are set (real, very) carefully with wide input and feedback.

7. very

8. She will deliver the keynote address at the plenary session and then preside (quiet, quietly) over three workshops.

8. quietly

9. It is her plan to help us in her (effective, effectively) way, coaching from the sidelines.

9. effective

10. I'm certain that her plan will work just (perfect, perfectly).

10. perfectly

11. All of those who attend her speech will feel (good, well) about their future.

11. * good

12. Our admired speaker will have done her work (good, well).

12. * well

PART D. Choose the correct word and write it in the space provided.

1. Our new copier runs (quieter, more quietly) than the old one.

1. _____

2. I (seldom ever, seldom) receive invoice numbers when customers send payment.

2. _____

3. Before accepting her current assignment, Sheila (formally, formerly) held the post of School District Superintendent.

3. _____

4. He has asked Douglas to complete the (recent, recently) approved work plan by next April.

4. _____

5. Wanda drove (slower, more slowly) than the other couriers and had fewer accidents.

5. _____

6. This division (may be, maybe) headed for an increase in its capital budget.

6. _____

7. Simpson wants the assignment (bad, badly).

7. _____

8. Rupio was (all ready, already) to turn in the proposal when she spotted an error.

8. * _____

9. Looking at Canon and Epson, we must select the (better, best) service plan.

9. _____

10. Dawson (sure, surely) put a positive spin on the company's current status.

10. _____

11. Pam felt (bad, badly) about the decision facing her.

11. _____

12. We earned $12,000 and $20,000 from investments and loans, (respectfully, respectively).

12. _____

13. The secretary always closed the minutes "(Respectively, Respectfully) yours."

13. _____

14. Teide was (all ready, already) aware of the board's decision.

14. _____

15. She was able to (formerly, formally) announce her position on Monday.

15. *_____

16. We cannot be (to, too) careful regarding tax reporting.

16. _____

17. The group considered three proposals and found yours the (more, most) feasible.

17. *_____

18. The administrative assistant could (not hardly, hardly) believe his good luck.

18. _____

19. I confess to reacting (bad, badly) when the news was made public.

19. _____

20. (Kindly, Please) send your second year goals to Dr. Ingram before Friday's meeting.

20. _____

21. Our office e-mail system is (rapid, rapidly) becoming unwieldy.

21. _____

22. Everyone in our department should feel (real, really) good about our progress.

22. _____

23. Our manufacturing giant is poised to move (quicker, more quickly) than its competitors.

23. _____

24. In one-to-one meetings, Janacek is (real, really) effective.

24. _____

25. Our web page needs hypertext that can link people to information (easy, easily).

25. _____

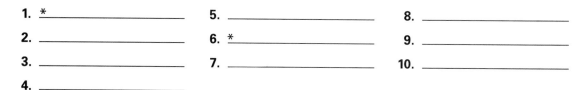

PART E. The following paragraph contains *ten* adverbs. In the answer spaces write them in the order they appear. If you are working collaboratively, be sure all partners agree on your final choices.

Clara Smith once had a co-worker who asked whether Smith had lived in a teepee before recently moving to her city. It may have been a very misguided comment, but Smith says society often views Native Americans from a purely white historical perspective and that modern native people are "invisible" to the larger population. While this problem might be enough of a barrier for native people, we know that they also live among people who believe almost all of the negative stereotypes about them. Smith wants to help gradually change these misperceptions and has started a business to do so. Her newly established Thornville company, called Art Alliance, creates products that charmingly educate people about Native American cultures.

1. *_____   5. _____   8. _____

2. _____   6. *_____   9. _____

3. _____   7. _____   10. _____

4. _____

OPTIONAL EXERCISES

OPTION 1   If you find an error, underscore it and write the correct word in the answer space. If there is no error, write C. If you're working collaboratively, be ready to convince your partners of your selection using material from the chapter.

1. It is critical that our work be done as flawless as possible.

   1. _____

2. Kadidlo does as good as her supervisor on all standard tests.

   2. * _____

3. Juarez has shown real positive leadership on the project.

   3. _____

4. The phone company promised that the upgrade would be completed as painless as possible.

   4. _____

5. How can we help employees who do not write very good?

   5. _____

6. Larpenteur seems to be moving slower these days.

   6. * _____

7. The air on the fourth floor smelled bad.

   7. _____

8. The client claims that the billing was not done fair.

   8. _____

9. She took the news of the merger pretty bad.

   9. _____

10. Hankins edited a page almost perfect in less than three minutes.

    10. _____

11. I could sure use a team approach on this task.

    11. _____

12. The driver took an agonizingly slow route to the airport.

    12. _____

13. Of the two supervisors, James is the most collaborative.

    13. _____

14. I was sure impressed by the group's work during Phase 1.

    14. _____

15. She will work slower at first and increase her speed later.

    15. _____

16. Erickson interviewed good for this position.

    16. _____

17. When will we know how bad the damage is?

    17. _____

18. The building was damaged bad in the hail storm.

    18. _____

19. When you work with others, you apologize excessive.

    19. _____

20. We were real sorry to hear about Garrison's father.

    20. _____

OPTION 2 Look at this paragraph from a business letter. Find eight errors, underscore them, and then write corrections for those errors in the spaces which follow the letter.

We are already to hire a man who applied for this position last week who's references are among the best we have ever seen. We seldom ever find ourselves with such a perfect candidate, but at last it has happened. It is almost to good to be true. He maybe the answer to our accounting department's present difficulties, as he was formally the chief accountant for Buringham's. His MAT and CPA scores are 94 and 162, respectfully. Do you wish to interview him before we offer him the position? Kindly let me know by tomorrow morning, so that I am able to plan our next moves.

1. _____   5. _____

2. _____   6. _____

3. _____   7. _____

4. _____   8. _____

OPTION 3 (CLASS DISCUSSION)   For many years grammarians warned us against the use of *badly* as an adjective. Modern dictionaries, however, now tell us that we may use the word after the linking verb *feel* in a construction such as this one: *He feels badly about the misunderstanding.* The *Random House Dictionary* claims that such usage in now standard. Lexicographers have yielded to the many people who struggled with the grammatical principle involved.

Feels badly (once considered grammatically incorrect) has always been used more frequently by college graduates than by high school dropouts. Discuss the reason for this phenomenon.

CHAPTER
21

Prepositions

■■■ POINT TO PONDER ──────────▶
Prepositions give clearer meaning to the
verbs or adjectives that they follow.

A preposition, you have learned, shows the relation of its object to another word in the sentence. Having read the preceding chapters of this text, you should have little difficulty in recognizing prepositions when you see them. You will recall that prepositional phrases function as modifiers.

> Many large banking institutions are located *in New York.* (Prepositional phrase modifies a verb.)
>
> He favors a bank *with many branches.* (Prepositional phrase modifies a noun.)
>
> He would like one *near his office.* (Prepositional phrase modifies a pronoun.)
>
> This institution is reliable *in every respect.* (Prepositional phrase modifies an adjective.)

Prepositions are not particularly difficult for the average writer or speaker to control. Here are several suggestions for their most effective usage:

1. Generally ignore prepositional phrases in deciding whether to use a singular or a plural verb in a sentence. Because a prepositional phrase is simply a modifier, it does not affect the *number* of the subject. Don't employ a plural verb simply because the object of a preposition is plural. (Note exceptions on pages 120 and 130.)

   A report of recent problems and grievances has been made. (Subject, *report,* and verb, *has been made,* are both singular.)

2. When you select a pronoun to serve as the object of a preposition, make certain it is in the objective case. Be especially careful when the preposition has a compound object.

> The form paragraphs were written by Mr. Whittaker and *me*.
> Lucy Gomez wants you to sit between Marie and *her*.

3. Avoid ending a sentence awkwardly with a preposition.

> AVOID: Whom did you give the letter *to?*
> USE: *To* whom did you give the letter?
> AVOID: This is the pen I wrote the letter *with*.
> USE: This is the pen *with* which I wrote the letter.

Some sentences will be made awkward if you *avoid the prepositional ending*. In such cases, it is wise to end with the preposition or to reword the sentence completely.

> AVOID: He does not know *for* what we are looking.
> USE: He does not know what we are looking *for*.

The beginning and the end of a sentence are positions of emphasis. A writer, therefore, will occasionally end a sentence with a preposition because he or she wants that word emphasized.

> Don't tell me what the report is *for;* tell me what it is *about*.

4. Avoid the use of unnecessary prepositions. You can weaken a sentence by inserting a preposition that is not needed.

> She does not know where the revised copy is *at*. (Omit *at*.)
> The paperweight fell off *of* his desk. (Omit *of*.)
> Where has he taken the booklet *to?* (Omit *to*.)

5. Avoid using the preposition *of* after *all* or *both* unless it is needed for clarity.

> DON'T USE: All *of the* bids must be submitted by noon. (The words *of* and *the* may be omitted.)
> USE: All bids *must* be submitted by noon.
> USE: Both executives favor the proposed change. (Not *Both of the executives*)
> USE: All *of* us were pleased with the results. (The preposition *of* is needed for clarity.)

6. Recognize clauses that serve as objects of prepositions. When such clauses begin with *whoever* or *whomever,* make your choice based on that clause's verb, not the preposition.

> You may assign that task to *whoever is presiding*. (A noun clause is the object of *to*. *Whoever* is the subject of the verb *is presiding*.)
> You may assign that task to *whomever you choose*. (A noun clause is the object of *to*. *Whomever* is the direct object of *choose*.)

7. Be especially careful in your use of these troublesome prepositions:

Among, Between   Use *among* in referring to more than two; use *between* in referring to only *two* objects or people.

> The estate was divided *among* the five heirs.
>
> Ms. Clark sat *between* the two attorneys.

In, Into   These words have many applications. In general, the preposition *in* is used with verbs that indicate place or position. *Into* is used with verbs that express motion or a change of condition.

> The signed documents are *in* the envelope.
>
> Put the signed documents *into* the envelope.
>
> He is *in* the room.
>
> Ms. Jackson's smile turned *into* a frown.

Like   The word *like* is often used as a preposition. It should not be used as a conjunction to join clauses.

> The new branch manager looks *like* Mr. Glass. (Last three words form a prepositional phrase.)
>
> It seems *as though* (not *like*) the building will never be completed. (Do not introduce a clause with *like*.)
>
> The new stationery is white, *as* (not *like*) you hoped it would be.

Per   This preposition is used primarily before Latin nouns or before weights and measures.

> The cost *per* capita is small.
>
> The maximum rate allowed is 55 miles *per* hour.
>
> She wants to talk with you about (not *as per*) your request.

8.   Recognize word groups that are used as prepositions. Here are a few examples of such prepositions with possible objects:

> *because of* the circumstances   *apart from* this minor problem
> *according to* the report   *instead of* the new edition

Note carefully the precise use of prepositions by well-educated speakers and writers—and use your dictionary frequently. Many a verb or an adjective must be followed by a particular preposition in order to convey clearly its intended meaning. In some instances another acceptable meaning will result if the preposition is changed. Hundreds of such words could be listed here, together with the prepositions that should be used with them. The few that follow will serve as examples.

1.	accompany by (a person)	The president was *accompanied by* the firm's chief counsel.
2.	accompany with (an object)	The blueprints were *accompanied with* the necessary specifications.
3.	acquaint with	I will be pleased to *acquaint* you *with* your new surroundings.
4.	acquit of (a charge)	He was *acquitted of* the charge against him.
5.	adapt from	The new model will be *adapted from* this sample.
6.	adapt to	Attempt to *adapt* yourself *to* this new environment.
7.	agree to (to consent or accede)	They *agreed to* the terms of the contract.

8.	agree with (to have same opinion)	I *agree with* what you have said.
9.	allude to	Please don't *allude to* my inexperience again.
10.	cognizant of	The auditor did not seem *cognizant of* the error.
11.	compare to (show similarity)	This office building may be *compared to* a small town.
12.	compare with (examine two objects or people)	Please *compare* this typewriter *with* the other.
13.	compensate for	The broker must be *compensated for* her services.
14.	comply with	He was willing to *comply with* my orders.
15.	consistent with	That error is not *consistent with* her usual performance.
16.	convenient for	Will four o'clock be *convenient for* you?
17.	convenient to (near)	Our office is *convenient to* the Capitol.
18.	conversant with	Few people are *conversant with* this new technique.
19.	correspond to (be similar)	This duplicator *corresponds to* the one we recently sold.
20.	correspond with (write)	We often *correspond with* our salesman in the Midwest.
21.	deal in (merchandise)	Their firm *deals in* earth-moving equipment.
22.	deal with (subjects)	The speaker seemed reluctant to *deal with* capital punishment.
23.	depend on (or *upon*)	You can *depend upon* our company to deliver the merchandise.
24.	differ from (to be unlike)	A living trust *differs from* a testamentary trust.
25.	differ with (disagree)	I *differ with* what she just said.
26.	different from (not *than*)	My desk is *different from* yours in many respects.
27.	encroach on (or *upon*)	A portion of this building *encroaches on* your neighbor's property.
28.	equivalent to	Her income is roughly *equivalent to* mine.
29.	identical with	Their computer is *identical with* ours.
30.	indicative of	That excellent sales total is *indicative of* the firm's efficient management.
31.	insist on (or *upon*)	We will *insist on* a new contract.
32.	liable for (responsible)	You will be *liable for* any damage done to the vehicle.
33.	liable to (susceptible)	His bout with pneumonia has made him *liable to* heart attacks.
34.	parallel to	The fence runs *parallel to* the sidewalk.
35.	reminiscent of	Today's meeting is *reminiscent of* one held two years ago.
36.	responsible for	All workers are held *responsible for* the tools they use.
37.	similar to	His bookcase is *similar to* mine.
38.	specialize in	We plan to *specialize in* sporting goods.
39.	talk to (one speaker)	The candidate *talked to* a large, attentive audience.
40.	talk with	The judge and the attorney *talked with* each other for several minutes.

_____WORKSHEET 21_____

PREPOSITIONS

PART A. Indicate whether each statement is true or false by inserting T or F in the space provided.

1. A sentence may begin or end with a prepositional phrase.

    1. *_____

2. A sentence must never end with a preposition.

    2. _____

3. A prepositional phrase always starts with a single-word preposition.

    3. _____

4. A preposition may have a clause as its object.

    4. _____

5. Prepositional phrases may modify verbs and nouns, as well as other parts of speech.

    5. _____

6. Prepositional phrases must have single-word objects.

    6. _____

7. It is wordy to use the expression *all of my children.*

    7. _____

8. Acceptable writing uses *like* in this way: *He looks like he is tired.*

    8. _____

9. *Accompany by* refers to things; *accompany with* refers to people.

    9. _____

10. *Different* and *differ* should be accompanied with the preposition *from,* not *than.*

    10. _____

PART B. If a sentence contains a preposition that is improperly used, underscore the preposition and write the correct word in the space provided. If the sentence contains no errors, place a C in the space. Argue for your decisions with your team partners.

Example: Your version of the incident is not consistent <u>to</u> Blakely's.

        with _____

1. Our office manager entered the information in the computer data base.

    1. *_____

2. She is cognizant with the fact that growing our database grows our market.

    2. *_____

3. We have a computer system identical to IBM's.

    3. *_____

4. The system manual alludes with IBM often.

    4. _____

5. Our spreadsheet patterns differ slightly with standard ones.

    5. _____

6. One of our part time systems analysts specializes on database troubleshooting.

    6. _____

7. He believes system advantages often run parallel with their disadvantages.

    7. _____

We worked and they read the newspaper.

The clock simply stopped or someone damaged it.

The job is difficult and it requires patience.

BUT: Ragoff wants the job, but he isn't eligible.

There were no customers, so we left early. (If the connective is something other than *and* or *or*, the comma is needed.)

CHOOSING CONJUNCTIVE ADVERBS

Because conjunctive adverbs both modify and connect, they should be chosen with care. Let's consider a few definitions:

Conjunctive Adverb	*Meaning*
therefore, consequently, hence	as a result; for that reason
however, nevertheless	in spite of this (or that); still; yet; but
moreover, furthermore, besides	in addition to that
otherwise	in other circumstances; in other respects; or else
thus	in this (or that) manner or way; because of this (or that)

Although some of these conjunctive adverbs are shown here as being synonymous, a good dictionary may indicate shades of difference in meaning. The word *however*, for example, suggests a moderate concession or a second point to be considered; *nevertheless* emphasizes direct opposition. Note carefully the use of conjunctive adverbs in these sentences:

The defendant was proved guilty; nevertheless (in spite of that fact), he was allowed to go free.

The new equipment is of superb quality; moreover (in addition to that fact), it will fit perfectly into the space available.

The shipment did come late; however (in spite of that fact), we were not inconvenienced.

She wrote the report; therefore (for that reason), she is responsible.

CORRELATIVE CONJUNCTIONS

Correlatives are conjunctions used in pairs to join coordinate words, phrases, and clauses. Occasionally an adverb and a conjunction are used as a pair to accomplish the same purpose. Here are a few common correlatives:

both . . . and   neither . . . nor

either . . . or   not only . . . but also

A pair of correlatives should be placed so that the sentence elements following them are *parallel* in form.

DON'T USE: He was asked *either* to buy supplies from the Lansing Corporation *or* the Boynton Company.

USE: He was asked to buy supplies from *either* the Lansing Corporation *or* the Boynton Company.

DON'T USE: Mr. Kelso is *not only* experienced *but also* has had five profitable years of college.

USE: Mr. Kelso is *not only* experienced *but also* well educated.

The meaning of *parallel in form* may be more apparent if we study a sentence that has been set up in this manner:

Hoxley should *either* ship the cement
or he should give us a reason for the delay.

You will note that the first correlative, *either,* is followed by the verb *ship;* but the second correlative, *or,* is followed by a pronoun that introduces an independent clause. We can easily eliminate any problem in parallelism by wording the sentence in this way:

Hoxley should *either* ship the cement
or give us a reason for the delay.

In this improved version, parallel structure has not been violated because both correlatives, *either* and *or,* are followed by verbs. This sentence, as a result, would be considerably more acceptable in today's business writing.

SIMPLE SENTENCES

A **simple sentence** is one that contains only one clause. Be careful not to mistake it for a compound sentence, which has at least two independent clauses. A clause, you will recall, has a subject-verb combination. An *independent* clause could be used as a sentence. Keep that thought in mind as you examine the following sentences. They are all *simple.*

The directors meet on the first Friday of each month.

The new textile plant in Jacksonville is now open.

The plaintiff and his attorney were embarrassed.

The judge hurried into the courtroom and took her place on the bench.

Ms. Blaine and Ms. Cone appeared in court but did not testify.

Mr. Crawford, having hired the guilty bookkeeper, felt responsible.

Note that no sentence on the preceding list has more than one subject-verb combination. If the last sentence were compound, it would read something like this: *Mr. Crawford hired the guilty bookkeeper; therefore, he felt responsible.* Bear in mind that a simple sentence may be long and have several phrases or compound elements—but only *one* clause.

FINAL THOUGHTS

It would be an excellent idea to memorize the short list of coordinating conjunctions that we have discussed. There are seven: *and, but, or, nor, for, so,* and *yet.*

Two simple sentences can often be joined to form a compound sentence. Here are two simple sentences: *The telegram arrived this morning. Mr. Lutz did not reveal its contents.* Most writers would prefer this compound sentence: *The telegram arrived this morning, but Mr. Lutz did not reveal its contents.*

The terms *conjunctive adverb* and *transitional phrase* are of minor importance. They refer, as you now know, to those words that we sometimes use to smooth the way from one independent clause to another. If the connecting word or phrase is anything other than a coordinating conjunction, a semicolon should be used.

Although the comma following a conjunctive adverb or transitional phrase is optional, most writers choose to insert it, as in this sentence: *Provost has the necessary qualifications; therefore, I voted for him.* You will be expected to insert optional commas in Worksheet 22.

Some grammarians think of connectives as the *glue* used to hold sentences and paragraphs together. In compound sentences they serve as *bridges* that help readers move smoothly from one independent clause to another. The readability of your writing and mine depends in part on our skillful use of connectives.

THE TEST OF REASONABLENESS

If you have taken a course in business arithmetic, you have probably learned to think in terms of *reasonableness.* You know that it would not be reasonable to add five large fractions and conclude that they total less than *one-half.*

Similarly, anyone taking a course involving communication would be wise to think in terms of reasonableness. The numbered sentences that follow were taken from a newspaper article. Whether you have a clear understanding of English grammar or not, you should be able to detect the illogical *(unreasonable)* portion of each one.

1. If you ask them what they think about that statement, you may find out what's going on in their own mind.
2. People will probably do what was done when they were a child.

--- **FOR CLASS DISCUSSION** ---

Tell how you would improve the foregoing sentences; then discuss why many people, even journalists, communicate in such unreasonable ways.

---

wWWw ============ **Watching the Web** ============

Back	Forward	Home	Reload	Images	Open

```
Download National News
To download our evening news broadcast directly onto your
hard drive, either press "download now" to begin the
process or you can return to this screen after checking
the other options on the menu.
```

[download now]   [I'll wait]

Name _Alisha_   Date _1-28-09_

———— WORKSHEET 22 ————

CONNECTIVES IN COORDINATE CONSTRUCTIONS

PART A. Indicate the kind of sentence by writing A or B in the answer space.

A. compound   B. simple

1. Set up the new account file; then begin entering the data.

       1. * ~~XXXX~~ A.

2. Every data field on every record must be complete and up-to-date.

       2. * B.

3. For customers outside of New York, enter the letter code ONY.

       3. B.

4. In the case of Manhattan customers, no code is necessary.

       4. B.

5. Customers from anywhere else in New York are identified by their 3-digit area code.

       5. B.

6. Account information is critical, but so far we have not tracked it well.

       6. A.

7. Our data staff is hard-working, yet they have been unable to maintain records.

       7. A.

8. The new entry system should make accurate recording easy and efficient.

       8. B.

9. The accounts manager is skeptical; however, I have vouched for this department.

       9. A.

10. We will be careful in managing this new system, and we will reap the benefits.

       10. A.

PART B. Add commas and semicolons according to the rules in Chapter 22. Insert all optional commas. In the answer space indicate the number of punctuation marks you have added. If no punctuation is needed, put 0 in the space. Convince your partners of the reasonableness of your choices.

Example: Mr. Luzak prepared a statement but he did not sign it.

      Mr. Luzak prepared a statement, but he did not sign it.

          _1_

1. Metropolitan Institute invites nominations and applications for the position of Vice President for Institutional Relations.

       1. * 0

2. This executive will report directly to and serve at the pleasure of the President of the Institute.

       2. 0

3. The vice president has responsibilities for government relations; conditionally public relations and media relations may be placed into this job description.

     additionally

       3. * 2

4. Minimum requirements include a baccalaureate degree and seven years of significant management experience in a complex organization.

       4. 0

5. The search committee desires the candidate to have additional qualifications these may include an advanced degree and executive-level experience in an educational setting.

5. * 1

6. Experience in managing complex internal and external communication strategies would be helpful but experience in higher education issues are the most critical qualification.

6. 1

7. The candidate should know about public relations issues affecting Metropolitan Institute however this knowledge can also be acquired on the job.

7. 2

8. The vice presidential candidate must be able to demonstrate success in creating and managing effective change efforts in complex organizations.

8. 0

9. Anyone seeking this position must be multi-faceted he or she must have formed successful partnerships with the business community in prior work.

9. 1

10. Interested candidates will have held public leadership positions in civic groups or on governing boards.

10. 0

11. They must be able to demonstrate a record of implementing principles for fair hiring and increasing diversity in the work force must be a priority.

11. 1

12. Susan Jackson has the job description contact her at the Institute's main campus.

12. 1

13. Applications will be reviewed beginning April 30 and accepted until the position is filled.

13. 0

14. Applications should include a cover letter and vitae and the address and telephone numbers of at least three references.

14. 0

15. References will be contacted without the approval of the candidate.

15. 0

PART C. In the space provided, write the connective that would be used logically in the sentence. Note the *punctuation* carefully. Make each choice from this list of connectives:

| and | therefore | furthermore |
| but | however | otherwise |

Example: Fill in every blank on the form; _____, we cannot consider your application.

_____otherwise_____

1. Our office can claim a 20 percent improvement, _____ this achievement will be recognized by headquarters.

1. * and

2. The blanks had not been filled in; _____, I refused to sign the contract.

2. * therefore

3. The software is colorful and interesting; _____, it is not user-friendly.

3. * however

4. The conference call feature is convenient, _____ it is too expensive.

4. * but

5. The trust agreement contains one minor typographical error; _____, it has been prepared perfectly.

5. otherwise

6. Her degree is in accounting; _____, she has experience as a CPA.

6. however furthermore

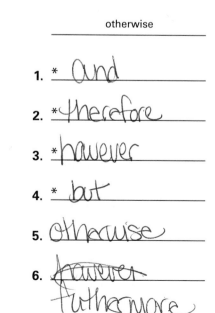

240   CONNECTIVES IN COORDINATE CONSTRUCTIONS

7. Your contract is about to expire, ____ the department needs to know if you intend to negotiate a new one.

8. Hirtle has no need for an insurance policy; ____, he will not buy one.

9. The strike will begin tomorrow; ____, it will involve all departments.

10. Our computer is down; ____, I could supply the report you requested on hard copy.

7. _and_____

8. _therefore_____

9. ~~however~~ _furthermore_

10. ~~otherwise~~ _however_

PART D. Underscore with a single line all simple sentences and with a double line all compound sentences in this memo paragraph.

All personnel are invited to attend the banquet and to bring a guest if they choose.* We especially welcome children and spouses. Our emphasis this year is on feeding the hungry, so please help us by bringing a nonperishable food item for the food shelf. It is our goal to gather 1,000 pounds of food, and for that we need your help. So bring a guest and a grocery item; you'll be giving support to your community. We look forward to seeing you at the banquet.

PART E. Write *compound* sentences on the subject of "Employee Evaluations." In each one you are to join independent clauses with the connective shown. (You are free to use your imagination in presenting any "facts.")

1. (furthermore) *_____

_____

_____

2. (accordingly) _____

_____

_____

3. (for example) _____

_____

_____

4. (otherwise) _____

_____

_____

5. (therefore) _____

_____

_____

PART F. Rewrite the following sentences. Make certain that what follows the first correlative is parallel to what follows the second one. (All correlatives are in italics.)

1. Either Yang will visit the manufacturer or not.

   * _____

   _____

2. We should acquire not only a scanner but also we need a more powerful search engine.

   _____

   _____

3. She wants both to send our materials to Endicott and ask him to edit them.

   _____

   _____

THE IMPACT OF LANGUAGE

THE UNDEPENDABLE EAR

An intelligent person may communicate with reasonable skill by applying the "sound test." Although a construction that *sounds* correct is likely to *be* correct, there are times when the human ear proves undependable. Consider this sentence taken from an article in *The Wall Street Journal:*

> He said there were an attempted robbery at the store two weeks earlier and a $160,000 robbery late last year.

———————————— FOR CLASS DISCUSSION ————————————

Justify the use of *were* in the preceding sentence, which *is* grammatically correct.

OPTIONAL EXERCISES:

OPTION 1   Add commas and semicolons as needed. In the answer space indicate the number of marks added. If no punctuation is needed, put 0 in the space. Insert optional commas. If you are collaborating, try each sentence independently and then confer about your answers.

1. Our company policy prohibits moonlighting however many workers do it.

1. *_____

2. Meet your deadline or lose $900 of your budget for next season.

2. _____

3. I will need help with the Zeller file I believe it extends back almost 15 years.

3. _____

4. Find the most common price per share accordingly plan the average expenditure.

4. _____

5. Taylor was responsible for the loss but not for the resulting customer dissatisfaction.

5. _____

6. Moving to larger quarters was hard work but it resulted in more efficiency.

6. *_____

7. Give Scheffer a reminder memo tell him he is expected at 2:00 P.M. sharp.

7. _____

8. No one expected much from her consequently we were delighted with her perfect record.

8. _____

9. Petrocelli is investigating a fraud case but he has uncovered no evidence.

9. _____

10. Darhmajhin has been nominated but is sure to decline the office.

10. _____

11. Two of our regional directors have flouted several policies yet nothing has been said.

11. _____

12. Seinfeld's family has been in shipping for four generations they understand embargoes.

12. _____

13. Higher fule costs were unanticipated and our prices will rise accordingly.

13. _____

14. Kendrick will speak about our mission statement and will cast a vision for the firm.

14. _____

15. Will you be driving a company car or will you use your own car and apply for mileage reimbursement?

15. _____

OPTION 2   Write four sentences. In each one you are to use the correlatives shown in parentheses.

1. (both . . . and) *_____

_____

_____

2. (either . . . or) _____

_____

_____

3. (neither . . . nor) _____

_____

_____

4. (not only . . . but also) _____

_____

_____

OPTION 3   (CLASS DISCUSSION)   You have read that the comma following a conjunctive adverb is optional. Tell why you would or would not place commas after the italicized connectives in these sentences:

1. The function keys on my keyboard are not labeled; *therefore,* (comma optional) I will need a user's manual.

2. Human services is holding a benefits workshop today; *consequently,* (comma optional) all department meetings will be postponed.

3. The company newsletter contained a classified section; *that is,* (comma optional) in those pages employees may advertise items they wish to sell.

4. Perkins cannot miss any of the next three sales meetings; *otherwise,* (comma optional) he will be removed from the team.

Do you feel that the addition of a comma, in each instance, will change the way in which the sentence is read? How much emphasis does the connective deserve?

Connectives in Complex Sentences

■■■ POINT TO PONDER

Complex sentences can add a professional touch to one's business writing.

In the preceding chapter we considered simple and compound sentences, how they are formed and how they are punctuated. This chapter will be concerned, for the most part, with complex sentences and the part played by conjunctions in forming them.

We have defined a **coordinating conjunction** as one that joins words, phrases, and clauses of equal rank or importance. A **subordinating conjunction** joins clauses of unequal rank, that is, an independent clause to a dependent (subordinate) clause. You may recall from your reading of Chapter 4 that a dependent clause cannot stand alone; it depends upon the main clause and is subordinate to it.

COMPLEX SENTENCES

A **complex sentence** has one independent clause and one or more dependent clauses. Many dependent clauses are introduced by subordinating conjunctions. In fact, it may be a conjunction that makes a clause subordinate. The words on the following list appear frequently as subordinating conjunctions, although some may also be used as other parts of speech.

after	as though	in order to
although	because	provided
as	before	since
as if	if	so that

than	until	wherever
that	when	whether
though	whenever	while
unless	where	

Adverb Clauses

Adverb clauses are dependent clauses generally used to modify verbs. They are introduced by subordinating conjunctions and answer questions such as *Why? Where? When? How? To what degree? Under what circumstances? For what purpose? With what result?*

The adverb clause may be placed after or before the main clause of a sentence. It seems natural to write the main clause first and then the adverb clause, which ordinarily modifies the verb in the main clause. It performs that function in these sentences:

> We listened intently *while Mr. Sieburn talked.* (The adverb clause, in italics, obviously modifies the verb *listened.*)
>
> No one was surprised *when Senator Peal proposed the legislation.*
>
> She rejected our offer *because she could not secure the necessary financing.*
>
> We hurried from the auditorium *as soon as the lecture had ended.*

Note that commas were not used in the foregoing sentences. Now let's transpose the clauses in each of the four sentences.

> *While Mr. Sieburn talked,* we listened intently.
>
> *When Senator Peal proposed the legislation,* no one was surprised.
>
> *Because she could not secure the necessary financing,* she rejected our offer.
>
> *As soon as the lecture had ended,* we hurried from the auditorium.

Each of the preceding sentences has been punctuated according to this rule:

RULE 1   Use a comma after an introductory adverb clause.

A clause of this type should be considered *introductory* if it precedes the main clause to which it refers.

Seasoned writers take liberties with many of the punctuation rules suggested by grammarians. Some fine writers do not use commas after adverb clauses if they feel there is no chance that the sentence will be misread. Most writers, however, prefer to follow the rule implicitly by setting off *all* introductory clauses of this type.

Ordinarily no comma is needed if the adverb clause follows the main (independent) clause. There are times, however, when punctuation must be used to satisfy the requirements of this rule:

RULE 2   Use commas to set off nonrestrictive clauses.

When a nonrestrictive adverb clause follows a main clause, it is likely to be used almost as an afterthought. Because it is *nonrestrictive,* it could be removed from the sentence without

Name _Alisha Hicks_ **Date** _1-30-02_

_____WORKSHEET 23_____

CONNECTIVES IN COMPLEX SENTENCES

PART A. Underscore the conjunction in each sentence; then write A or B to indicate whether it is _subordinating_ or _coordinating._

A. subordinating conjunction   B. coordinating conjunction
   or relative pronoun   FANBOYS

Example: He now works in electronics, <u>but</u> he may change jobs in
                 April.

                                                                              B

1. Because our division has done so well this year, the C.E.O. will
   make a presentation to us at the convention.   1. * _A._

2. We expect her to give us a certificate, or an engraved company clock. 2. * _B._

3. Our marketing approach was solid, and our sales staff has worked
   hard.   3. _B._

4. Most departments can excel if those two factors are working well. 4. _A._

5. Since we will be award recipients, we have all decided to attend the
   convention.   5. _A._

6. Those who can afford it will take their family vacations at that time. 6. _A._

7. They will converge on Chicago, where this year's convention will be
   held.   7. _A._

8. Others will take two days off work and visit the Windy City for the
   presentation.   8. _B._

9. It will be memorable to have families around us when the C.E.O.
   makes her speech.   9. _A._

10. As soon as we return, the award will be placed prominently in our
    department.   10. _A._

PART B. In the space provided, write the word(s) modified by the clause in italics.

Example: The surplus airplane parts _that you want_ will
                 be sold at auction on Saturday.   parts

1. Auctions are commonplace in the regions _where_
   production is commonplace.   1. ~~Auctions~~ regions

2. For example, a person _who is looking for tractors_
   goes to John Deere country.   2. a person

3. Sometimes the city and the bank hold an auction
   after a business failure.   3. * hold

4. Sometimes businesses decide to sell off merchandise *that hasn't sold well.*

5. *As long as people have surplus goods,* we will have auctions.

4. ~~Merchandise~~

5. ~~Auctions~~ will have

PART C. In each sentence one of the words in parentheses is correct. Write that word in the answer space.

1. Thoma read (that, where) the company would downize within the year.

2. This action is essential (except, unless) profits suddenly soar.

3. All current grants will still be (disbursed, dispersed) as planned.

4. Administrators will try (and, to) keep their divisions from panicking.

5. Speculation about layoffs creates anxiety, (and, but) good leaders can prevent much overreaction.

6. They will communicate immediately (so, so that) fears can be allayed.

7. The 90,000 employees of this multinational corporation are (disbursed, dispersed) throughout the world.

8. None of us have any doubt (that, but what) we have time to build profits.

9. We must be sure (and, to) make sensible decisions this season.

10. If we work hard and remain confident, we may not (loose, lose) our jobs.

1. * that

2. * unless

3. ~~dispersed~~ disbursed

4. to

5. but

6. So that

7. ~~disbursed~~ dispersed

8. that

9. ~~and~~ to

10. lose

PART D. Insert commas and semicolons, including those that are considered optional. In the space provided, indicate the number of punctuation marks you have added. Write 0 if no punctuation is needed. If you are collaborating, decide together on the best punctuation choices.

1. Some office groups are considering customizing shifts; such planning can yield many benefits.

2. Shift customizing can ease burdens on parking, because people come and go at times other than rush hour.

3. Parents can build in longer lunch hours, if their families need mealtime help.

4. Customized shifts cut down heavy elevator traffic during peak times, and most workers discover that they spend less waiting time, as a result.

5. Although shift customization is fairly easy to accomplish, it does require what Victor Bono calls *lateral thinking.*

6. Instead of managers setting shift expectations, shift customization begins its planning with the majority of the employees, those who comprise the major workforce.

1. * 1

2. ~~0~~ 0

3. ~~0~~ 0

4. * ~~1~~ 1

5. 1

6. ~~0~~ 2

7. Work teams think together about what they need, then they consider the most logical way to get work done.

7. _____

8. After they have made their best suggestions, they pass them along to another team of shift planners.

8. _____

9. This team looks at available space resources, they also consider current and projected production plans, and they draft a customized schedule.

9. _____

10. As soon as the second team's draft is done, it is sent back to the original work teams, they see which of their expectations have been met.

10. _____

11. They also look at the big picture of production while they consider personal and departmental desires.

11. _____

12. If there is enough leeway in the draft, the original teams approve it, and that plan typically begins the following month.

12. _____

13. If there are too many difficulties with the draft, the original teams create a new draft of their own for the second team's consideration.

13. _____

14. In the end, all the involved planners feel ownership of the plan, and it stands a far better chance of solving resource and scheduling problems.

14. _____

PART E. Find and underscore the ten errors in word choice in the following paragraph from a business letter and then, on a separate sheet of paper, edit it into a better paragraph with your collaborative team.

The new finance manager looks underqualified on paper, but I think we may have trouble with him. I heard from someone who worked with him two years ago where he would try and save time at the end of every fiscal period by dispersing account funds himself rather than leaving it to the account executives. The person who told me this had no doubt but what this procedure caused problems with record keeping and was responsible for his loosing significant profit. I think we should discuss this matter with him and tell him that he cannot stay with our firm except he follows our established rules for dispersement. We need to have that conversation so he knows we really do want him to remain with us providing he rises to our standards.

PART F. Rewrite each of the following compound sentences to make it complex.

Example: Mr. Wilson owns five oil wells, and he has given considerable money to charity.
Mr. Wilson, who owns five oil wells, has given considerable money to charity.

1. Mr. Grant is an excellent landscape artist, and he plans to join our firm.

   _____

   _____

   _____

2. Janet Hosmer has a law degree, and she visited every European country on her recent trip.

   _____

   _____

   _____

3. The tractor had broken down four times within a month, so we sold it.

   * _____

   _____

   _____

4. Our microcomputer may be somewhat small, but it is capable of handling this job.

   _____

   _____

   _____

5. Our senior accountant lost his wife and his daughter in an automobile accident, and he is uneasy about driving at high speeds.

   _____

   _____

   _____

_____ FOR CLASS DISCUSSION _____

(if time permits)

The skillful use of conjunctions, relative pronouns, and appropriate punctuation will allow a writer to combine ideas in a variety of ways. Can you think of at least five different sentences, either compound or complex, that combine these thoughts:

Mr. Silverman is 65 years old. He will retire in June.
Tell what punctuation you would use in each sentence.

THE IMPACT OF LANGUAGE

Quiz (Chapters 20 through 23)

NAME _____

DIRECTIONS

Your instructor may ask you to examine any four of the sentences that follow. Some contain errors in wording; others contain errors in punctuation. On the lines provided, you are to express in complete statements the rules or principles that have been violated. Be careful to spell every word correctly. If you are collaborating, make each decision together before answering.

1. The four of you may divide the profit between yourselves.
2. He was unwilling to confide in Mr. Hixson and I.
3. Ms. Whitney does not enjoy her work like she once did.
4. Either Mr. Tilman should cooperate or resign.
5. Operating costs have increased drastically but Ms. Webb is not alarmed.
6. Ms. Welby was real sorry to hear about your accident.
7. Briggs & Lowe, Inc., produces the pistons, we manufacture the iron housing.
8. When the telephone rang, which desk were you sitting at?
9. I read in this book where the atmosphere is changing.
10. Some brands of cough syrup really taste badly.
11. My project can be completed quicker than yours.
12. Lee Kralick who wrote the memorandum is not working today.

Sentence No._____ Answer:_____
_____
_____
_____

Sentence No._____ Answer:_____
_____
_____
_____

Sentence No._____ Answer:_____
_____
_____
_____

Sentence No._____ Answer:_____
_____
_____
_____

THE IMPACT OF LANGUAGE

ALL THE PREPOSITIONS?

A vice president of a national retail department store chain served with me on an advisory committee. When he discovered I was an English teacher, he stood up and announced that he knew all the prepositions. Then he recited the list. Although the words he recited may function as more than one part of speech, I was impressed that he remembered them all. I have no doubt his mastery of the list is not in vain. He will know for certain any word on his list is a preposition *if it is followed by an object.*

about	between	like	since
across	beyond	near	through
after	by	of	throughout
against	concerning	off	to
along	down	on	toward
among	during	opposite	under
around	except	outside	until
at	for	over	up
before	from	past	upon
beneath	in	per	with
beside	inside	plus	within
besides	into	regarding	without

———————————— FOR CLASS DISCUSSION ————————————

All words listed here are frequently used as prepositions. Can you use at least five of them as other parts of speech?

Review

People who can use language effectively land the most lucrative positions in corporations.

Following is a review of the most important principles covered in Chapters 17 through 23. The material treated in that portion of the text—adjectives, adverbs, prepositions, and conjunctions, as well as verbals—may well prove challenging. Before you begin Worksheet 24, make certain that you have memorized these definitions:

1. An adjective is a word that modifies a noun or a pronoun.
2. An adverb is a word that modifies a verb form, an adjective, or another adverb (or any adverb equivalent).
3. A preposition is a word (or word group) that shows the relation of its object to some other word in the sentence.
4. A conjunction is a connective used to join words, phrases, or clauses.
5. A verbal is a verb form used as a noun, an adjective, or an adverb. Infinitives, gerunds, and participles are verbals.

FREQUENTLY MADE ERRORS

Each of the following numbered sentences would be unacceptable in its present form. Attempt to determine precisely *why* it would be unacceptable before you read the explanation that has been provided.

1. She likes to occasionally take dictation.

Did you recognize the split infinitive in the preceding sentence? The adverb *occasionally* has been placed between the two words that make up the infinitive *(to take),* and the resultant construction is awkward. A careful writer would word the sentence in this manner: *She likes to take dictation occasionally.*

2.   We had not heard about Carl receiving the award.

In this sentence the gerund *receiving* is the object of the preposition *about; award* is the object of *receiving.* (Although they are verbal *nouns,* gerunds can take objects.) You may remember that a noun or a pronoun used to modify a gerund must be in the possessive case. We can improve the sentence by simply changing *Carl* to *Carl's.*

3.   Taking his rapid dictation, it is impossible to avoid errors.

This sentence contains an excellent example of a dangling verbal phrase. The introductory participial (verbal) phrase is logically a modifier, but there is nothing for it to modify. Here is a more acceptable wording: *Taking his rapid dictation, I could not avoid making errors.* In this improved version the verbal phrase modifies *I.*

4.   He is shorter than anyone in his family.

This sentence seems to suggest that *he* is not a member of his own family. Note carefully these two acceptable versions: *He is shorter than anyone else in his family* and *He is shorter than any other person in his family.*

5.   He refused to pay the agreed upon price.

This sentence may be difficult to understand because a hyphen has been omitted in the compound adjective *agreed-upon.* Remember that two or more words may be joined to form a compound adjective if they come before the word modified and carry the force of a single modifier. Some professional writers tend to omit such hyphens when they feel that the meaning of a particular sentence is perfectly clear without them. To be certain that *your* meaning is not obscure, make it a habit to insert hyphens in constructions such as *agreed-upon price.*

6.   Nancy Washington handled the situation real good.

The verb *handled* should be modified by the adverb *well,* not the adjective *good.* Remember that adverbs are used to modify verbs, adjectives, and other adverbs. The word *real,* which careful writers employ as an adjective, should not have been used to modify an adverb. The last two words (*real good*) should be changed to *very well.*

7.   Most employees do not want to begin in sales like I did.

In this sentence the word *like,* which generally functions as a preposition or verb, has been used to introduce a short clause. The conjunction *as* should be substituted; in other such constructions *as if, as though,* or *that* may prove more acceptable. Remember to avoid the use of *like* if the word that follows is the subject of a verb.

8.   Either help with the addressing of envelopes or the proofreading of letters.

This sentence lacks parallel structure in that the correlative conjunctions have been used improperly. *Either* is followed by a verb; *or* is followed by an adjective. Study carefully this acceptable version: *Help with either the addressing of envelopes or the proofreading of letters.*

    9.   The shelves are deep enough, however, they are somewhat narrow.

Did you recognize the foregoing as a compound sentence? Because the second independent clause has been introduced with a conjunctive adverb, the first comma should be changed to a semicolon.

    10.   My oldest brother who lives in this city plans to run for councilman.

This sentence, you will undoubtedly agree, should be punctuated with two commas, one after *brother* and one after *city.* The word *oldest* identifies the brother being discussed; therefore, the *who* clause simply provides some additional information and must be considered nonrestrictive. A clause of this type, which must be set off with commas, can be removed from a sentence without materially changing the meaning of the main clause.

    11.   She only gave us ten minutes to arrive at an answer.

As you may have detected, the placement of the word *only* in this sentence is not entirely satisfactory. Because it logically modifies the word *ten,* the sentence should be changed to read *She gave us only ten minutes to arrive at an answer.*

    12.   He responds quicker than most of our students.

In this sentence the use of *quicker,* which is basically an adjective, should be challenged. Because the word has been used to modify a verb *(responds),* most business writers would substitute an adverb, as in this wording: *He responds more quickly than most of our students.*

    13.   Those kind are produced by a local manufacturer.

It is illogical to combine *those,* which is a plural form of an adjective, with *kind,* a singular noun. This sentence should begin in either of these ways: *That kind is produced* or *Those kinds are produced.*

    14.   The house needs a coat of paint, the garage is in excellent condition.

Note that no coordinating conjunction has been used to join the independent clauses in this sentence. The comma, of course, should be changed to a semicolon.

    15.   When everyone had been seated Mr. Cole began his talk.

Because the dependent clause in this complex sentence precedes the main clause, a comma should be placed after the word *seated.* Remember that introductory adverb clauses are generally set off by commas.

TERMINOLOGY

In Chapters 17 through 23 there are several grammatical terms that you may have found unfamiliar. Take a few moments to check your understanding of these:

verbal	gerund
infinitive	participle
split infinitive	dangling modifier
misplaced modifier	coordinating conjunction
absolute phrase	subordinating conjunction
positive degree	conjunctive adverb
comparative degree	transitional phrase
superlative degree	correlative conjunctions
compound adjective	introductory adverb clause
coordinate adjectives	restrictive clause (or phrase)
simple sentence	nonrestrictive clause (or phrase)
compound sentence	noun clause
complex sentence	adjective clause
compound-complex sentence	

REVIEW CHART

concept	Ch. ____ page ____	first critical point to remember	example	second critical point to remember	example
adjectives					
adverbs					
modifier placement					
sentence types		simple compound complex compound–complex			
prepositional phrases					
conjunction types		coordinating subordinating correlative conjunctive adverb			
verbals		gerunds participles infinitives			

_____WORKSHEET 24_____

REVIEW

PART A. Indicate the kind of sentence by writing *simple, compound, complex,* or *compound-complex* in the answer space. Convince your partner(s) of your selection using ideas from the chapter.

1. The "What Business Thinks III" poll was conducted by Bob McReynolds.

   1. * _____

2. McReynolds is a cofounder of Polling Incorporated, an on-line survey firm.

   2. _____

3. He augments poll research by inviting focus groups of business executives to discuss what they believe are the relevant issues of the day.

   3. _____

4. The focus results are given to public policy makers; these unfiltered reactions of business persons then affect a wide variety of policy issues.

   4. * _____

5. When these groups meet, they can get behind the "facts" of the poll to the values that determine why respondents behave the way they do.

   5. _____

6. The most vital groups devote about an hour to the issue of the day and then devote another "unofficial" hour to a wide range of issues that matter to them.

   6. _____

7. These ruminations tend to include some good stories, and the best ones are published.

   7. _____

8. Some interesting conversations this year found their way into *Business Journal,* but far more interesting were the exchanges that never made it to the page.

   8. _____

9. These discussions dwelled primarily on the challenges of working in an economy of virtually full employment.

   9. _____

PART B. Note the word in italics and indicate its part of speech by writing the appropriate letter.

   A. an adverb   C. an adjective
   B. a conjunction   D. a preposition

1. The package should reach Butte *within* two days.

   1. * _____

2. We need one more actuary *and* one more claims examiner.

   2. _____

3. *After* Saturday these items will not be on sale.

   3. _____

4. *Because* Monday was a holiday, my letter did not reach you by the 14th.

   4. * _____

5. Immel's ideas are not *really* conservative.

5. _____

6. Ms. Gold should have stayed at home if she is not *well.*

6. _____

7. Call me immediately *if* you hear from Trowbridge.

7. _____

8. He asked me some interesting questions *about* microchips.

8. _____

9. Ramon does his work rather *lackadaisically.*

9. _____

10. Every copy that this machine produced is *perfect.*

10. _____

PART C. Decide together which *letter* indicates the truth about each sentence.

   A. This sentence has a gerund improperly modified.
   B. This sentence has a dangling verbal phrase.
   C. This sentence has an awkward split infinitive.
   D. This sentence contains no errors.

1. Mr. Gault complained about Mert refusing to work overtime.

1. *_____

2. By driving at 60 miles an hour, the trip took only two hours.

2. _____

3. We would like to, as you know, modernize this building.

3. _____

4. We appreciated him helping with the terminology.

4. _____

5. In preparing the document, Faraday omitted a few crucial figures.

5. _____

PART D. Identify the sentence that would be most acceptable in a business communication by writing the appropriate *letter.* Pay particular attention to the words in italics.

1. (A) Our latest book will open a new market, just *as we forecasted.*
   (B) Our latest book will open a new market, just *like we forecast.*
   (C) Our latest book will open a new market, just *as we forecast.*

1. *_____

2. (A) We've never sold to teens; *but* this book will appeal to them.
   (B) We've never sold to teens; *however,* this book will appeal to them.
   (C) We've never sold to teens; *and* this book will appeal to them.

2. *_____

3. (A) Initially I differed *with* the head of marketing that certain figures corresponded *to* market share.
   (B) Initially I differed *with* the head of marketing that certain figures corresponded *with* market share.
   (C) Initially I differed *from* the head of marketing that certain figures corresponded *to* market share.

3. _____

4. (A) I believed that the market was divided *evenly between* the five consumer age brackets.
   (B) I believed that the market was divided *even between* the five consumer age brackets.
   (C) I believed that the market was divided *evenly among* the five consumer age brackets.

4. _____

5. (A) I was comparing past sales *to* the new strategy recently *adapted* by Bookhouse.
   (B) I was comparing past sales *with* the new strategy recently *adopted* by Bookhouse.
   (C) I was comparing past sales *to* the new strategy recently *adopted* by Bookhouse.

5. _____

6. (A) Then Peters demonstrated to Hall and *me that* our situation is quite different.

   (B) Then Peters demonstrated to Hall and *I that* our situation is quite different.

   (C) Then Peters demonstrated to Hall and *I where* our situation is quite different. **6.** _____

7. (A) Bookhouse's strategy deals *in* store sales; our strategy deals *in* catalog orders.

   (B) Bookhouse's strategy deals *with* store sales, our strategy deals *with* catalog orders.

   (C) Bookhouse's strategy deals *with* store sales; our strategy deals *with* catalog orders. **7.** _____

8. (A) At first having this oversight revealed made me angry *at* Peters.

   (B) At first having this oversight revealed made me angry *with* Peters.

   (C) At first having this oversight revealed, made me angry *with* Peters. **8.** _____

9. (A) Shortly thereafter, *however,* I realized *all of* our marketing people were right.

   (B) Shortly thereafter, *however;* I realized *all* our marketing people were right.

   (C) Shortly thereafter, *however,* I realized *all* our marketing people were right. **9.** _____

10. (A) We now anticipate a *rise* in revenue; success is *imminent.*

   (B) We now anticipate a *raise* in revenue; success is *imminent.*

   (C) We now anticipate a *rise* in revenue; success is *eminent.* **10.** _____

PART E. By writing the appropriate *letter* in the answer space, identify the sentence that has been correctly punctuated. If you are collaborating, make a case to your partner(s) for your choice.

1. (A) David Wong, who sells fine linens can be trusted completely.
   (B) David Wong, who sells fine linens, can be trusted completely.
   (C) David Wong who sells fine linens, can be trusted completely. **1.** *_____

2. (A) We should attend the seminar, however we have no time.
   (B) We should attend the seminar; however, we have no time.
   (C) We should attend the seminar, however, we have no time. **2.** _____

3. (A) Any letter that Ms. Stavros writes is likely to be satisfactory.
   (B) Any letter, that Ms. Stavros writes is likely to be satisfactory.
   (C) Any letter that Ms. Stavros writes, is likely to be satisfactory. **3.** _____

4. (A) We had completed our business, therefore, we left early.
   (B) We had completed our business, therefore we left early.
   (C) We had completed our business; therefore, we left early. **4.** _____

5. (A) Ms. Fazio has many talents, for example, she is an excellent photographer.
   (B) Ms. Fazio has many talents; for example, she is an excellent photographer.
   (C) Ms. Fazio has many talents, for example she is an excellent photographer. **5.** _____

PART F. Indicate the preferred choice by writing the appropriate *letter* in the space provided.

1. *My New Job* is designed
   (A) to significantly help your job search.
   (B) to help your job search significantly.

   1. *_____

2. As you complete the worksheets,
   (A) proceed purposefully.   (B) precede purposively.

   2. *_____

3. Recall your job history, but do not dwell
   (A) on the past.   (B) on the passed.

   3. _____

4. When you have reached the end, you will
   (A) sure be ready.   (B) surely be ready.

   4. _____

5. First, you need to claim which of your last two jobs fit you
   (A) best.   (B) better.

   5. *_____

6. Identify what made you
   (A) really fulfilled.   (B) real fulfilled.

   6. _____

7. List the five skills that you used
   (A) most in that occupation.   (B) more in that occupation.

   7. _____

8. Begin
   (A) carefully to complete the resume worksheet.
   (B) to carefully complete the resume worksheet.

   8. _____

9. If you use the chronological template, include the dates of
   (A) all of your prior work.   (B) all your prior work.

   9. _____

10. If you use the functional template, claim job skills by category
    (A) waving any dates.   (B) waiving any dates.

    10. _____

11. When drafting your actual resume, remember that
    (A) the less pages you use, the better.
    (B) the fewer pages you use, the better.

    11. _____

12. Resumes that begin with personal contact data read
    (A) more smoothly than others.   (B) smoother than others.

    12. _____

13. Be sure
    (A) to place references on a separate sheet.
    (B) and place references on a separate sheet.

    13. _____

14. Although inkjet cover letters are acceptable, resumes must be laser copies or
    (A) formerly type set and printed.
    (B) formally type set and printed.

    14. _____

15. In the end, you must be able to claim, "The person described on this page is
    (A) I."   (B) me."

    15. _____

16. While it takes quite a while to create a fine resume, writing a cover letter goes
    (A) much quicker.   (B) much more quickly.

    16. _____

17. An effective cover letter contains no more than three paragraphs,
    (A) twenty-five sentences at most.
    (B) twenty five sentences at most.

    17. _____

18. The cover letter represents more of your personality
    (A) than does a resume.   (B) then does a resume.   **18.** _____

19. Its purpose is to link you, describe you, and
    (A) altar the recipient's schedule for you.
    (B) alter the recipient's schedule for you.   **19.** _____

20. It links you to a person or publication by showing how you
learned about the job
    (A) for which your applying.   (B) for which you're applying.   **20.** _____

21. It describes you by letting you list experience and argue that
    (A) you working for this company would be desirable.
    (B) your working for this company would be desirable.   **21.** _____

22. Setting a date for a telephone conversation,
    (A) the letter alters the recipient's schedule.
    (B) the recipient's schedule is altered.   **22.** _____

23. This telephone conversation will be an opportunity for you
    (A) to again present yourself, this time by voice.
    (B) to present yourself again, this time by voice.   **23.** _____

24. An excellent resume and cover letter can set you apart from the
many candidates
    (A) among whom employers must choose.
    (B) between whom employers must choose.   **24.** _____

25. A flawed resume and careless cover letter are, in the end,
    (A) too expensive.   (B) to expensive.   **25.** _____

PART G. Find and underscore the ten word choice errors in this memo paragraph. In the blanks below, suggest how you would correct each error to produce a more acceptable piece of writing.

Regarding the purchase of office supplies, I would like to make two suggestions:

    1. Please order from the smallest of the two suppliers in town, Clancy Brothers, as we have had less problems with them than with their competitors and invoicing seems to go smoother with them than with anyone else in town. We have seldom ever had problems with their merchandise, and all of the salepersons are quite helpful. Their competitors charge to much for most everything.

    2. Remember to turn in your receipts within 24 hours of making a purchase. The accounting department reports where some people wait a week or more to turn in receipts. When these kind of things happen, both billing and reimbursements maybe delayed and our whole system becomes inefficient. Thank you for working with us to streamline office supply purchasing.

1. _____   **6.** _____

2. *_____   **7.** _____

3. _____   **8.** _____

4. _____   **9.** _____

5. _____   **10.** _____

A PUZZLING SUBJECT

When communicating, many people make errors because they ignore this cardinal rule of grammar: A verb and its subject must agree in number. If one is plural, the other must be plural. To apply the rule, a person must be able to *identify* subjects.

Here, in the form of a puzzle, is an excellent suggestion for anyone who would like to analyze a sentence.

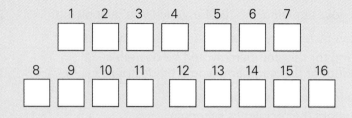

Each of the following numbered sentences contains a single word that functions as a simple subject. You are to put the first letter of that word in the square that bears the same number.

1. In the morning his fiduciary will look into the matter.
2. When should I plan to meet you?
3. Their need for new equipment should be discussed seriously.
4. In the center of her office is a huge walnut desk.
5. In a desk drawer was found an ultramodern white telephone.
6. The hall seems unusually narrow.
7. In May of this year our chief electrician will retire.
8. Our old, irreparable Varityper is no longer in use.
9. Her enthusiasm for the job impressed Mr. Slavick.
10. What did our representative tell you?
11. At exactly 9 A.M. the brochures were placed on my desk.
12. The finding of an astute financial consultant may be difficult.
13. The senior partner's initiative was never doubted.
14. Her latest resolution is to master this IBM computer.
15. In less than 45 minutes my secretary completed the mailing.
16. His most difficult task will be to acquire the software.

---

wWw ════════ Watching the Web ════════

Back	Forward	Home	Reload	Images	Open

Today's Headline News
Filed in the Oval Office under Campaign Funding, the President's assistant today found the missing figures requested by the Senate Investigating Committee. He turned the information over to the committee chair this afternoon.

| read on | | next headline |

Building Sentences: What to Work Toward

Assembling a sentence takes as much care
as assembling a machine.

A well-known professional writer once admitted that most sentences in his books have been rewritten at least five times. His continual rewriting does not impress me as being strange or unusual. There are many ways to combine words to form sentences, and the first combination that comes to one's mind may be less than adequate. This chapter will offer a few suggestions for building sentences that communicate ideas in the most effective way possible. You will note that some of the principles included here have been touched upon in previous chapters; some will not be found elsewhere in this text. Perhaps the most obvious mark of a skillful writer is the ability to distinguish between complete sentences and sentence fragments. We assume that you have that ability.

Variety

Certainly you recognize the importance of variety in all mature writing. Our finest writers, as you know, use simple, compound, and complex sentences of varying lengths to hold the interest of their readers. A series of short, choppy simple sentences can be just as dull and uninspiring as a series of long, involved compound sentences. Consider a few of the ways in which a skillful writer may combine these two closely related ideas: (1) *Ward graduated from Columbia University in June.* (2) *He now works for a New York brokerage firm.* Here are several alternatives:

1. Compound sentence with coordinating conjunction

   Ward graduated from Columbia University in June, and he now works for a New York brokerage firm.

2. Simple sentence with participial phrase

   Having graduated from Columbia University in June, Ward now works for a New York brokerage firm.

3. Complex sentence with adjective clause

   Ward, who graduated from Columbia University in June, now works for a New York brokerage firm. OR Ward, who now works for a New York brokerage firm, graduated from Columbia University in June.

4. Simple sentence with appositive

   Ward, a June graduate of Columbia University, now works for a New York brokerage firm.

5. Complex sentence with adverb clause

   Since Ward graduated from Columbia University last June, he has been working for a New York brokerage firm.

Unity

In building a sentence, include only closely related ideas. A sentence is said to lack *unity* if it includes ideas that are not closely related. A lack of unity, or *oneness of aim,* can unduly challenge the reader. Consider these sentences:

AVOID: This entire mailing could have been completed in less than three hours, and we may purchase a laptop computer. (The two ideas expressed in this sentence are not *closely* related.)

USE: We may purchase a laptop computer that would complete a mailing of this size in less than three hours.

AVOID: Graham has three dependents, and life insurance is a wise investment. (The two ideas are not *closely* related.)

USE: Because Graham has three dependents, he should purchase a life insurance policy.

Conciseness

In building a sentence, work toward being concise. Build upon the idea of unity above, taking care to include only pertinent information for your reader. The following sentence should prove troublesome to any reader, not because it seriously lacks unity but because it lacks conciseness.

Ms. Dixon, who answered the president's buzzer, the usual signal that he wanted a stenographer, took the notes he dictated on the arsonist's conviction for setting fire to two apartment buildings in which ten people were injured (most of the residents managed to get out safely) and transcribed four letters.

Several lines of thought are expressed in this long, loosely connected sentence. Written as a paragraph, it could be made more forceful and easier to understand.

Because the president had buzzed for a stenographer, Ms. Dixon went to his office. His dictation concerned the conviction of the arsonist who had set fire to two apartment buildings and, in the process, injured ten persons. Ms. Dixon transcribed four letters from her notes.

Parallel Structure

Make certain that sentence elements *with similar functions* are parallel in structure. If, for example, the first of three such elements begins with a verb, each of the other two should begin with a verb. If the first element is a gerund, the others should be gerunds. Such uniformity in the expression of similar sentence parts will help a writer to avoid awkwardness. (See discussion of parallel structure on pages 236–237.)

This rule can be applied too rigidly. Occasionally a minor breach of parallelism will help to convey a complicated idea clearly and succinctly. In the majority of cases, however, a reader will be disturbed by such a breach. The parts that make up a compound subject, object, or complement should generally be parallel, just as all items in a series should be parallel.

AVOID: He worries too much about his family, his studies, and about what the future will bring.

USE: He worries too much about his family, his studies, and his future.

AVOID: We would rather pay cash now than sending a check later.

USE: We would rather pay cash now than send a check later.

AVOID: The action that he took and what he said seemed inconsistent.

USE: What he did seemed inconsistent with what he said.

AVOID: Either the orange crates are in the warehouse or on the loading platform.

USE: The orange crates are either in the warehouse or on the loading platform. (What follows one correlative conjunction must be parallel to what follows the other.)

Subordination

Subordinate an idea of secondary importance by expressing it in the dependent (subordinate) clause of a complex sentence. Ideas expressed in the main clauses of a compound sentence are given equal emphasis. The expert use of subordination will help a writer to avoid the excessive use of conjunctions such as *and, but,* and *so.*

AVOID: Operating costs have increased, so we will appeal to the Public Utilities Commission for authority to change our rates.

USE: Because operating costs have increased, we will appeal to the Public Utilities Commission for authority to change our rates.

AVOID: The government allows a substantial exclusion, and Lloyd will not have to pay a federal tax on his father's estate.

USE: Because the government allows a substantial exclusion, Lloyd will not have to pay a federal tax on his father's estate.

AVOID: This vast plateau is rich in oil, and it has been purchased by the Tidewater Company.

USE: This vast plateau, which is rich in oil, has been purchased by the Tidewater Company. (Another writer might choose to deemphasize the oil company by using this version. *This vast plateau, which has been purchased by the Tidewater Company, is rich in oil.*)

Emphasis

To gain emphasis, place important words at the beginning of a sentence or, even better, at the end. Transitional words such as *however* and *for example,* as well as other words and phrases of relatively minor importance, can often be placed within a sentence rather than at the beginning or end.

ACCEPTABLE:	For example, our file clerk cannot spell accurately.
PREFERRED:	Our file clerk, for example, cannot spell accurately. (In this construction less emphasis is placed on the phrase *for example*.)
ACCEPTABLE:	For some undisclosed reason the credit manager questioned Ted's honesty.
PREFERRED:	The credit manager, for some undisclosed reason, questioned Ted's honesty. (The prepositional phrase has been deemphasized.)

If items in a series are not of equal importance, you can build emphasis appropriately by placing them in the order of their significance—with the most important item at the end.

| AVOID: | You will have that opinion if you work here for 50 years, for 10 years, or for 1 year. |
| USE: | You will have that opinion if you work here for 1 year, for 10 years, or for 50 years. (Items have been arranged in a climactic order.) |

Emphasis can occasionally be achieved by the use of a balanced construction to express contrast between two ideas in a sentence.

| UNBALANCED: | Some people are always on time, and others never arrive on time for an appointment. |
| BALANCED: | Some people are always on time; some are always late. |

Two ideas presented in previous chapters may help you to secure proper emphasis: (1) Choose an exact word in preference to a vague one. (2) Use the active voice more often than the passive. In your attempt to achieve proper emphasis, don't sacrifice clarity, smoothness, or variety in your writing.

Which sentence building error can you detect here? How would you make this message more rhythmic and direct?

```
wWWw ══════════ Watching the Web ══════════

   Back      Forward     Home      Reload      Images      Open

   ONLINE PHOTOS
   Never again drive to the photo shop, wait and wonder
   about your prints, and receive inferior quality
   workmanship! You want clean photos. You want crisp
   color. You want a great value for your money. Check us
   out today!


   [ check us out ]                                    [ no thanks ]
```

_____WORKSHEET 25_____

BUILDING SENTENCES: WHAT TO WORK TOWARD

PART A. In the space provided, write the word that would make the sentence correct.

1. A sentence containing ideas that are not closely related is said to lack _____.

   1. *_____

2. Most sentences may be classified as simple, compound, or _____.

   2. _____

3. Sentence elements that perform similar functions should be _____.

   3. _____

4. Placing words most important to your meaning at the beginning or end of a sentence helps you clarify your _____.

   4. _____

5. Placing a primary idea in a main clause and a secondary idea in a dependent clause gives your sentence correct _____.

   5. _____

PART B. The following sentences lack unity. Attempt to rewrite each one to show a relationship between ideas. Add words if necessary.

Example: Bruno Hoffman is an excellent architect, and the Draper Building has ten stories. Bruno Hoffman, an excellent architect, designed the ten-story Draper Building.

1. Several teamsters' negotiators were stranded in Cleveland, and labor talks began this morning in New York.

   *_____

   _____

   _____

2. The LAX Daily Planner is quite expensive, and people ought to learn what sort of planner will work best for them.

   _____

   _____

   _____

3. Significant profit this year came from stock investments, and our broker is a genius.

   _____

   _____

   _____

PART C. Break this long piece of writing into ten distinct, correctly punctuated sentences, rewriting the paragraph on the lines below.

when job hunting an applicant must be well prepared in several ways a little research at the city employment bureau and the public library can be valuable an applicant can discover the salary range of jobs in his or her field the number of such positions in that metro area and even sometimes an idea of the turnover rate for those positions of course a prepared applicant will have an excellent resume most authorities suggest that the resume cover no more than one page and yet sum up the applicant's talents and skills surely there will be much that goes unsaid in a resume that "left out" information can be contained in a portfolio which is shown during a job interview in fact the resume's chief job is to get the applicant an interview the applicant more than anything else wants to get a foot inside the door then all the preparation will have paid off

_____

_____

_____

_____

_____

_____

_____

_____

_____

_____

_____

_____

_____

_____

PART D. You are to build a single complex sentence from each of the following pairs of simple sentences. The less important idea, which appears in italics, should be subordinated.

Example: _This engine has been used continually since 1985._ It is still in excellent condition.
Although this engine has been used continually since 1985, it is still in excellent condition.

1. Our marketing division has expanded to twice its original size. It is responsible for a 40 percent increase in sales.

* _____

_____

2. I like the way Anderson conducts staff meetings. I believe three hours is too long for weekly progress checks.

_____

_____

3. We need time to build a team. It is only as a team we will be able to design and market our products competitively.

_____

_____

PART E.   Rewrite the following sentences to achieve greater emphasis.

Example: The explosion resulted in ten deaths, as you may know.
             The explosion, as you may know, resulted in ten deaths.

1. For example, this computer could solve your problem in less than three minutes.

_____

_____

2. (Arrange items in a climactic order.) He was honored as the graduate who had done

the most for his state, his country, his school, and his city. _____

_____

_____

_____

3. (Use a balanced construction.) Dr. O'Grady handles the large accounts, and her partner

always takes care of the small ones. _____

_____

_____

PART F.   As a collaborative team, discover two different ways to combine these two ideas into a single sentence: (1) David Ling proved to be a fine administrator. (2) He has just been elected chairman of our group.

1. _____

_____

2. _____

_____

THE IMPACT OF LANGUAGE

WHERE'S THE ACTION?

You may have noted that linking verbs do *not* express action. The predicate adjective that follows such a verb will usually modify the subject of the clause, as in *Marie seems happy.* Adverbs are generally used to modify action verbs, as in *He walked slowly* or *She talked rapidly.* As you cope with each of the following sentences, select an adverb if the verb expresses action and an adjective if it does not express action.

The young man looked (guilty, guiltily) to me.
The thief looked (guilty, guiltily) at his victim.
She felt (bad, badly) about the accident.
He felt (careful, carefully) along the dark wall for an opening.
The percolating coffee smells (delicious, deliciously).
The dog smells his food (careful, carefully) before eating.

_____ FOR CLASS DISCUSSION _____

As you study each of the foregoing sentences, determine which one of the two options is correct and also *what word it modifies.*

CHAPTER

26

Building Sentences: What to Avoid

■■■ POINT TO PONDER

Most business writers are guilty, at least *occasionally,* of wasting words.

This chapter contains additional suggestions for the building of strong sentences. These ideas are not offered as hard-and-fast rules that a writer should follow at any cost. As you refine your own style of writing, you may occasionally find it advisable to ignore one or more of these suggestions. If you do so and the resultant sentence proves to be unsatisfactory, rewrite your copy to conform with the principles discussed in this chapter. They serve as guidelines for many fine writers.

Omission of Words

Avoid the omission of words needed to complete the meaning of a sentence. The wording of that statement rightfully implies that judgment is involved. Some words are important to the meaning of a sentence, and others are not. Note that the words in parentheses could safely be omitted from these sentences: *I hope (that) he understands my message. My father and (my) mother are interior decorators. Hodges is better informed than I (am).* Words needed to clarify meaning, however, should always be expressed.

AVOID: Perhaps you noticed Felton used no notes. (Meaning is obscured by the omission of *that.*)

USE: Perhaps you noticed *that* Felton used no notes.

AVOID: Murray has served and will again if no one else volunteers. (The word *served* is inaccurately implied after *will.*)

USE: Murray has served and will *serve* again if no one else volunteers.

AVOID: The agent offered us more than Salvi. (This sentence may confuse a reader.)

USE: The agent offered us more than Salvi offered us. OR The agent offered us more than he offered Salvi.

AVOID: On Thursday Cooper was too busy. (In business writing, comparisons should generally be completed.)

USE: On Thursday Cooper was too busy to *complete your questionnaire.*

AVOID: We should trade in our opaque projector and tape recorder. (This wording seems to imply that one piece of equipment serves two functions.)

USE: We should trade in our opaque projector and *our* tape recorder.

Shifts in Tense

Avoid illogical shifts in tense. Good writers may find it necessary to use verbs of dissimilar tenses in a single sentence. They will, however, guard against any change in tense that may result in an awkward construction or that may obscure the intended meaning.

AVOID: She accepted the merchandise and pays the seller with a personal check. (The shift from past tense to present tense is illogical.)

USE: She accepted the merchandise and paid the seller with a personal check.

AVOID: I will be on the platform, and he is going to be in the audience. (Construction is awkward because of change in tense.)

USE: I will be on the platform, and he will be in the audience. (Both verbs logically belong in the future tense.)

Unnecessary Words

A careful business writer will omit any words that do not contribute to the meaning of the sentence, for no one enjoys reading a long, rambling message. It is certainly not businesslike for a writer to express in many words a thought that requires only a few. Most executives would agree that in business today *time is money.* The ten expressions that follow illustrate one type of wordiness you should avoid in your writing.

Wordy	*Improved*
A check in the amount of $10	A check for $10
In regard to	About
Due to the fact that	Because
At a later date	Later
Until such time as	Until
In the event that	If
Enclosed herewith is	Enclosed is, Here is
For the duration of a month	For a month
In reference to	About
Will you be so kind as to	Please

Look for opportunities to omit unnecessary words in your own writing. Exercise judgment, though. Don't eliminate words that are needed to make your meaning clear, and don't omit words that are needed for the sake of courtesy.

Misplaced Modifiers

In building a sentence, make certain that every modifier is appropriately placed. You have been reminded several times in this text to be careful about the placement of modifiers. A descriptive word, phrase, or clause should be so placed that it clearly and logically modifies the intended word. You may recall that a phrase too far removed from the word it modifies is said to be misplaced (see Chapter 17). As you consider this principle of effective writing, don't pay undue attention to terminology. Your ability to identify elements such as participial phrases is of minor importance. You will use such elements correctly if (1) you can recognize them simply as modifiers and (2) you can determine which words they modify. Pay particular attention to the italicized words in these sentences:

AVOID: We *only* want you to lend us a few dollars.
USE: We want you to lend us *only* a few dollars.
AVOID: Janasek qualifies for any one of the four available positions *with her computer background.*
USE: With her computer background Janasek qualifies for any one of the four available positions (The prepositional phrase *with her computer background* modifies Janasek.)
AVOID: We need a machine for the dispensing of postage stamps *that can be placed on the counter.*
USE: We need a postage-stamp dispenser *that can be placed on the counter.*
AVOID: *Reading at that speed,* I suppose you could finish the 250 pages in an hour.
USE: *Reading at that speed,* you probably could finish the 250 pages in an hour. (The participial phrase properly modifies *you.*)

Unclear Reference of Pronouns

The proper reference of pronouns was discussed in Chapter 10. It is mentioned again here because of its importance in the building of sentences. No one enjoys reading a sentence a second or third time to determine the antecedent of *she, he, it, we,* or *they.* In business correspondence, pronouns should generally refer to specific persons, places, and things. If the reference is perfectly clear, however, the pronoun *this, that, it,* or *which* may be used with a preceding clause or sentence as its antecedent. In *Come at a later hour if that would be more convenient,* the main clause serves as the antecedent of *that.* Although such constructions are common in informal writing and speaking, they should be employed in business correspondence only when the meaning is perfectly clear. In the following sentence, the vague reference of *which* would not be considered appropriate in business writing.

AVOID: She may be assigned the Alabama territory, *which* would please her husband.
USE: Her husband will be pleased if she is assigned the Alabama territory.
AVOID: He is attending medical school because he believes *it* is a fine profession.
USE: He is attending medical school because he believes that medicine is a fine profession.
AVOID: In the report does *it* say anything about transportation facilities?
USE: Does the report say anything about transportation facilities?

Some authorities frown upon the use of a pronoun that refers to a noun in the possessive case. Others make use of such antecedents when there is no chance for confusion. Certainly it would be difficult to find fault with a sentence as clear as this one: *If you want Mr. Gray's opinion, ask him.*

A Final Note

In business writing, avoid the use of an indefinite *they* or *you* in sentences such as these:

They say that Andrew Carnegie was generous with his money. (BETTER: Andrew Carnegie, according to his biographers, was generous with his money.)

They say that there is no iron ore in this part of the country. (BETTER: Geologists claim that there is no iron ore in this part of the country.)

Do you need experience to get a job as an installer with the telephone company? (BETTER: Must a person have experience to get a job as an installer with the telephone company?)

Expand   This verb means "to increase the size, volume, or scope of; to enlarge upon." *Expand* means "to spend; to use up; to consume."

>   We may have to *expand* our production facilities.
>   Management may not want to *expend* the necessary funds.

Percent   This word, which indicates an exact number of hundredths, should generally be used with a specific number. Use *percentage* when the number is not given.

>   Thirty *percent* of our sales are made to industrial users.
>   What *percentage* of our gross profit will be paid in taxes?

Principal   When used as an adjective, this word means "chief, main, first in rank or importance." As a noun it may refer to the chief administrator of a school, the amount of an investment or indebtedness (minus interest), a main actor or performer, a person who employs another as his or her agent, and so forth. Do not confuse it with *principle,* which is most often used to mean "fundamental truth" or simply "integrity, uprightness."

>   The coming inspection is our *principal* concern right now.
>   Both *principal* and interest must be paid in full by January 15.
>   Our treasurer does not fully understand the *principles* of cost accounting.
>   We recommend Walt because he is a man of *principle.*
>   His sister is the *principal* of a grade school.

Reason Is Because   This informal wording should always be avoided in business writing. Use *that* in place of *because.* Also, avoid the use of *reason why,* which is redundant.

>   The reason for our not voting is *that* (not *because*) we lacked a quorum.
>   (Better) We did not vote on the motion because we lacked a quorum.
>   I want to know *why* (not *the reason why*) sales were poor in March.

Same   Do not use this word in place of the pronoun *it.*

>   Your bill arrived on March 11, and we paid *it* (not *same*) immediately.

Their   Be careful to spell this personal pronoun correctly. Do not substitute the adverb *there.* Be especially careful in writing the contraction *they're,* which means *they are.*

>   Both Kathryn and Frances feel that *their* jobs are secure.
>   I wish that you had been *there* with me.
>   *They're* attempting to duplicate our production technique.

Wait On   In some parts of the country this expression is used too often in place of *wait for.* To *wait on* a person is to serve him or her in some way.

>   Please *wait for* me if I do not arrive by seven o'clock.
>   The waitress is too busy to *wait on* us right now.

_____**WORKSHEET 26**_____

BUILDING SENTENCES: WHAT TO AVOID

PART A. An important word has been omitted from each of the following sentences. You are to (1) insert a caret (∧) to indicate where it should appear and (2) write the word in the space provided.

Example: This morning the machine was repaired, and
500 copies∧run.

were
_____

1. He observed Mr. Wells did not take notes at the meeting.

    1. *_____

2. Your manuscript arrived in Friday's mail, but have not had time to read it.

    2. _____

3. The new employees will probably be a systems analyst and engineer.

    3. _____

4. The computer is perfectly efficient, but the software disks faulty in some way.

    4. _____

5. Ten designs were submitted, but only one accepted.

    5. _____

PART B. Select the correct word and write it in the space provided. Help your collaborative partner(s) learn why you would make each choice.

1. The reason he returned is (because, that) he had forgotten his key.

    1. *_____

2. A small (percent, percentage) of our stockholders voted against the merger.

    2. _____

3. (There, Their, They're) will be a full investigation.

    3. _____

4. My monthly payment on the loan reduced the (principal, principle) by $205.10.

    4. _____

5. Okada and Pappas share an office, but (there, their, they're) friendship is cool.

    5. _____

6. In all business matters Mr. Pennick proved to be a man of (principal, principle).

    6. _____

7. If we (expand, expend) the necessary capital, we will notice short term losses and long term gains.

    7. _____

8. Our systems programmer was once a high school (principal, principle).

    8. _____

9. The reason I couldn't adjourn the meeting was (that, because) Gorley continued to talk.

9. _____

10. My marketing advisor understands the (principals, principles) of retailing.

10. _____

PART C. Each of the following sentences contains an unnecessary or illogical shift in tense. Rewrite each one in a more acceptable form.

Example: She ran off 100 copies but leaves the machine uncovered.
She ran off 100 copies but left the machine uncovered.

1. Graves looked directly at me and tells me to sign the contract. _____

_____

_____

2. I will write the memorandum, and I am going to tell him about the drainage problem.

* _____

_____

3. We have met your agent, and we gave her our answer. _____

_____

_____

4. Ames received the crates on Monday but doesn't open them until today. _____

_____

_____

PART D. Each of the following sentences is weak in that it (1) violates parallel structure, (2) contains a misplaced or dangling modifier, or (3) employs a pronoun with an indefinite antecedent. Rewrite each one in a more acceptable form.

1. While addressing the stockholders at our annual meeting, I understand that Mr. Wallace contradicted himself twice.

* _____

_____

_____

2. Having completed the mailing, it was inevitable that Cunliffe would take his morning break.

_____

_____

_____

3. Ms. Brimley immediately began reading my report and to make marginal notes.

_____

_____

_____

4. The field superintendent took credit for every idea submitted by his crew, which is why Bragan protested.

_____

_____

_____

5. To make certain that everyone understood his proposal, we observed that Mr. Lassiter used a few line drawings.

_____

_____

_____

6. I understand that they manufacture these trucks in Japan, which you failed to mention.

_____

_____

_____

7. The interviewer asked Norman about his education, his work experience, and she wanted to know about his plans for the future.

_____

_____

_____

8. The visitors from Germany were not only impressed with our machinists but also our office personnel, which pleased me.

_____

_____

_____

9. I met a young businessman while stranded in North Dakota who is interested in carrying our line of products.

_____

_____

_____

10. Mr. Osborne only gave me 30 minutes to proofread the four pages, correcting any errors, and running off 50 copies for the staff.

_____

_____

_____

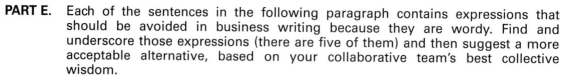

PART E. Each of the sentences in the following paragraph contains expressions that should be avoided in business writing because they are wordy. Find and underscore those expressions (there are five of them) and then suggest a more acceptable alternative, based on your collaborative team's best collective wisdom.

Each and every person at the sales conference was asked to purchase a handbook for the price of $20. Most of them were upset due to the fact that this required purchase had never been mentioned in advance publicity. In the event that you want us to participate in your conference next year, will you be so kind as to notify us in advance of any required purchases, or simply include them in a higher conference fee.

1. _____   4. _____

2. _____   5. _____

3. _____

_____ FOR CLASS DISCUSSION _____

(if time permits)

To achieve maximum clarity, a writer must use transitional elements skillfully. These connectives, which were discussed at length in Chapter 22, serve as the binding that ties together the parts of a sentence or paragraph; thus, they add coherence to one's writing.

Attempt to use each one of the following transitional elements to join independent clauses in a compound sentence.

as a result	in addition	on the other hand
consequently	in other words	otherwise
for example	meanwhile	that is to say
furthermore	nevertheless	then

OPTIONAL EXERCISES

OPTION 1 Write the *letter* that indicates the error made in each sentence. If you are collaborating, your entire group must agree on each one.

A. This sentence lacks parallel structure.
B. A pronoun in this sentence needs a specific antecedent.
C. This sentence contains a misplaced modifier.
D. This sentence lacks unity.

1. We only wanted to use his camcorder for ten minutes.

1. * _____

2. Bess recently met Karl Sundheim, according to what she said yesterday, who invented this timing device.

2. * _____

3. Thank you for helping to solve our problem, and we hope to visit your city in July.

3. _____

4. The ideal place for our October convention either would be Roanoke or Charlotte.

4. _____

5. Addison proposed a merger and Drabek opposed the idea, but it didn't seem right.

5. _____

6. When they talked on Tuesday, Harry and Gerald discussed my problem, but he did not suggest a solution.

6. _____

7. Estrada has several responsibilities: greeting visitors, answering the telephone, he sometimes uses the computer, filing correspondence, and to help with the payroll.

7. _____

8. Our head office is in Philadelphia, but my son is not interested in electronics.

8. _____

9. Stillwell will be a valuable addition to this staff with her background in architecture.

9. _____

10. When I arrived, McCormack had a huge office and Trabeck had a tiny one, and this bothered me.

10. _____

11. I would rather make the telephone call now than putting it off until tomorrow.

11. _____

12. Standing on the roof, the distant fire could be seen clearly by both of us.

12. _____

OPTION 2 Write one or more smoothly worded paragraphs on the subject of "Women in Business."

_____

_____

_____

Two sentence building errors in this short message jumped out at us. Can you find them?

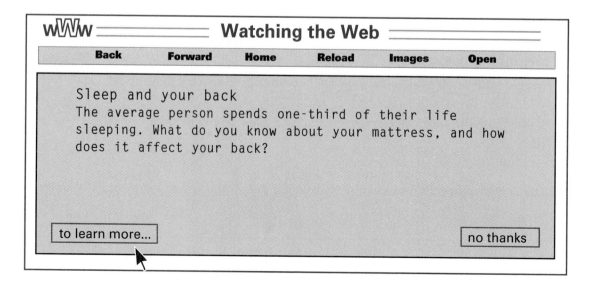

CHAPTER

27

The Writing of Numbers

▶ POINT TO PONDER

A long number expressed in words may prove unnecessarily difficult to comprehend.

It is extremely difficult to find two authorities who agree completely on how numbers should be written in business correspondence. In fact, our best writers vary their procedures according to the nature of a communication and the emphasis desired. The individuals who prepare an annual report are inclined to express almost all numbers as figures rather than words—and with good reason. They know that the stockholders who read the report will be vitally interested in those figures; consequently, they want them to stand out. Having scrutinized several hundred business letters chosen at random, I must conclude that today's business writers *generally* favor the use of figures.

The ideas offered in this chapter represent the consensus of today's best writers. Please bear in mind that these suggestions pertain, for the most part, to business correspondence. *All* numbers used in statements, invoices, vouchers, check registers, sales slips, and the like should ordinarily appear as figures. In sentences, however, they are likely to be written in accordance with the suggestions that follow.

NUMBERS AS WORDS

1. Generally spell out isolated numbers from *one* to *ten.*

   The discussion lasted for *ten* minutes.

   We will be gone for *six* days.

   The program will begin at *eight* o'clock. (Spell out all numbers used with *o'clock;* the figure *8* would be used with A.M. *or* P.M.)

2. Unless you want to emphasize them, spell out *indefinite* numbers that may be expressed in one or two words.

The auditorium will accommodate several *thousand* people.

She will probably retire when she is in her early *seventies.*

We received *hundreds* of responses to our advertisement.

3. Spell out a number that introduces a sentence. If the number is long, recast the sentence to avoid awkwardness.

AVOID: *21* of the instruments had been damaged.
USE: *Twenty-one* of the instruments had been damaged.
AVOID: *471* people were in the auditorium.
USE: There were *471* people in the auditorium.

4. Spell out short common fractions that are used alone.

He refused to accept his *one-fourth* share.

More than *one-third* of us accepted the challenge. (A writer should, however, use figures in writing a mixed number: *We offered him a discount of $2\frac{1}{2}$ percent.*)

5. Spell out all numbers in very formal invitations and announcements.

. . . on Sunday, the *twenty-seventh* of February . . .

6. To achieve greater clarity, write out only the **shorter** of two consecutive numbers if no punctuation mark intervenes.

We plan to build 24 *twelve*-room residences in this tract.

He asked for *fourteen* 79-cent pens.

How long will it take you to read these *32 fifteen*-page reports?

7. In legal documents, express amounts of money in both words and figures.

. . . Four Hundred Fifty Dollars ($450)

8. Generally spell out an ordinal number (first, second, third, etc.) that can be expressed as one word. EXCEPTIONS: Use figures for all dates and for street names above *Tenth,* and where clear and appropriate in titles and graphics, as on the cover of this book. (Note that when this book's title is cited in the preface, the hyphenated ordinal number is spelled out.)

We are starting our *fortieth* year of operations.

He lives on *Seventh* Street in Oklahoma City.

Our office is on the corner of 32nd Street and *First* Avenue.

Many of these changes took place in the *nineteenth* century.

Our head buyer will be in New York on the *2nd* (or *2d*) of June.

9. In isolated round numbers, spell out *million* or *billion* to make reading easier.

The winning candidate received a plurality of 1.2 *million* votes.

This tax legislation would increase revenue by $7 *billion.*

NUMBERS AS FIGURES

1. Generally use figures to express exact numbers above *ten*.

The Novikoff file has been missing for *30* days.

She distributed *1,325* copies of the bulletin.

This booklet contains *100* suggestions for improving public relations.

Our firm recently purchased *13* Canon copiers.

2. In business writing, generally use figures to express each of the following:

    a. amounts of money (except *one cent*)

The knife can be purchased for only *89* cents. (In expressing amounts less than a dollar, generally write out the word *cents*. Do not, as a rule, use the symbol ¢ in connected matter. Do not use a decimal, such as *$.49,* except to achieve uniformity in a series of numbers.)

The irate customer asked for a refund of her *$49.50.*

We have only *$25* in petty cash. (Do not use a decimal point and two zeros when an isolated figure expresses an even amount in dollars.)

    b. market quotations

The common stock in question closed yesterday at 25 7/8.

    c. dimensions

Our smallest boxes are 6 by 8 by 3 inches. (When several dimensions are given, as in an invoice, express them in this manner: 6″ × 8″ × 3″.)

    d. degrees of temperature

In our freezer the temperature is now 5 degrees Fahrenheit (or 5° F).

    e. decimals and percentages

Wilson typed the sentence in 4.25 seconds.

We have already used 35 percent of the sheet metal delivered on Monday.

Please add these figures: 2.92, 3.74, and 5.12.

We spent only 0.8 percent of our gross sales for advertising.

The average annual return on our investment was a meager .09 percent. (If a zero follows the decimal point, it is not necessary to place a zero before it.)

    f. street numbers

Carbo lives at 126 Willow Street; Epstein lives at 8 Wickfield Court.

    g. pages and divisions of a book

The picture appears in Volume 8, page 214.

h. time (hour of the day) when *A.M.* or *P.M.* follows (The abbreviations may also be expressed in lowercase letters: *a.m., p.m.*)

> The class was in session from 10 A.M. until 1 P.M. (If one figure expresses minutes, the other figures should be expressed in a uniform manner: *We talked from 9:30 A.M. until 11:00 A.M.,* not *from 9:30 A.M. until 11 A.M.*)

i. weights and measures

> This oil drum, which weighs exactly 18 pounds, will hold only 10 gallons.

j. identification numbers

> The accident on Route 5, according to the news commentator on Channel 7, resulted in several deaths.

SPECIAL SITUATIONS

1. If several numbers in a sentence perform similar functions, express them uniformly. If one should be written as a figure, write all as figures.

> The inventory shows *21* ranges, *9* refrigerators, *37* washers, and *10* dryers.
>
> Our cell phones sell for *$55.00, $69.50, $79.50,* and *$95.00.* (Note the consistent use of decimal points and zeros to achieve uniformity as well as clarity.)
>
> BUT: The *32* tables sold in *five* days. (The numbers do not perform similar functions.)

2. Generally use figures in writing dates.

> We plan to meet on September 7, 2002. (If the year follows the day, do not add *st, nd, rd,* or *th* to the figure designating the day.)
>
> The office was closed on August 15. (Inasmuch as the year was not expressed, *August 15th* would be equally acceptable.)

3. When an ordinal number is used to designate the day, it should be expressed as a figure, in this manner:

> Business has been poor since the *9th.*
>
> We have not seen him since the *26th* of July.
>
> Call me again on the *15th* of November.

————WORKSHEET 27————

THE WRITING OF NUMBERS

PART A. Assume that each of the following items appears in a sentence with no other numbers. If the form used is not acceptable, write the preferred form. If it is acceptable, write C.

1. Suite Seventeen   1. * _____
2. the last three months   2. _____
3. four thirty A.M.   3. _____
4. in his early 30s   4. * _____
5. ninth of May   5. * _____
6. a 1/8 share   6. _____
7. 5th Street West   7. _____
8. five hundred dollars   8. _____
9. thousands of visitors   9. _____
10. Volume Six, page 411   10. _____
11. Twenty-sixth Avenue   11. _____
12. $49.75 and $80   12. _____
13. four by five feet   13. _____
14. for the low price of $.99   14. _____
15. 3 P.M. or 3:45 P.M.   15. _____
16. 7 people witnessed the accident.   16. _____
17. fifteen degree programs   17. _____
18. precisely twelve kilograms   18. _____
19. July 10   19. _____
20. $862.00   20. _____
21. two three-hour commutes   21. _____
22. ten percent   22. _____
23. .5 percent   23. _____
24. $51,600,000   24. _____
25. the fifth discipline   25. _____

PART B. Examine the number(s) in each of the following sentences. If no change should be made, write C in the answer space. If a number has been expressed inappropriately, write the preferred form. If you are working collaboratively, remember to agree on each answer.

Example: Hunter left for Boise on the 4 of April.   4th

1. The firm dismissed 15 workers.   1. * _____

2. The flight arrived at 8:13 P.M.   2. * _____

3. During the winter, parking on Level Four is limited.   3. * _____

4. The home equity interest rate was set at $5\frac{1}{2}$ percent.   4. _____

5. We ordered 15 50-cent tape dispensers.   5. _____

6. The cab was sent to Six Elm Street.   6. _____

7. Workers in their 60s will not be forced to retire.   7. _____

8. I rose to the 3 salary level.   8. _____

9. She checked the FedEx rate for a two pound 6 ounce package.   9. _____

10. He hoped for a 3 and a half percent raise.   10. _____

11. The software upgrade included 6 disks.   11. _____

12. The office measures only 8 by 11 feet.   12. _____

13. The vendor is located at Fairview and 62nd Street.   13. _____

14. This is our 12 research conference.   14. _____

15. Our client will be here at 10:00 A.M.   15. _____

16. You will find $10.00 in the cash box.   16. _____

17. Over 3/4 of our customers pay by check.   17. _____

18. There are key tax advantages in the 8 ward.   18. _____

19. The 4 executives negotiated the merger.   19. _____

20. In Volume Three, section 11, you will discover the liability clause.   20. _____

PART C. Find and underscore five errors in the writing of numbers in this section from a rental agreement. Correct these errors in the five blanks that follow the selection.

Because this property management firm owns an industrial park, 2 shopping malls, and eight four-unit apartment buildings, we have strict and fair business policies which all our tenants must agree to observe. All rent must be paid by the 30 of the month. Business clients may rent no more than 3 consecutive units, although they may remodel as they choose within that number. Apartment tenants, in addition to their apartment unit, are entitled to one of the 16 45-square foot storage lockers in the basement of their building, which must be kept clean and hazard-free at all times.

1. _____
2. _____
3. _____
4. _____
5. _____

PART D. Rewrite each of the following sentences in a more acceptable form.

1. 556 employees are covered by the insurance carrier named in the lawsuit. * _____

_____

_____

2. To fit current desk space, your tower cannot exceed twenty by eight inches. _____

_____

_____

3. Calendar refills for company executive planning systems sell for $5, $15, or 21.95.

_____

_____

4. Benediro made amendments to the 1st, 2nd and 5th meeting agendas. _____

_____

_____

5. I counted twelve ink jet cartridges, sixteen reams of laser pager, and 21 storage CDs.

_____

_____

6. We worked on the web page design from 10:00 A.M. until six-thirty P.M. _____

_____

_____

7. You'll recognize the courier; she is six feet two inches tall. _____

_____

_____

8. Our bank has authorized a line of credit for our remaining debt of four thousand
dollars. _____

_____

_____

9. With the Euro, you can visit the same 6 countries and exchange money only 2 times.

_____

_____

10. Create a table that will accommodate variable figures such as one-half, 4 1/8 and six.

_____

_____

11. The Chunnel offers two departures after 7 o'clock. _____

_____

_____

12. For computer efficiency, keep the room temperature below seventy-six degrees.

_____

_____

_____ **FOR CLASS DISCUSSION** _____

(if time permits)

One of the most overworked adjectives in our language is the word *nice*. It has been used to describe people, vehicles, houses, games, food, scenery, pets—everything from peanuts to pyramids.

The following numbered sentences would be clearer if the word *nice* had been avoided. You are to suggest at least eight different words that could be substituted to provide a more meaningful ending.

1. The new office manager is *nice*.
2. Her new seven-room home is really *nice*.

A WORD TIP FROM THE REAL WORLD

An exceptionally capable college student habitually used substandard English in the classroom. The instructor reminded him that he would soon be applying for employment and that such language would jeopardize his chances for success. The student claimed that he would have no difficulty using flawless English when the situation demanded it. I do not know if he was successful. I do know that our college placement office worries when students fail to speak and write well as they leave for job interviews. Such students don't do themselves any favors, and they build a poor reputation for the school.

_____ **FOR CLASS DISCUSSION** _____

Do you feel that a person who habitually uses unacceptable language can communicate effectively on special occasions?

CHAPTER

28

Uses of the Comma

■■■ POINT TO PONDER

In using punctuation marks, most people feel insecure.

In the preceding chapters of this text, you were introduced to several important uses of the comma and the semicolon. In this section of eight chapters, all marks of punctuation will be discussed; their uses will be explained and illustrated. This chapter and the two immediately following are concerned with the use of the comma.

The average person is probably unfamiliar with most rules governing the use of commas. It is certainly possible for a writer with a logical mind to punctuate fairly well without knowing those rules—but is *fairly well* good enough? Anyone who guesses about the use of commas may convey a meaning that was not intended. Note the importance of appropriate punctuation in these sentences:

> If you agree to help Peterson, we will not pursue the subject. (The writer is *referring to* Peterson.)
>
> If you agree to help, Peterson, we will not pursue the subject. (The writer is *addressing* Peterson.)
>
> All committee members favoring the change met to discuss the cost. (*Some* committee members favor the change.)
>
> All committee members, favoring the change, met to discuss the cost. (*All* committee members favor the change.)

The foregoing examples suggest that the meaning of a sentence often depends upon its punctuation. They suggest also that no one should be satisfied to *guess* how writing should be punctuated.

You are probably aware that some sentences or paragraphs may be correctly punctuated in more than one way—even within the framework of the rules. The emphasis you place upon a particular expression may, in some instances, be determined by the punctuation you choose. Keep in mind also that the best punctuation tends to be inconspicuous. Readers become conscious of punctuation only when the meaning of a passage is not clear. Let's look now at three rules for the use of the comma.

RULE 1   Use commas to separate three or more items in a series.

The items may be words, phrases, or clauses of equal grammatical rank. Note that in the following examples commas are not used before the first item in the series or after the last item. They are used to separate the items *from one another.*

> We were impressed with his poise, his understanding, and his honesty. (nouns in a series)
>
> The work was done quietly, quickly, and satisfactorily. (adverbs in a series)
>
> In his leisure time he swims, reads, and jogs. (verbs in a series)
>
> The young man seemed enthusiastic but uninformed, energetic but untrained, willing but not able. (pairs of words in a series)
>
> We cannot complete this project in an hour, in a day, or even in a week. (phrases in a series)
>
> She favored Model D, I favored Model A, but the firm purchased Model B. (short clauses in a series)

The use of a comma before the conjunction in series such as these is optional. It is recommended, however, that you place a comma before the conjunction because its absence may confuse a reader, particularly in this kind of construction: *The novels that he reviewed were written by Creighton, Molinski, Trevino, Lindstrom and Boggs.* (Did Lindstrom and Boggs write separate novels, or are they coauthors of a single novel?)

COORDINATE ADJECTIVES

The punctuation of adjectives in a series deserves special attention. Unless such adjectives are coordinate, commas should not be used to separate them. There is no ideal way to determine whether adjectives are coordinate or not. Two tests, however, are commonly recommended: (1) If the word *and* logically could be placed between two adjectives, consider them to be coordinate and insert a comma. (2) If adjectives logically may be transposed (reversed), consider them to be coordinate and insert a comma between them. Observe the italicized adjectives in these sentences:

> She is engaged in *dangerous, exciting* work. (We could say *dangerous and exciting work* or *exciting, dangerous work.*)
>
> He was in a *thoughtful, introspective* mood.
>
> *These five old manual* typewriters should be donated to charity. (Apply the tests to prove that these adjectives are not coordinate.)

Don't be confused in writing such adjectives. A natural pause comes between coordinate adjectives and suggests strongly the need for punctuation.

A Few Don'ts

Do not use a comma when only two words or phrases are joined by a coordinating conjunction, as in these examples:

Lewis *and* his partner are excellent appraisers.

We plan to go to Concord *or* to Manchester on Tuesday.

If a conjunction is used at each joining in a series, commas are not necessary.

He was asked to wait *and* observe *and* reconsider.

If an ampersand (&) is used in a company name, do not use a comma before the ampersand.

Haynes, Cord & Staley is an old, reliable firm.

> **RULE 2** Use a comma before a coordinating conjunction that joins two main (independent) clauses in a compound sentence.

The foregoing rule, you may recall, was discussed in Chapter 22. The most common coordinating conjunctions were identified as *and, but, or,* and *nor,* although *for, so,* and *yet* are also used occasionally to join independent clauses. Observe the punctuation in these sentences:

The accident occurred in a busy intersection, but no one claimed to have seen it. (The main clauses of a compound sentence could serve as separate sentences.)

The final session came to a close, and the legislators left for their homes.

In applying this rule, make certain that a clause (which must contain both a subject and a verb) follows the conjunction. These sentences are *simple* even though they have compound predicates:

We reported our findings to Gentry and went on to our next job. (This sentence cannot be divided into two clauses because it lacks a second subject; it is *simple,* not compound.)

Tillman recognized the three delegates but could not recall their names. (Note that no comma is needed.)

You were told in Chapter 22 that a comma is not needed if the independent clauses are very short and joined by *and* or *or.*

He walked and she rode. (No comma is needed).

A comma should be placed before a coordinating conjunction that joins the main clauses of a *compound-complex* sentence. Sentences of this type have at least two main clauses and at least one dependent clause.

We were impressed with the gentleman who delivered the main address, but we felt that the master of ceremonies was unprepared.

The punctuation of compound sentences will be discussed again when the use of semicolons is presented in Chapter 31.

An introductory element (word, phrase, or dependent clause) that is placed before the main clause of a sentence should generally be followed by a comma. Rule 3, however, is concerned only with introductory verbals, which may appear as single words or in phrases. You may recall that Chapter 17, which covers verbals, provides a few examples similar to those that follow.

Looking to the future, he opened a money market account. (Introductory phrase contains the verbal *looking*. It is not necessary to recognize *looking* as a participle to punctuate the sentence correctly.)

Driven for only 730 miles, this tank truck is practically new. (Introductory phrase contains the verbal *Driven,* a participle.)

Before leaving, speak to the senior project engineer about your plans. (Introductory phrase contains the verbal *leaving,* a gerund.)

To make matters worse, Belnick was unable to analyze the system failure. (Introductory phrase contains the verbal *to make,* an infinitive.)

Agitated, he stomped out of the conference room. (The verbal *Agitated,* a participle, modifies *he.*)

Relieved, we began to talk of more pleasant things.

A verbal used as a subject is, of course, an essential part of a clause and should not be set off with a comma.

To satisfy my employer is not easy. (Verbal phrase is the subject.)

Worrying will not help matters. (Verbal, *Worrying,* is the subject.)

Some writers prefer not to place a comma after a short introductory prepositional phrase that contains a verbal. Consider this sentence:

In his writing(,) Shipley did not mention the present crisis.

Although the use of a comma after *writing* is optional, please insert commas after all such verbal phrases as you complete the worksheets that follow.

Executives' Choice

Beside   Careful business writers do not interchange this word with *besides,* which means "in addition to." The common definition of *beside* is "by the side of."

Reinhardt sat *beside* his employer.

We have several colors *besides* this one.

In Back Of   This expression is somewhat wordy. In some constructions it is too informal for business use. The word *behind* can generally be substituted.

This corporation will always stand *behind* (not *in back of*) its products.

In Regards To   This expression is not grammatical. Use either *in regard to,* or, better still, *about.*

     Iverson would like to talk with you *about* (not *in regards to*) her proposed amendment.

Irregardless   Avoid the use of this nonstandard substitute for *regardless.*

     We plan to start production in June *regardless* (not *irregardless*) of the pending litigation. (The term *irrespective,* however, is acceptable in business writing.)

Pair   This word is singular. Do not use it to refer to more than one.

     We have only *20 pairs* (not *pair*) of trousers in stock.

Party   This word is used correctly to refer to a group of people. Only in legal writing may it be used to refer to one person.

     The hotel could not provide accommodations for a *party* of ten.

     Do you have the name of the *person* (not *party*) who returned this merchandise?

Shape   This word is too informal for business writing when it is used as a substitute for *condition* or *state.*

     The men would not tire so easily if they were in better *condition* (not *shape*).

THE IMPACT OF LANGUAGE

THE COMMA DILEMMA

Assume that you are writing a report concerning an incident that recently took place in a local store. You know what your final sentence will be, but you are not certain how you should punctuate it. Here are your alternatives:

1. The police officer, who carried a shotgun, arrested two suspects.
2. The police officer who carried a shotgun arrested two suspects.

_____ FOR CLASS DISCUSSION _____

Tell precisely how you will decide whether or not to use commas in your sentence.

A WORD TIP FROM THE REAL WORLD

Connie runs a travel agency. She makes a commission on every major trip she sells, and her agency flourishes by encouraging travelers to participate in tour packages. "Descriptions are everything," Connie maintains. "I put only my best describers on the phone with clients who are looking for vacation packages. The people who have a flair for accurate and extensive descriptions beyond the words that are printed in the brochures are the ones who sell the trips and the ones who get the commissions. I ought to know. It's the way I became appreciated by customers and earned my reputation. My reputation built my client base and allowed me to open my own agency." It seems that careful word choice can lead to exciting places.

Name _____ Date _____

_____WORKSHEET 28_____

USES OF THE COMMA

PART A. Indicate whether the statement is true or false by placing T or F in the space provided.

1. All compound sentences have only two independent clauses.   1. __F__

2. An independent clause could be used as a separate sentence.   2. __t__

3. Every compound sentence contains a coordinating conjunction.   3. __F__

4. Verbals are verb forms used as other parts of speech.   4. __t__

5. Gerunds, infinitives, and participles are all verbals.   5. __t__

6. A series of clauses should never be separated with commas.   6. __F__

7. If the last two items in a series are joined with a conjunction, a comma should not be used before the conjunction.   7. __f__

8. It would be illogical to join two coordinate adjectives with *and.*   8. __f__

9. There is never more than one correct way to punctuate a sentence.   9. __f__

10. Coordinating conjunctions are used in compound sentences only.   10. __f__

PART B. By writing the appropriate letter(s) in the answer space, indicate the rule (or rules) justifying the punctuation used in the sentence. Agree as a collaborating team first; then write your answer. Some items will have two letters as answers.

    A. Two independent clauses joined by coordinating conjunction
    B. Introductory verbal or verbal phrase
    C. Items in a series

1. We selected a digital camera and a plain paper fax, but neither one was in stock.   1. * __A__

2. Entering the figures, I skipped a line, but I have since corrected the error.   2. __B, A__

3. To be a good teammate, I must be supportive, but I must also critique fairly.   3. * __B, A__

4. To process forms more quickly, he ordered a sheetfed scanner.   4. __B__

5. Power surges are affecting computer memory, color monitors, and fax transmissions.   5. __C__

6. Heartened by the rise in the price of our stock, our board made big plans.   6. __B__

7. This cell phone has 2-hour talk time, 20-hour stand-by, and digital readout.   7. __C__

8. To insure best printer performance, order a quality printer cable for each port.

8. __B__

9. We were sent the bid this morning, and I called in Pima, Kells, and Olson.

9. __A,C__

10. You'll like our electronic organizer, and you may also appreciate our dictionary.

10. __A__

11. We must finish our estimate by Friday, or we will certainly lose our client.

11. __A__

12. I respect her work, yet I am hesitant to trust her personally.

12. __A__

13. The AAA account executive used to work here, but she moved to Hudson.

13. __A__

14. In attempting to save money, we have compromised quality.

14. __B.__

PART C. Insert all necessary commas in each of the following sentences. In the space provided, indicate the number of commas you have inserted. Write 0 if no commas are necessary.

1. Stunned by her reaction, Paulson didn't know how to respond.

1. * __1__

2. The proposed grant budget was approved, but we received no funds.

2. __1__

3. Our multifunction copier is state-of-the-art, but most people are afraid to use it.

3. * __1__

4. The configuration should include an internet keyboard, a 4.0 GB hard drive, 48 MG RAM, a 56K modem, and 32X CD ROM.

4. __4__

5. Our department will be open on Tuesday, Wednesday, and Thursday each week.

5. * __2.__

6. Our designers suggest these color combinations: dark green on white, blue on crimson, black on yellow, and dark red on tan.

6. __3__

7. While trying to decrease everyone's anxiety, Victor made some poor jokes.

7. __1__

8. In deciding on the best marketing plan for the new product, I studied data on the target audience, received bids from several agencies, held three focus groups, and then told O'Malley to launch the television campaign he had proposed.

8. __4__

9. In December our profits are projected at $35,000.

9. __0__

10. While looking for the data disk he found a spare ink cartridge, several envelopes, and a CD ROM dictionary missing for two months.

10. _____

11. Tucked into the book was $500, but Grayson was not even tempted to keep it.

11. __1__

12. Al bought a new attaché case in order to make a favorable impression on his clients.

12. _____

13. Every chair he tested was either too wide or too narrow too dark or too light too expensive or too shoddy.

13. _____

14. To better serve our customers we will now offer our catalog on-line.

14.   1

15. I want to have lunch with Bozeman on Monday and Canning on Wednesday.

15.   0

16. The group approved but he resigned.

16.   0

17. Prices will need to rise before June or we will be short of operating capital.

17.   1

18. I should talk to Henrich check the proposal with Keifert edit it with Malcolm and submit it to van Gelder.

18.   3

19. Encouraged by her team's approval she moved into Phase 2 of the project.

19.   1

20. Having worked in that division I know the politics of the management team.

20.   1

PART D. Read through this paragraph from a business letter, underscoring the six expressions that would be unacceptable in good correspondence. Supply correct choices in the blanks which follow the paragraph. Persuade your partner(s) about your choices.

We value your patronage and are sorry to hear that you had trouble with a shipment of our merchandise. The material was in excellent shape when it left the factory. We always stand in back of our products. We hope that the party who wrote to alert us of this problem will accept a new shipment from us, because we want to satisfy every customer irregardless of whether the damage was our fault or the delivery company's fault. There were several other shipments beside yours that were damaged this month. Please notify us immediately in regards to any similar problem in the future. We want to respond to such needs immediately. Thank you.

1. _____

2. _____

3. _____

4. _____

5. _____

6. _____

PART E. In the spaces provided, write the 15 words that should be followed by commas. Put them in their proper order.

Stuart Bennington has always been willing to work hard to achieve his goals. While attending college in Michigan he took courses in marketing merchandising economics statistics and finance. He knew even then that there was a place for him in the corporate world and he wanted to be prepared. To earn money for tuition and books he worked in the college dining room three afternoons a week. In his junior year he started a small printing business and it provided him with enough money to cover his college expenses. To get started he had bought some printing equipment that was damaged but it served his needs. He worked long hours studied until late each night and still managed to enjoy life. After graduating with a B+ average he was offered employment by three prestigious corporations. His choice of Ford was not surprising for he has always been interested in automobiles. By working hard he assured his success with the company.

1. * _____
2. * _____
3. * _____
4. _____
5. _____
6. _____
7. _____
8. _____
9. _____
10. _____
11. _____
12. _____
13. _____
14. _____
15. _____

_____ FOR CLASS DISCUSSION _____

(if time permits)

Here is a familiar quotation: "I don't know a single rule, but people have no difficulty in understanding what I write. Good punctuation is simply a matter of inserting a comma whenever there is a pause."

1. How effective is the "pause" test in helping a writer to punctuate effectively?
2. Why do so few people take time to learn punctuation rules?

29

Uses of the Comma (continued)

■■ POINT TO PONDER

Punctuation marks work almost invisibly in a paragraph that is correctly punctuated.

In this chapter you will find four more excellent rules for the use of commas. Although those that involve complex sentences were presented earlier, they are repeated here because of their importance to the careful business writer.

RULE 4 Use commas to separate the items in a date or an address from one another, and then use a comma to separate the date or address from the rest of the sentence which follows.

The company moved to 1260 Turner Street, Wichita, Kansas, sometime last year.

On May 14, 1992, we celebrated our fortieth anniversary.

The historic meeting took place at 10 A.M. on Tuesday, July 2, 1990, in the Blackstone Hotel.

Do not use commas to set off the year if the day of the month is not indicated *(May 1965.)* Dates in military correspondence generally appear in this form: *14 August 1990* (no comma needed within the date, but a comma will still need to separate the date from any words which follow it).

RULE 5 Place a comma after an introductory adverb clause.

This rule was presented in Chapter 23, where complex sentences were introduced. You may recall that a comma is generally needed if an adverb clause precedes the main clause to which it refers. Such clauses are said to be *transposed.* Don't forget that adverb clauses are introduced with subordinating conjunctions (*if, since, because, when, while, as, provided, after, before, unless,* etc.).

> Before data processing came into use, checks were sorted by hand.
>
> If we advertise in trade magazines, our sales will certainly increase.
>
> As he read the fine print in the contract, his hand began to shake.

It was noted in Chapter 23 that some writers do not use a comma if the introductory clause is short or if there is little chance for a misreading. You will do well, however, to follow the rule implicitly by placing commas after all adverb clauses that introduce sentences.

As you know, no comma is usually needed if an adverb clause follows the main clause of a sentence. Rule 6, however, suggests the need for judgment. Occasionally a comma should be placed after the main clause if an adverb clause follows.

RULE 6   Use commas to set off nonrestrictive clauses and phrases.

You may recall that a similar, but less inclusive, rule was presented in Chapter 23, which is concerned solely with complex sentences. Because this new rule pertains to several types of modifiers (some of which you will recognize), our discussion is divided into three parts:

1. An adverb clause that follows a main clause is, in most instances, restrictive and should not be set off with a comma. If, however, such a clause is only loosely connected to the main clause, it should be considered nonrestrictive and set off. You will find that the idea expressed in a nonrestrictive clause could be expressed in another sentence. Read these examples carefully:

    > We failed to reach our quota of 550 sales in December, *although we made a determined effort.*
    >
    > The firm is being forced into bankruptcy, *as you have probably guessed.*
    >
    > We find it advisable to vote against Lane, *however experienced he may be.*

Unless the adverb clause that follows a main clause is clearly nonrestrictive, do not set it off with a comma. The adverb clauses in these sentences are restrictive:

> You will be well pleased *when you see the new advertising layouts.*
>
> Hudson will be seriously considered for promotion *if his fine work continues.*
>
> Strand talked with several eyewitnesses *before he entered his plea.*
>
> We hesitated *because several lives were at stake.*

If you find it difficult to determine whether such adverb clauses are restrictive or nonrestrictive, don't be dismayed. Your own good judgment is likely to serve you well. Fortunately, a natural pause will commonly come before an adverb clause that should be set off with a comma.

2. An adjective clause, as you know, may be restrictive or nonrestrictive. Such clauses may be used to modify nouns or pronouns; they are frequently introduced with relative pronouns such as *who, whose, whom, which,* and *that.*

If the adjective clause is needed to identify the word modified, it should be considered *restrictive.* Restrictive clauses are never set off with commas. If, on the other hand, the adjective clause simply adds information that is not needed to identify the word modified, it is nonrestrictive. Such clauses can generally be omitted without changing the meaning of the main clause. They should always be set off with commas.

Adjective clauses introduced with the pronoun *that* are restrictive and should not be set off. Note the restrictive and nonrestrictive clauses in these sentences:

RESTRICTIVE: The mistake *that you made* can be corrected easily. (It is not natural to pause before reading a restrictive clause.)

RESTRICTIVE: The man *who meets all your qualifications* will never be found. (Note that the restrictive clause identifies the person being discussed.)

RESTRICTIVE: The gentleman *whose property I damaged* treated me with kindness and understanding. (If the restrictive clause were omitted, the reader would not know what gentleman the writer had in mind.)

NONRESTRICTIVE: Toland, *who will head our delegation,* is a born leader. (The nonrestrictive clause simply adds information. It is not needed for identification.)

NONRESTRICTIVE: This ornate building, *which has 28 stories and 950 offices,* was built with federal funds. (The adjective *this* identifies the building.)

NONRESTRICTIVE: My only son, *whom you met on Thursday,* has enrolled at New York University. (The nonrestrictive clause could be omitted without changing the meaning of the main clause.)

NONRESTRICTIVE: We should meet in this office on Saturday, *when no* work will be in progress. (An adjective clause introduced with *when* or *where* is generally nonrestrictive. *When* is more often used in adverb clauses.)

NONRESTRICTIVE: The three telegrams, *all of which were mailed in Columbus,* told of her good fortune. (Adjective clauses introduced with *all of which,* *each of whom,* and similar expressions are always nonrestrictive.)

Adjective clauses that follow proper nouns are almost always nonrestrictive. Occasionally, however, we use this kind of construction: *I am talking about the Albert Jones who works in your office.* The adjective clause in such a sentence is restrictive because the name (Albert Jones) does not adequately identify the person under discussion.

3. Nonrestrictive *phrases* should be set off with commas. We have already discussed the importance of setting off introductory verbal phrases, which are usually nonrestrictive. When such a phrase appears elsewhere in a sentence (not at the beginning), we should determine whether it is restrictive or nonrestrictive. Those that are nonrestrictive should be set off.

RESTRICTIVE: The student *helping to address envelopes* is a volunteer.
RESTRICTIVE: The material *to be destroyed* has absolutely no value to the firm.
RESTRICTIVE: He purchased the transistor radio *made in Brooklyn.*
NONRESTRICTIVE: Grace Munson, *having worked in a law office,* was able to answer my question.
NONRESTRICTIVE: Olson, *in order to save time,* sent the package by air freight.
NONRESTRICTIVE: This right front wheel, *obviously mounted improperly,* is the source of your problem.

NONRESTRICTIVE:	*In fact,* no one on our governing board objected to the change. (A transitional phrase that relates to a preceding thought should be set off.)
NONRESTRICTIVE:	*For example,* several of our technicians have college degrees.

RULE 7 Use commas to set off parenthetical expressions.

Because nonrestrictive phrases and clauses have already been discussed, Rule 7 may appear to be somewhat superfluous. Parenthetical expressions *are,* as a rule, *nonrestrictive,* but they are distinctive enough to deserve a place of their own in our discussion of commas. A parenthetical expression (which may be a word, a phrase, or a short clause) tends to interrupt the natural flow of a sentence because it is somewhat abruptly inserted. Here are a few expressions that are often used parenthetically:

as a consequence	I believe	moreover
as a result	if necessary	nevertheless
as a rule	in addition	of course
as well as _____	in brief	on the contrary
as you know	in fact	on the other hand
by the way	it has been said	therefore
for example	it seems	to be sure
however	I understand	together with _____

Unless such an expression blends in very smoothly with the sentence it interrupts, it should be set off with commas. You will be wise to set off all parenthetical expressions that you find on the worksheets that follow this chapter. Observe how parenthetical expressions interrupt the flow of thought in these sentences:

He was told, *it seems,* that no more money would be available.

Handley, *by the way,* has several excellent ideas for improving our service.

The new engine, *together with a small box of tools,* will be shipped to you on Wednesday.

If you attempt to sell your home now, *however,* you may experience some difficulty.

Our firm has, *I believe,* the industry's most efficient blast furnace.

Adverb clauses may be used parenthetically. If such a clause interrupts the flow of a sentence, it should generally be set off with commas.

Several of us, because we had heard the report, expressed concern about the future.

We realized, as the vote clearly indicated, that Denton was well regarded by her colleagues.

Name _____ **Date** _____

_____WORKSHEET 29_____

USES OF THE COMMA
(continued)

PART A. Answer the following questions by writing T for true or F for false in the space provided.

1. Adverb clauses are usually introduced with coordinating conjunctions.

    1. * F

2. All adverb clauses should be set off with commas.

    2. F

3. Clauses are said to be transposed if an adverb clause precedes a main clause.

    3. T

4. Adverb clauses can be restrictive.

    4. T

5. Adjective clauses cannot be restrictive.

    5. F

6. A nonrestrictive clause should be set off with commas.

    6. T

7. If a restrictive clause is taken from a sentence, the meaning of the main clause generally changes.

    7. T

8. Some parenthetical expressions do not require the use of commas.

    8. T

9. Clauses are the only type of word group used as parenthetical expressions.

    9. F

10. If a nonrestrictive clause is taken from a sentence, the meaning of the main clause generally remains unchanged.

    10. T

PART B. Insert all commas that are needed in the following sentences. Justify your punctuation by writing the appropriate *letter* in the space provided.

    A. Commas are used to set off a nonrestrictive clause.
    B. Commas are used to set off an introductory adverb clause.
    C. Commas are used to set off a parenthetical expression.
    D. No commas are needed.

Example: When we submit our expenses, reimbursement can follow

    B

1. No matter what their occupation, almost all workers need a team of assistants.

    1. * C, B?

2. Almost never are average employees given such a support team.

    2. * D.

3. Management, however, often has the benefit of think tanks and task forces.

    3. C.

4. These groups assist the manager, who benefits from their critique.

    4. * A.

5. If every worker had such a coaching team what would the business world be like?

5. _B_

6. Is it possible to support and critique every member of the staff?

6. _D_

7. Whenever a staff takes a quality approach to project management the answer is yes.

7. _B_

8. In a major publishing firm in the midwest every project is taken on by a team.

8. _C._

9. This team which can number four to six is gathered for its expertise and availability.

9. _A._

10. The team chooses one member who will act as the project executive.

10. _D._

11. That person as I understand it is the one who will sign off on all deadlines.

11. _C._

12. The team is accountable to that person to provide timely and accurate work.

12. _D._

13. The project executive in turn finds needed assistance and oversees outcome.

13. _C._

14. As we look at the project executive's role we see that he or she should be a "big picture" thinker.

14. _B._

15. However being aware of details and knowing what questions to ask is also key.

15. _C._

16. When firms use this approach the executive writes a budget for time and money.

16. _B_

17. The cost of a project can be accurately estimated if the team is experienced.

17. _D._

18. Checkpoints of course are established along the timeline of the project.

18. _C._

19. The project executive coaches the team and critiques the work as it progresses.

19. _D._

20. As a result the entire team produces better work with good advice in timely ways.

20. _C._

PART C. Insert all commas that are needed in these sentences. In the space provided, indicate the number of commas you have inserted. Write 0 if no commas are needed. If you are collaborating, discuss your answers with your teammates before deciding what will be your group's set of shared answers.

1. A recent book about consulting was written for anyone who consults.

1. * _0_

2. The author interestingly enough defines consulting as trying to improve a situation while lacking control of implementation.

2. * _2_

3. Those who have direct control are managers of course.

3. _1_

4. Those who do not on the other hand are consultants.

4. _2_

5. The author concentrates on helping a consultant to gain leverage and impact.

5. _0_

6. When a consultant has leverage and impact her or his expertise is used.

6. * _1_

308   Uses of the Comma (continued)

Name _____ Date _____

7. As a result, her or his recommendations are accepted. **7.** 1

8. The book teaches skills that lead to job satisfaction for clients and consultants alike. **8.** 0

9. The author maintains that anyone can consult, either internally to his or her own organization or externally to others. **9.** 1

10. He is a veteran of countless staff skills training workshops around the country. **10.** 0

11. He has worked with engineers, personnel workers, purchasing agents, and auditors. **11.** 3

12. Because of his experience, he has led entire organizations to changed behavior. **12.** 1

13. He has also helped single departments within larger companies. **13.** 0

14. The principles, he says, are the same for almost all organizations. **14.** 2

15. This book gives its major attention to the work of internal consultants. **15.** 0

16. Internal consultants, as you might guess, are those who work from within to change a system. **16.** 2

17. The book is loaded with examples, illustrations, case studies, and cartoons. **17.** 3

18. It cuts across employment status hierarchy, and it offers good advice to anyone. **18.** 1

19. This reviewer believes it should be required reading for all business majors. **19.** 0

20. In addition, she believes that management should encourage workers to read it and enact it, for their profit and working environment will improve if they do. **20.** 2

PART D. As you read the following paragraph, underscore every comma that has been used incorrectly. There are six errors.

Mr. Neilson, our treasurer, read his quarterly report, but omitted several important figures pertaining to the recent merger. Ms. Frabetti would certainly have objected, if she had been at the meeting. Those directors who were present, expressed their approval of current plans to review our obsolete, accounting procedures. Because our offices close for several days during December, Mr. Neilson suggested that quarterly reports be sent to stockholders in January, April, July, and October, of each year. Mr. Tanaka, who generally helps to prepare such reports, supported the idea enthusiastically. One member of our group, however, vehemently opposed every new proposal, that was made.

HOW TO TREAT *HAROLD*

Some writers make it a practice to use no commas in such expressions as *my son Jim, my daughter Susan,* or *my cousin George.* Others, however, prefer to insert commas if the names prove to be nonrestrictive appositives (see Chapter 30). A man with only one son might use commas in this sentence: *My son, Harold, plans to study medicine.* (The name is nonrestrictive because the words *my son* identify the person being discussed.)

_____ FOR CLASS DISCUSSION _____

If you were asked to write the italicized sentence, would you choose to set *Harold* off with commas? State your reason. (Assume, of course, that you have only one son.)

---

wⱮⱮw ═══════════ Watching the Web ═══════════

| Back | Forward | Home | Reload | Images | Open |

Have you surfed the net, looking for the right business opportunity and never found it? Have you become discouraged between jobs and felt as though you'd never land another one? Well friend this page is written just for you. Here is the chance you've been waiting for.

`read on`   `no thanks`

OPTIONAL EXERCISES

OPTION 1　Insert commas. In the answer space write the number of marks you have added.

1. To reach her goal, Andrews, my project manager, has worked overtime all week.

   1. * *3*

2. Since we had record attendance this year, we will begin planning next year's conference now.

   2. *1*

3. Two envelopes were delivered today, but I don't know which one Jackson wants.

   3. *1*

4. No, Mr. Savoy, we are not hiring keyliners, lithostrippers, or press workers.

   4. * *4*

5. David Cleary, Jr.'s assessment of the situation was astute, wasn't it?

   5. *2*

6. To be honest, I feel Wentworth's agency has let us down, down, down.

   6. *3*

7. In fact, unless third quarter earnings are up dramatically, we'll have to take a loss for the entire year.

   7. *2*

8. If you have anything to suggest suggest it now before we submit this revised, reduced budget.

   8. *1*

9. The more I watch Fitch work on the telephone, the more I'm convinced that we should hire him.

   9. *1*

10. Diana Severson, smiling and nodding, walked through that gathering in a way that said aloud, "I will be the winner."

    10. *3*

11. "Yes," said Polk, "you'll find the office at 8219 Oxborough Avenue, Bloomington."

    11. *3*

12. Mansfield believes that International Systems, Ltd., of Worthington, England, could be of enormous help with our operation in Fort Wells, Australia.

    12. *5*

13. Igelewsky will attend every conference, training, and promotion from now on.

    13. *2*

14. Because she is so fast, accurate, energetic, and personable, Santos will go far.

    14. *4*

15. Mark my words, dear colleagues, our pay raises are but a month away.

    15. *2*

OPTION 2 Insert 20 missing commas in the following paragraph. Your collaborative team needs to agree on comma placement each time.

Most people, it seems, find punctuation rules difficult to understand and, as a result, difficult to apply. Some rules, of course, are more challenging than others. Most people can easily recognize items in a series, but the same people may have trouble with verbal phrases or nonrestrictive clauses. If you sincerely want to learn the rules, you can. After you have studied the ten comma rules, you should start thinking in terms of those rules *every time you write.* When you prepare homework papers for classes in economics, history, geography, literature, or any other discipline, keep the rules in mind and apply them. If you are unsure of yourself, look at the rules again. Study the examples of adverb clauses, nonrestrictive elements, parenthetical expressions, and compound sentences. Learn to recognize them at a glance. If you apply a rule, it will become more familiar to you. Eventually all ten rules will be yours to command, and writing will be less challenging.

OPTION 3 (CLASS DISCUSSION) A number of researchers have concluded that high-ranking executives generally spend more time *listening* than they spend speaking or writing. It was also discovered that the average person in our society is not a very efficient listener; in fact, workers who were given listening tests did not do at all well.

With these findings in mind, do you feel that courses in listening should be offered routinely in colleges throughout the country? Discuss briefly.

THE IDEAL VACATION SPOT

While watching television recently, I noticed that one commercial featured a sign bearing these words:

LAKE TAHOE

LIKE NO PLACE ON EARTH

———————————— FOR CLASS DISCUSSION ————————————

Do you suppose that Lake Tahoe is really in outer space, as the sign suggests? Comment.

THE IMPACT OF LANGUAGE

NAME _____

DIRECTIONS

Your instructor may ask you to examine any four of the ten sentences that follow. You are to write the rule that governs the punctuation of each one chosen. Working as a collaborative team, you must reach consensus about your answers.

1. Mr. Marconi, having already made his decision, did not read our report.
2. Unless you have a college degree, you will not be considered for the position.
3. He read most of the chapter, but he skipped the most important part.
4. On May 3, 1979, he was living at 134 Center Street, Dover, Delaware.
5. I have been told that our chief teller, Ms. Chavez, is a fine musician.
6. In repairing the engine, he burned his hand badly.
7. This office will be closed on Monday, Tuesday, and Wednesday of next week.
8. Several of our employees, it seems, are unhappy with working conditions.
9. Margaret Lasky, who proposed the change, is certainly willing to compromise.
10. Besides David, Thomas and his partner will join our group.

Sentence No. _____ Rule: _____

_____

_____

_____

Sentence No. _____ Rule: _____

_____

_____

_____

Sentence No. _____ Rule: _____

_____

_____

_____

Sentence No. _____ Rule: _____

_____

_____

_____

COMMAS IN BRIEF

RULE: Use a comma or commas . . .	EXAMPLE
1. . . . to separate items in a series.	He has never been in Pittsburgh, Memphis, or New Orleans.
2. . . . before a coordinating conjunction that joins two independent clauses.	The package arrived on Monday, but the contents had been damaged in transit.
3. . . . after an introductory verbal (word *or* phrase).	Before entering the building, Harold stopped to have his shoes shined.
4. . . . to separate the items in a date or an address.	They met on Saturday, January 6, 1989, in Portland, Oregon.
5. . . . after an introductory adverb clause.	If she had made the sale, she would have earned an excellent commission.
6. . . . to set off nonrestrictive phrases and clauses.	Mr. Ross Williams, who once worked for General Motors, will be our new vice president.
7. . . . to set off parenthetical expressions.	There are, I understand, at least four more items to be discussed.
8. . . . to set off words that are independent of a main clause or clearly nonrestrictive.	This project, Mr. Daniels, may take a week or more. No, it cannot be completed in two or three days.
9. . . . when they are needed simply to prevent misreading.	Without Edna, Thomas may find it difficult to stay in business.
10. . . . when they are needed to secure emphasis.	The letter of commendation was, belatedly, sent to his home address.

CHAPTER

31

Uses of Semicolons and Colons

■■ POINT TO PONDER

Most people, unfortunately, never learn to use semicolons correctly.

THE SEMICOLON

The break, or pause, that a **semicolon** represents in a sentence is somewhat greater than the break indicated by a comma. In some of its functions the semicolon could be considered a "weak period." The rules governing its use can be mastered easily by anyone who can identify clauses and phrases in a sentence.

> **RULE 1** Use a semicolon to separate the main clauses of a compound sentence if a coordinating conjunction does not connect them.

You have learned to place a comma before *and, but, or, nor, for, so,* or *yet* when one of these conjunctions joins the clauses of a compound sentence. Rule 1 refers to closely related coordinate clauses not joined by such conjunctions. Note these examples:

> The raw materials were supplied by our Akron plant; the finished product was made in our Los Angeles branch.
>
> Cambridge is simply *near* Boston; it is not a part of that city.
>
> The brochures have already been printed; they have not yet been distributed.

A semicolon should be used when the second clause of a compound sentence is introduced with a conjunctive adverb or a transitional phrase. The pause that normally precedes either of these connectives suggests the need of a strong mark of punctuation. The following are frequently employed in compound sentences as conjunctive adverbs or as transitional phrases.

accordingly	henceforth	next
also	however	on the contrary
as a consequence	in addition	on the other hand
as a result	in fact	otherwise
besides	in other words	still
consequently	instead	that is (i.e.)
for example (e.g.)	likewise	that is to say
for instance	meanwhile	then
furthermore	moreover	therefore
hence	nevertheless	thus

The use of a comma after any one of the preceding transitional words or phrases will cause a reader to pause and to place added emphasis upon that connective. Many business writers today prefer to insert that comma except after conjunctive adverbs of only one syllable (*thus, hence, then,* etc.). Note carefully the punctuation in these compound sentences:

The meeting has been in progress for two hours; however, several important matters have yet to be introduced.

The Federal Housing Administration has appraised the property at $300,000; therefore, we do not feel that Clark's offer is reasonable.

Production at our Louisville plant came to a standstill during the recent strike; nevertheless, we managed to eke out a small profit for the fiscal year.

He tried to make amends; that is, he offered me the use of his car.

Monday is a national holiday; hence, we will have a three-day weekend. (Some writers never place the optional comma after *hence, thus,* or *then.* The mark, of course, results in a pause.)

Note: The expressions we have been discussing sometimes appear in sentences that are not compound. Observe the absence of semicolons in these simple sentences:

The firm needs some new leadership, that is, a more knowledgeable president.

Roy Tortelli, in other words, is well suited to his job. (The expression *in other words* has been used parenthetically.)

> **RULE 2**   Use a semicolon to separate items in a series when the items themselves contain commas.

Readers are likely to be confused when they encounter commas *within* items in a series and also *between* such items. Note the clarity that results when sentences of this type are punctuated properly.

We will present pins denoting 20 years of service to Kay Witham, an economist; Bert Kaplan, an accountant; Sally Covello, a teller; and Carrie Haynes, a loan officer.

We were visited this summer by people from LaGrange, a suburb of Chicago; Troy, a small college town in Georgia; and Austin, the capital of Texas.

The four most important dates in our firm's history are probably January 12, 1888; August 2, 1905; September 25, 1922; and December 1, 1998.

We were led to believe that Renko, Hayden, and the others would act favorably upon our application; that Gene Poston, our chief engineer, would receive full credit for his invention; and that our company would soon begin producing this revolutionary new product.

RULE 3 Use a semicolon before an expression such as *for example* (e.g.), *that is* (i.e.), *for instance, that is to say,* or *namely* when it is used to introduce an enumeration. Place a comma after such an expression.

Davila used a few terms that the new cost estimator may not understand; for example, *duplexing, control character,* and *crossfooting.*

Our products have sold exceptionally well in four New England states; namely, Massachusetts, Rhode Island, Connecticut, and New Hampshire. (Some business writers prefer to use a colon in a sentence of this type.)

If the enumeration appears within a sentence, not at the *end,* dashes or parentheses should be used in this manner:

A few of the older employees—namely, Scott, Pafko, and Genovese—disapprove of these innovations. (The use of dashes tends to place emphasis on the names.)

A few of the older employees (namely, Scott, Pafko, and Genovese) disapprove of these innovations. (Words that appear in parentheses tend to be deemphasized.)

Several of the expressions mentioned in Rule 3, you may recall, are also used in building compound sentences.

On Monday morning we faced several serious problems; for example, we could not use the scanner because of a power outage.

BUT: We have made a number of excellent purchases in the past month, for example, this spreadsheet software. (A semicolon was *not* used because the transitional expression was not followed by an enumeration or an independent clause.)

RULE 4 (OPTIONAL) Use a semicolon before a coordinating conjunction that separates two independent clauses if commas are within those clauses.

Some professional writers apply this rule only when they feel that a semicolon is needed to eliminate any possible lack of clarity. Because the use of a comma would also be considered correct, the worksheet that follows this chapter will not test your mastery of Rule 4.

Woodson, as you may have heard, contributed several dollars to the gift; (comma optional) but Manley contributed nothing.

His determination, his courage, and his sincerity could not be denied; (comma optional) but his methods, as you know, were often questioned by his colleagues.

The semicolon is an excellent mark of punctuation if used sparingly. Don't allow your mastery of this mark to tempt you into writing long, unwieldy sentences. Don't use a semicolon when a period would be more logical or when the following clauses should be subordinated to the main idea.

THE COLON

The function of a **colon,** which directs a reader's attention to what follows, is quite different from that of a semicolon, which acts as a separator.

RULE 1   Use a colon after a formal introduction to the words that follow.

The colon specializes in introducing explanations, examples, quotations, and enumerations. To direct the reader's attention, words such as *the following, as follows, thus, these items,* or *this response* may be used or simply implied. Study carefully the functions of the colons in these sentences:

We hope to open a branch office in each of the following states: Nebraska, Wisconsin, Arizona, and Colorado.

Only three pieces of furniture remain in our showroom: a sofa, an end table, and a bookcase. (Only *the following* three pieces of furniture: . . . etc.)

I have one serious objection to your project: it may prove to be very expensive. (I have *the following* serious objection: . . . etc.)

He seems to have forgotten this rule: Use commas to separate items in a series. (If a sentence that follows a colon is to be emphasized, it should begin with a capital letter.)

He claimed that only one kind of work would ever satisfy him: acting. (The use of a comma or a dash would be informal.)

The money collected during the campaign was distributed thus: $2,000 for clerical help, $5,000 for postage, $7,000 for stationery and printing, and $87,500 for the underprivileged.

You will be pleased to hear the good news: Enzio has passed the bar examination.

Ortiz used these exact words: "Don't ignore the facts." (A quotation that is a complete sentence should begin with a capital letter.)

Do not place a colon after a verb or a preposition that is followed by a series. Note that a colon is not needed in these sentences:

Our equipment will undoubtedly include a tractor, a large crane, and a ditch digger. (A colon should not be placed after *include.*)

Copies of the memorandum were sent to their production foreman, their purchasing manager, and their engineering designer. (A colon should not be placed after *to.*)

Use a colon, however, if items in a series following a verb or a preposition are listed on separate lines. Also, capitalize each word on the list.

At tomorrow's meeting we will probably discuss:
(1) The new union contract.
(2) Our revised office procedures.
(3) Our declining production figures.

CAPITALIZING AFTER A COLON

Do not capitalize the first word of an independent clause that follows a colon if that clause simply explains or illustrates the idea expressed before the colon. *(He expressed one minor complaint: his office needs more file cabinets.)* Use a capital, however, if the material following the colon meets any of these criteria:

1. It is a quoted sentence. (See example on p. 326.)
2. It requires special emphasis, possibly because it states a rule or principle. (See example on p. 326.)
3. It consists of two or more complete sentences.

> The new schedule has two distinct advantages: It allows the technicians more time for research. It provides the sales team with excellent incentives. (Note that both sentences following the colon begin with capital letters.)

4. It begins on a new line, perhaps in the form of a list. (See example on p. 326.)
5. It is introduced with a single word such as *Note* or *Remember.*

> Note: The audit will be delayed until Monday.

When a short direct quotation is preceded by introductory words such as *She said* or *The agent replied,* the verb is likely to be followed by a comma. A colon should generally be used if the quotation is long (at least two sentences) or if it is attributed to something inanimate, as in *The last line stated* or *The final paragraph read.*

> In concluding her speech, Senator Vance said: "The young people of today will be our nation's leaders of tomorrow, and in their hands will rest the destiny of the greatest republic that this world has ever known. We are supremely confident that they will prove equal to the monumental task that lies before them."

> The report concluded: "It is strongly recommended that the appropriate action be taken before the end of this fiscal period." *(Report* names something inanimate.)

RULE 2 Use a colon after the salutation of a business letter.

Dear Mr. Ames: Ladies and Gentlemen:

EXCEPTION: If *open punctuation* is used, no mark should follow the salutation.

RULE 3 Use a colon to separate the hours from the minutes when time is expressed in figures.

10:45 A.M. 2:20 P.M.

RULE 4 Use a colon to separate a title from a subtitle.

American Business Enterprise: The Role of Retailers

> **RULE 5**   Use colons in footnotes and bibliographies if the style being followed suggests such usage.

Authors and publishers have not agreed upon a standard style. Here is one popular technique:

Krause, Frederick. *Investments,* 5th ed., Englewood Cliffs, NJ: Prentice Hall, Inc., 1989.

> **RULE 6**   Use a colon to separate (1) chapter from verse in a biblical reference or (2) the parts of a mathematical ratio.

Genesis 2:8 $10{:}2 = 30{:}x$

A WORD TIP FROM THE REAL WORLD

Language that well-educated people consider to be grammatically unacceptable is often used in newspaper, magazine, and television advertising. The public is being continually exposed to constructions such as these:

". . . more satisfying than *any* [rather than *any other*] beer sold."
". . . to shave a man as *smooth* as this."
"If Nestea *wasn't* 100% tea . . . "
". . . for people who want to cook *easy* and still cook *good*."

Pamela, a market researcher, interviews consumers every day about wording in advertisements and on packaging. She claims that in over half the interviews she conducts, consumers are concerned that wording may be misleading, ungrammatical, or inaccurate. Many of her interviewees even try to rewrite the survey questions so that they reflect more closely their opinions about the products.

———————————— FOR CLASS DISCUSSION ————————————

Why do copywriters frequently ignore the rules of grammar? Because young people tend to accept without question the wording of any advertisement, should copywriters be careful to use constructions that are grammatically acceptable?

————WORKSHEET 31————

USES OF SEMICOLONS AND COLONS

PART A. Indicate whether the statement is true or false by inserting T or F in the space provided.

1. A semicolon could be considered a weak period.

   1. _____

2. A semicolon might be used in a sentence that employs a coordinating conjunction to join its main clauses.

   2. _____

3. The word *moreover* may be used as a conjunctive adverb.

   3. _____

4. Semicolons may be used to separate items in a series.

   4. _____

5. The most common coordinating conjunctions are *and* and *but*.

   5. _____

6. An expression such as *for example* should always be followed by a colon when it appears within a sentence.

   6. _____

7. Several semicolons must never appear in a single sentence.

   7. _____

8. Semicolons should be used to separate the hours from the minutes in the expression of time.

   8. _____

9. A colon may not be followed by a quotation.

   9. _____

10. Colons and commas have similar functions in sentences and can often be interchanged.

    10. _____

PART B. Insert all commas, semicolons, and colons that are needed in each of the following sentences. In the space provided, indicate the number of punctuation marks you have added. Include optional commas.

1. When a small business is stretched to its limits it is wise to consider reorganization.

   1. _____

2. Sometimes that reorganization involves cuts or layoffs sometimes it involves duty reassignments.

   2. *_____

3. Employees should examine three aspects of their work realistically use of time use of materials and revenue production.

   3. *_____

4. They should keep tabs on these aspects over a given time most advisors suggest three months as a reasonable period.

   4. *_____

5. The entire staff should meet once or twice during this period to check their work on two key points time spent and revenue produced.

   5. _____

6. No one is better suited to this evaluation than the staff members themselves.

   6. _____

7. The periodic staff meetings can be brief one group met from 8 00 A.M. until 8 15 A.M. each Monday during the evaluation period for updates and encouragement.

7. _____

8. During a difficult time regular non-anxious communication makes a real difference in climate some say it holds people together for better decisions.

8. _____

9. When such an evaluation period is complete the staff shares a much more complete picture of the company and strategic planning is much more realistic.

9. _____

10. Often an interesting side benefit occurs people take ownership of particular tasks and discover or devise better ways of accomplishing them.

10. _____

11. Sometimes this deep ownership shows that someone else is better suited to the work than the current staff member sometimes the current work is simply affirmed.

11. _____

12. If the entire staff discusses the costs and benefits of each company project they can grow the two factors needed for future success creativity and teamwork.

12. _____

13. One small business president has put it this way "It wasn't until we were almost bankrupt that we learned what we were really good at. Now we sell that and nothing else!"

13. _____

14. As you know many factors contribute to the success or failure of small businesses however one of the most destructive is lack of shared vision.

14. _____

15. Although lack of money is almost always cited as the reason for business collapse it is often the second most critical factor not the first.

15. _____

16. A great inventor of products services or ideas must be able to share her vision with three key groups investors colleagues and clients.

16. _____

17. Occasionally it takes a calamity in business to get a team to discover what it is really selling that calamity can mean death or vigorous new life.

17. _____

18. One business consultant has a wish for all struggling companies that they conduct this three-month evaluation now before things get rough in order to claim their vision.

18. _____

19. He believes that such work shared across the whole staff builds a prime asset shared vision.

19. _____

20. "This asset will equip even the smallest organizations for the tough times" he claims.

20. _____

PART C. The following memo paragraph was punctuated with commas only. Five of the commas are inappropriate and should be replaced with colons or semicolons. Find and underscore the five incorrect commas and then indicate, in proper order in the blanks below the memo paragraph, whether they should be replaced with colons or semicolons.

The interoffice e-mail system from XTECH requires users to be prepared with several pieces of information at the time of installation, department code numbers, three speed-address preferences, a screen name, and a password. All users must create their own passwords, by all means keep these passwords secret. Every user must also be prepared at two-month intervals to change passwords, this frequent change cuts down considerably on confidentiality leaks. If a department has ten or more users online, it should supply its users with two pieces of data, a two-digit numerical prefix for the department and a four-digit departmental internet access code, to track departmental use of the online time. Since the system will be installed at 12,01 A.M. on January 1, 1997, users may begin their individual station installation at any time after that.

1. *_____   4. _____

2. *_____   5. _____

3. _____

PART D. Write the *letter* indicating the punctuation mark that should follow the word in italics. If you're collaborating, support your choices with chapter ideas until your team comes to a consensus on answers.

A. comma   B. semicolon   C. colon

Example: The project was extremely *difficult* but we managed to
complete it in less than three hours.

A
_____

1. Some annuities are based upon the life of one *person* others are
based upon the lives of more than one.

1. *_____

2. Two of the most popular types are *these* the cash refund annuity
and the joint survivorship annuity.

2. *_____

3. Premiums may be paid on a monthly *basis* or the entire amount
due may be paid in a single lump sum.

3. _____

4. Some annuities provide an income for a limited period of *time*
some provide an income for the remainder of one's life.

4. _____

5. All large insurance companies sell these *contracts* but their
charges are likely to vary.

5. _____

6. The principal advantage of a typical annuity contract is probably
this the annuitant cannot outlive his or her income.

6. _____

7. Annuities may be purchased by *individuals* and they may be
purchased by companies for their pension plans.

7. _____

8. Insurance executives sometimes divide annuities into these two
categories immediate and deferred.

8. _____

9. One insurance agent likes to sum up the value of these contracts in three *words* peace of mind.

9. _____

10. My contract is with *Metropolitan* his contract is with Prudential.

10. _____

11. The return on a fixed annuity is *predetermined* the return on a variable is not.

11. _____

12. In recent years single-premium life annuities have become extremely *popular* for they offer excellent tax savings.

12. _____

13. One feature that prospective buyers dislike is *this* a penalty is generally imposed for an early withdrawal.

13. _____

14. Some companies allow annuitants to withdraw funds without penalty after the first *year* some will impose a penalty for any withdrawal during the first five years.

14. _____

15. Sandberg works for a mutual life insurance *company* Lapchik works for a stock company.

15. _____

PART E. Write a short, smoothly worded paragraph on the subject of "Work Environments." Use at least two semicolons and circle each one.

_____

_____

_____

_____

_____

_____

_____

_____

_____

_____

_____

_____

_____

_____

_____

_____

_____

_____

_____ **FOR CLASS DISCUSSION** _____

(if time permits)

Do you feel that it is easier for the average person to learn how to *speak* well or to *write* well? Suggest a few challenges that are faced by writers but not by speakers.

CHAPTER

32

Review

■ POINT TO PONDER ⟶

The rules of grammar are not easily forgotten by those who put their knowledge to use daily.

Chapters 25 through 31, as you know, are concerned with sentences, numbers, commas, semicolons, and colons. This chapter will give you an opportunity to assess your understanding of the rules and suggestions you encountered in that unit of work. You will find that the format of this chapter is similar to that found in other review chapters contained in this text.

FREQUENTLY MADE ERRORS

Each of the following sentences would be considered unacceptable in its present form. Before you read the explanation that has been provided, make a serious attempt to determine how the sentence could be improved.

    1.   Traveling at that speed, the accident was inevitable.

Did you recognize *Traveling at that speed* as a verbal phrase? It seems to function as a modifier, but there is no word for it to modify. Here is a perfectly acceptable wording: *Traveling at that speed, you were certain to have an accident.* In this version the verbal phrase modifies *you.*

    2.   Some banks are open on Saturday, which you may already know.

The word *which,* as used in this sentence, is a pronoun—a pronoun that would logically refer to a specific antecedent. Ideally, it will follow the noun or noun equivalent that serves as the

333

antecedent. In our sentence *which* refers vaguely to the entire preceding clause. Here is a more acceptable wording: *You may already know that some banks are open on Saturday.* (In this version the use of *which* is avoided entirely.)

3. We observed Mr. Locke has a new associate.

The omission of an important word can make a sentence unnecessarily difficult to understand. This sentence would be perfectly clear if the word *that* were inserted after *observed.*

4. 49 of our employees refused to sign the petition.

A number that comes at the beginning of a sentence should be expressed as a word, not as a figure; for example, *Forty-nine of our employees refused to sign the petition.* If the number cannot be expressed in one or two words, use a figure, but recast the sentence so that it will not come at the beginning.

5. Our Duluth plant will be closed for 6 days.

In this sentence the only number has been expressed as a figure. You may recall reading, however, that business writers generally spell out isolated numbers from *one* to *ten.* Here is the preferred version: *Our Duluth plant will be closed for six days.*

6. We purchased the old residence, and made it into an office.

Can you detect something wrong with the foregoing sentence? Note that it is simple, not compound, because it contains only one clause. Even though that clause has a compound predicate, there is no reason to place a comma after the word *residence.*

7. George Yamamoto, who sells real estate can probably answer your question.

Have you discovered something missing in sentence 7? Perhaps you recognized *who sells real estate* as a nonrestrictive clause that should be set off with two commas. Of course, a nonrestrictive clause that comes at the end of a sentence can be set off with one comma. In our sentence, however, commas should be placed after *Yamamoto* and *estate.* Any adjective clause that follows a proper noun is likely to be nonrestrictive.

8. Alan Goldberg our letter consultant wrote the final paragraph.

Sentence 8 lacks important punctuation. *Our letter consultant* is a nonrestrictive appositive; therefore, it should be set off with commas, one after *Goldberg* and one after *consultant.*

9. This truck belongs to the company, the other one is mine.

Did you identify the two *independent* clauses in this compound sentence? Because they are not joined by a coordinating conjunction, a semicolon, not a comma, should be placed after the first clause.

10. We plan to open branches in London, England, Paris, France, and Lisbon, Portugal.

Although this sentence may prove understandable to the average reader, the punctuation leaves much to be desired. Because the items in a series contain commas within themselves, we can achieve maximum clarity by separating those items with semicolons. Study this more acceptable version: *We plan to open branches in London, England; Paris, France; and Lisbon, Portugal.*

11. The reason for her anger is because you were late.

Most careful writers consider the use of *reason . . . is because* much too informal for business use. Here is a more acceptable wording: *She is angry because you were late.*

12. Arnold completed the report for Major Conti, filled out several requisitions, and I believe that Kevin helped him.

The foregoing sentence apparently contains three items in a series, but only two of the items are parallel in structure. A careful writer would probably use one of these possibilities: *Arnold completed the report for Major Conti and filled out several requisitions. I believe that Kevin helped him.* OR: *I believe that Kevin helped Arnold complete the report for Major Conti and fill out several requisitions.*

13. When she saw the tax collector, she turns abruptly and leaves the office.

In this sentence the shift from past tense to present tense is highly illogical. A careful writer would have expressed all three verbs in the past tense, as in this wording: *When she saw the tax collector, she turned abruptly and left the office.*

14. Will you be so kind as to send me a check in the amount of $10?

This kind of wordiness has no place in American business today, and most business executives avoid its use. The sentence in question would carry a greater impact if it read *Please send me a check for $10.*

15. We will probably purchase 24 90-cent notebooks.

When two numbers are used consecutively and no punctuation mark intervenes, the careful business writer will spell out the shorter of the two in order to achieve maximum clarity. Sentence 15 would be written in this way: *We will probably purchase 24 ninety-cent notebooks.*

TERMINOLOGY

In Chapters 25 through 31 you found only a few grammatical terms that do not appear in earlier parts of the text. Those on the following list, however, were prominently mentioned in these chapters. Before you take the next examination, make certain that you understand each of them.

unity	items in a series
excessive detail	coordinate adjectives
parallel structure	independent clause
shift in tense	verbal phrase
shift in voice	parenthetical expression
subordination	direct address

Two of the chapters being reviewed contain sections headed "Executives' Choice." If you have studied carefully the material presented in those sections, your business writing will not include expressions such as these:

small percent	in back of the desk
principle goal	in regards to
man of principal	irregardless
reason is because	four pair
there office	party who wrote
990 others beside me	in fine shape

REVIEW CHART

concept	Ch. _____ page _____	first critical point to remember	example	second critical point to remember	example
what sentence writers should strive for		unity conciseness		subordination parallel structure emphasis	
what sentence writers should omit		word omission tense problems		wordiness misplaced modifiers faulty pronoun referents	
using numbers					
using commas		in series in a compound sentence in dates and addresses after introductory adverb clauses		with nonrestrictive clauses or phrases with direct address or appositive elements when needed for emphasis or to prevent misreading	
using colons					
using semicolons					

———— WORKSHEET 32————

REVIEW

PART A. By writing the appropriate *letter* in the answer space, indicate the response that explains the use of a comma (or *commas*).

    A. introductory adverb clause
    B. items in a series
    C. a nonrestrictive appositive
    D. a nonrestrictive adjective clause
    E. a parenthetical expression
    F. separating clauses in a compound sentence
    G. a verbal phrase

1. Drawing 300 candidates to a job fair was a dream for Donna Gallo, who claims that 10 percent of technology positions go unfilled every year.

    1. _____

2. That's exactly what happened when OpenDoors, a new employment service, sponsored its first on-line job fair last summer.

    2. *_____

3. At the job fairs, which last 30 days, job seekers can visit participating companies on-line through virtual tours and employee testimonials.

    3. _____

4. They can complete brief on-line interviews, and they don't have to put on a suit.

    4. *_____

5. If candidates like what they see, they can forward their resumes electronically and be on the phone with a human resources representative in minutes.

    5. *_____

6. The on-line fairs allow companies and organizations to market themselves, show off their strengths, and gather information about promising candidates at the same time that job seekers are looking at companies.

    6. _____

7. "If people weren't changing jobs, they were preparing to change," says OpenDoors President Donna Gallo.

    7. *_____

8. "Now is the time to market your shop, your company, and your technologies to people," she continues.

    8. _____

9. "When technology workers arrive at work one day and discover they've been terminated, they usually already know where they want to be employed next."

    9. _____

10. Created as a division of Job Labs Inc., OpenDoors got its start in late 1997 by developing a local job-recruitment Web site that posts vacancies from 180 companies.

    10. _____

11. OpenDoors, besides listing jobs at on-line job fairs, posts openings continuously.

    11. _____

12. In addition to visiting the site periodically, jobseekers can fill out a profile so that they can be notified by e-mail when jobs matching their requirements are posted.

12. _____

13. "We built OpenDoors so that users could come in at no cost and also remain anonymous, a very important feature," Gallo says.

13. _____

14. "Registering with us, they won't be flooded with telephone calls but instead can create a stream of information flowing toward them."

14. _____

15. To post job openings with OpenDoors, a company pays $1,500 for three months or $4,500 for a year.

15. _____

16. Employers may, at their own discretion, post an unlimited number of positions from their own Web browser.

16. _____

17. To participate in an on-line job fair, companies pay between $6,000 and $9,000.

17. _____

18. As you might guess, OpenDoors has also created job fairs for individual clients.

18. _____

19. Other products include college-recruitment sites, designed specifically for candidates fresh out of college, and custom-designed employment sites.

19. _____

20. OpenDoors currently has 11 employees, and they expect to double or triple in size in the next year.

20. _____

PART B. By writing the appropriate letter in the answer space, indicate the sentence that has been correctly punctuated.

1. (A) Building a team or quality circle takes several resources: commitment, time, and energy.
   (B) Building a team or quality circle, takes several resources; commitment, time, and energy.
   (C) Building a team or quality circle takes several resources; commitment, time, and energy.

1. *_____

2. (A) The group needs to commit time, and energy to the process of getting to know one another and understanding each member's styles and habits.
   (B) The group needs to commit time and energy to the process of getting to know one another, and understanding each member's styles, and habits.
   (C) The group needs to commit time and energy to the process of getting to know one another and understanding each member's styles and habits.

2. *_____

3. (A) Groups often use a style indicator such as the MBTI; this helps them to become aware of their own biases and patterns.
   (B) Groups often use a style indicator such as the MBTI; which helps them to become aware of their own biases and patterns.
   (C) Groups often use a style indicator, such as the MBTI; to help them become aware of their own biases and patterns.

3. _____

4. (A) Taking such an evaluation instrument can be easy and fun, sharing the results with the whole group can lead to a dramatic rise in understanding.
   (B) Taking such an evaluation instrument can be easy and fun; and sharing the results with the whole group can lead to a dramatic rise in understanding.
   (C) Taking such an evaluation instrument can be easy and fun; sharing the results with the whole group can lead to a dramatic rise in understanding.

4. _____

5. (A) For one thing, people understand that co-workers' habits might be deeply ingrained; not simply arising out of their whimsy or carelessness.
   (B) For one thing, people understand that co-workers' habits might be deeply ingrained, not simply arising out of their whimsy or carelessness.
   (C) For one thing, people understand that co-worker's habits might be deeply ingrained, not simply arising out of their whimsy or carelessness.

5. _____

6. (A) Additionally workers with particular habits might be put to different sorts of tasks, for which those habits might be quite helpful.
   (B) Additionally, workers with particular habits might be put to different sorts of tasks for which their sets of habits might be quite helpful.
   (C) Additionally workers with particular habits might be put to different sorts of tasks for which their sets of habits might be quite helpful.

6. _____

7. (A) Everyone claims his or her style, preferences, and habits honestly so that the team can do it's best work.
   (B) Everyone claims his or her style, preferences, and habits honestly, so that the team can do its best work.
   (C) Everyone claims his or her style, preferences, and habits honestly so that the team can do its best work.

7. _____

8. (A) It is critical that group members, who have begun to form their team in this way, not consider the exercise a one-time activity.
   (B) It is critical that group members who have begun to form their team in this way not consider the exercise a one-time activity.
   (C) It is critical that group members who have begun to form their team in this way, not consider the exercise a one-time activity.

8. _____

9. (A) Group members need to remind one another of their commitment, their progress, and their appreciation at all times in the group's work together.
   (B) Group members need to remind one another of their commitment, their progress, and their appreciation at all times in the groups work together.
   (C) Group members need to remind one another of their commitment, their progress, and their appreciation at all times in the groups' work together.

9. _____

10. (A) Mutual respect and understanding, this is how individuals become a team.
    (B) Mutual respect and understanding; this is how individuals become a team.
    (C) Mutual respect and understanding: this is how individuals become a team.

10. _____

PART C. By writing the appropriate letter in the answer space, indicate the sentence that would be most acceptable in a business communication. Be careful to note word choices, grammar, spelling, and punctuation.

1. (A) The large boiler began hissing and to vibrate.
    (B) The large boiler began hissing, and to vibrate.
    (C) The large boiler began to hiss and to vibrate.   1. *_____

2. (A) I insisted that Celia show us both an old picture and recent one.
    (B) I insisted that Celia show us both an old picture and a recent one.
    (C) I insisted Celia show us both an old picture and recent one.   2. _____

3. (A) We shipped 100 pair of bookends on March 4, 1993.
    (B) We shipped 100 pairs of bookends on March 4th, 1993.
    (C) We shipped 100 pairs of bookends on March 4, 1993.   3. _____

4. (A) The accused, according to this 8-page report, was not a man of principle.
    (B) The accused, according to this eight-page report, was not a man of principle.
    (C) The accused, according to this eight-page report, was not a man of principal.   4. _____

5. (A) He resigned because he isn't well.
    (B) The reason he resigned is that he is in bad shape.
    (C) The reason he resigned is because he isn't well.   5. _____

6. (A) Twenty items on this counter are priced at $10.
    (B) 20 items on this counter are priced at $10.00.
    (C) Twenty items on this counter are priced at $10.00.   6. _____

7. (A) These calendars now sell for only $.98.
    (B) These calendars now sell for only 98 cents.
    (C) These calendars now sell for only ninety-eight cents.   7. _____

8. (A) To save time the software was sent by Federal Express.
    (B) To save time we sent the software by Federal Express.
    (C) To save time, we sent the software by Federal Express. 8. _____

9. (A) Brady is satisfied with our present business, Hagen wants us to expend into the Midwest.
    (B) Brady is satisfied with our present business, Hagen wants us to expand into the Midwest.
    (C) Brady is satisfied with our present business; Hagen wants us to expand into the Midwest.   9. _____

10. (A) Because Gail is using the copier, I have not finished my project.
    (B) Gail is using the copier, which is why I haven't finished my project.
    (C) Because Gail is using the copier I have not finished my project.   10. _____

PART D. By writing the appropriate *letter* in the space provided, indicate the sentence that would be more acceptable in business.

1. (A) Our new office is spacious, but it still seems crowded.
    (B) Our new office is spacious but it still seems crowded.   1. *_____

2. (A) Orders have increase for four years. That explains our profitability.
   (B) Our profitability has been caused by an increase in orders over four years.

2. _____

3. (A) The columnist observed Hayward earns twice the salary of her rival.
   (B) The columnist observed that Hayward earns twice the salary of her rival.

3. _____

4. (A) The Consumer Safety Bureau approves and stands behind this product.
   (B) The Consumer Safety Bureau approves and stands in back of this product.

4. _____

5. (A) They say that you need ten years' experience beyond entry level.
   (B) Employment experts claim that jobseekers need ten years' experience beyond entry level.

5. _____

6. (A) John has a robust voice and we need someone to record our commercial.
   (B) Because John has a robust voice, he should record our commercial.

6. _____

7. (A) Our meeting lasted for two hours; we had only ten minutes for your proposal.
   (B) Our meeting lasted for two hours; we only had ten minutes for your proposal.

7. _____

8. (A) CNA Airways' flights are often late, which gives them a poor reputation.
   (B) CNA Airways has a poor reputation because their flights are often late.

8. _____

9. (A) I delayed your project's approval because it lacked thorough data.
   (B) The reason I delayed your project's approval was because it lacked thorough data.

9. _____

10. (A) Our staff meeting must be adjourned promptly at eleven o'clock.
    (B) Our staff meeting must be adjourned promptly at 11 o'clock.

10. _____

PART E. In the following business letter paragraph, underscore the five word choice errors and provide an appropriate replacement word in the blanks which follow the paragraph. Keep the replacements in order.

During this period of transition, we must take special care to see that our records remain in good shape. Even a small percent of faulty invoices could be very damaging in an audit. Our interim evaluators will expand much energy in an attempt to make certain we are doing excellent work, so when their in our offices, our principle duty is to show them that we are competent and honest.

1. _____   2. _____

3. _____   4. _____

5. _____

PART F.   With your partner(s), decide which is the appropriate letter for the sentence that has been correctly punctuated and write it in the answer space.

1. (A) Our firm has taken on the interesting and somewhat costly job of sponsoring a local athlete in her bid for the Olympics.
   (B) Our firm has taken on the interesting, and somewhat costly job of sponsoring a local athlete in her bid for the Olympics.

   1. *_____

2. (A) She competes in a new breed of speed skating; skate sprinting.
   (B) She competes in a new breed of speed skating: skate sprinting.

   2. _____

3. (A) She is astonishingly fast and has won several regional and national competitions.
   (B) She is astonishingly fast, and has won several regional and national competitions.

   3. *_____

4. (A) To be eligible for Olympic competition, she needs considerable financial backing.
   (B) To be eligible for Olympic competition, she needs considerable, financial backing.

   4. _____

5. (A) This money pays for: training fees, ice time, and enormous travel expenses to world-class competitions which lead up to the Olympics.
   (B) This money pays for training fees, ice time, and enormous travel expenses to world-class competitions which lead up to the Olympics.

   5. _____

6. (A) Know this: there are no guarantees.
   (B) Know this, there are no guarantees.

   6. _____

7. (A) She may fall prey to injuries, or she simply may be outclassed by other athletes, who are judged to be faster or cleaner in their skating.
   (B) She may fall prey to injuries, or she simply may be outclassed by other athletes who are judged to be faster or cleaner in their skating.

   7. _____

8. (A) But the president of our firm and our board of directors all believe she has a chance and so have developed a budget for her sponsorship.
   (B) But the president of our firm and our board of directors all believe she has a chance, and so have developed a budget for her sponsorship.

   8. _____

9. (A) The employees have become her biggest fan club, and the firm receives plenty of publicity whenever she appears in public to speak or to skate.
   (B) The employees have become her biggest fan club; and the firm receives plenty of publicity, whenever she appears in public to speak or to skate.

   9. _____

10. (A) After all, our logo appears on her jacket, and in any program published for those who attend competitions.
    (B) After all, our logo appears on her jacket and in any program published for those who attend competitions.

    10. _____

11. (A) The situation has benefits for her and for us, and we are pleased to be involved in her life and potentially in sports history.
    (B) The situation has benefits for her and for us and we are pleased to be involved in her life and potentially in sports history.

    11. _____

12. (A) When these competitions are finished, we intend to do it all again.
    (B) When these competitions are finished we intend to do it all again.

    12. _____

Uses of Dashes, Parentheses, and Brackets

Too many dashes in advertising copy is like too much shouting on radio commercials.

The dash is a more emphatic mark of punctuation than any we have already discussed. Dashes, in many of their functions, are used as substitutes for commas, parentheses, semicolons, or colons. You will note that, like commas and parentheses, they may be used in pairs to set off elements within sentences. They are created by typing two side-by-side hyphens

RULE 1 Use dashes to set off any nonrestrictive element that deserves special emphasis.

My supervisor—as well as 3 million other quality-minded Americans—owns this make of automobile.

This phenomenal new entry—the most versatile and dependable operating system ever produced—is exactly what your office needs.

Although a parenthetical expression or an appositive is usually set off with commas, a writer who wants to place special emphasis upon such an element will employ a stronger mark of punctuation, as in the foregoing examples. Advertising copywriters frequently demand such emphasis.

If a nonrestrictive element contains commas within itself, it should generally be set off with either dashes or parentheses, since the addition of two more commas may prove confusing to a reader. Greater emphasis will be secured if dashes are employed, as in these examples:

The three competing firms—Gaston Bros., Zenith Controls, and Century Motors—were asked to submit bids. (Less emphasis would be placed upon the appositive if we enclosed it in parentheses.)

The company—as Chen, our union representative, had predicted—refused to grant the requested increase in wages. (By using parentheses, we could deemphasize the mention of Chen and his prediction.)

RULE 2 Use a dash before a word (*these, any, each, all,* etc.) that sums up a preceding series.

The broken boiler, the missing ledger, the late shipment—all these problems will demand my attention.

Joe Kaufman, Eileen O'Brien, Don McGuire—each of them knows the combination to the safe.

RULE 3 Use a dash to indicate an afterthought, an abrupt change in thought, or an emphatic pause.

The budgeting of personal finances is not an easy task—even for the very rich.

You should consider investing in Vulcan Materials, Dow Chemical, General Electric, Goodyear—but you have your own ideas.

The farmers were ready to give up their struggle—and then the rains came.

The work will be finished by—Let me check with the supervisor.

RULE 4 Use a dash before the name of an author or a work that follows a direct quotation and indicates its source.

"By working faithfully eight hours a day, you may eventually get to be boss and work 12 hours a day."—Robert Frost

"Since dictionaries have changed much, we need not be surprised if they change more."—*Webster's New World Dictionary*

RULE 5 Use dashes to emphasize an independent clause that abruptly interrupts another clause.

Four leading institutions—you know their names—will cooperate with us in this extensive research. (Use parentheses to set off such elements without emphasis.)

The parent firm—no one can understand why—refused to grant financial aid to its subsidiary during the recent crisis.

RULE 6 Use a dash before a word or phrase that has been repeated with greater emphasis.

Industry leaders should unite in seeking the solution—the solution that will lead to greater production in our mills and improved morale among our workers.

She was slow in data entry—painfully slow.

RULE 7 Use a dash before introductory expressions such as *namely* or *for example* if the following words are to be emphasized.

There were several unwelcome guests—for example, the reporter who had criticized our policies.

These generators have a number of serious deficiencies—in other words, we have no intention of buying one.

Dashes Used with Other Marks

Generally no other mark of punctuation should immediately precede or follow a dash. There are, however, several exceptions to that general rule. Observe the punctuation in these sentences:

Only one local firm—Murdoch & Agassi, Inc.—made a substantial contribution to the fund. (Period in an abbreviation may precede a dash.)

Ethan Grossweiler—have you heard?—will be our chief executive officer. (Question mark or exclamation point may precede a dash.)

Mausser said—according to three reliable sources—"I will not take the position if it is offered to me." (Quotation mark may follow a dash.)

The dash is a relatively informal mark of punctuation. It should, therefore, be used sparingly in a formal business communication. Because it is frequently employed to secure emphasis, a writer will minimize its effectiveness by using this mark too often. Make it a habit to employ commas whenever you feel that commas and dashes would be equally acceptable in a given construction.

PARENTHESES

Parentheses may sometimes enclose sentence elements that would ordinarily be set off with commas or dashes. The writer's choice will depend upon the degree of emphasis he or she intends to convey. When such a choice exists, you will do well to use parentheses if the words in question are of minimum importance. Parentheses tend to deemphasize the material they enclose. The first of the rules that follow involves such a choice.

> **RULE 1** Use parentheses to enclose nonrestrictive elements that should be deemphasized.

Because Hingston failed to attend the seminar (possibly because of illness), his notes are incomplete. (When a comma and a closing parenthesis come together in a sentence, always write the parenthesis first.)

She has decided to leave early on Saturday morning (as you suggested) and to stay in Phoenix for five days. (*As you suggested* would bear greater emphasis if it were set off with either commas or dashes.)

Crane's experience with the National Labor Relations Board (see page 502) may prove of interest to you. (Note that the word *see* does not begin with a capital letter.)

The street on which our warehouse is located (Madison) carries heavy traffic during work hours.

The incident occurred on May 21 (or was it May 22?) at the Biltmore Hotel in Los Angeles. (Note the use of a question mark *inside* the closing parenthesis.)

5. To indicate an emphatic pause

6. To enclose figures that follow a spelled-out number

7. To emphasize an independent clause that abruptly interrupts another clause

8. To precede the name of an author following a direct quotation

5. _____

6. _____

7. _____

8. _____

PUSHED PAST HER LIMIT

After five months as a secretary, a person who had been a fine Business English student felt completely frustrated. Her employer, it seems, insisted on using language in "his way"—and "his way" included too many constructions that violated the rules she had mastered in college. Being responsible for publishing reports that contained "serious grammatical errors" was so irritating that she decided to see a counselor to talk about her job.

FOR CLASS DISCUSSION

What would your attitude be if your boss insisted upon violating the rules of grammar?

OPTIONAL EXERCISES

OPTION 1 Use only dashes and commas as you punctuate the following ten sentences. In the answer space indicate the number of marks you have added.

1. Chicken beef fish   those are the only entrees available at the banquet.   1. *_____

2. You will need to bring the system serial number the licensing agreement the original software disks   but you already know how to register for an upgrade.   2. _____

3. Our new personnel director   a woman of great character humor and intelligence   will begin her performance evaluations next week.   3. _____

4. As he spoke Howard   not to mention every man and woman in the audience   knew he was making history.   4. _____

5. "A sale is only as good as the relationship behind it."   David Gillard   5. _____

6. We placed giveaway CD roms   an encyclopedia a graphics pack and an internet navigator   randomly in the guests' conference folders.   6. _____

7. The stock market took a plunge   a plunge that sent other world markets into panic.   7. _____

8. Chester F. Brake   he's Preston's advisor   must sign off on every contract.   8. _____

9. The new C.E.O. hails from the west coast   he certainly isn't a Bostonian   and will maintain a home there.   9. _____

10. The price per share   by the way our broker predicted this trend is rising sharply.   10. _____

OPTION 2 Use only parentheses and commas as you punctuate the following six sentences. In the answer space indicate the number of marks you have added.

1. Our team leader met Simpson he's the marketing chairman but they could not agree on a plan.   1. *_____

2. Two employers FranOptical and AAA Motors were named in the lawsuit.   2. _____

3. Saronski asked Parker to 1 proofread the letter 2 make any necessary corrections and 3 send the letter by next day air.   3. _____

4. The foreclosure auction was held on Friday you may recall that it rained on Thursday and all the machinery was sold.   4. _____

5. The PC comes fully loaded see the list of software on page 3 and sells for less than $1,500.   5. _____

6. The buyer Maude E. Clampett agrees to deposit in escrow the sum of Twenty Thousand Dollars $20,000 .   6. _____

OPTION 3   Write one or more paragraphs in answer to this question: As we attempt to judge the acceptability of language, should we consider popular usage to be the determining factor?

_____

_____

_____

_____

_____

_____

_____

_____

_____

_____

_____

_____

_____

_____

_____

_____

_____

_____

_____

_____

_____

_____

_____

_____

_____

OPTION 4   (CLASS DISCUSSION) My abridged dictionary lists over a hundred definitions for the word _run_, which may be used as a verb, a noun, or an adjective. It is obvious that this word has taken on dozens of new meanings since it first became a part of our language.

Consider the word _chauvinism_, which once was defined simply as "militant devotion to and glorification of one's country; fanatical patriotism." The French soldier Nicholas Chauvin, it seems, was extremely devoted to Napoleon.

Perhaps no one knows exactly when or how the expression _male chauvinism_ originated, but it certainly added a new definition for the word. By using your imagination, attempt to reconstruct what happened. Who might have been first to use the word in this new way, and why did he or she do so? Why did others accept the new usage and popularize it?

HEADLINES

**NEW MOREAU FILM
IS ALL HER'S**

*Benevolent Mayor
Finds Forgives and Forgets
Nasty Parking Tickets*

**New Punting Rule to Stay
Despite Coaches Objection**

**CRISES HITS
HIGH SCHOOLS**

*There's No surprises Left
for State Finance Director*

**Wife of Heir Neither
Captive or Captivated;
Files Divorce**

**DEATH AND
DESTRUCTION
STILL REIGNS
IN STREETS**

*New Book Hits
Market on Baseball*

——————————— FOR CLASS DISCUSSION ———————————

These headlines were taken from eight newspaper stories. As a collaborative team, attempt to determine the error that was made in each one. When you have convinced one another, share your findings with the rest of the class.

Across

1. Kind of verb that may take an object
5. Tense used to express a general truth
8. A noun substitute
9. Progressive form of *set*
11. Writers should _____ (leave out) unnecessary words.
12. Superlative degree of *tall*
14. Mark that follows salutation of letter
15. Abbr. used at beginning of subject line in letter
16. Abbr. used with a diagonal to mean *account*
18. Mark used to set off an afterthought
20. The plural form of *datum*
21. Principal parts: _____, *lay, lain*
22. Abbr. for *et cetera*
24. Form of *be* used with singular subject in third person
25. A sentence that refers to two or more unrelated ideas lacks _____.
27. All intransitive verbs are in the _____ voice.
28. Any name (part of speech)
32. Do not _____ yourself into thinking that grammar is unimportant.
35. Another name for a *verbal noun*
36. Past tense of *nag*
37. The salutation *Dear* _____ is somewhat obsolete.
38. Generally write out numbers from *one* to _____.
39. Comparative degree of *easy*
42. Your response may be written or _____.
43. Prefix that means *before*
45. Pronoun (first person, plural, possessive)
47. The opposite of *slow*
51. Correlative conjunction used with *either*
52. Adverb derived from *near*
53. Abbr. for *route*
54. Progressive form of *bid*
55. Past participle of *do*

Down

1. The verb *went* is in the past _____.
2. One of the three *articles*
3. Mark sometimes used to separate two independent clauses
4. Infinitives, participles, and gerunds
5. Kind of noun that is capitalized
6. Coordinating conjunction used informally to mean *therefore*
7. The pronoun *we* is in the _____ case
10. The plural of *that*
13. Principal parts: _____, *saw, seen*
17. The pronoun *him* is in the objective _____.
19. Pronoun (third person, singular, nominative, masculine)
20. Past tense of the verb *dot*
21. Subject complements follow _____ verbs.
23. The first word in most infinitives
25. Prefix that means *not*
26. Compound pronoun (second person, singular)
29. Many dictionary entries contain _____ labels.
30. *Big, bigger, biggest* are _____ of an adjective.
31. Group of related words without a subject-verb combination
33. Adjective derived from *elder*
34. The pronoun *she* is in the feminine _____.
40. Past tense of the verb *race*
41. Her absence was _____ to illness.
44. Past participle of the verb *tear*
45. The number of clauses in a simple sentence
46. Past tense of the verb *run*
48. The most common coordinating conjunction
49. Prefix that means *three*
50. Abbr. for *organization*

LET'S DANGLE A PARTICIPLE

When a writer or speaker uses a participle (verbal adjective), there should be no doubt about what it modifies. A sentence such as *Working feverishly for two hours, the job was finally completed* is both ambiguous and illogical. It should, of course, be changed to something like this: *Working feverishly for two hours, we finally finished the job.*

Believe it or not, there are some dangling participles that many fine writers and speakers consider to be acceptable. A number of grammarians would not object to sentences such as these:

Strictly speaking, this is not a warehouse.

Allowing for traffic delays, the trip should take about an hour.

Judging by his attire, the new service manager is anything but conservative.

_____ **FOR CLASS DISCUSSION** _____

The preceding sentences contain participles (*speaking, allowing, judging*) but no words that they can logically modify. Attempt to justify the acceptability of such sentences.

Uses of Quotation Marks, Ellipses, and Apostrophes

■ POINT TO PONDER

The ethical writer always uses quotation marks when employing someone else's words.

The proper use of quotation marks is extremely important in several areas of business. Editors, reporters, and legal secretaries must learn to use them skillfully. All business writers, of course, should familiarize themselves with accepted practice so that their work will be technically correct. The following rule is probably basic enough to be recognized by all readers.

RULE 1 Use quotation marks to enclose material that is quoted directly.

"Our industry is vital to the American economy," said Paulson. (Note the placement of the comma inside the closing quotation mark.)

"Our industry," said Paulson, "is vital to the American economy." (Note that two pairs of quotation marks are needed in this type of construction.)

Schumacher used these exact words: "We have no intention, nor have we ever had any intention, of attempting to create a monopoly." (Note the placement of the period inside the closing quotation marks.)

Richardson said, "Send me five dozen of these units by April 15"; Darrow said nothing. (Note the placement of the semicolon after the closing quotation mark.)

In his closing remarks the speaker referred to "the magnificent contributions of these self-sacrificing men and women." (A quotation need not be a complete sentence.)

This was her answer: "We have been short of materials since our credit was curtailed in early June. We most urgently need plastic sheeting and copper wire." (Although two sentences are quoted, only one pair of quotation marks is needed.)

"This multicolored brochure is being revised," she said. "The improved version will be ready by Friday." (Two pairs of quotation marks are needed. Note that the second quoted sentence begins with a capital letter.)

Following are a few notes concerning current business practices that involve the handling of direct quotations.

1. Words that have been quoted indirectly should not be placed in quotation marks.

   She asked me whether the information will be stored in a data base.
   Bates said that he had seen our advertisement in the Yellow Pages.
   BUT: Bates said, "I saw your advertisement in the Yellow Pages."

2. A long quotation may be handled in either of the following ways:
   a. You may single-space and use a shorter typing line than for the remainder of your copy. No quotation marks will be necessary.
   b. If you maintain a uniform line length, you should place a quotation mark at the beginning of each paragraph and at the end of the final paragraph only. Any quotation marks used *within* these paragraphs should be single quotation marks (').

3. In reporting a conversation, a writer should begin a new paragraph each time the speaker changes.

   "If the lumber arrives by noon tomorrow, how soon will the cabinets be ready?" asked Garrison.
   "We have several other jobs to finish first," said the foreman.
   "Can you guarantee shipment by November 1?" persisted Garrison.

4. Business writers occasionally make use of a quotation *within* a quotation. If you employ this type of construction, remember to use double quotation marks for the first quotation and single marks for the quotation it contains. If the second quotation contains quoted matter, revert to the use of double marks. This type of complicated writing should generally be avoided in business correspondence.

   The final paragraph read: "You would do well to heed Mr. Purdin's advice: 'Give the public what the public wants, and you will be in business for a long time. Mr. Wanamaker suggested the only attitude that can lead to sustained success in retailing when he said, "The customer is always right."'"

5. A question used at the end of a sentence should not be set off in quotation marks unless it is someone else's words.

   The question is, Does our work require a letter-quality printer?

6. Only the exact word or words that have been taken from another source should be placed in quotation marks.

   Shantz referred to the "devastating effect" of this new directive.

7. The words *yes* and *no* should not be placed in quotation marks unless the writer is actually quoting another person.

We are hoping that he says yes to our offer.

Fuentes is not likely to respond with a simple yes or no.

BUT: When we asked her if she could program the computer, she said, "No."

RULE 2   Use quotation marks to enclose the titles of minor works (articles from magazines, songs, essays, short stories, short poems, one-act plays, lectures, sermons, chapters, motion pictures, television shows).

You will note that the rule does not include the names of books, magazines, newspapers, long musical works, or book-length poems. It is accepted practice to underscore the names of these longer works or to print them in italics.

This week's issue of *U.S. News & World Report* contains an article entitled "Changing Role of World Powers."

If you read Graham and Dodd's *Security Analysis,* you will find the chapter "Investment and Speculation" to be particularly interesting.

Lloyd asked, "Was the poem 'If' written by Rudyard Kipling?"

RULE 3   Use quotation marks to enclose words used in an unconventional manner.

If we continue in our present spending habits, this firm will soon go "down the tubes." (When slang is used for effect, it should be enclosed in quotation marks.)

You could persuade your son to go to college if you tried a little "consumer motivation." (Technical and trade terms may be enclosed in quotation marks when they are used in unconventional contexts.)

Although words referred to simply as words may be enclosed in quotation marks, most business writers prefer to underscore them. (In print they would appear in italics.)

Does the word <u>run</u> really have 140 different meanings?

The expression *each and every* should be avoided in business writing.

A closing quotation mark will frequently come together with another mark of punctuation. In inserting such marks, make sure that you follow these rules:

1.   Always place a period or a comma inside (before) a closing quotation mark.
2.   Always place a colon or a semicolon outside a closing quotation mark.
3.   If a question mark, an exclamation point, or a dash applies to the quoted matter, place it inside a closing quotation mark; otherwise, place it outside.

"What is the circulation of your magazine?" he asked. (The quoted portion is a question.)

Did he say, "Our circulation will soon exceed one million"? (The entire sentence is a question, but the quoted portion is not.)

Were you present when he asked, "Why don't we discontinue production?" (Use only one question mark even though the quoted portion and the entire sentence are both questions.)

"I can't believe it!" shouted the happy winner.

"If the patent is granted—" are the only words I heard.

THE ELLIPSIS

> **RULE**   Use the ellipsis (three periods) to indicate that words are being omitted from a quoted passage.

If the omission of words follows a complete statement, it will be necessary to use four periods—one to terminate the sentence and three to form the ellipsis. When typing, space after each period in the ellipsis.

> These were his words: "We could not have achieved final victory without the full cooperation of firms like . . . the Ballard Engineering Corporation."
>
> She gave you these instructions: "Check the balance of our account with Ramsey Motors. . . . Cancel my appointment with Mr. Solano."

An ellipsis may be used at the end of an unfinished thought.

> If you succeed, you will be rewarded handsomely, but if you fail . . . (The use of a dash would be considered less formal.)

THE APOSTROPHE

Before you attempt to do the worksheet that follows, it may be wise to review Chapter 7, which sets forth the rules that govern the use of possessive nouns; those rules will not be repeated here. The following rule should serve simply as a reminder.

> **RULE 1**   Use the apostrophe correctly in forming the possessive case of nouns and certain pronouns.

> We could not understand *Drew's* attitude toward her work.
>
> The *plumbers'* union may be forced to increase monthly dues.
>
> I did not understand *Davis's* reference to *Socrates'* death. (Why were these singular nouns made possessive in different ways?)
>
> *Stanley and Albert's* new real estate office has attracted considerable attention.
>
> In this office *one's* work is never done.

> **RULE 2**   Use an apostrophe in a contraction to indicate the omission of letters or numbers in a contraction.

> We *haven't* time to fill these orders today.
>
> He graduated with the class of *'88.*
>
> It is two *o'clock.*
>
> *Don't* send the cement pipe until October 15.

In writing contractions, make certain that you place the apostrophe where the omission has been made. In a word such as *didn't,* the apostrophe takes the place of the *o* in *did not.*

If it is needed to prevent misreading, use an apostrophe in forming the plural of a letter or of a word referred to simply as a word.

He does not always pronounce his *r*'s. (Plurals of lowercase letters always require apostrophes.)

She received *A*'s in her three most difficult courses. (Apostrophes should be used in the plural forms of vowels that are capitalized.)

There are three *T*s and two *L*s in his last name. (Although the modern trend is away from the use of apostrophes in such readable plural forms, some authorities may still prefer to insert them, as in *T*'s and *L*'s.)

You would have a better paragraph if you eliminated a few of the *so*'s. (The apostrophe is needed to prevent misreading.)

His one short paragraph on microcomputers contained five *and*s. (The word *and*s is readable without an apostrophe.)

Molinski is not yet familiar with the *do*'s and *don't*s of data processing.

Trends of the Times

Until recent years it was common to add an apostrophe and *s* when forming the plural of a number expressed as a figure or of an abbreviation made up of individual letters. Today's business writers, however, are likely to add only an *s*.

You will find *YMCA*s in most parts of this country.

We have several *M.D.*s working in our research laboratories.

The depression of the early *1930*s must never be repeated.

The column is difficult to add because his *7*s and *9*s look alike.

He quoted the *CEO*s of three major corporations.

Although the apostrophe is used less frequently today than in former years, it will continue to have these primary functions:

1. To build possessive-case forms of nouns
2. To indicate omitted letters in contractions
3. To form plurals that would otherwise be easily misread

Typists, of course, use the apostrophe as a *single* quotation mark (see page 360), and anyone preparing an invoice, order form, or similar communication may use an apostrophe as a symbol for *feet* (8' × 4' plywood).

THE IMPACT OF LANGUAGE
SHOULD WE APPLY THE BRAKES?

The late Dwight MacDonald, who was a highly respected essayist and critic, once noted that language does indeed change. He felt, however, that there must be some *brakes,* which should be applied by teachers, writers, and lexicographers. It is their function, according to him, to make it difficult for new words and usages to get into circulation "so that the ones that survive will be the fittest."

Lexicographers who prepare dictionaries for the Oxford University Press would probably agree with Mr. MacDonald. One editor, a woman, had this to say: "We rather think things are changing away from permissiveness." With that thought in mind, she refused to list the word *chairperson. Chairman,* she claimed, may still be used to designate a member of either sex. Oxford dictionaries, in spite of modern trends, also caution people to distinguish between *less* and *fewer, due to* and *because of,* and so forth.

_____ **FOR CLASS DISCUSSION** _____

Do you agree that an attempt should be made to resist changes in our language? State your reasons.

---

wWWw ═══════ **Watching the Web** ═══════

| Back | Forward | Home | Reload | Images | Open |

Retire Early with a Fortune!
You too can discover how to build up cash for early
retirement. Its a matter of a few hours a week and a few
phone calls a day to reap benefit's youve never imagined!

| want to see more? click here | | no thanks |

_____WORKSHEET 34_____

USES OF QUOTATION MARKS, ELLIPSES, AND APOSTROPHES

PART A. Answer each of the following questions by writing Yes or No in the space provided.

1. Is there only one kind of quotation mark (") that may be used? **1.** * _____

2. Should the title of a short story usually be enclosed in quotation marks? **2.** _____

3. Is it correct to enclose the title of a novel in quotation marks? **3.** _____

4. Would it make sense to enclose a portion of a sentence in quotation marks? **4.** _____

5. Do ellipses indicate that something has been added to a quotation? **5.** _____

6. Should an ellipsis always consist of three periods? **6.** _____

7. If a colon and a closing quotation mark come together in a sentence, should the colon be written first? **7.** _____

8. If a comma and a closing quotation mark come together in a sentence, should the comma be written first? **8.** _____

9. If a question mark and a closing quotation mark come together in a sentence, is it always correct to write the question mark first? **9.** _____

10. Can apostrophes be omitted in the plural forms of many abbreviations? **10.** _____

PART B. Punctuate the following sentences. In the space provided, indicate the number of punctuation marks you have added. (Count both opening and closing quotation marks.) Do *not* punctuate for emphasis. If you're working collaboratively, the team must agree on each answer.

1. Wendy Andreas was recently interviewed for   PC NOW   an article in *PC Journal.* **1.** * _____

2. She said   Most PCs come with Web browsers and e-mail software. **2.** _____

3. She added that most include some sort of offer for Internet access. **3.** _____

4.   If you are not an online veteran   she suggested   you may want to select a PC with easy sign-up and several months of free service. **4.** * _____

5. Andreas described some models that have keyboards with special buttons that connect users rapidly with the Net. **5.** _____

6. This is a real convenience at least according to most of my colleagues   she observed.   6. _____

7. Andreas opinion is that a buyer should know clearly what is needed before shopping.   7. _____

8. In her consumer book *Shopping for Your PC* she actually cites brand names.   8. * _____

9. Compaq Hewlett-Packard IBM Gateway and other companies all offer computers with these features for under $1 300.   9. _____

10. As a concrete example Andreas noted that this month one retailer was selling an excellent brand-name computer printer and monitor for $1 199.   10. _____

11. This computer which is being phased out   she said   is still quite powerful.   11. _____

12. At the same time a competitor was offering a computer with a slightly different configuration for $999 via mail order.   12. _____

13. For an extra $114 Andreas observed   the buyer could double the memory and hard disk capacity.   13. _____

14. There will always be something with more power at a good price just around the corner.   14. _____

15. If you need a new PC right now you don t have to wait Andreas said.   15. _____

16. She also said that people don t have to buy a top-of-the-line model for fear of obsolescence.   16. _____

17. Andreas best advice   Just know what you want. That will help enormously.   17. _____

18. You can go with the six big names   names like IBM HP Compaq   or you can find good deals with lesser-known brands she believes.   18. _____

19. The key according to this expert seems to be to buy just what you need at the time that you need it.   19. _____

20. Don't let marketers fool you Andreas concludes. Keep your own needs clear and you'll do just fine.   20. _____

PART C. In the following passage from a memo, five apostrophes are needed. There are currently eight apostrophes in the passage. Find and underscore the three apostrophes that should be omitted.

Jackson's work on Bailey's account has been excellent. However, we cannot afford to allow Jackson to use any more hour's on that project, since Jackson's own account's are likely to suffer. Let's invite Jackson to a brief meeting on Wednesday to discuss strategy's before it's too late.*

PART D. Write the letter that identifies the correctly punctuated sentence.

1. (A) Javonovitch said, "I'm certain that the report was sent last night."
   (B) Javonovitch said "I'm certain that the report was sent last night."   1. _____

2. (A) What do you suppose made her ask, "When *will* it arrive—Christmas?"
   (B) What do you suppose made her ask, "When *will* it arrive—Christmas"?   2. *_____

3. (A) Harvey ordered the most expensive gadget reviewed in the newsletter column "Sweet Deals:" the hand-held date minder.
   (B) Harvey ordered the most expensive gadget reviewed in the newsletter column "Sweet Deals": the hand-held date minder.   3. _____

4. (A) Several IBM's were purchased last spring.
   (B) Several IBMs were purchased last spring.   4. *_____

5. (A) Did the quotation read, "The market will be frozen until September"?
   (B) Did the quotation read, "The market will be frozen until September?"   5. _____

6. (A) I remarked that I had never seen the plant in full operation.
   (B) I remarked that "I had never seen the plant in full operation."   6. _____

7. (A) The philosophy of the company is taken from the book *The Fifth Discipline.*
   (B) The philosophy of the company is taken from the book "The Fifth Discipline."   7. _____

8. (A) The board member's votes will be tallied and their decision announced Monday.
   (B) The board members' votes will be tallied and their decision announced Monday.   8. _____

9. (A) The company intends to diversify, adding a division for womens' shoes.
   (B) The company intends to diversify, adding a division for women's shoes.   9. _____

10. (A) "Never again," he replied. "Never again"!
    (B) "Never again," he replied. "Never again!"   10. _____

PART E. One word in each sentence needs an apostrophe. In the answer space write the correct spelling of that word.

1. Johnson is aware of Greens trouble with dyslexia.   1. _____

2. Managements workload has increased for the third straight month.   2. _____

3. Thomas is unaware of Garloughs running unopposed for chairperson.   3. _____

4. We havent seen Caruso since his presentation last month.   4. _____

5. It was fortunate that the meeting could be moved to the Larsons.   5. _____

6. The scanner came from merchandising; the printer
is Terrys.

6. _____

7. Jeanne wont have her report ready until at least
5:30 P.M.

7. _____

PART F.

1. Write a sentence that contains a quoted question.

_____

_____

2. Write a sentence that contains one apostrophe and a pair of quotation marks but no
quotation.

_____

_____

_____

WHAT ELSE IS NEW?

Apparently the problem of poor spelling is not new to American business. Here's a
direct quotation from the *Champion Spelling Book,* written by Warren Hicks and published by
the American Book Company in 1909:

For years, teachers, principals, superintendents, and school boards everywhere have
been wearied by the cry of business: "The boys that you send to us can't spell."

_____ **FOR CLASS DISCUSSION** _____

Why, in your opinion, do some people continue to spell poorly after years of exposure to the
English language?

OPTIONAL EXERCISES

OPTION 1   The following letter contains the ten errors listed. To the right of each paragraph, put the *number* that identifies any error made. The first answer has been provided. If you're collaborating, be sure your team members arrive together at their final answers.

1. Misspelled word
2. Pronoun in wrong number
3. Misused colon
4. Apostrophe missing
5. Unnecessary apostrophe

6. Comma missing
7. Verb in wrong number
8. Hyphen omitted
9. Unnecessary comma
10. Number incorrectly expressed

July 19, 2000

J. K. Denisovich
1456 Woodlawn Avenue
Chicago, IL 60606

Dear Ms. Denisovich:

We are happy to respond to your request for information about holding your next national conference at the Duluth Convention Auditorium Complex.

The Auditorium Complex was built ten years ago and have accomodated at least a dozen major conferences each year since then. The complex consists of several multipurpose buildings on a large lot adjacent to beautiful Duluth harbor. These buildings range in size from 20,000 to 150,000 square feet and it may be broken internally into hundreds of smaller meeting and display spaces.

7 ☐ ☐ ☐

In addition: Duluth offers ninety hotels, motels, and bed-and-breakfasts within ten miles of the Auditorium Complex. Visitors will have at least 100 options for food, from fine dining, to fast food, from gourmet to deli. Many of these places have arranged catering services to the Auditorium Complex, with great success over the year's.

☐ ☐ ☐ ☐

We hope to hear from you soon to arrange a date because our next years calendar is now filling. If I can be of further help as you plan please call me.

☐ ☐

Sincerely,

Marvin Edquist

OPTION 2 Write one or more smoothly worded paragraphs on the subject of "Physical Fitness."

_____

_____

_____

_____

_____

_____

_____

_____

_____

_____

_____

_____

_____

_____

_____

_____

_____

_____

_____

_____

_____

_____

_____

_____

_____

_____

_____

_____

_____

_____

_____

OPTION 3 (CLASS DISCUSSION)   A student approached me after class and said, "I work with a young woman who has true executive potential. She will probably get the promotion she deserves if her English doesn't disqualify her. Because she is a friend of mine, I find myself wanting to correct her every time she uses _good_ for _well,_ but she is a sensitive person and may be offended. What should I do?"

What _should_ she do? Do you have any suggestions?

Uses of Periods, Question Marks, and Exclamation Points

■ POINT TO PONDER

Exclamation points become ineffective when used too frequently.

The marks discussed in this chapter have one thing in common: they are all used to end sentences. Each, however, has other important applications.

THE PERIOD

RULE 1 Use a period after a statement, a command, or a request.

This software can be used with your computer.

Check every figure on this invoice.

Please let me know if you hear from the agency.

Would you please hand me the pen. (Although this sentence is worded as a question, it is actually a request. No verbal response would be expected.)

If a statement or a command is enclosed in parentheses and written within another sentence, no period should follow it.

When Mr. Redgrave enters the banquet room (you will recognize him by his bushy eyebrows), bring him to my table. (Note that no period is used after *eyebrows*.)

> **RULE 2**   Use a period after words that logically substitute for a complete sentence.

Such fragments are most acceptable when they serve as answers to questions.

No, not at all.
In July, of course.

> **RULE 3**   Use periods in writing some abbreviations.

In recent years periods have been eliminated from a considerable number of abbreviations. Those that denote single words and those expressed in lowercase letters are likely to require periods.

etc.	Ms.	e.g.	Sept.	Inc.
i.e.	Sr.	qr.	Mon.	l.c.d.

Abbreviations that are made up of capital letters are likely to be written without periods. Following is a random list of common abbreviations that are generally written as shown.

CPA	YMCA	FCC	TVA	USSR	mpg
UFO	YMHA	NATO	ICC	USA	mph
FDIC	YWCA	FTC	NAACP	UN	rpm
IRS	AAA	FBI	NAM	AMA	rps

Postal authorities, as you may know, have provided us with a two-letter, period-free abbreviation for each state (MA, NY, NC, PA, OH, MO, AZ, NJ, etc.).

If you check more than one dictionary to determine how an abbreviation should be written, you may discover that they are not in agreement; for example, one may list *rpm* while another lists *r.p.m.* As you make your choice, keep in mind that the abbreviation without periods is likely to be the more current version.

> **RULE 4**   Use the period as a decimal point.

We discovered that 36.7 percent of their customers purchased furniture for cash; the other 63.3 percent bought on time.
Pulaski bought a color printer for $549.95.

> **RULE 5**   In preparing an outline, place a period after a letter or a number that marks a division but is not enclosed in parentheses.

   I. Type of securities
      A. Stock
         1. Preferred
            a. Participating
            b. Nonparticipating

Additional Notes on Use of the Period

1. Do not place periods after headings (titles) or after items in a topic outline (see foregoing portion of an outline).
2. Do not use consecutive periods at the end of a sentence.

> Our mail generally arrives before 11 A.M. (Final period completes the abbreviation and ends the sentence.)
>
> The display room is open each day for three hours (1 P.M. to 4 P.M.). (Final period is necessary because parenthesis mark follows the abbreviation.)

3. Do not use a period after a contraction (don't, can't) unless the contraction ends the sentence.
4. Do not use periods after items on a list unless they form complete sentences.

THE QUESTION MARK

> **RULE 1** Use a question mark at the end of a direct question.

> How many barrels of oil did the well produce during January?
>
> Which of our 50 states is smallest in population?
>
> The most important question is, Why did you make the purchase?

A sentence may be worded as a statement although it is actually a question. The final mark of punctuation will determine the writer's intent.

> You did remember the tickets?
>
> The watch keeps accurate time?

If several questions begin in the same way, they may be expressed in this abbreviated form:

> Where were you living in 1964? in 1974? in 1984?

A short question may be appended to a statement by the use of a comma.

> You still want the silverware, don't you?

A question that has been enclosed in parentheses or dashes should be followed by a question mark.

> The law of diminishing returns (have you heard of it?) may provide the answer to your problem.

If a question ends with an abbreviation that requires a period, be certain to insert the period before the question mark.

> Do you ever make use of the abbreviation *e.g.*?

A statement that includes an indirect question should be followed by a period, not a question mark.

Monique Bray asked me how to prepare an affidavit.

> **RULE 2**   Use a question mark enclosed in parentheses to express doubt.

He was wearing a gray Botany (?) suit when he left the office.

Keep in mind the suggestions made in the preceding chapter concerning the use of question marks with quotation marks. If necessary, review that material before attempting Worksheet 35.

THE EXCLAMATION POINT

> **RULE**   Use an exclamation point after a word or group of words that expresses strong feeling.

The exclamation point is used frequently, perhaps too frequently, in today's sales literature. Used sparingly, it adds emphasis or importance to the words it follows. This mark may suggest anger, relief, fright, exasperation, excitement, surprise, or any other intense feeling.

What a day!	Watch out!	Save me!
How incredible a story!		Don't touch that!

You will recall from your reading of Chapter 34 that the exclamation point should be written before a closing quotation mark only if it applies to the quoted matter.

"Halt!" the guard shouted.
What a stirring rendition of "America, the Beautiful"!

A WORD TIP FROM THE REAL WORLD

Mike, head of security for an investment firm, had plenty of experience in guard work when he applied for a position at his present company. But so did the many other applicants for that job. Mike was curious about why in the end he had been selected for the entry-level position when so many others had not. He was told by his new employer, "I was impressed with your record of service in past jobs, it's true, but I was equally impressed with the state of your resume. The format and the attention to detail were striking. I decided that if you were that conscientious about the way you presented yourself on paper to our office, you'd be even more conscientious about doing your job for us once we hired you." If pure in-field qualifications are equal, it may be the resume that sets you apart from your competition.

_____WORKSHEET 35_____

USES OF PERIODS, QUESTION MARKS, AND EXCLAMATION POINTS

PART A. In the space provided, write T or F to indicate whether the statement is true or false.

1. A period should not ordinarily follow a sentence beginning with *Please.*

    1. _____

2. A period can be used after words that do not constitute a complete sentence.

    2. _____

3. A command is sometimes but not always followed by an exclamation point.

    3. _____

4. A statement enclosed in parentheses within another sentence should not be followed by a period.

    4. _____

5. In the name H. P. Glander, the *H* and the *P* are followed by periods because they are abbreviations.

    5. _____

6. If a sentence ends in an abbreviation, two consecutive periods are not necessary.

    6. _____

7. To be considered a question, a sentence need not be worded as a question.

    7. _____

8. A period should ordinarily follow a sentence that contains an indirect question.

    8. _____

9. A question enclosed in parentheses within another sentence should omit its question mark.

    9. _____

10. An exclamation point should always be written inside a closing quotation mark.

    10. _____

PART B. Punctuate the following sentences. Periods, question marks, and exclamation points are emphasized, but they are not the only marks that must be added. In the space provided, indicate the number of punctuation marks you have used.

1. Does this fax machine come in beige   in black   in smoke

    1. _____

2. This printer has a few flaws   e g   it doesn't sheet feed labels or large envelopes

    2. _____

3. One supplier was it Reliable Products   offered a discount and free cookies

    3. *_____

4. Will your company charge for shipping   for rush delivery   for special orders

    4. *_____

5. We hear that one local company we won't mention the name is about to close

5. _____

6. Please tell us the truth about your company's long-range plans for the area

6. _____

7. If your plans are to remain like R J Nobles we will give you our business

7. _____

8. The Office Inc which sells by catalog has a stable clientele

8. *_____

9. Geraldo asked   Can we order ink jet transparencies next time

9. *_____

10. Last month No 2601 labels were out of stock weren't they

10. _____

11. Did you say   Buy three colored ink cartridges for the printer

11. _____

12. What variety What quality What a display

12. _____

13. Be sure to call me Tom when the Mr Magic Whiteboard Markers arrive

13. _____

14. Don't worry about the cost we can get markers at a 22 5 percent discount

14. _____

15. (a question) Did you place the order for copier toner yesterday Kayla

15. _____

16. Terrific That means it should arrive this morning before the meeting

16. _____

17. We purchase one cartridge for $10 50 a three-pack costs $28 95

17. _____

18. Harrison orders them from OfficeCom on E River Road

18. _____

19. Katherine J Mooney was a Brand Bros representative for many years

19. _____

20. When Thornbush finally got his order of neon copier paper he said   Wow

20. _____

PART C. This memo paragraph includes too many exclamation points. To be appropriate for standard business use, it should use only one or two. Which ones could you safely replace with periods? Which ones should be omitted entirely? Underscore the replaceable exclamation points.

Our department is over budget!! We must take steps immediately to cut back on expenses!! Please conserve on paper, online time, and general office products; we have used our entire year's allotment for these items already and we are only into the third quarter! I know that with everyone's help, we can reduce our expenses, but we must all begin today!

_____

_____

_____

PART D. As a collaborative team, decide on the letter that identifies the sentence with the more acceptable punctuation and write it in the blank.

1. (A) The question is, Will we profit from the media exposure?
   (B) The question is, "Will we profit from the media exposure"?

1. *_____

2. (A) When the fax jammed, the assistant sighed, "What else can go wrong"?
   (B) When the fax jammed, the assistant sighed, "What else can go wrong?"   2. _____

3. (A) How many checks arrived on this Friday? on last Friday? on the Friday before?
   (B) How many checks arrived on this Friday, on last Friday, on the Friday before?   3. _____

4. (A) You took notes on your conversation with Billings, didn't you?
   (B) You took notes on your conversation with Billings. Didn't you?   4. *_____

5. (A) Our new partners include firms in several states (Ohio, Idaho, Iowa, etc.)
   (B) Our new partners include firms in several states (Ohio, Idaho, Iowa, etc.).   5. _____

6. (A) K G Johnson used to serve with the F.B.I.
   (B) K. G. Johnson used to serve with the FBI.   6. _____

7. (A) Dr. Ford (his first name is Henry) is not related to the car manufacturer.
   (B) Dr. Ford (his first name is Henry.) is not related to the car manufacturer.   7. _____

8. (A) Would you please mail the data base disk to our colleague in Princeton?
   (B) Would you please mail the data base disk to our colleague in Princeton.   8. _____

9. (A) The selling price of our software—have you heard?—will rise next month.
   (B) The selling price of our software—have you heard—will rise next month.   9. _____

10. (A) Dennison (have you met her) is well-acquainted with our staffing needs.
    (B) Dennison (have you met her?) is well-acquainted with our staffing needs.   10. _____

PART E. In this exercise you are to write the meaning of each abbreviation. (Your dictionary may or may not make use of the periods shown.)

Example wk.   _____week_____

1. FDIC   1. *_____

2. NASA   2. _____

3. gm.   3. *_____

4. CDT   4. _____

5. etc.   5. _____

6. FAA   6. _____

7. e.t.a.   7. _____

8. CEO   8. _____

9. CD (banking)   9. _____

10. NYSE 10. _____

11. SUV 11. _____

12. Lt. (military) 12. _____

13. wpm 13. _____

14. PM (political title) 14. _____

15. Ph.D. 15. _____

FOR CLASS DISCUSSION

(if time permits)

Contemporary dictionaries seem to have eliminated a surprising number of hyphens from words that were once hyphenated. They have removed also a substantial number of periods from common abbreviations. *Webster's Collegiate* provides these entries (without periods): ltd, ltr, lub, lb, ea, inc, FOB, cwt, cv, oz, pp, and ppd. I checked more than fifty abbreviations in that work and found only three with periods (Mr., Mrs., and Ms.).

Presumably those of us who use the English language determine what changes will be made; dictionaries simply record those changes. Do you approve of the trend toward writing almost all abbreviations without periods? Can you suggest a logical reason for this trend?

MEDIUM OR MEDIA?

The noun *medium* has several meanings, one of which is "a means of mass communication, such as newspapers, magazines, television, or radio." Too often we hear the preferred plural form, *media,* used inappropriately. Most authorities would object to the wording of this sentence: *Television has become an extremely effective media.* The singular form, *medium,* should be used in such constructions.

A writer or speaker, however, may refer to all forms of mass communication as *the media.* Note this correct usage: *The media have reported every important detail of the recent disaster.*

CHAPTER

36

The Division of Words

■ **POINT TO PONDER** ⟶

Hyphens and dashes are used in significantly different ways.

Most computers allow us to select a menu option to make the right-hand margin of a letter or a report perfectly even. The option for this function is likely to be labeled *JUSTIFY.*

A writer who, for any reason, does not enjoy the luxury of such an option is going to be faced with the problem of word division; that is, he or she will occasionally have to break a word at the end of a line to avoid an excessively uneven right-hand margin. If a word is broken in an acceptable manner, a reader will have no difficulty in mentally joining the two parts. If, however, a word is broken illogically, the reader's task will become unnecessarily challenging.

A person with sound judgment should be able to divide words satisfactorily. Common sense suggests that abbreviations and figures, unless exceptionally long, should never be divided. It tells us also that, to facilitate reading, we should type as much of a word as possible before using the hyphen. You would be wise to familiarize yourself with the 12 rules that follow, for they have been well accepted by today's finest business writers.

RULE 1   Avoid excessive word division.

Some business writers are taught never to divide a word at the end of a line of typing. Such a solution to the problem of word division seems extreme. It is true, however, that a writer should choose to divide a word only when really necessary to maintain an acceptable margin.

379

Before attempting to divide a word, pronounce it to yourself slowly and carefully. If it contains only one sound, write it in solid form. Because each of the following words contains only one syllable, or sound, none of them should be divided.

brought	sighed	strength
freight	straight	thirst
friend	strange	through

RULE 3   Divide only between syllables.

A writer can sometimes determine the proper syllabication of a word simply by pronouncing it slowly. Some words, however, will offer two possible alternatives, such as a choice between *in for ma tion* and *in form a tion* or *re sid u al* and *re si du al*. Any logical division of such words should prove satisfactory to a reader. The careful writer would probably eliminate any doubt by checking a reliable dictionary, which is generally considered the final authority in such matters. Note the manner in which the dictionary divides each of these words.

ac knowl edg ment	de vel op	lat er al
ad mo ni tion	e ro sion	pu ri fi ca tion
be hav ior	har mo nize	sea son al ly
be liev er	ig ni tion	tab u la tor

RULE 4   Do not divide a word unless it has at least six letters.

Even words of six letters should not be divided unless the need is readily apparent. Don't consider such a division unless each syllable contains three letters, as in these words:

ask ing	lis ten	pen cil
fil ter	man tel	tab let

RULE 5   Do not divide one or two letters from the remainder of a word.

A writer who divides a word after the first or second letter does little toward improving the appearance of the margin. Furthermore, the reader may experience a slight difficulty in coping with such a division. A writer would also have no logical reason to divide a word before the final letter or two letters. To apply this rule, you would always write words such as the following in solid form, never dividing them as they have been divided here:

a gainst	de cant er	in sert ed
a gend a	de ceased	op tion al
be troth al	ex changed	re signed
be tween	ex plor er	re solved
death ly	ex port er	un changed

Some writers will occasionally divide a word after a prefix containing only two letters (*re-solved, un-necessary,* etc.). Such divisions, however, are not recommended. You will find that a rigid application of this fifth rule will keep you from dividing words that contain fewer than six letters.

Most careful writers would divide a word such as continuance (*con tin u ance*) *after*, rather than *before*, the *u*. Here are a few other words to which the rule would apply.

sim i lar i ty	o bit u ar y	re tal i ate
mu nic i pal	re cip i ent	spec u late

If the one-letter syllable is part of a common suffix, such as *able* or *ible*, carry the suffix over to the next line (*reli-able, convert-ible*, etc.). In some instances the syllabication of a word will not permit you to keep the suffix intact (*ca-pa-ble, pos-si-ble*, etc.).

RULE 7 If a consonant is doubled where syllables join, generally divide the word between the consonants.

admis sion	rebel lion	repel lent
confer ring	rebut tal	submit ted
plan ning	recol lect	supres sion
progres sive	recom mend	transmit tal

RULE 8 If a suffix has been added to a root word that ends in a doubled letter, ordinarily divide before the suffix.

This rule could be considered an exception to the one preceding. A word such as *tell-ing* is made up of the root *tell* and the suffix *ing*. It would logically be divided after the second *l*. Here are several other words that would be governed by this rule:

cross ing	fall ing	small est
drill ing	install ers	spell ers
dwell ing	miss ing	stress ing

RULE 9 Divide a hyphenated word only at the hyphen.

self-explanatory	quasi-judicial
pre-emptive	court-martial

RULE 10 Do not end more than two consecutive lines with hyphens.

Because words should be divided only when really necessary, you should have little difficulty in adhering to this rule.

RULE 11 Do not divide the last word of a paragraph or the last word on a page.

RULE 12 Avoid the division of names.

Proper nouns should be divided only when absolutely necessary. It is generally better to leave a line slightly short than to break a word such as *Prendergast* or *Massachusetts*.

Divide proper-noun groups so that they can be read with ease. The name *Donald S. Crenshaw* might be typed with *Donald S.* at the end of one line and *Crenshaw* at the start of the next. *The Honorable Charles P. Lucas* might be divided after *Honorable* or after the *P.* The person who simply applies good judgment in typing names will not mislead the reader.

A Reminder Concerning Compound Adjectives

You will recall from your reading of Chapter 19 that a compound adjective should generally be hyphenated when it precedes the noun it modifies. Note the use of hyphens in these sentences:

> We hope to dispose of this *hand-feed* copier.
>
> He does not have change for a *ten-dollar* bill.

In writing a word such as *hand-feed* or *ten-dollar* at the end of a line, remember to divide it only at the hyphen.

THE IMPACT OF LANGUAGE

A PERPLEXING HEADLINE

Most people would find the following newspaper headline difficult to understand. *Jane Drake,* a fictitious name, has been substituted for the name that actually appeared in the newspaper.

JANE DRAKE LED COURT STRIKES DOWN KEY PROPOSITION 13 PROTECTION FOR TAXPAYERS

——————————— FOR CLASS DISCUSSION ———————————

What must be added to this headline to make it readily understandable?

_____ **WORKSHEET 36** _____

THE DIVISION OF WORDS

PART A. In the space provided, write T or F to indicate whether the statement is true or false.

1. A one-syllable word may be divided.

    1. *_____

2. A word should not be divided immediately before a one-letter syllable.

    2. *_____

3. If a root word ends in a double consonant, divide before an added suffix.

    3. _____

4. Six-letter words are the shortest words that ought to be divided.

    4. _____

5. A word should not be divided after a first syllable of only two letters.

    5. _____

6. When dividing the word *repressing,* avoid dividing it between the *s*'s.

    6. _____

7. Hyphenated words may be divided at any of several spots.

    7. _____

8. One or two letters may be divided from a word to make a line of text even.

    8. _____

9. Divide words between syllables, checking with a current dictionary.

    9. _____

10. More than two consecutive lines may end in hyphens.

    10. _____

PART B. Assume that each word in this exercise appears at the end of a line and is to be divided. In the space provided, write the *letter* that indicates the best way shown to divide the word. If two answers are acceptable, choose the one that shows the greater number of syllables before the hyphen. Use your dictionary when necessary.

Example: (A) re-consider (B) rec-onsider (C) recon-sider

    C
    _____

1. (A) as-sessment (B) assess-ment (C) ass-essment

    1. _____

2. (A) selfcon-cept (B) sel-fconcept (C) self-concept

    2. *_____

3. (A) boi-sterous (B) boister-ous (C) bois-terous

    3. _____

4. (A) re-turning (B) return-ing (C) retur-ning

    4. *_____

5. (A) gymnas-tic (B) gym-nastic (C) gymnast-ic

    5. _____

6. (A) regu-lation (B) re-gulation (C) regul-ation

    6. *_____

7. (A) auto-matic (B) au-tomatic (C) automat-ic

    7. *_____

8. (A) install-ing (B) insta-lling (C) instal-ling

    8. _____

9. (A) compro-mise (B) com-promise (C) comp-romise

    9. _____

10. (A) parti-cular (B) par-ticular (C) partic-ular   10. _____

11. (A) glob-alism (B) glo-balism (C) global-ism   11. _____

12. (A) sim-ilarity (B) simi-larity (C) similar-ity   12. _____

13. (A) int-erstate (B) in-terstate (C) inter-state   13. _____

14. (A) un-convinced (B) uncon-vinced (C) unconvinc-ed   14. _____

15. (A) manda-tory (B) man-datory (C) mandat-ory   15. _____

16. (A) in-finitive (B) infin-itive (C) infini-tive   16. _____

17. (A) pro-grammer (B) program-mer (C) prog-rammer   17. _____

18. (A) a-nalogous (B) anal-ogous (C) analo-gous   18. _____

19. (A) regis-tered (B) re-gistered (C) register-ed   19. _____

20. (A) lawa-biding (B) law-abiding (C) lawabid-ing   20. _____

21. (A) sequenc-ing (B) sequen-cing (C) se-quencing   21. _____

22. (A) un-popular (B) unpop-ular (C) unpopu-lar   22. _____

23. (A) tradition-al (B) trad-itional (C) tradi-tional   23. _____

24. (A) anti-aircraft (B) an-tiaircraft (C) antiair-craft   24. *_____

25. (A) with-drawal (B) withdraw-al (C) withdra-wal   25. _____

26. (A) stat-utory (B) statu-tory (C) sta-tutory   26. _____

27. (A) re-plication (B) repli-cation (C) replica-tion   27. _____

28. (A) kil-owatt (B) kilo-watt (C) ki-lowatt   28. _____

29. (A) fre-quencies (B) freque-ncies (C) frequen-cies   29. _____

30. (A) be-coming (B) beco-ming (C) becom-ing   30. _____

31. (A) dia-meter (B) diame-ter (C) diamet-er   31. _____

32. (A) de-cid-ing (B) decid-ing (C) deci-ding   32. _____

33. (A) cor-poration (B) corpo-ration (C) corpora-tion   33. _____

34. (A) un-touchable (B) untouch-able (C) untoucha-ble   34. _____

35. (A) arbitra-tion (B) arbi-tration (C) arbit-ration   35. _____

PART C. One word division rule has been broken five times in this short passage from a conference program. Find the five problem spots and write the five words correctly in the blanks which follow the passage.

> Contributors to the continuity fund include Dr. Edna Morgen-
> stern, Mr. and Mrs. Edward Glenn Brookfield, Mr. John Thomp-
> son, Mrs. Delilah Jenkins, Mr. and Mrs. Terrence Storm-Fergu-
> son, Ms. Sheila Partridge-Guttmann, Dr. Edmund Smiley, Dr. Alan
> James Scannell McCornick, Mrs. Jane Bengston, Mr. John Berg-
> quist, Mr. and Mrs. Harrison Sundberg, Dr. Camille Maria Rodri-
> guez, and Ms. Heleni Panayotopouloi.

_____   _____

_____   _____

_____

PART D. In the space provided, show how the word should be divided into syllables. If you are collaborating, prove that your answer is a good one by using different dictionaries whenever necessary.

Example: accountant _____ ac count ant _____

1. paralegal   1. * _____
2. reservation   2. _____
3. collegiality   3. * _____
4. excessive   4. * _____
5. phenomenon   5. _____
6. guardianship   6. _____
7. interpret   7. _____
8. foreclosure   8. _____
9. security   9. _____
10. lenience   10. _____
11. currency   11. _____
12. hazardous   12. _____
13. synergism   13. _____
14. maintenance   14. _____
15. officiate   15. _____
16. proprietary   16. _____
17. paralysis   17. _____
18. expelling   18. _____
19. beginning   19. _____
20. prevaricate   20. _____

PART E. Write three complete sentences.

1. Tell where you would divide the word *separate* (sep a rate) at the end of a line and why you would divide it in that way.

_____

_____

_____

2. Tell where you would divide the word *respectively* (re spec tive ly) and why you would divide it in that way.

_____

_____

_____

3. Tell where you would divide the word *deductible* (de duct i ble) and why you would divide it in that way.

_____

_____

_____

---

wWWw ============ **Watching the Web** ============

| **Back** | **Forward** | **Home** | **Reload** | **Images** | **Open** |

```
On a job hunt?
Turning up few opportunities?
If you're not finding what you really want,
if rejection is hurting your selfes-
teem, take this short course on finding your own
constellation of talents, recommended by the author of
What Color is MY Parachute.
```

| read on | | no thanks |

37

General Vocabulary Study for Business Use

POINT TO PONDER

The C.E.O. of a large corporation is almost certain to have an excellent vocabulary.

Researchers have discovered that the boss in any job situation—particularly in the business world—almost always has a more extensive vocabulary than his or her subordinates. Recent studies have also revealed that by college age the average student has almost abandoned the quest for new words. You are not likely to add a significant number of new words to your vocabulary unless you undertake an organized program for improvement. If you have not already set up such a program, this chapter may serve as your beginning.

A Few Steps to Follow

Anyone who seriously wants to gain control of an increased number of words would do well to follow these steps:

1. Jot down in a pocket-size notebook any reasonably common words that you have encountered but do not really understand. Your best entries will be words that appear in print with some frequency, for these are the words you will need in order to read with understanding.
2. Make time to sit down with a good dictionary to determine the definitions of the words on your list, and enter those definitions in a permanent notebook.
3. Study the words and definitions you have entered.
4. Use the words as you speak and write. Unless you put them to use, it is doubtful that you will master them.

Words to Describe People

The following 20 words, each of which appears frequently in print, could serve as the beginning of a basic vocabulary list. Each, you will note, is an adjective that could be used to describe a fellow employee.

AMIABLE (ā′ mē a bel)　You could use this word to describe a fellow worker who is thoroughly likable. It means "having a friendly, sociable, and congenial disposition."

DIFFIDENT (dif′ e dent)　Don't ask a *diffident* colleague to speak before a large group of people. This adjective means "lacking self-confidence; timid."

EFFERVESCENT (ef fer ves′ ent)　Most work teams include at least one person who could be described as effervescent—"lively, high-spirited, vivacious."

ERUDITE (er′ yoo dīt)　Use this word to describe the person who has a wide knowledge gained from reading. It means "learned, scholarly."

INDEFATIGABLE (in di fat′ i ga ble)　Do you know anyone who can work or play indefinitely without getting tired? Such a person may be described as indefatigable, which means "tireless, inexhaustible, energetic."

INDOLENT (in′ dō lent)　Here's a word to describe someone whose principal pastime is avoiding work. It means "lazy, idle."

INTREPID (in trep′ id)　If you need someone to face a roomful of angry reporters, choose a person who is intrepid, which means "not afraid; bold; fearless; brave."

IRASCIBLE (ir as′ e bel)　No one really enjoys working for an irascible employer, that is, one who is "quick-tempered; easily angered."

LOQUACIOUS (lo kwa′ shus)　If you enjoy listening, spend your coffee breaks with a loquacious colleague, for that person is "very talkative; fond of talking."

METICULOUS (me tik′ yoo lus)　If a particular job must be done perfectly, give it to a meticulous employee, that is, someone who is extremely careful about details. That person may be described as "finical, scrupulous, precise."

MUNIFICENT (myoo nif′ e sent)　A munificent employer would undoubtedly reward an exceptionally loyal employee with occasional bonuses. *Munificent* means "extremely liberal in giving; very generous."

OFFICIOUS (o fish′ us)　Use this word to describe the person who insists upon offering unwanted advice or services. The officious individual is "meddlesome, obtrusive."

PUGNACIOUS (pug nā′ shus)　How would you describe the type of employee who constantly provokes arguments with coworkers and thoroughly enjoys a good fight? This person is pugnacious, which means "quarrelsome, combative, given to fighting."

RECALCITRANT (ri kal′ si trant)　Recalcitrant employees may not be able to hold their jobs for long. They have their own ideas about how things should be done. They are the ones who refuse to obey authority, rules, or regulations. Think of them as being "stubbornly defiant, obstinate, rebellious."

RESOURCEFUL (ri sors′ ful)　If your office staff is faced with an unusual problem, the resourceful employee may be called upon to cope with it. This adjective means "able to deal promptly and effectively with problems, difficulties, and so forth."

SOLICITOUS (se lis′ e tes)　A worker's illness may be easier to bear if his or her employer is solicitous, which means "caring; attentive; concerned; showing anxious desire."

TACITURN (tas′ i turn)　Any large office is likely to have one or two people who seldom say a word. Such people are taciturn, which means "habitually silent; uncommunicative."

UBIQUITOUS (ū bik′ wi tus)　To the insecure employee, the boss may appear to be ubiquitous, which means "seeming to be present everywhere at the same time."

VERSATILE (vur′ sa til)　Here's a word to describe the person who can do many things well. It means "many-sided, competent in many things."

VINDICTIVE (vin dik′ tiv)　Use this word to describe the person who, when insulted or injured by another, just cannot wait to retaliate. It means "revengeful, disposed to take revenge."

1. Don't believe anything that Terence Mayes just told you. He is a _____.

1. * _____

2. Alfonso, who relishes fine dining, actually studies the menus of expensive French restaurants. He is a _____.

2. _____

3. Waxman, our night watchman, lives in a remote part of town and seldom leaves his small home except to go to work. He is a _____.

3. _____

4. The office manager gave me a tongue lashing and threatened to fire me because I had taken an extra five minutes on my coffee break. He is a _____.

4. _____

5. McAfee often disrupts the office with his practical jokes and untimely attempts at humor. He is a _____.

5. _____

6. Quigley, who treats the boss as if he were a king, will do just about anything to gain his approval. He is a _____.

6. _____

7. Takemoto's manner and behavior did not alert us in any way to the fact that he was suffering severe abdominal pain. He is a _____.

7. _____

8. Tompkins will probably make a few mistakes during the coming week because he is such a _____.

8. _____

9. Our data entry clerk will never do *today* what he can do *tomorrow.* He is a _____.

9. _____

10. Bonelli's stories delighted everyone who attended the company's annual banquet. Bonelli is a _____.

10. _____

PART E.   This drill will test your understanding of words related to those defined in this chapter. Write six short sentences, each one to contain the word shown in parentheses.

1. (recalcitrance) _____

_____

_____

2. (vindictiveness) _____

_____

_____

3. (irascibility) _____

_____

_____

4. (indolence) * _____

_____

_____

5. (amiably) _____

_____

_____

6. (effervescence) _____

_____

_____

TRENDS OF THE TIMES

As you begin to write a word like *coexist,* do you ever find yourself wondering whether or not a hyphen should be used after the prefix? Many people do. I have certainly checked my dictionary on many occasions to determine the precise spelling of such words. You may be pleased to learn that the trend today is to place *no hyphen* after common prefixes. Your dictionary is likely to spell each word on the following list just as it is shown here.

antiaircraft	coauthor	reactivate
antibiotic	coeducation	reaffirm
anticlimax	coefficient	reappoint
antifreeze	coexist	reassess
antihero	cohabit	reattempt
antihistamine	cooperate	reestablish
antiknock	copilot	reevaluate

If a prefix is followed by a capitalized word, however, a hyphen should be used, as in *pro-American.* It is also correct to use a hyphen when it is needed to prevent misreading, as in this sentence: I will *re-ally* myself with these dedicated people. (See page 204 for additional notes on the hyphen.)

Some Terms Commonly Used in Business

■ POINT TO PONDER

Vocabulary power is generally regarded as an excellent predictor of success in business.

If you are employed in the business world, you should attempt to master those challenging terms that are of special importance in your own field. Because the words defined in this chapter are important in more than one field, there is a strong possibility that you will encounter them often. The following words, added to those discussed in Chapter 37, represent an excellent beginning for a businessperson's basic vocabulary list.

Action Words for Business

Let's begin with 20 verbs chosen at random from several areas of business. In all likelihood you will see and hear many of these words even if you never enter the business world.

ARBITRATE (ar′bi trāt), *v.t.* and *v.i.*   Labor and management often arbitrate their differences. This word means "to submit a dispute to a disinterested third person (or group) for solution" or "to act as a judge (or *arbitrator*)."

AUDIT (o' dit), *v.t.*   An independent accounting firm may be called upon to audit the financial records of a business. This word means "to examine, verify, or correct (accounts, records, or claims)."

CONFISCATE (kon' fis kāt), *v.t.*   Law enforcement officers often confiscate weapons or narcotics that are illegally held. This word means "to seize by or as by authority."

DEFAULT (de folt'), *v.i. and v.t.*   A person who defaults in making payments on a mortgage is likely to lose his or her property. This word means "to fail to make a payment that is due; to fail to do something or be somewhere when expected."

EMBEZZLE (im bez' l), *v.t.*   Employees may embezzle funds belonging to the firms for which they work. This word means "to steal property entrusted to one's care; to take by fraud for one's own use."

ENJOIN (in join'), *v.t.*   A judge may enjoin a firm from using false or misleading advertising. This term means "to prohibit or forbid, especially by legal injunction; to order (someone) to do something."

ESCHEAT (es chēt'), *v.i. and v.t.*   If a person who dies has no will and no legal heirs, that person's property will escheat to the state. This word means "to revert (as to the government)."

GARNISHEE (gar ni shē'), *v.t.*   A merchant, with the cooperation of the court, may garnishee a portion of the wages of a delinquent charge customer. This word means "to attach (property, wages, etc.) by authority of a court so that a debt may be satisfied."

INDEMNIFY (in dem' ni fī), *v.t.*   A businessperson may have an insurance company indemnify every building owned by the firm. This word means "to protect against loss; insure" or "to compensate for a loss; reimburse."

INDICT (in dīt'), *v.t.*   A grand jury may indict a person suspected of having committed a crime. This word means "to charge with the commission of a crime; especially, to make a formal accusation on the basis of positive evidence."

LAPSE (laps), *v.i.*   A life insurance policy will generally lapse 32 days after the due date of an unpaid premium. This word means "to become forfeit or void because of the holder's failure to pay the premium on an insurance policy."

LEASE (lēs), *v.t.*   A business manager may choose to lease, rather than purchase, a factory or warehouse. This word means "to acquire the use of the property (land, buildings, etc.) for a specified time and for fixed payments." The contract involved is called a *lease*.

LIBEL (lī' bel), *v.t.*   Reporters must be careful not to libel those about whom they write. This word means "to publish, write, or print unfavorable, injurious, or false statements about."

LIQUIDATE (lik' wi dāt), *v.t. and v.i.*   A merchant in financial difficulty may decide to liquidate. This word has several meanings: "(1) to clear up the affairs of (a bankrupt firm), (2) to pay (a debt), (3) to convert into cash."

MORTGAGE (mor' gij), *v.t.*   A businessperson may mortgage real estate in order to raise capital. This word means "to pledge (property) to a creditor as security for the payment of a debt."

NEGOTIATE (ni go' shē āt), *v.t.*   Any large furniture manufacturer would want to negotiate a favorable contract with a lumber supplier. This word means "to make arrangements for, settle, or conclude (a business transaction); to transfer, assign, or sell (negotiable paper)."

PERJURE (pur' jer), *v.t.*   Dishonest persons may perjure themselves while on the witness stand in court. This word means "to lie while under oath."

POSTDATE (pōst dāt'), *v.t.*   A person may decide to postdate a check because this week's deposit will not be made until tomorrow. This word means "to place on an instrument a date later than that on which the instrument is drawn."

RECONCILE (rek' en sīl), *v.t.*   When the members of a management team have a heated dispute, they should seriously attempt to reconcile their differences. This word means, "to reestablish friendship between; to settle or resolve, as a dispute."

REDEEM (re dēm'), *v.t.*   A person may leave a coin collection as security for a loan and later attempt to redeem it. This word means "to buy back; to pay off (a mortgage or note); to exchange for money or goods."

Fifteen Nouns for Business

The following nouns, like the verbs already discussed, were chosen because they are used in many areas of business.

APPRAISER (a prāz′ er)   If you request a real estate loan, the lending institution will probably send an appraiser to inspect your property. This professional is "a person given authority to estimate the value of property or goods."

BENEFICIARY (ben e fish′ er ē)   A merchant is likely to be named beneficiary when a customer purchases insurance to cover the amount of a credit purchase. A beneficiary is "a person named to receive the benefit from an insurance policy or a will."

BOYCOTT (boi′ kot)   A merchant may find that sales have declined because of a boycott, which is "a joining together (as of union members) in refusing to deal with, so as to punish, an organization or a person."

DEPRECIATION (di prē shē ā′ shun)   A good business manager will allow for the depreciation of buildings and equipment. Depreciation is "a decrease in the value of property through wear or obsolescence" or "the allowance made for such wear and obsolescence."

DISBURSEMENT (dis burs′ ment)   A business manager must be careful about the disbursement of funds. This word refers to "a paying out; an expenditure."

EQUITY (ek′ wi tē)   If you are making payments toward the purchase of property, your equity in that property should increase with each payment. The word *equity* means "the value of property beyond the amount owed on it."

FIDUCIARY (fi dōo′ shē er ē)   A fiduciary may be named to act in behalf of a person who is mentally incompetent or a minor. The word means "a trustee; one empowered to act in behalf of another or to hold property in trust for another."

INFLATION (in flā′ shun)   Some economists have predicted a prolonged period of inflation. This word means "a decrease in the value of money and a rise in prices, often because of an increase in the amount of currency in circulation."

LIEN (lēn)   Unpaid taxes are considered a lien against real estate. This word means "a claim on property against the payment of a just debt."

LOCKOUT (lok′ out)   An unhappy employer may make use of a lockout to accomplish a particular purpose. A lockout is "the refusal of an employer to allow employees to come to work unless they agree to certain terms."

MARKUP (mark′ up)   In discount houses the markup on goods tends to be small. *Markup* refers to "the amount added to the cost to cover overhead and profit in arriving at the selling price."

MERGER (mur′ jer)   Corporation officials generally hope for greater profits when they propose a merger. This word means "the union, or combining, of two or more commercial interests (corporations, etc.)."

MIDDLEMAN (mid′ l man)   A retailer or a wholesaler would be considered a middleman. This word refers to "a trader who buys and sells commodities (hoping for a profit) to other middlemen or to ultimate consumers."

RECIPROCITY (res i pros′ i tē)   A lumber dealer and a furniture maker could easily practice reciprocity by buying from each other. The word means "an exchange of favors, privileges, or business for the mutual benefit of those involved."

UNDERWRITER (un′ der rit er)   A business manager who has a question about the firm's fire insurance should call the underwriter. This word refers to "a person or agent who signs an insurance policy, thus assuming liability in the event of specified loss or damage" or "a person who guarantees the purchase of stocks or bonds to be made available to the public for subscription."

Related Words

If you understand the 35 words discussed in this chapter, you should be ready to use these 24 related words:

appraisal	disburse	lessee	negotiator
appraise	embezzler	lessor	perjury
arbitrator	garnishment	libelous	reciprocate
auditor	indemnification	liquidation	reconciliation
confiscation	indictment	mortgagor	redeemable
depreciate	inflationary	negotiation	underwrite

A Final Note

Several of the words treated in this chapter have additional meanings that were intentionally omitted. The definitions offered in this text are those that should prove most helpful to anyone who functions in the business community. If you have read the chapter carefully, you should have no difficulty in understanding sentences such as these:

If the union refuses to accept this proposal, we will be forced to call in an *arbitrator.*

The *embezzler* proved to be a trusted employee who had worked here for 18 years.

Since their stories conflict, at least one of the witnesses is guilty of *perjury.*

Tivoli is extremely unhappy about the *garnishment* of his wages.

The lease impressed me as being perfectly fair, but the *lessor* refused to renew it.

FRONT-PAGE NEWS

The following sentence was found on the front page of one of our leading newspapers.

The poll of 450 people was done after Morgan's release by the Gordon S. Black Corporation.

Having read that statement, a friend of mine concluded that someone named Morgan had been released by the Gordon S. Black Corporation. Actually, Morgan had been paroled from prison. The placement of modifiers, however, tends to obscure the intended message.

_____ FOR CLASS DISCUSSION _____

Reword the sentence in question so that its meaning is perfectly clear. Be sure to include all ideas.

————WORKSHEET 38————

SOME TERMS COMMONLY USED
IN BUSINESS

PART A. Each of the 16 verbs listed can be used once in the sentences that follow. Write the correct choices in the spaces provided.

arbitrate	audit	default	escheat	embezzle	garnishee
indemnify	indict	lapse	lease	libel	mortgage
perjure	postdate	reconcile	redeem		

1. Mahoney Media Group wishes to _____ its two studio buildings for $1 million through American Insurance Corporation.

   1. *_____

2. The bank may require us to _____ our building as a way of raising capital for our new publishing venture.

   2. _____

3. With all of the circumstantial evidence against Ellerbe, it looks likely that the grand jury may _____ her.

   3. *_____

4. When tabloids drag the good name of a business through the journalistic mud, causing harm to reputation, that business can sue for _____.

   4. _____

5. It is in the best interests of all parties that our two employers _____ their differences and come to an agreement to settle this dispute.

   5. _____

6. When thieves are caught and haven't the means to pay for what they've stolen, the court often decides to _____ their wages.

   6. _____

7. It is considered white collar crime to _____ funds from the company for which one works; it is often a very sophisticated form of theft.

   7. _____

8. Since our deposit will go to the bank early tomorrow morning, we can surely write and _____ a check this evening.

   8. _____

9. This complex accounting system makes it possible to _____ on our utilities payment and not discover the error until the lights are turned out.

   9. _____

10. With a sudden windfall, some people spend wildly while others systematically _____ bank notes and mortgages.

   10. _____

11. In some unresolved labor troubles a mediator is selected to _____ the dispute; both parties may be bound to accept the decision.

   11. _____

12. One must, under oath, speak the truth as he or she knows it; doing otherwise, people _____ themselves.

12. _____

13. When the tax accountant and the IRS disagree on payment amounts, an _____ is one way to reach a solution.

13. _____

14. It is more cost effective for this firm to _____ a small fleet of vans than to buy them outright.

14. _____

15. Insurance payments must be kept current or policies _____.

15. _____

16. Without a will or heirs, our CEO's property, including all assets in this business, will _____ to the state of Oregon.

16. _____

PART B. In the space provided, write the letter that identifies the correct definition.

1. redeem	**A.** to prohibit or forbid	**1.** *_____
2. audit	**B.** to fail to make a payment that is due	**2.** _____
3. confiscate	**C.** to publish statements that damage another's reputation	**3.** *_____
4. default	**D.** to examine or verify (accounts, records)	**4.** _____
5. embezzle	**E.** to seize by or as by authority	**5.** _____
6. enjoin	**F.** to lie while under oath	**6.** _____
7. escheat	**G.** to rent property for specified time and payments	**7.** _____
8. garnishee	**H.** to clear up the affairs of (a bankrupt firm)	**8.** _____
9. perjure	**I.** to steal property entrusted to one's care	**9.** _____
10. indict	**J.** to attach or seize (as property or wages)	**10.** _____
11. negotiate	**K.** to pledge for payment of a debt	**11.** _____
12. lease	**L.** to buy back	**12.** _____
13. libel	**M.** to settle or conclude (a business transaction)	**13.** _____
14. liquidate	**N.** to revert (as to the government)	**14.** _____
15. mortgage	**O.** to charge with a crime	**15.** _____

PART C. In this excerpt from a memo about retail property, five terms from the chapter are misspelled. Underscore them and correct their spelling on the blanks which follow the excerpt.

Our retail morgage agreement states that, if we should try to leese another property in competition with this one, the corporation can place a lein on our merchandise and other holdings. If we want to change that clause, we must negociate with a corporate lawyer to reckoncile any differences.

1. *_____   4. _____

2. _____   5. _____

3. _____

PART D. Each of the 15 words listed can be used once in the sentences that follow. Decide as a collaborative team which word fits best in which blank and write the team's choices in the spaces provided.

appraiser	depreciation	fiduciary	lockout	middleman
beneficiary	disbursement	inflation	markup	reciprocity
boycott	equity	lien	merger	underwriter

1. We hired an independent property _____ to confirm the value of our office furnishings and electronic equipment.

   1. *_____

2. We get a tax allowance for the yearly _____ of our computers.

   2. *_____

3. With the current _____ on import ore from that nation, manufacturing dependent on ore must find alternative sources quickly.

   3. _____

4. Our publishers have a _____ agreement with certain book merchants; publishers make overstock available and merchants sell more books.

   4. _____

5. If our traveling sales force purchases tickets directly from the carriers, there is no need for a _____ such as a travel agent.

   5. _____

6. The moment the storm damaged our outdoor equipment, Susan called our insurance _____ to determine whether we had a claim.

   6. _____

7. Our entire division was named as a _____ in his will.

   7. _____

8. It is possible to borrow against the value of property, as long as the borrower has accrued some _____ by paying down a good share of the mortgage.

   8. _____

9. The _____ of your market study grant will take place next week; at that point, you'll have the cash to continue your research efforts.

   9. _____

10. Under our current business plan, the _____ of our banking firm and our marketing company will produce excellent bank promotions.

   10. _____

11. When our CFO was a minor, Senator Woodson acted as her _____.

   11. _____

12. We have received official notice that the tree removal service has placed a _____ on our property until their exorbitant invoice is paid in full.

   12. _____

13. Analysts predict high _____ this year in gas and oil prices due to a shortage of workers in the fields of exploration and processing.

   13. _____

14. Pilots imposing a _____ prevented other airline employees from carrying out their responsibilities last week.

   14. _____

15. Large catalog merchants can offer very low prices because their operating expenses are low; they need not exceed a 50 percent _____.

   15. _____

PART E. This drill will test your understanding of words closely related to those defined in this chapter. Write six short sentences, each one to contain the words shown in parentheses.

1. (appraisal) *_____

_____

2. (depreciate) _____

_____

3. (disburse) _____

_____

4. (indictment) _____

_____

5. (inflationary) _____

_____

6. (libelous) _____

_____

FOR CLASS DISCUSSION

(if time permits)

As you increase your vocabulary, make certain that you pronounce each new word correctly. The following list is composed of common words that are frequently mispronounced, even by professional men and women. How do you pronounce them?

1. affluent	**5.** facade	**9.** grievous	**13.** irrevocable	**17.** preferable
2. almond	**6.** fracas	**10.** indict	**14.** mischievous	**18.** respite
3. comparable	**7.** genuine	**11.** infamous	**15.** museum	**19.** subtle
4. disheveled	**8.** gibe	**12.** irreparable	**16.** often	**20.** succinct

---

wWWw ========= **Watching the Web** =========

Back	**Forward**	**Home**	**Reload**	**Images**	**Open**

Attention all lease-holders on office machinery:
If you lease your copier, printer, fax, or scanner,
prepare to tear up that paper and send those
machines back!
Calling all leasors! You don't need to lease when you can
own for less. Check out our prices on HP, Sony, and other
brand multi-function tools.

read on   no thanks

Executives' Choice

■ **POINT TO PONDER**

It is infinitely more satisfying to *know* that a particular construction is right than to *guess.*

Y ou have found throughout this text brief sections entitled "Executives' Choice." These sections have presented English words and word combinations that are often used inappropriately in business. This chapter will simply bring these expressions, together with examples of correct business usage for each, into a single alphabetized list. Chapter numbers are given to indicate where explanations and definitions may be found. This list, of course, is not intended to include *all* expressions that pose problems for the business writer. It does, however, include the most common.

1. ACCEPT, EXCEPT   (See Chapter 12.)

    Because the shipment was late, we refused to *accept* it.
    Everyone *except* Blatnick was in the office on Monday.

2. ADAPT, ADOPT, ADEPT   (See Chapter 10.)

    Perhaps we can *adapt* this software to our use.
    Perhaps we should *adopt* a new retirement policy.
    He is not particularly *adept* at proofreading.

3. ADVICE, ADVISE   (See Chapter 14.)

    You would do well to take Ramon's *advice.*
    I *advise* you to prepare a statement in advance.

4. AFFECT, EFFECT   (See Chapter 12.)

The new promotion policy will not *affect* me.
The new policy will have an *effect* upon several office workers.
We hope to *effect* a change in his thinking.

5. A HALF A   (See Chapter 9.)

The discussion will last about *a half* (not *a half an*) hour.

6. ALLOWED, ALOUD   (See Chapter 10.)

No one was *allowed* in the building after 10 P.M.
The clerk of the court read the charges *aloud*.

7. ALREADY, ALL READY   (See Chapter 20.)

The morning train to Baltimore has *already* left.
The visitors from Gary are *all ready* to leave.

8. ALTER, ALTAR   (See Chapter 19.)

If it rains on Tuesday, we will have to *alter* our plans.
We used a fine grade of oak to build the *altar* of the church.

9. ALTOGETHER, ALL TOGETHER   (See Chapter 10.)

Wayne was *altogether* unhappy when he heard the news.
We were *all together* in this room when the accident occurred.

10. AMOUNT, NUMBER   (See Chapter 10.)

He ordered a large *amount* of sand.
He ordered a large *number* of concrete blocks.

11. AND, BUT   (See Chapter 23.)

The manager's office is large *and* luxurious.
Blackwell's office is small *but* adequate.

12. AND ETC.   (See Chapter 9.)

We purchased several items (folders, envelopes, *etc.*).
NOT: . . . (folder, envelopes, *and etc.*).

13. ANGRY, MAD   (See Chapter 9.)

When he set fire to the building, we knew he was *mad*.
The customer was obviously *angry* with the salesperson.

14. APPRAISE, APPRISE   (See Chapter 12.)

The property must be *appraised* before we make an offer to buy it.
Why wasn't Golden *apprised* of these findings?

15. ASSISTANCE, ASSISTANTS   (See Chapter 9.)

He programmed the computer without any *assistance* from me.
My two *assistants* will not be available on Monday.

16. BANK ON   (See Chapter 9.)

You can *depend* (not *bank*) on us for support.

17. BEING THAT, BEING AS   (See Chapter 9.)

Because (not *Being as* or *that*) the shipment is damaged, I cannot accept it.

18. BESIDE, BESIDES   (See Chapter 28.)

He sat down *beside* Chesterton.
No one *besides* Jacobs has read the report.

19. BET   (See Chapter 9.)

I *suppose* (not *bet*) you found errors in the Spangler report.
Our salespeople occasionally *bet* on football games.

20. BREAK, BRAKE   (See Chapter 14.)

Be careful not to *break* any of these fragile items.
We will work for two hours and then take a short *break*.
When the light changed to red, I immediately applied the *brake*.

21. BUT WHAT   (See Chapter 23.)

I have no doubt *that* (not *but what*) the sale will be a success.

22. CAN, MAY   (See Chapter 12.)

Galworthy *can* operate any kind of office machine.
May I go with you to the conference in New Orleans?

23. CANVAS, CANVASS   (See Chapter 12.)

The boat cover is made of *canvas*.
We should *canvass* this neighborhood for orders.

24. CAPITOL, CAPITAL   (See Chapter 14.)

They took a picture on the steps of the *Capitol* in Jackson.
We have insufficient *capital* to go into business.

Jackson is the *capital* of Mississippi.
Many people are opposed to *capital* punishment.

25. CITE, SIGHT, SITE   (See Chapter 15.)

The attorney could not *cite* a similar case.
The speeding car is now out of *sight.*
This is an ideal *site* for our new plant.

26. COARSE, COURSE   (See Chapter 18.)

This material is too *coarse* for our purpose.
You will, of *course,* be entitled to a discount.

27. CONFIDANT, CONFIDENT   (See Chapter 14.)

Simmons would be an excellent *confidant.*
We are *confident* that the patent will be granted.

28. CONSENSUS OF OPINION   (See Chapter 14.)

The *consensus* (not *consensus of opinion*) is that Hale will win.

29. CONTACT   (See Chapter 15.)

We will *telephone* (rather than *contact*) you on Friday. (Try to be as specific as possible.)

30. CONTINUAL, CONTINUOUS   (See Chapter 18.)

His *continual* complaining annoys the other employees.
The engine has been running *continuously* for three hours.

31. CORPORATION, COOPERATION   (See Chapter 9.)

This *corporation* has been in business for 72 years.
We cannot finish this project without your *cooperation.*

32. COULD OF   (See Chapter 15.)

With your help we could *have* (not *of*) finished before noon.

33. COUNSEL, COUNCIL   (See Chapter 14.)

You should engage him as your legal *counsel.*
He would *counsel* you in your business affairs.
The city *council* meets on Wednesday nights.

34. DATA   (See Chapter 14.)

The *data are* (not *data is*) in the envelope.

35. DEAL   (See Chapter 14.)

> AVOID: Perhaps we can make a *deal*.
> USE: Perhaps we can come to an *agreement*.

36. DISBURSE, DISPERSE   (See Chapter 23.)

We cannot *disburse* the money without authorization.
We will *disperse* our sales representatives throughout the world.

37. DISINTERESTED, UNINTERESTED   (See Chapter 18.)

A *disinterested* attorney was asked to give his opinion.
We are *uninterested* in your investment program.

38. DUE TO, BECAUSE OF   (See Chapter 15.)

The argument was *due to* a misunderstanding.
We postponed the lecture *because of* the rain.

39. EITHER, ANY   (See Chapter 14.)

Either of the two machines may be used.
Any of the club's members would have helped you.

40. EMINENT, IMMINENT   (See Chapter 18.)

An *eminent* industrialist addressed the group.
The report suggested that war was *imminent*.

41. ENTHUSE   (See Chapter 15.)

> AVOID: We *enthused* over the new machinery.
> USE: We *became enthusiastic* about the new machinery.

42. EVERYDAY, EVERY DAY   (See Chapter 10.)

His *everyday* activities would prove exciting for most of us.
I thoroughly enjoyed *every day* that I spent at General Electric.

43. EXPAND, EXPEND   (See Chapter 26.)

We may issue new stock if our business continues to *expand*.
Wheaton refused to *expend* the money needed for repairs.

44. EXPECT, SUPPOSE   (See Chapter 15.)

We will *expect* delivery on Monday.
I *suppose* (not *expect*) you talked with Harrington.

45. FORWARD, FOREWORD   (See Chapter 18.)

If the loan is granted, we will go *forward* with our plans.
The author mentioned my name in the *foreword* of his book.

46. FORMALLY, FORMERLY (See Chapter 20.)

We have not been *formally* introduced.
He *formerly* worked for T. R. Wright, Inc.

47. FORTH, FOURTH (See Chapter 9.)

The strange mixture sent *forth* a disagreeable odor.
At least a *fourth* of the items have already been sold.

48. GOT (See Chapter 15.)

We *received* (not *got*) your message in this morning's mail.

49. GUESS (See Chapter 15.)

I *suppose* (not *guess*) we should sign the contract.
Please do not ask me to *guess* your age.

50. HAD OUGHT (See Chapter 15.)

AVOID: The dispatcher *had ought* to write more legibly.
USE: The dispatcher *should* write more legibly.

51. IMPLY, INFER (See Chapter 15.)

The speaker *implied* that no action would be taken.
I *infer* from what you said that the plan has been abandoned.

52. IN BACK OF (See Chapter 28.)

We stand *behind* (not *in back of*) our products.

53. IN REGARDS TO (See Chapter 28.)

Nothing was done *about* (not *in regards to*) the damaged shipment.

54. INTELLIGENT, INTELLIGIBLE (See Chapter 18.)

Bondi is the most *intelligent* person I know.
Because of the static the announcer's words were not *intelligible*.

55. IRREGARDLESS (See Chapter 28.)

He will buy the lathe *regardless* (not *irregardless*) of my opinion.

56. KINDLY, PLEASE (See Chapter 20.)

Please (not *Kindly*) send us the figures for March.

57. LOOSE, LOSE (See Chapter 23.)

The mechanic discovered that the air filter was *loose*.
If you cannot provide the software, you will *lose* the Soji account.

58. MAYBE, MAY BE   (See Chapter 20.)

Maybe we should offer to help organize the program.
Clarkson *may be* able to obtain the information.

59. MOST, ALMOST   (See Chapter 18.)

Most of this firm's employees seem happy.
Almost everyone in the room seemed surprised.

60. NICE   (See Chapter 18.)

The assistant manager gave *an informative* (not *a nice*) report.

61. PAIR, PAIRS   (See Chapter 28.)

We have only one *pair* of scissors left.
We have ten *pairs* of scissors left.

62. PARTY, PERSON   (See Chapter 28.)

The *person* (not *party*) in the gray suit is my supervisor.
I would like accommodations for a *party* of four.

63. PASSED, PAST   (See Chapter 19.)

A Greyhound bus just *passed* this building.
We are not really interested in *past* events.

64. PERCENT, PERCENTAGE   (See Chapter 26.)

Her commission will be 20 *percent.*
What *percentage* does your firm pay?

65. PERSONAL, PERSONNEL   (See Chapter 18.)

This portfolio is for your *personal* use.
The *personnel* in this department are certainly accommodating.

66. PHONE, TELEPHONE   (See Chapter 19.)

Ames will *telephone* (not *phone*) you this afternoon.

67. PRINCIPAL, PRINCIPLE   (See Chapter 26.)

His *principal* goal is to lead the department in sales.
He is a good producer, but he lacks *principle.*

68. PROCEED, PRECEDE   (See Chapter 19.)

You may *proceed* with your work.
The lieutenant will *precede* you in line.

69. PROVIDED, PROVIDING   (See Chapter 23.)

He will go *provided* you accompany him.
We are *providing* the necessary equipment.

70. RAZE, RAISE   (See Chapter 18.)

We will *raze* the condemned structure and erect an office building.
He asked me to *raise* the window a few inches.

71. REAL, VERY   (See Chapter 18.)

The ring is obviously made of *real* gold.
This machine is *very* (not *real*) efficient.

72. REASON IS BECAUSE   (See Chapter 26.)

AVOID: The *reason* she left early *is because* she is ill.
　USE: She left early *because* she is ill.

73. RESPECTFULLY, RESPECTIVELY   (See Chapter 20.)

We *respectfully* request your presence.
Bill, Ted, and Dick scored 580, 615, and 595, *respectively.*

74. SAME   (See Chapter 26.)

Because the property is perfectly located, you should purchase *it* (not *same*).

75. SELDOM EVER   (See Chapter 20.)

We *seldom* (not *seldom ever*) see their sales representative.

76. SHAPE   (See Chapter 28.)

AVOID: The economy right now is in great *shape.*
　USE: The economy right now is in fine condition.

77. SHOULD OF   (See Chapter 19.)

General Foods *should have* (not *should of*) canceled the order.

78. SO, SO THAT   (See Chapter 23.)

Discuss the project with Evans *so that* (not *so*) he will understand.

79. STATIONARY, STATIONERY   (See Chapter 18.)

The platform will remain *stationary.*
The letter was written on expensive *stationery.*

80. SUSPICION, SUSPECT   (See Chapter 19.)

There is a legitimate reason for our *suspicion.*
We *suspect* a part-time employee of the theft.

81. THEIR, THERE, THEY'RE   (See Chapter 26.)

A few employees are unhappy with *their* working conditions.
There are several topics to be discussed.
I understand that *they're* hoping to sell a million units.

82. TO, TOO, TWO   (See Chapter 20.)

He walked *two* miles *to* the Steed Building.
We plan *to* make the trip *too*.
Do not wait *too* long before leaving.

83. TRY AND, BE SURE AND   (See Chapter 23.)

Please *try to* (not *try and*) finish the work before you leave.
Be *sure to* (not *sure and*) sign both copies of the contract.

84. UNLESS, EXCEPT   (See Chapter 23.)

Fraley will not hear the story *unless* (not *except*) you tell him.

85. WAIT FOR, WAIT ON   (See Chapter 26.)

Please *wait for* me in front of the building.
It is generally wise to tip people who *wait on* you.

86. WAIVE, WAVE   (See Chapter 18.)

I was asked to *waive* my rights to the property.
Wave to me when you reach the top of the building.

87. WEATHER, WHETHER   (See Chapter 19.)

We will go ahead with our plans if the *weather* doesn't change.
He asked me *whether* or not I would drive my own car.

88. WHERE, THAT   (See Chapter 23.)

I heard *that* (not *where*) more stringent motor vehicle laws are being considered.

89. WRIGHT, WRITE, RIGHT   (See Chapter 19.)

Terranova is an excellent *playwright*.
Pelletier will *write* the report sometime this week.
Machado may be able to provide the *right* answer.

ON THE USE OF WHOSE

The word *whose* is the possessive form of the pronoun *who,* which is used to refer to people. Most dictionaries and handbooks of English tell us that we may sometimes avoid an awkward construction by using *whose* to refer to an inanimate object or an animal. The following sentences have been offered as acceptable examples of such usage.

It is the first poem whose publication he ever sanctioned.
He saw rocks whose surfaces glistened with mica.
The play, whose style is rigidly formal, is typical of the period.

More than a hundred language authorities were asked to comment on the acceptability of the preceding sentences. A fourth of them objected to the use of *whose* to refer to the word *play.* All three sentences impress me as being somewhat awkward, primarily because of the manner in which *whose* has been employed.

————————————————— FOR CLASS DISCUSSION —————————————————

Reword the three sentences in question without using the word *whose;* then decide whether your sentences are as acceptable as those that you changed.

A WORD TIP FROM THE REAL WORLD

Have you ever uttered a word worth thousands of dollars? A couple of years ago a physician with a major health care provider made the statement in a television interview that insurance coverage for maternity stays was being decreased and, as a result, the average length of stay was also being decreased. He said that most mothers really were not in need of the sort of *vacation* a three-day stay gave them. The television station was immediately flooded with calls, and the provider company received thousands of angry calls and letters and lost many patients. Not only that, the provider took out newspaper advertisements and sent letters to each family on its patient list, apologizing for the physician's poor choice of words. It was a costly word-choice error for the physician and his entire company, costly to the tune of an estimated $11,000!

_____**WORKSHEET 39**_____

EXECUTIVES' CHOICE

PART A. If the sentence contains an incorrect word, underscore it and write the correct word in the answer space. If the sentence has no error, put a C in the answer space. If you are collaborating, decide as a team what the best answer is.

Example: Be sure <u>and</u> sign your name at the bottom of the page.

_____to_____

1. We were all ready working when David arrived.

1. * _____

2. This supply budget allows for a higher amount of orders in June.

2. * _____

3. I cannot concentrate when telephone calls continuously come in.

3. _____

4. We must keep the furniture in good shape or else we lose our deposit.

4. _____

5. Bozeman will precede with the agenda as soon as Kendall returns.

5. _____

6. You must be able to site the particular portion of the tax code that deals with interstate commerce and transport as it affects our case.

6. _____

7. Our billing system adds each client to the data base irregardless of whether the order comes in person, by fax, by phone, or by e-mail.

7. _____

8. For our department to expend, we will need to sell more books.

8. _____

9. Please appraise me of Henson's availability.

9. _____

10. She will need to alter her afternoon appointment schedule today.

10. _____

11. To reach an agreement, the factions asked an uninterested manager to mediate further conversations.

11. _____

12. We raised capitol by selling shares and by inviting donations.

12. _____

13. The author waved all copyright privileges and permitted duplication.

13. _____

14. She will vote for him whether or not he makes productive changes.

14. _____

15. Be sure and sign the bank signatory card this morning.

15. _____

PART B. In this passage from a memo, discover and underscore thirteen errors in word choice.

The consensus of opinion in the office is that a large amount of applicants will right to us in regards to the open position. I have no doubt but what the process will be all together to much time and my two assistance will be board. The personal department will only have one week to find a party to fill the opening, and the continuous interruptions make the task almost impossible.

PART C. Each of the following sentences contains two or more expressions that would be inappropriate in a business communication. Rewrite each sentence in acceptable form. Note carefully the language usage recommended in this chapter.

1. Urbana banked on the film's success at the box office, of coarse.

   *_____

_____

_____

2. Capitol gains this year will be taxed at an all together unbelievable rate.

_____

_____

_____

3. Will you be able to take a brake from canvasing the neighborhood today?

   *_____

_____

_____

4. The advertising department ordered a large amount of markers recently; they must loose them frequently.

_____

_____

_____

5. Her management decisions are always based on principal and are real well received.

_____

_____

_____

6. We seldom ever have to wait on the downtown couriers; they are quite reliable.

_____

_____

_____

7. The reason we hired him is because someone in personal recommended him.

_____

_____

_____

8. She is an imminent foreign trade consultant who can council us well.

_____

_____

_____

9. When Junker leaves, I expect I will lose my confident.

_____

_____

_____

10. Everyday people in this office get mad about not being aloud in the staff lounge.

_____

_____

_____

11. I doubt but what your team will need to altar the budget very much.

_____

_____

_____

12. My assistants was not needed to affect the repairs on the system.

_____

_____

_____

13. I crave your advise about whether to adapt a new HMO policy.

_____

_____

_____

14. Cheryl could of excepted Andrew as a colleague if he hadn't enthused so much.

_____

_____

_____

15. We can move foreword toward making a deal if the principle players assent.

_____

_____

_____

(if time permits)

If you have been conscientious in your work, you should now be thoroughly familiar with the parts of speech. Here is a short review exercise:

1. Suggest a sentence in which the word *head* is used as a noun, another in which it is used as an adjective, and a third in which it is used as a verb.
2. Suggest a sentence in which the word *since* is used as a preposition, another in which it is used as a conjunction, and a third in which it is used as an adverb.

General Review

■ **POINT TO PONDER**

No one should ever feel self-conscious about using correct grammar.

In this final chapter of the text we will first concentrate upon 20 errors that are commonly made in business writing. The term *error* is, of course, relative. Language that is acceptable in the home may be unacceptable in the office. The language uses discussed in this chapter are *errors* in that they are inappropriate to business and, therefore, inappropriate to the academic community. They have been detected in business letters, business talks, college assignments, and classroom discussions. They have not been listed in order of importance or frequency. Because these problem areas have been covered elsewhere in this text, chapter numbers will be given to indicate where additional information may be found. Here are the 20 errors:

1. **The misuse of plural nouns in the possessive case**   If a noun to be made possessive denotes *more than one,* make certain that you determine the correct plural form before you attempt to make it possessive. Don't forget to add just the apostrophe if the plural form ends in *s;* add an apostrophe and *s* (*'s*) if the plural form ends in another letter of the alphabet. (See Chapter 7.)

    AVOID: The *plumber's* union will not meet this month.
    USE: The *plumbers'* union will not meet this month.

2. **The use of the objective case to modify a gerund**   A noun or pronoun that modifies a gerund must be in the possessive case; such a noun or pronoun really functions as an adjective. Not many college students have mastered this important use of the possessive case. (See Chapter 17.)

    AVOID: We heard about *Brent* failing to pass the examination.
    USE: We heard about *Brent's* failing to pass the examination.

3. **Omission of a hyphen in a compound adjective that precedes the noun modified**
This error has been discovered many times in business writing that is otherwise accurate. The lack of a needed hyphen may thoroughly obscure the meaning of a sentence. (See Chapter 19.)

AVOID: His *rags to riches* background should appeal to the voting public.
USE: His *rags-to-riches* background should appeal to the voting public.

4. **The use of *less* for *fewer*** Many people simply do not make use of the word *fewer*—in spite of its importance to our language. It should be used, as you have learned, to modify most plural nouns. *Less* is used correctly to modify nouns that indicate quantity in bulk. (See Chapter 19.)

AVOID: We have received *less* orders this month.
USE: We have received *fewer* orders this month.
USE: We were paid *less* money than we deserved.

5. **The use of the comparative degree of an adjective to modify a verb** Verbs, as you know, must be modified by adverbs, not adjectives. Even well-educated speakers, however, tend to have difficulty in using the comparative degree of adverbs. (See Chapter 20.)

AVOID: This printer runs *smoother* than that one.
USE: This printer runs *more smoothly* than that one.

6. **The use of *real* for *really*** The word *real* is basically and historically an adjective. As such, it should be used to modify nouns and pronouns. In recent years it has been used as an adverb by people in all walks of life. In spite of its present popularity, the use of *real* as an adverb is not good business practice. (See Chapter 20.)

AVOID: Kane's new secretary is *real* efficient.
USE: Kane's new secretary is *really* (or *very*) efficient.

7. **The use of a plural pronoun when *everybody* (or *everyone*) is the antecedent** This error is made by some of our finest speakers. It seems to be the type that just "slips out" before a person realizes what he or she has said. Keep in mind that *everybody* (or *everyone*) is singular, takes a singular verb, and must be referred to with a singular pronoun. (See Chapter 11.)

AVOID: Everybody will please do *their* own work.
USE: Everybody will please do *his or her* own work.

8. **The use of a nominative-case pronoun as an object** When a verb or a preposition has more than one object, make certain that all object pronouns are in the objective case. (See Chapter 9.)

AVOID: Promotions were given to Lipton, Palley, and *I*.
USE: Promotions were given to Lipton, Palley, and *me*.

9. **The use of the superlative degree in comparing only two objects or people** Like the others, this error occurs with great frequency. We should use an adjective or an adverb in the superlative degree only when we refer to *more than two*. (See Chapter 19.)

AVOID: Of the two investment programs analyzed, I like yours *best*.
USE: Of the two investment programs analyzed, I like yours *better*.

10. **The use of *whom* as a subject when a parenthetical expression follows** The use of *whom* poses a problem for most people. It is especially important for the business writer to use this word accurately. The choice between *who* and *whom* seems most difficult when a parenthetical expression follows the subject *who*. (See Chapter 11.)

> AVOID: *Whom* do you think will attend the convention in Dallas?
> USE: *Who* do you think will attend the convention in Dallas?

11. **The use of a pronoun such as *which* or *that* with no specific antecedent** A single word or expression should generally serve as the antecedent of a pronoun. Too often a pronoun introducing an adjective clause refers vaguely to a preceding clause or sentence. (See Chapter 25.)

> AVOID: We just addressed 2,500 envelopes, *which* wasn't easy.
> USE: We just addressed 2,500 envelopes, *which* must now be sealed.
> USE: We just completed the difficult task of addressing 2,500 envelopes.

12. **The use of a needless *a* or *an* in expressions such as *type of person*** The indefinite article (*a, an*) is frequently employed when it contributes nothing to the meaning of the sentence. (See Chapter 18.)

> AVOID: What kind of *a* program are you planning?
> USE: What kind of program are you planning?

13. **The omission of *other* or *else* in comparing a person or thing with others in the same group** It seems surprising that a word as important as *other* or *else* is so often omitted by business writers who make such comparisons. (See Chapter 19.)

> AVOID: The president has a larger vocabulary *than any* executive in our firm.
> USE: The president has a larger vocabulary *than any other* executive in our firm.

14. **The use of *lay* for *lie*** This error may be the most common one of all, yet the average adult has no good excuse for confusing these two words. The rules should not pose a great challenge. (See Chapter 15.)

> AVOID: You should *lay* down for a few minutes.
> USE: You should *lie* down for a few minutes.

15. **The use of the past tense for the past perfect tense** The past perfect tense tends to be neglected. It should be employed to express an action that was completed at a specific time in the past. (See Chapter 14.)

> AVOID: I *left* the office by the time the auditor arrived.
> USE: I *had left* the office by the time the auditor arrived.

16. **The use of *was* for the subjunctive *were*** Too many people fail to understand that the subjunctive mood should be used to express ideas that are contrary to fact. *Were* is the usual sign of the subjunctive. (See Chapter 12.)

> AVOID: The manager would be upset if she *was* here now.
> USE: The manager would be upset if she *were* here now.

17. **The misplacement of the word *only*** Since the word *only* may function as an adjective or an adverb, it is used to modify nouns, pronouns, adjectives, and verbs. As a

result, a speaker or writer must give careful thought to its placement in a sentence. It should be placed so as to modify the word intended. (See Chapter 18.)

AVOID: We *only* have five branch offices.
USE: We have *only* five branch offices.

18. **The use of *like* as a conjunction**   The word *like,* which is perfectly acceptable as a verb, an adjective, or a preposition, should not be employed to introduce a clause. The use of *like* as a conjunction is considered to be illiterate or, at best, informal. Certainly such usage is not recommended in business. (See Chapter 21.)

AVOID: It seems *like* the plans will be accepted.
USE: It seems *as if* (or *that*) the plans will be accepted.

19. **The use of *between* for *among***   The word *between* is often used inappropriately to refer to more than two people or objects. (See Chapter 21.)

AVOID: The jury members will discuss the case *between* themselves.
USE: The jury members will discuss the case *among* themselves.
USE: He was asked to choose *between* the two leading brands.

20. **The use of *than* after *different***   Authorities agree upon the use of *from* as a preposition following the word *different. Different than* is sometimes used in informal writing if a clause follows immediately. (See Chapter 21.)

AVOID: This periodical is different *than* the others.
USE: This periodical is different *from* the others.

Another 20 Reminders

In this chapter and the one preceding, we have reviewed specific constructions and word choices discussed in earlier parts of the text. We will now look at several other important parts of the text—but in a more general way. It would be impossible, in a single short chapter, to touch upon *all* the principles, rules, and suggestions presented in a text of this length. It is possible, however, to bring to your attention again the rules and concepts that tend to give the greatest difficulty to students of business English. If you need additional information concerning the 20 items reviewed here, use your index to find the appropriate pages.

1. To find the simple subject of a clause, find the verb; then ask *Who (verb)?* or *What (verb)?* For example, in the sentence *Notice to evacuate the building was given on Monday,* the verb is *was given.* You would find the subject by asking the question *What was given?* Because the subject (*notice*) is singular, a singular verb was chosen.

2. To find the direct object of a verb, first find the verb; then ask *(Verb) what?* or *(Verb) whom?* For example, in the sentence *Fisher recommended Becker and me for promotion,* the verb is *recommended.* You would find the direct objects (*Becker, me*) by asking the question *Recommended whom?* Because all objects must be in the objective case, *me* (not *I*) was used.

3. Remember that a prepositional phrase is just a modifier. As such, it cannot affect the number (singular/plural) of the subject. Consider this sentence: *A man with several years of experience and an immense capacity for work is difficult to find.* In spite of the long prepositional phrase, the simple subject is *man,* which is singular. The verb, *is,* you will note, is also singular.

4. Remember that a singular noun is generally made possessive by the addition of an apostrophe and *s* (*'s*); for example, *manager's, lady's, Mr. Cross's, Charles's.* If the singular noun has more than one syllable and ends in the sound of *s* or *z,* the addition of *apostrophe s* (*'s*) may lead to a very awkward pronunciation. The apostrophe alone may be added in such cases; for example, *Ulysses', Diogenes', Gonzalez'.*

5. Remember that some indefinite pronouns—*some, all, any, none*—may be singular or plural, depending upon their reference. *Some of the men* would be a plural subject because *some* refers to a plural noun. *Some of the money* would be considered singular because *some* refers to *money,* a singular noun.

    Some of the guests (plural) *have* left.
    Some of the ink (singular) *has* spilled.

6. Remember that personal pronouns in the possessive case are *not* written with apostrophes.

    We took *ours* and they took *theirs.*

7. Remember that pronouns serving as subject complements (after linking verbs) should be in the nominative case.

    The delegates will be Busch, Dawes, and *I.*
    The oldest person here is either *he* or Dobson.

8. Remember that the active voice of a verb is generally stronger than the passive. It is sometimes awkward to employ both active and passive voices in the main clauses of a compound sentence.

    AVOID: We will meet Donley, and an attempt to collect the money will be made.
    USE: We will meet Donley and attempt to collect the money.

9. Know the difference between transitive and intransitive verbs. The use of a transitive verb in the active voice but with no object is extremely awkward. The use of an intransitive verb *with* an object may be just as bad.

    AVOID: I am going to *set* here for a few minutes.
    USE: I am going to *sit* here for a few minutes.
    AVOID: I am going to *defer* for a few days.
    USE: I am going to *defer judgment* for a few days.

10. Remember that verbs are used in three moods: indicative, imperative, and subjunctive. The indicative mood is used to make statements and to ask questions; the imperative, to issue commands and make requests; the subjunctive, to express ideas that are contrary to fact.

    INDICATIVE MOOD: She *enjoys* her work.
    IMPERATIVE MOOD: *Help* him lift the cabinet.
    SUBJUNCTIVE MOOD: I wish he *were* more capable.

11. Recognize the difference between restrictive and nonrestrictive adjective clauses. A restrictive clause cannot be removed from a sentence without seriously changing the meaning of that sentence. Such clauses must never be set off with commas.

    RESTRICTIVE CLAUSE: The employee *who works hard* will get ahead.
    NONRESTRICTIVE CLAUSE: Ben Cord, *who works hard,* will get ahead.

PART E. Select the preferred method of writing numbers.

      A. The italicized number should be written as a figure and should be followed by *nd, rd, st,* or *th.*

      B. The italicized number should be written in figures as shown.

      C. The italicized number should be written as a word (or words).

Example: The meeting was held on May *19,* 1992.   B
_____

1. The program will begin at *8* o'clock.   1. _____

2. *27* people voted against the motion.   2. *_____

3. You will need 50 *10*-cent stamps.   3. _____

4. The address of the Marvin Company is *10* Maple Avenue.   4. _____

5. By the *23* of August we should have the information.   5. _____

6. We made a small profit for *4* consecutive years.   6. _____

7. We hope to finish our work by *5* P.M.   7. _____

8. There is a shortage of *9* items.   8. _____

9. This store will not be open on the *6* of May.   9. _____

10. You have *$435.64* in your checking account.   10. _____

PART F. You are to underscore each error that you find and write the correct form in the space provided. Look for errors in punctuation, as well as in grammar and word usage. If the sentence contains no errors, put a C in the space.

Example: The large bookcase is Mr. Burns's, the small one is mine.   _____;_____

         We received <u>less</u> orders on Tuesday than on Monday.   _____fewer_____

1. It seems like we ought to postpone this project.   1. *_____

2. Did Hendrix say, "The office will be closed on Monday"?   2. _____

3. I work slower on these documents than I did on the spreadsheets.   3. *_____

4. Chen, who improved our software will not attend the grand opening.   4. _____

5. The last time I saw the report, it was laying on the file cabinet.   5. _____

6. I had not heard about Kingsley Company merging with DataWeb.   6. *_____

7. The new health insurance forms are different than the old ones.   7. _____

8. Office Shipping, Inc., made a real important difference in our service.   8. _____

9. Fontana was part of the much maligned firm of Gentry Associates.

9. _____

10. When everybody makes their year-end report, we must collect them.

10. _____

11. Young would head this task force if she was still in this department.

11. _____

12. (name is Jones) Copies of the Jones report were sent to Hall, Scheerer and me.

12. _____

13. They've donated a refrigerator to use for the employee's lunches.

13. _____

14. He asked, "Where does the budget discussion fall on the agenda"?

14. _____

15. Headquarters acquiesced to their demands but not to our's.

15. _____

16. Our six voting member's seats were empty at the 2:00 recess.

16. _____

17. Were Wilson more conscious of his colleagues, he would see their anger.

17. _____

18. Looking at Mac and IBM only, Mac has the strongest "kid appeal."

18. _____

19. Jenson is always on time, Samuels is always late.

19. _____

20. Certainly we knew about Harding taking over Southpark Enterprises.

20. _____

21. Our proposal presentation was well rehearsed, and the board loved it.

21. _____

22. Our sales teammates feel like they lose in each planning meeting.

22. _____

23. What would Krupke do if he was here now?

23. _____

24. (name is Allen) Allens' plan was received well by both parties.

24. _____

25. By next Tuesday we will finish the tax computations.

25. _____

26. These data were collected using a new method of research.

26. _____

27. Laminated covers give a real polished appearance.

27. _____

28. The only ones having chicken kiev at the banquet were Davis and I.

28. _____

29. Whom do you believe will perform better than they did last year?

29. _____

30. Grace will be at the 9:00 A.M. meeting; I will join her at 10:00 A.M.

30. _____

PART G. Rewrite the following sentences, each of which contains one or more of the errors discussed in this chapter.

1. There have been less breakdowns this month than last, which pleases our production supervisor.

   *_____

   _____

2. The actuarys convention went real good, just like you said it would.

   _____

   _____

3. The component you need is laying on my desk between several other items.

   _____

   _____

4. Mr. Cracow asked me about Leon only working one day last week.

   _____

   _____

5. Whom did Ms. Tregasis say is a more dedicated worker than anyone on earth?

   _____

   _____

6. The fittings you sent are different than the ones described in your catalog, which is why we returned them.

   _____

   _____

7. It seems like Kanitz mailed the stockholder's proxies out a week to late.

   _____

   _____

8. If everybody uses their own computers, we will only have to supply the software.

   _____

   _____

9. We are real pleased to hear about Norris getting the promotion, for he is more deserving than any employee of the firm.

   _____

   _____

10. This company bought corn futures in the commodities market, which was a wise thing to do.

   _____

   _____

PART H. This paragraph from an interoffice memo passed the computer spellcheck test. All of its words are real, English words. However, as you are about to discover, many of them are used incorrectly. Try to find and underscore the twelve errors in this brief paragraph, and then remind yourself that faulty word choice is often missed even with the best of computer aids.

No one knows better then me how difficult life in this office can be; employees, who work real hard are sometimes overlooked irregardless of there talent and effort. In regards to this problem, I would like to institute a new program, just between the twelve of us in the shipping department. Everyone of us will submit the name of one of our co-workers each month for special recognition. We'll draw the name of one employee out of a hat on the first day of each month, and that party will win a gift certificate to The Cafe on Lake Street. This is a small prize, but I hope it will keep us from continuing to loose moral. Let's recommend one another generously and have a real good time doing it!

_____ FOR CLASS DISCUSSION _____

(if time permits)

This textbook contains many rules—too many for the average reader to remember easily. Those that are needed most frequently, such as the ones that govern plural forms, are likely to be mastered first. Can you recall the rules that tell how the plural forms of the following singular nouns should be spelled?

1. switch	**3.** subsidiary	**5.** piano	**7.** sister-in-law
2. pulley	**4.** curio	**6.** analysis	**8.** Murphy

THE IMPACT OF LANGUAGE

WHAT'S IMPLIED?

It is interesting to note that the conjunction *than,* although frequently followed by a pronoun in the nominative case, is sometimes followed by a pronoun in the objective case. Note these two acceptable constructions:

1. No one is more trustworthy than *she.*
2. The supervisor trusts no one more than *her.*

_____ FOR CLASS DISCUSSION _____

In sentence 1 the word *is* has obviously been implied after *she.* Justify the use of *her* in sentence 2 by determining the words that have been implied.

HOW TO IDENTIFY A COMPLEMENT

A friend of mine once asked me why the word *burning* would not be considered a subject complement in the sentence *The house is burning.* Although it does seem to modify the subject (the *burning house*), grammarians would consider it to be part of the phrase *is burning,* which is a progressive form of the verb. We will recognize *burn* as a verb if we attempt to conjugate it (I burn, you burn, he burns, etc.).

If, however, the sentence read *The house is unattractive,* we would have to consider the word *unattractive* to be an adjective used as a subject complement and the word *is* to be a linking verb. There is no way that we can conjugate *unattractive.* Can you pick out the subject complements in two of these sentences?

The proposed plan will be adopted in June.
Several workers in the stenographic pool are unhappy.
Only one person in the class is failing.
The new office building will be magnificent.

A WORD TIP FROM THE REAL WORLD

When you're out in the real world, for example, standing in line at a fast food place, and the person in front of you is placing an order, notice what runs through your head as the cashier says, "$2.96. Have you got a penny?" and the person in front of you says, "No, I don't got one." What do you think about that person? Most people would probably notice the ungrammatical remark and react in a slightly, not excessively, negative way. Most people would think the person careless or perhaps a bit lazy. We wouldn't attack the person's character or integrity, but we probably would not give the person credit for much experience in learning.

It's too bad, but that's exactly what happens when an otherwise intelligent person lets ungrammatical speech slip out when conversing with someone who knows what sounds proper. The person with the good ear will never decide not to trust the ungrammatical person's character, but some deep and troubling judgment is made about intelligence and diligent effort. If it's true when you're standing in line at Burger King, it's true in the business world at large.

POSTTEST (OPTIONAL)

DIRECTIONS: Consider carefully each of the 25 sentences that follow. Underscore any word, word combination, punctuation mark, or abbreviation that would be unacceptable in business; then write the preferred form in the space provided. If a sentence is perfectly acceptable as printed, place a C in the space.

Example: Orson discussed the project with Shelby
and I.

_____me_____

1. Neither your office or Collins's is large enough to accommodate 20 people.

1. _____

2. Sol told me about Casey's enrolling in three Economics classes.

2. _____

3. The plastic is manufactured here, the valves are manufactured in Salt Lake City.

3. _____

4. Neither Lujack nor I am willing to move to the west.

4. _____

5. Farley & Lenz, Inc., is not likely to reduce their price.

5. _____

6. Gorski, as well as her administrative assistant, is from the State of Kansas.

6. _____

7. My brother-in-laws both work at our plant in the South.

7. _____

8. Mr. Ruiz's team members will be Remick, Holtz, and me.

8. _____

9. He will be called as the principle witness at both courts-martial.

9. _____

10. The Murphys appeared to be uninterested in Hawkins's problem.

10. _____

11. Our group of 22 people is in Washington to attend a session of Congress.

11. _____

12. Kulak's new word processor corresponds with mine.

12. _____

13. Fertig's leaving certainly had a negative affect upon the group.

13. _____

14. He assumed a holier than thou attitude to make me feel bad.

14. _____

15. Their real conservative accountant is the more reliable of the two men.

15. _____

16. Dora Lemkey is one of the ten applicants who has been interviewed.

16. _____

17. He will probably give the samples to whoever wants them.

17. _____

18. Please try and get Curtis's attention.

18. _____

19. There are a desk and a typewriter that you can use for the next hour.

19. _____

20. If Sam was as near retirement as I am, he would be uninterested in the merger.

20. _____

21. My copy of the report is different from the one laying there on your desk.

21. _____

22. Before leaving for Cincinnati, she lay down for 15 minutes.

22. _____

23. Kirsten assured me that Georgia was farther south than Kentucky.

23. _____

24. I imply from your remark that you haven't heard about Mario's being selected.

24. _____

25. All four and five-bedroom houses in this tract have been sold.

25. _____

WHO IS *YOU?*

The executive vice president of a textile firm received a memorandum from an accountant in her department. It contained this message:

We were hoping that the software related to cost accounting would be compatible with our new Apple computer. It appears, however, that you cannot use the two together. Jefferson, who ordered the software because it was generously discounted, will undoubtedly want to return it. I told him that you should always be careful to ask about compatibility before ordering.

_____ FOR CLASS DISCUSSION _____

The word *you* is among those words most frequently misused in our language. It should not have been employed in the preceding paragraph; yet it appears twice. Tell why it should not have been used and then attempt to reword the sentences in question.

KEY ITEMS

WORKSHEET 1

PART A   In this exercise we highlight nine colloquialisms.

PART B
1. failure   There are, of course, other possible answers to each of the items in Part B.
3. had to settle for

PART C
1. about   There are other possible answers to each item here.
2. except
3. $1,000

PART D
1. A
2. B
3. B
4. A
5. A

PART E
1. du   Note that the phonetic spelling, which ordinarily appears in parentheses, follows the main entry word in your dictionary. The accent mark generally follows the syllable to be stressed. In a few dictionaries it precedes the stressed syllable.
2. ra
3. mis

PART F
2. B   Your dictionary undoubtedly shows *ec-sta-sy.*
3. D

OPTION 1
3. Old Norse   To find the derivation of a word, look at the etymology [in brackets]. The language mentioned *last* is likely to be the language in which the word originated.
5. noun, verb, and adjective   Note the abbreviations *n, vt.,* and *adj.*
8. slēve   The phonetic spelling is shown in a dictionary entry in parentheses.

OPTION 2
1. C
2. A

Watching the Web—Chapter 1

    Make Money from your Home

    Don't wait another day. Start to use your at-home time to make you rich. Many people have already discovered success. Please use this opportunity to take the chance to get to know us, and we are sure that you will see we're on the level.

    On the level is a phrase that is too casual for business use but commonly used in conversation.

WORKSHEET 2

PART A
2. outwitted, outwitting   See Rule 2 in Chapter 2.
7. occurred, occurrence
12. permitted, permitting

PART B
1. judgment—an exception to Rule 3
4. encouragement   Because the suffix begins with a consonant, the final *e* in *encourage* should not be dropped.

435

11. peaceable   The root word ends with the soft sound of *ce*. The final letter should not be dropped if *able* or *ous* is added to a word that ends with the soft sound of *ce* or *ge*.

PART C   **3.** deceiving   See Rule 4.

4. neighbor   The *ei* combination in this word is pronounced with the sound of long *a*.

PART D   **1.** inaudible

3. illegible

PART E   The two errors in the date and address lines and the eight errors in the body of this letter would not all be caught by a computer spell-check program. Read carefully.

PART F   **1.** aggressive

4. occasionally

OPTION 2   **1.** Leave this line blank. There is no error.

2. knowledge

3. convenient

4. eminent

5. Leave this line blank. There is no error.

WORKSHEET 3

PART A   **1.** verb

2. conjunction

PART B   **1.** N   Remember that all names are nouns.

2. P   *It* substitutes for workshop in sentence 1.

3. N

14. P   Words like *anyone* and *someone* are pronouns.

PART C   **1.** A   Bronson is a name (noun).

2. C   *Said* expresses a kind of action.

3. B

4. C   The verb *was* expresses a *state of being*.

5. A

PART D   **1.** quickly (B)   The adverb *quickly* modifies the verb *learned*.

2. well (B)   This adverb modifies *does organize*.

3. enthusiastic (A)   This adjective modifies the noun *Rankin*. It follows a linking verb and may be referred to as a predicate adjective.

PART E   **1.** or (B)   *Or*, like all conjunctions, is a connective.

2. on (A)   *On the platform* is a prepositional phrase.

3. but (B)   The two most common conjunctions are *and* and *but*.

PART F   **1.** When   The word *when* can join clauses (discussed in next chapter).

2. and

7. or   The word *or* is always a conjunction.

PART G   **1.** Underscore *in foreign businesses*.   This phrase modifies *investments*.

2. Underscore *to questionable factories*.   This phrase modifies *ties*.

3. Underscore *in some cases*.   This phrase modifies *operate*. Keep in mind that prepositional phrases are used to modify, limit, or describe— just as adjectives and adverbs are.

8. Underscore *from them*.   This phrase modifies *learn*.

PART H   **1.** B   Strong resumés use clear action verbs to demonstrate confidence and competence.

5. A   School subjects are considered nouns and feature prominently in a resumé's *Education* section.

OPTION 1   **1.** has decided

2. Complete

8. Will vote

OPTION 3   **1.** A   **2.** B   The adjective *enormous* modifies the noun *salary*. The adverb *recently* modifies the verb *was given.*

            3. B   **4.** A   *Compelling* modifies the noun *speech.*

WORKSHEET 4

PART A	**1.**	B
PART B	**1.**	Underscore *good problem solving skills* since it contains no subject or verb.
PART C	**1.**	A Note the absence of a subject-verb combination.
	2.	B This fragment *does* contain a subject-verb combination; therefore, it is a clause.
	3.	C
	4.	A
	5.	A
PART D	**1.**	people To find the subject, ask, *Who takes?* The underscored phrases are simply modifiers.
	2.	packages Ask the question *What are currently available?*
	3.	some Ask the question *What offers a system?*
	5.	type
PART E	**1.**	conference To find the direct object, ask, *Will host what?*
	2.	*location* *Didn't learn what?*
	3.	*plans* *Is making what?*
OPTION 1	**1.**	B *Takes* answers *What does planning a meeting do?*
	2.	A *Planning* answers *What pays good dividends?*
	4.	C *Purpose* answers *Should evaluate what?*
	14.	C *Notes* has as its object *them; checks* has as its object *appropriateness.*
OPTION 2	**3.**	A possible response: Thomas Aguilar has been an attorney for more than 20 years.
OPTION 3	**1.**	A possible response: The book he chose was written by Charles Dickens, a novelist of the nineteenth century.

WORKSHEET 5

PART B	**1.**	Underscore *Mother.* Put a 1 in the answer space.
	5.	Underscore *Purchasing* and *Agent.* Put a 2 in the answer space.
	16.	Underscore *Executive, Assistant,* and *Councilwoman.* Put a 3 in the answer space.
PART D	**1.**	An acceptable response: The embroidery used tiny french knots.
	2.	An acceptable response: Final approval rests with the French government.

Watching the Web—Chapter 5

     Limited time offer! Exquisitely reconditioned cars available now!
No matter whether you come from North, East, West, or South, when you see this offer <u>your</u> not going to believe your eyes.
*The underscored *your* should read *you're.*

WORKSHEET 6

PART A	**2.**	CPAs Underscore *CPA's*
	6.	portfolios Underscore *portfolioes.*
PART B	**4.**	valleys If a singular noun ends in *y* preceded by a vowel, simply add *s* to make it plural.
	5.	radios If a noun ends with *o* preceded by a vowel, simply add an *s.*
PART C	**1.**	banjos Follow principle 6b.
PART D	**1.**	are Underscore *crises,* the simple plural subject.
PART E	**3.**	An acceptable response: These bacteria are not really harmful.

WORKSHEET 7

PART A	**2.**	Claus's Clauses' See rule 2, page 76.
PART B	**2.**	board members' beliefs
	7.	Jones's (or Jones') reply
PART C	**3.**	B The sentence refers to *this* company (singular).
	7.	C This sentence refers to the *questions* of clients (plural).
PART D	**1.**	years' Underscore the word *year's*.
	3.	conventions Underscore the word *convention's*.

WORKSHEET 8

PART A	**1.**	F
	2.	F
	3.	T
PART B	**1.**	B
	5.	D The prepositional phrase in the sentence is *about meetings*.
PART C	**2.**	B Because *men* is already plural, simply add *'s* to denote a locker room for many men.
	4.	C
	6.	C
	7.	A *Rabinowitzes* has not been used in the possessive case. An *es* is added to make a proper noun ending in a *z* sound plural.
PART D	**7.**	B There is no reason to capitalize *tax base*.
	10.	C

Watching the Web—Chapter 8

CD-ROM Encyclopedia of Cooking
This is the last cookbook you'll ever need. The <u>reason</u> you'll love it is <u>because</u>, on one CD, we have included over 7,000 recipes, many with full-color photographs, for your family's enjoyment! You'll love it. You have our guarantee.
*This is a redundancy. Only one of the two underscored words is needed. We could rewrite the sentence in any of several ways: *The reason you'll love it is, on one CD, . . .* or *You'll love it because, on one CD, . . .*

WORKSHEET 9

PART A	**1.**	A Underscore *I*, which is the subject of *will be*.
	2.	C Underscore *me*, the object of the preposition *to*.
	3.	B Underscore *them*, the object of the verb *add*.
PART B	**1.**	she The antecedent of *she* is Sara Belize.
	2.	him *Except him* is a prepositional phrase.
PART D	**2.**	him and me Use the objective case after the preposition *to*.
	5.	themselves Use the compound pronoun to refer to the noun *visitors* which closely precedes it.
	6.	him *Him* is the object of the preposition *except*.
PART E	**1.**	angry The word *mad* means "mentally deranged."
OPTION 1	**1.**	first
	2.	neuter
OPTION 2	**1.**	A possible response: This company opened *its* doors in 1940.

Watching the Web—Chapter 9

Visit the website voted "most interesting" by TAO: Travel Agents Online. See our special offers for travel in and out of Europe for this summer. Order air, hotel, car, or rail coupons online. If you need <u>assistants</u> in accessing the hyperlinks on this site, click here:
*Here *assistants* should read *assistance*.

WORKSHEET 10

PART B
1. candidate
2. firm . . . certain of the *firm's* subsidiaries.

PART C
1. his or her   *Many a business person* is singular.
2. their   *Brokers* is plural.
4. his or her   *Anyone* is singular.
6. his or her   *No one* is singular.

PART E
1. In order to reach Macy's personnel division, a person must walk through the store.

WORKSHEET 11

PART B
1. his or her   *Each,* the subject, is singular. The prepositional phrase (*of our conference managers*) is simply a modifier.
2. her or his   *Everyone,* the antecedent, is singular.
6. anyone   This expression, like *someone* and *everyone,* should be written as two words only if an of-phrase follows.

PART C
1. his or her   *Either* is the antecedent of this item; either is always singular.

PART D
6. whom   This pronoun is correct because it serves as the object of the preposition *to.*
7. who   *Who* is the subject of the verb *ordered* and is in the nominative case.
11. A noun clause, *Whoever controls the budget,* serves here as the subject of the verb *controls.* The subject of that clause is *Whoever;* the direct object is *budget.*

PART E
3. *Who's* means *who is.* Here the writer wants the possessive form of *who: whose.*

OPTION 1
15. hers, her   The antecedent is *each,* which is always singular. The pronoun *her* must agree with *each.*

WORKSHEET 12

PART A
1. is   The subject, *analyst,* is singular.

PART B
5. (p) Ginsberg, mother

PART C
5. is   The simple subject is *exposure* (singular). Ignore the phrase *not to mention the commanding view.*
6. give   The subject is plural: *view* and *center.*
7. agrees   The subject (*Rosa Lopez*) is singular. Ignore the modifying phrase between the subject and the verb.

PART D
1. *Are* is plural verb; it cannot be used with the singular subject, *Clinton and Clinton Electric.*

PART E
2. was   Our group was indeed smaller at one time. The idea expressed is not contrary to fact.
4. were   Use the subjunctive *were* to express an idea that is contrary to fact. The wording of the sentence tells us that our previous manager is not still here.

PART F
1. Change *was* to *were.* Write something like this: The subjunctive (*were*) should be used to express an idea that is contrary to fact.

OPTION 1
13. B   Any subject modified by *every* is singular.
14. A
17. B   Any subject modified by *each* is singular.

Watching the Web—Chapter 12

Tandy's Sales Seminars
<u>Every one one of Tandy's certified trainers absolutely guarantee</u> that you will finish your on-line seminar fully equipped to sell your product in three new markets in the coming month, or your money back.

*This is an error in agreement. The subject is *every one* (singular), yet the verb is *guarantee* (plural). Adding an s to the verb would solve the problem (*every one . . . guarantees*).

WORKSHEET 13

PART A example   A   The subject, *person,* will do the answering.

      1.   P   The subject, *Williams,* did not send anything. Someone is sending Williams.

      3.   P   Compare with active voice: I will invite you.

PART B   **2.**   I   The verb *seem* is a linking verb.

      7.   T   The subject, *research,* was acted upon; therefore, the verb is in the passive voice. Verbs in the passive voice are *always* transitive.

      9.   I   The verb has no object. It is followed by prepositional phrases.

PART C   Remember, to change a passive construction into active voice, look first for the one who is acting or doing something. Then make sure that word is the subject of the sentence. Next, follow it with an action verb.

PART D   **2.**   Underscore *have had.* Find the direct object by asking the question *Have had what?* Write *information* (DO).

      5.   Underscore *are,* the verb. In the answer space write *busy* (SC). The complement modifies the subject (*Analysts*).

PART E   **2.**   At our meeting this afternoon Mr. Ramirez will answer your questions concerning personal computers.

Watching the Web—Chapter 13

Gentlemen, Wouldn't you love to have a full head of hair again? Wouldn't you love to get it with no nasty side <u>affects</u>? Just click here to <u>recieve</u> some information that might just make your day!

*An easy-to-miss spelling error: *receive*

An error of word choice: use *effects,* not *affects*

WORKSHEET 14

PART A   **5.**   E   All verbs in the past perfect tense include the helping verb *had.*

      6.   C

PART B   **1.**   is

      2.   were demonstrating   Use the past progressive tense because the action was in progress for several days.

PART C   **2.**   had gone   The past perfect tense is used here to express an action (the going) that came before another past action.

      5.   will have begun   The *beginning* will take place before another future action (the reaching of Paris).

PART D   **1.**   present perfect   The helping verb *have* or *has* is used to build the present perfect tense.

      4.   present (emphatic)

PART E   **1.**   appreciated   will appreciate

PART F   **1.**   A possible response: He has learned his lesson.

PART G   **1.**   counsel is correct

      2.   consensus

Watching the Web—Chapter 14

Enroll in our on-line investment club today. You will receive the most up-to-the-minute market information daily. You will discover market patterns that have until now been known and understood only by investment professionals. You will also read expert <u>advise</u> from top brokerage firms in our new commentary section. Interested? Click here.

Advise should be spelled *advice,* since it is used here as a noun, not a verb.

WORKSHEET 15

PART A   **1.**   T

      2.   T

PART B   **3.**   lay   The simple form of the present tense has been used. Note that the object of this transitive verb is *groundwork.*

      5.   laid

PART C	2.	spent Use the past participle with a helping verb (*are*).
	4.	shaken
	8.	struck or stricken Either word is acceptable.
PART E	1.	dug dug
	2.	froze frozen
	4.	swam swum
PART F	1.	An acceptable response: One book on this list has been banned in Boston.

WORKSHEET 16

PART A	1.	we
PART B	2.	Underscore *was sold*. The verb is in the passive voice because the subject, *connector*, did not *act* in any way. Put a *P* in the space.
	6.	Underscore *have put*. The subject, *we*, did the acting (the *putting*). Put an *A* in the answer space.
PART C	2.	I The verb must be intransitive because it is in the active voice and it has no object.
	9.	T The verb *make* must be transitive because it is in the active voice and has an object, *case*.
PART D	1.	B The word *apprise* means "to notify" or "to inform."
PART E	1.	A
	2.	B
	19.	B *The number* is always singular.
	27.	B Use the subjunctive, since the speaker is not in the old place.

Watching the Web—Chapter 16

CIGN Search Engine for Windows 97

"The best engine you can get for the money!" CyberWeekly

Every web user needs to check out this great offer, get out their MasterCard or Visa number, and order today.

*This is an error in agreement. The subject is *every web user* (singular), yet later in the sentence the possessive pronoun is *their* (plural). Using *his or her* would solve the problem (*every web user . . . his or her MasterCard . . .*). Another solution would be to remain entirely in the plural: All web users need to check out this great offer, get out their MasterCard or Visa numbers, and order today.

WORKSHEET 17

PART A	1.	B The word *writing* is a gerund because it is a verb form, it ends in *ing*, and it has been used as a noun (a subject).
	2.	D
PART B	1.	Jenkins's Use the possessive-case form of a noun or pronoun to modify a gerund *(handling)*. In this instance the gerund serves as the object of the verb enjoy.
	2.	Having been This form of the participle was used because its action took place prior to the action of the main verb (*was hired*). Jenkins was a consultant before she was hired here.
PART C	1.	to gain
	3.	to have originated Use the perfect infinitive because its action (the originating) took place prior to the action of the main verb, *is believed*, which is in the present tense.
PART D	1.	A Underscore *to visit*
	2.	B The infinitive is *to plan*. Underscore those two words. The infinitive is split by the words *more effectively*.
PART E	1.	B The verbal phrase, *Looking for a bargain*, modifies the word *people* and is properly placed.
	2.	A The verbal phrase relates to the word *you (understood)* or to some other consumer, not to premiums or policies.
PART F	1.	To do the job properly, you should use a power drill.

WORKSHEET 18

PART B	**1.**	Underscore *kind of a.* Write *kind of* in the answer space.
	5.	Underscore *only waited.* Write *waited only* in the answer space.
PART C	**1.**	an Use *an* because a vowel sound follows.
	2.	a The word *hall* begins with a consonant.
PART D	**3.**	pressed past Although *rose above* does tell the reader that Kozinski exceeded his goals, it is more hackneyed than *pressed past,* which contains more vivid imagery.
PART E	**3.**	have only
PART F	**1.**	foreward—replace with forward
	2.	eminent—replace with imminent

WORKSHEET 19

PART A	**2.**	most We can assume there are more than two accounts.
	3.	any other
	4.	*Well hidden* is at the end of the question.
PART C	**1.**	should have *Have,* not *of,* is a verb.
	10.	fewer *Less* should not be used with plural nouns that are countable, such as *pages.*
PART E	**5.**	past The adjective *past* modifies the noun *decade.*

Watching the Web—Chapter 19

How's your mileage?
If you're paying today's higher gas prices but getting <u>less</u> miles to the gallon, here's something you've been waiting for: ME<u>A</u> (mileage extender additive)
*Use *fewer* rather then *less* for countable things like miles.

WORKSHEET 20

PART A	**1.**	A If you had been asked to complete the sentence, you probably would have suggested an adverb like *well* or *satisfactorily.*
PART B	**1.**	profitably
	6.	typically If an adjective ends in *al (typical),* the adverb will ordinarily end in *ally.*
PART C	**11.**	good The adjective follows the linking verb *will feel.*
	12.	well Underscore the verb, *have done.* Note that we have chosen an adverb to modify a verb.
PART D	**8.**	all ready
	15.	formally
	17.	most
PART E	**1.**	once
	6.	also
OPTION 1	**2.**	Underscore *good.* Write *well* in the answer space.
	6.	Underscore *slower.* Write *more slowly* in the answer space. The adverb is needed to modify *moving.*

WORKSHEET 21

PART A	**1.**	T
PART B	**1.**	Underscore *in.* Write *into* in the answer space.
	2.	Underscore *with* and write *of.* The adjective *cognizant* is always followed by the preposition *of.*
	3.	Underscore *to* and write *with.*
PART C	**1.**	The preposition *like* should not be followed by a subject and verb. If it is, it should be replaced with the conjunction *as.*
PART D	**2.**	with
	5.	to
PART E	**1.**	On what day will Dawes start?

Watching the Web—Chapter 21

New 70,000 Image ArtPak

Choose <u>from between</u> our four new CD's, all packed with images you've been asking for. Make letters, posters, and ads <u>just like the professionals do!</u> See three sample images now.

*Since there are four CD's, either use *from among* or simply *from*.

*The word *like* is not a conjunction, but it is used here to start a clause containing a subject (*professionals*) and a verb (*do*). Replace *like* with a real conjunction, *as* (*just as the professionals do*) or with the words *the way* (*just the way the professionals do*).

WORKSHEET 22

PART A	1.	A
	2.	B
PART B	1.	Put a 0 in the answer space.
	3.	Place a semicolon after *relations* and a comma after *additionally.* Put a 2 in the answer space.
	5.	Place a semicolon after *qualification.* Put a 1 in the answer space.
PART C	1.	and The comma after *improvement* tells us that a coordinating conjunction should be used to join the clauses.
	2.	therefore Note the use of a semicolon and a comma.
	3.	however
	4.	but
PART D		The first sentence is simple; it does contain two infinitive phrases but only one subject and verb.
PART E	1.	A possible response: Employee evaluations can be painful; furthermore, they can be blatantly unfair.
PART F	1.	Either Yang will visit the manufacturer or she will not.
OPTION 1	1.	Place a semicolon after *moonlighting* and a comma after *however.* Put a 2 in the answer space.
	6.	Place a comma after *work.* Put a 1 in the answer space.
OPTION 2	1.	A possible response: Both the recession and the strike contributed to our problems during the past year.

Watching the Web—Chapter 22

Download National News

To download our evening news broadcast directly onto your hard drive, either press "download now" to begin the process or <u>you can return to this screen</u> after checking the other options on the menu.

*This is a problem of parallel structure. Since the clause begins with *either press*, it should follow with *or return to this screen,* omitting the words *you can.* In this way, both conjunctions are directly followed by parallel verbs.

WORKSHEET 23

PART A	1.	Underscore the word *because.* Put an A in the answer space.
	2.	Underscore the word *or.* Put a B in the answer space.
PART B	3.	hold The adverb clause *after a business failure* modifies the verb in the main clause.
PART C	1.	that
	2.	unless
PART D	1.	Place a semicolon after *shifts.* Put a 1 in the answer space.
	4.	Place a comma after *times* to separate the two independent clauses. Put a 1 in the answer space.

WORKSHEET 24

PART A	1.	simple There is only one subject.
	4.	compound There are two independent clauses.
PART B	1.	D *Within two days* is a prepositional phrase.

4. B If we transpose the two clauses in this sentence, it will be more obvious that *because* is a connective (conjunction).

PART C **1.** A *Mert* should be in the possessive case (*Mert's*).

PART D **1.** C

2. B

PART E **1.** B Two commas are needed to set off the adjective clause.

PART F **1.** B

2. A

5. B Use the comparative form because you are deciding between two jobs.

PART G **2.** fewer problems *Problems* is plural and countable, so the adjective *fewer* applies here.

Watching the Web—Chapter 24

Today's Headline News
<u>Filed in the Oval Office under Campaign Funding, the President's assistant today found the missing figures</u> requested by the Senate Investigating Committee. He turned the information over to the committee chair this afternoon.
*Notice the misplaced modifying phrase. *Filed in the Oval Office under Campaign Funding* must modify what it is closest to in the sentence, in this case *the President's assistant.* But we believe it is meant to modify *the missing figures.* The sentence needs to be rewritten so that the modifier is not misplaced: *The President's assistant today found the missing figures filed in the Oval Office under Campaign Funding.*

WORKSHEET 25

PART A **1.** unity

PART B **1.** Here is an acceptable response: When labor talks began this morning in New York, several teamsters' negotiators were stranded in Cleveland.

PART D **1.** A possible answer: Our marketing division, which has expanded to twice its original size, is responsible for a 40% increase in sales.

Watching the Web—Chapter 25

Online Photos
Never again drive to the photo shop, wait and wonder about your prints, and receive inferior quality workmanship! You want clean photos. You want crisp color. <u>You want a great value for your money.</u> Check us out today!
*This good advertisement would have far more impact if it stayed parallel: *You want great value.*

WORKSHEET 26

PART A **1.** that Place a caret after *observed.*

PART B **1.** that An even better sentence would be this: He returned because he had forgotten his key.

PART C **2.** I will write the memorandum and tell him about the drainage problem. (The words *I will* are implied after the word *and.*)

PART D **1.** One possibility: I understand that Mr. Wallace, while addressing the stockholders at our annual meeting, contradicted himself twice.

OPTION 1 **1.** C The misplaced modifier is *only,* which modifies the word *ten* and should be placed before that word.

2. C The clause *who invented this timing device* modifies *Karl Sundheim* and should follow that name.

Watching the Web—Chapter 26

Sleep and your back
The average person spends one-third of <u>their</u> life sleeping. What do you know about your mattress, and how does <u>it</u> affect your back?
*First, the subject is *person* (singular) and the possessive pronoun is *their* (plural). Either change the subject and verb into plural form *(average people spend)* or change the pronoun into singular form *(his or her).* Second, the first sentence is not parallel with the second one. One could rewrite it so that both use *you: If you're an average person, you spend one-third of your life sleeping.*

WORKSHEET 27

PART A.
1. Suite 17
4. in his early thirties
5. 9th of May

PART B
1. C
2. C
3. 4

PART D
1. A total of 556 employees are covered by the insurance carrrier named in the lawsuit. (The sentence is edited to begin with words, not numerals.)

WORKSHEET 28

PART B
1. A
3. B, A

PART C
1. Set off the introductory verbal phrase by placing a comma after *reaction.* Put a 1 in the answer space.
3. Separate the two independent clauses by placing a comma after *state-of-the-art.* Put a 1 in the answer space.
5. Separate items in a series by placing commas after *Tuesday* and *Wednesday.* Put a 2 in the answer space.

PART E
1. Michigan
2. marketing
3. merchandising

WORKSHEET 29

PART A
1. F

PART B
1. Place a comma after *occupation* to set off the parenthetical expression. Put a C in the answer space.
2. No commas are needed. Put a D in the answer space.
4. Place a comma after *manager* to set off the nonrestrictive clause. Put an A in the answer space.

PART C
1. 0
2. 2 Place commas after *author* and *enough* to set off the parenthetical expression.
6. 1 Place a comma after *impact* to set off the introductory adverb clause.

WORKSHEET 30

PART B
1. Place commas after *printer* and *compact.* Put a 2 in the answer space.
4. Place commas after *analyst, Lewinski,* and *York.* Put a 3 in the answer space.

PART C
1. Place commas after *supervisor, courageous, meeting, note,* and *statement.* Put a 5 in the answer space.
2. Place a comma after *Corporation.* Put a 1 in the answer space.
9. Place commas after *Press* and *CDT.* Put a 2 in the answer space.

PART E
1. A possible response: Vincent Stalowski, who is a Dartmouth graduate, will be your replacement.

PART F
1. noun in direct address (*Mr. Mikado*)
3. introductory adverb clause (*if my memory serves me correctly*)
5. parenthetical expression (*I understand*)

OPTION 1
1. Place commas after *goal, Andrews,* and *manager.* Put a 3 in the answer space.
4. Place commas after *No, Savoy, keyliners,* and *lithostrippers.* Put a 4 in the answer space.

Watching the Web—Chapter 30

Have you surfed the net, looking for the right business opportunity and never found it? Have you become discouraged between jobs and felt as though you'd never land another one? <u>Well friend</u> this page is written just for you. Here is the chance you've been <u>waiting</u> for.

*Set *friend* off with commas on either side: *Well, friend, . . .*

WORKSHEET 31

PART B

2. *Sometimes that reorganization involves cuts or layoffs; sometimes it involves duty reassignments.* Put a 1 in the answer space.

3. *Employees should examine three aspects of their work realistically: use of time, use of materials, and revenue production.* Put a 3 in the answer space.

4. *They should keep tabs on these aspects over a given time; most advisors suggest three months as a reasonable period.* Put a 1 in the answer space.

PART C

1. :

2. ;

PART D

1. B   This compound sentence has no connective.

2. C

WORKSHEET 32

PART A

2. C

4. F

5. A

7. A

PART B

1. A

2. C

PART C

1. C   It would be acceptable to omit the *to* before *vibrate.*

PART D

1. A

PART F

1. A

3. A

WORKSHEET 33

PART B

2. It was too humid—the dewpoint was 69—for the exterior finish of the building to be applied on Thursday, June 29. Put a 3 in the answer space.

3. The witness arrived from San Antonio (or was it El Paso?) on July 10th. Put a 3 in the answer space.

4. "We have nothing to fear but fear itself."—Roosevelt. Put a 1 in the answer space.

PART D

4. Underscore the comma following *MBA* and write something like this: A dash should be used before a word or phrase that is repeated with greater emphasis.

5. Underscore the comma following *Picard* and write something like this: Dashes should be used after *accountants* and *Picard* to set off the appositive that contains commas within itself.

OPTION 1

1. Chicken, beef, fish—those are the only entrees available at the banquet. Put a 3 in the answer space.

OPTION 2

1. Our team leader met with Simpson (he's the marketing chairman), but they could not agree on a plan. Put a 3 in the answer space.

WORKSHEET 34

PART A

1. No

PART B

1. Put 4 in the answer space. Note: *PC Journal* may be underscored or printed in italics.

4. "If you are not an online veteran," she suggested, "you may want to select a PC with easy sign-up and several months of free service." Put a 6 in the answer space.

8. Put a 3 in the answer space. Note: "Shopping for Your PC" may be underscored or printed in italics.

PART C

The three apostrophes that should be omitted can be found in *hour's, account's,* and *strategy's.* These should be plural nouns instead: *hours, accounts,* and *strategies.*

PART D   **2.**   A

                 4.   B

PART E   **1.**   Green's

Watching the Web—Chapter 34

> Retire Early with a Fortune!
> You too can discover how to build up cash for early retirement. <u>Its</u> a matter of a few hours a week and a few phone calls a day to reap <u>benefit's</u> <u>youve</u> never imagined!
> *Three apostrophe errors can be found here. *Its* should read *It's*; *benefit's* is not possessive, merely plural (*benefits*); *youve* needs an apostrophe (*you've*).

WORKSHEET 35

PART B   **3.**   *One supplier (was it Reliable Products?) offered a discount and free cookies.* Put a 4 in the answer space.

                 4.   *Will your company charge for shipping? for rush delivery? for special orders?* Put a 3 in the answer space.

                 8.   *The Office, Inc., which sells by catalog, has a stable clientele.* Put a 5 in the answer space.

                 9.   *Geraldo asked, "Can we order ink jet transparencies next time?"* Put a 4 in the answer space.

PART D   **1.**   A

                 4.   A

PART E   **1.**   Federal Deposit Insurance Corporation

                 3.   gram

WORKSHEET 36

PART A   **1.**   F

                 2.   T

PART B   **2.**   C

                 4.   B

                 6.   A

                 7.   A   Here A is correct; C shows a greater number of syllables before the hyphen, but the final syllable has only two letters and should remain with the rest of the word.

                24.   A is the best choice, since this word used to be hyphenated and that sense remains. However, C will become more acceptable as the word loses its former hyphenated image.

PART D   **1.**   par a le gal

                 3.   col le gi al i ty

                 4.   ex ces sive   This word is an exception to Rule 7, since the root, excess, ends in a double consonant. Most dictionaries break it between the double *s*.

Watching the Web—Chapter 36

> On a job hunt? Turning up few opportunities? If you're not finding what you really want, if rejection is hurting your <u>selfes-teem</u>, take this short course on finding your own constellation of talents, recommended by the author of *What Color is MY Parachute.*
> *Always hyphenate compounds words beginning with *self* after *self* (*self-esteem*).

WORKSHEET 37

PART A   **1.**   effervescent

                 2.   recalcitrant

PART B   **1.**   E

                 3.   A

PART C   **1.**   munificent   Replace with *magnificent* or *breathtaking,* for example.

PART D   **1.**   prevaricator

4. An acceptable response: This office on a Friday afternoon is the picture of indolence.

Watching the Web—Chapter 37

For the first time on the Web! The World Book of Famous Quotations
Give your writing real style and flair by using this <u>officious</u> guide to familiar quotations for any occasion.
*More than likely, the advertiser meant to use *official* rather than *officious.*

WORKSHEET 38

PART A	**1.**	indemnify
	3.	indict
PART B	**1.**	L
	3.	E
PART C	**1.**	mortgage
PART D	**1.**	appraiser
	2.	depreciation
PART E	**1.**	Here is another acceptable response: An appraisal of this property will be made by a local banker.

Watching the Web—Chapter 38

Attention all lease-holders on office machinery:
If you lease your copier, printer, fax, or scanner, prepare to tear up that paper and send those machines back! Calling all <u>leasors</u>! You don't need to lease when you can own for less. Check out our prices on HP, Sony, and other brand multi-function tools.
*A person who lends or provides a lease (owns the item) is a *lessor,* not a *leasor;* however, this advertisement is aimed at *lessees,* person who use leased machinery. It should probably say *Calling all lessees!*

WORKSHEET 39

PART A	**1.**	already Underscore *all ready.*
	2.	number Underscore *amount.*
PART C	**1.**	Urbana depended on the film's success at the box office, of course.
	3.	Will you be able to take a break from canvassing the neighborhood today?

WORKSHEET 40

PART A	**1.**	C
PART B	**1.**	E
	2.	C
	3.	D
PART C	**1.**	C
	2.	A
PART D	**1.**	A
	7.	A is the correct response if de Silva is the person being referred to in the sentence. B is the correct response if de Silva is someone being spoken to (direct address).
PART E	**2.**	C
PART F	**1.**	Underscore *like.* Write *as if* or *as though.*
	3.	Underscore *slower.* Write *more slowly.*
	6.	Underscore *Company.* Write *Company's.*
PART G	**1.**	Here is one acceptable response: Our production supervisor is pleased that there have been fewer breakdowns this month than last.

GLOSSARY

ABBREVIATION   A shortened version of a word. Examples: *mdse., amt., mfr.*

ABSOLUTE ADJECTIVE   An adjective that cannot be compared because it represents an extreme. Examples: *perfect, unanimous.*

ABSOLUTE PHRASE   A phrase that consists of a noun or pronoun and a participle. It modifies a whole clause. Example: *The meeting having ended,* we returned to our desks.

ABSTRACT NOUN   A noun that names a quality, idea, or action rather than anything concrete. Examples: *love, enthusiasm, stamina.*

ACTIVE VOICE   A designation used to indicate the relation of a verb to its subject. If a verb is in the active voice, the subject *acts.* Example: I *signed* the report. (See Passive Voice.)

ADJECTIVE   A word used to modify (limit, describe) a noun or a pronoun.

ADJECTIVE PHRASE OR CLAUSE   A phrase or a clause that is used as an adjective, that is, to modify a noun or a pronoun.

ADVERB   A word used to modify a verb, an adjective, an adverb, or an adverb-equivalent.

ADVERB PHRASE OR CLAUSE   Any phrase or clause that functions as an adverb—usually to modify a verb.

AGREEMENT   Similarity in number, case, gender, or person of two or more grammatically connected elements, such as subject and verb, pronoun and antecedent.

ANTECEDENT   The word or group of words to which a pronoun refers.

ANTONYM   A word with a meaning opposite to that of another word.

APOSTROPHE   A mark of punctuation used primarily in possessive-case forms and contractions.

APPOSITIVE   A noun or noun-equivalent that immediately follows another noun or noun-equivalent to explain (or rename) the first one. Example: John Simmons, *the supervisor.*

ARTICLE   Any of these three adjectives: *a, an, the.*

AUXILIARY VERB   A helping verb, used before a main verb to build a verb phrase. Example: *has been* completed.

BALANCED CONSTRUCTION   A sentence with grammatically equal structures used to obtain emphasis of two or more ideas.

BRACKETS   Marks used by writers or editors to enclose their own comments in material being quoted.

CASE   The form of a noun or pronoun (nominative, possessive, objective) that indicates its relation to other words in the sentence.

CLAUSE   A group of related words containing a subject and a verb.

COLLECTIVE NOUN   A word that, in its singular form, names a group. Examples: *family, jury, committee.*

COLLOQUIALISM   An informal expression, often more acceptable in conversation than in business writing.

COLON (:)   The mark of punctuation that usually follows a formal introduction.

COMMA (,)   The punctuation mark most commonly used to set off sentence elements or to separate them from the rest of the sentence.

COMMAND   An imperative sentence, one that orders someone to do something. Example: *Read the entire report.*

COMMON GENDER   Form of a pronoun that refers to a person but does not indicate that person's sex. Example: Someone left *his* pen on the table.

COMMON NOUN   A word that indicates a general class of persons, places, objects, conditions, or qualities. Examples: *man, building, floor.*

COMPARISON   Changes in the forms of adjectives and adverbs to indicate degrees (positive, comparative, superlative). Example: *fast, faster, fastest.*

COMPLEMENT   A word or words that follow a linking verb and rename or modify its subject. Also, any word or words that appear in the predicate to complete the meaning of the verb.

COMPLEX SENTENCE   A sentence that contains one independent clause and one or more dependent clauses.

COMPOUND   A sentence element that consists of two or more parts. Examples: *Alan* and *Ted* cooperated. Mr. Gant referred to *you* and *me.*

COMPOUND-COMPLEX SENTENCE   A sentence with two or more independent clauses and one or more dependent clauses.

COMPOUND PERSONAL PRONOUN   An intensive or reflexive pronoun, both of which end in *self* or *selves.* Examples: *himself, themselves.*

COMPOUND SENTENCE   A sentence with two or more independent clauses.

CONCRETE NOUN   A noun that names something capable of being perceived by the senses. Examples: *book, desk, lamp.*

CONJUGATION   A listing of the forms that a verb takes to reflect changes in tense, number, person, voice, and mood.

CONJUNCTION   A connective that is generally used to join words, phrases, and clauses.

CONJUNCTIVE ADVERB   A word that joins two independent clauses and also functions as a modifier. Examples: *therefore, however, consequently.*

CONNECTIVE   A word or phrase that joins sentence elements. Examples: *and, therefore, in other words.*

CONSTRUCTION   The manner in which words are arranged in a grammatical element.

CONTRASTING EXPRESSION   A sentence element that begins with *not, never,* or *seldom* and expresses an idea contrary to the one preceding it. Examples: *not Boston, never at night, seldom on Sunday.*

COORDINATE ADJECTIVES   A series of two or more descriptive adjectives that perform a similar function and should be separated by commas.

COORDINATING CONJUNCTION   A word used to join sentence elements (words, phrases, or clauses) that are of equal importance or rank.

CORRELATIVES   Conjunctions used in pairs to join coordinate words, phrases, or clauses. Examples: *either . . . or.*

DANGLING MODIFIER   A modifier (often a verbal phrase) that cannot logically modify any other word in the sentence. A modifier is sometimes considered *dangling* if it is simply too far removed from the word it would logically modify.

DASH (—)   A mark of punctuation used to set off sentence elements emphatically or to indicate an abrupt change in thought.

DECLENSION   A listing of all variant forms of a noun or pronoun.

DEMONSTRATIVE PRONOUN   Any one of these pronouns: *this, that, these, those.*

DEPENDENT CLAUSE   A clause (often referred to as *subordinate*) that cannot stand alone. It may function as an adverb, an adjective, or a noun.

DETERMINER   A word that is typically followed by a noun. Example: *a, an, the, my, our.*

DIAGRAMMING   The use of line graphs to show the relationship of each sentence part to other parts of a sentence.

DIRECT ADDRESS   The use of the name (or an appropriate substitute) of the person to whom a message is intended. Example: Let me know, *Louis,* if you would like to go.

DIRECT OBJECT   A noun (or noun-equivalent) that completes the meaning of a transitive verb and receives its action. Example: I mailed the *letter.*

DIRECT QUOTATION   A repeating of the exact words of another person.

DOUBLE NEGATIVE   The unacceptable addition of a negative word to an expression that is already negative. Example: *I don't have none.*

ELLIPSIS (. . .)   The omission of words from a quotation (indicated by three spaced periods).

ELLIPTICAL CONSTRUCTION   A construction in which one or more words are clearly implied but not expressed. Example: *He is taller than I* (am).

EUPHEMISM   A thoroughly acceptable expression that is substituted for an expression considered to be harsh or offensive.

EXCLAMATION POINT (!)   The punctuation mark that follows an exclamation, which may be a sentence or a fragment expressing strong feeling.

EXPLETIVE   A word that is used to fill out a construction without contributing to its meaning. Example: *There* is no time left. The word *expletive* may also refer to an exclamation or oath (often to profanity).

FUTURE PERFECT TENSE   A verb phrase that uses *will have* or *shall have* as helping verbs to express action that will be completed before a specific future time or action. Example: *will have called, shall have finished.*

FUTURE TENSE   A verb phrase that uses *will* or *shall* as a helping verb to express future time. Examples: *will come, shall write.*

GENDER   Classifications of nouns and pronouns that indicate sex (masculine, feminine) or the absence of sex (neuter). A pronoun that may refer to either a male or a female is considered to be of *common gender.*

GERUND   A verb form that ends in *ing* and functions as a noun (subject, object, or complement). Example: *Running* is healthful exercise.

GOBBLEDYGOOK   Language that is unclear, repetitious, and wordy, such as that used in many government publications.

HYPHEN (-)   A short line used to connect the parts of some compound words or to divide words at the ends of lines.

IDIOM   A construction that means something quite different from what a literal interpretation of the words would suggest. Example: *He is dying to meet you.*

IMPERATIVE MOOD   A designation used to describe verbs that issue commands or make requests.

INDEFINITE PRONOUN   A pronoun that does not refer to a particular person or thing. Examples: *everybody, anybody.*

INDEPENDENT CLAUSE   A clause that can stand alone.

INDICATIVE MOOD   Designation of verbs used to make statements or ask questions.

INDIRECT OBJECT   A noun or noun-substitute that precedes a direct object and tells to whom or for whom something is done. Example: Give *me* the watch.

INDIRECT QUOTATION   Reference to a statement not being quoted word for word. Example: *He said that he will return our check.*

INFINITIVE   A verbal that is generally made up of two words (*to* plus a verb form) and that functions as a noun or as a modifier. Examples: *to write, to have written.*

INFLECTION   The process of changing a base word (noun, pronoun, verb, modifier) in order to express its various functions. Examples: *walk, walks, walking, walked; slow, slower, slowest.*

INTENSIVE PRONOUN   A compound (*-self*) pronoun that is used to add emphasis to another word. Example: The manager *himself* spoke with me.

INTERJECTION   A word (part of speech) that expresses nothing more than emotion or feeling. Examples: *oh, wow, hurray.*

INTRANSITIVE VERB   A verb that does not require another word (such as an object) to complete its meaning. Linking verbs are intransitive.

IRREGULAR VERB   A verb that does not form its past tense and past participle in the usual way, that is, by the addition of *d* or *ed* to the present-tense form. Example: *go, went, gone.*

ITALICS   A style of printing used for words to be emphasized. Letters are usually sloped to the right.

ITEMS IN A SERIES   Three or more words, phrases, or clauses used consecutively to perform a similar function.

LINKING VERB   A verb that relates a following complement (noun, pronoun, or adjective) to the subject. Examples: *am, is, has been, seems.*

MAIN (INDEPENDENT) CLAUSE   A clause that can stand alone.

MODIFIER   Any word, phrase, or clause that limits, qualifies, or describes another word or combination of words.

MOOD   One of three forms (indicative, imperative, subjunctive) that are used to indicate how the action of a verb is expressed.

NOMINAL   Performing the function of a noun (used as a subject, object, etc.).

NOMINATIVE CASE   The case form of a noun or pronoun that functions as a subject or subject complement.

NONRESTRICTIVE   Not necessary to the meaning of the sentence. Nonrestrictive elements are usually set off by commas.

NOUN   The name of anything (person, place, thing, action, idea, etc.). One of eight parts of speech.

NOUN CLAUSE OR PHRASE   A dependent clause or phrase that functions as a noun, generally as a subject, object, or complement.

NUMBER   Designation of a part of speech as *singular* or *plural.*

OBJECT   A noun or noun-equivalent that completes the meaning of a transitive verb in the active voice or of a verbal (infinitive, participle, gerund). The *object of a preposition* is a noun or noun-equivalent that is related by the preposition to another word or group of words.

OBJECTIVE CASE   The case form of a noun or pronoun that functions as the object of a verb, the object of a preposition, or the subject of an infinitive.

PARALLELISM   The use of similar grammatical elements to express sentence parts that are similar in function, such as the use of four gerunds to express four items in a series.

PARENTHESES ( )   Punctuation marks used in pairs to set off sentence elements, particularly elements that are to be deemphasized.

PARENTHETICAL EXPRESSION   A word or group of words that has been placed in a sentence as an aside and tends to interrupt the natural flow. Example: There are, *it seems to me,* better ways to solve our problem.

PART OF SPEECH   Any of eight classifications of words according to function (noun, pronoun, verb, adjective, adverb, preposition, conjunction, interjection).

PARTICIPLE   A verb form that is used as an adjective (the *finished* product, the picture *taken* on Monday) or as part of a verb phrase (is *walking,* has *done*).

PASSIVE VOICE   Form of a transitive verb phrase (*was told, has been told,* etc.) that usually requires the subject to receive the action of the verb.

PAST PERFECT TENSE   A verb phrase that includes the auxiliary *had* (*had left, had been left,* etc.) and expresses action completed before another past action or before a specific past time.

PAST TENSE   Form of verb used to indicate that action was completed prior to the present.

PERIOD (.)   A terminal mark of punctuation used after statements, commands, abbreviations, and so forth.

PERSON   A classification that indicates whether a personal pronoun refers to the speaker (first person), the person spoken to (second person), or the person (or thing) spoken about (third person).

PERSONAL PRONOUN   Any one of these pronouns: *I, my, mine, me, you, your, yours, he, his, him, she, her, hers, it, its, we, our, ours, us, they, their, theirs.*

PHRASAL PREPOSITION   A combination of words that functions as a preposition. Examples: *according to, instead of.*

PHRASE   A group of related words not containing both a subject and a verb.

PLURAL   Any form of a noun, pronoun, or verb that suggests more than one. Examples: *books, they, we.*

POSITIVE DEGREE   The basic form of an adverb or adjective *(fast)* in contrast to the compared forms *(faster, fastest).*

POSSESSIVE CASE   The case form of a noun or pronoun that may be used to show ownership, possession, authorship, brand, kind, or origin. Examples: *Lucy's* handwriting, *my* typewriter, *Darwin's* theory.

PREDICATE What is said about the subject. It consists of the main verb (simple predicate) or the main verb plus its modifiers and complements (complete predicate).

PREDICATE ADJECTIVE An adjective that follows a linking verb and modifies the subject of that verb. Example: This report is *excellent.*

PREDICATE NOMINATIVE A noun or pronoun that follows a linking verb and renames the subject of that verb. Examples: Hawkins is our *representative.*

PREFIX One or more syllables (*un, mis, hydro,* etc.) placed before a word or combining form to build a new word.

PREPOSITION A word (part of speech) used to show the relation of its object to another word in the sentence.

PREPOSITIONAL PHRASE A group of related words containing a preposition, its objects, and (sometimes) modifiers.

PRESENT PARTICIPLE An *ing* form of a verb that is used as an adjective (a *selling* point) or as part of a progressive-form verb (I am *listening*).

PRESENT PERFECT TENSE A verb phrase that includes the helping verb *have* or *has* (*have left, have been left,* etc.) and expresses (1) an action just completed, (2) an action beginning in the past and continuing into the future, or (3) a past action that may occur again.

PRESENT TENSE A verb form used to indicate a general truth, a present action, or a habitual action.

PRINCIPAL PARTS OF A VERB The four basic verb forms used in building tenses: present *(do),* past *(did),* past participle *(done),* and present participle *(doing).*

PROGRESSIVE FORM OF A VERB Verb phrase that consists of a form of the verb *be* and a present participle *(am going, are walking, is writing).*

PRONOMINAL ADJECTIVE A word that is generally considered to be a pronoun form although it is used to modify a noun. Examples: *his* home, *my* problem, *which* answer.

PRONOUN A word that is used as a noun substitute. Examples: *he, them, anyone, everybody, which.*

PROPER ADJECTIVE An adjective that is based upon a proper noun. Example: *Swedish* (from *Sweden*).

PROPER NOUN A noun that should be capitalized because it names a specific person, place, or thing. Examples: *Thomas Paine, Nashville, September.*

QUESTION MARK (?) Mark of punctuation that follows a direct question (one that requires a verbal response). It is also used to express doubt.

QUOTATION MARKS (" ", ' ') Punctuation marks that are used to enclose words being quoted directly.

REDUNDANCY An expression that contains more words than are needed to convey the intended meaning. Examples: *blue in color, consensus of opinion.*

REFLEXIVE PRONOUN A compound pronoun that refers to or renames a preceding noun or pronoun (usually the subject). Example: He repeated *himself.*

REGULAR VERB A verb to which *d* or *ed* is added to form both the past tense and the past participle. Example: *walk, walked, walked.*

RELATIVE PRONOUN A word that substitutes for a noun and introduces a subordinate clause. Examples: *who, whose, whom, which, that, what, whoever, whatever, whomever, whichever.*

RESTRICTIVE ELEMENT A word, phrase, or clause that cannot be removed from a sentence without changing the essential meaning being conveyed.

SEMICOLON (;) A punctuation mark that is used primarily to separate independent clauses or items in a series (if the items contain commas within themselves).

SENTENCE An independent group of words that contains at least one subject and one predicate.

SINGULAR The form of a noun or pronoun that refers to only one person or object. Also, the verb form used with subjects that refer to only one.

SUBJECT A word or word group about which something is said (or asked) in the predicate.

SUBJECT COMPLEMENT A noun, pronoun, or adjective that follows a linking verb and either renames or modifies the subject.

SUBJUNCTIVE The verb form used to express either an idea that is clearly contrary to fact or a *that* clause of recommendation, demand, suggestion, desire, request, necessity, or resolution.

SUBORDINATE CLAUSE   A dependent clause that functions as a noun, an adjective, or an adverb and relates to another part of the sentence.

SUBORDINATING CONJUNCTION   A conjunction that normally introduces a dependent clause and connects it to an independent clause.

SUFFIX   One or more syllables (*-ment, -able,* etc.) added at the end of a word to change its meaning.

SUPERLATIVE DEGREE   The form of an adjective or adverb that suggests an extreme. Examples: *coldest, most ambitious, least helpful.*

SYNONYM   A word with a meaning approximately the same as the meaning of another word.

SYNTAX   The grammatical structure of words, phrases, and clauses.

TENSE   A category of verb inflection that indicates time.

TRANSITIONAL PHRASE   A short phrase used either to link sentences or to link two independent clauses in a compound sentence. Example: Several of our machines need repairs; *for example,* this engine is inoperative.

TRANSITIVE VERB   A verb that, in the active voice, requires an object to complete its meaning.

VERB   A word (part of speech) that expresses action or state of being.

VERB PHRASE   A word group that functions as a single verb. Examples: *has been gone, will be working.*

VERBAL   A verb form that functions as a noun, an adjective, or an adverb.

VOICE   Classification that indicates the relation of a transitive verb to its subject. Voice may be *active* or *passive.* Examples: (active) Gary *made* the necessary repairs. (passive) The necessary repairs *were made* by Gary.

Index